STREET ATLAS

Bristol
and Bath

published in 1995 as
ol and Avon' by

's, a division of
us Publishing Group Ltd
eron Quays, London E14 4JP

olour edition 2001
ed impression 2002

0-540-07806-9

ilip's 2001

Ordnance Survey®

roduct includes mapping data licensed
Ordnance Survey® with the permission
Controller of Her Majesty's Stationery
e. © Crown copyright 2001. All rights
ved. Licence number 100011710

ed and bound in Spain
yfosa-Quebecor

Contents

III **Key to map symbols**

IV **Key to map pages**

VI **Route planning**

VIII **Administrative and Postcode boundaries**

1 **Street maps** at 2½ inches to 1 mile

140 **Street maps of Bristol and Bath city centres** at 5 inches to 1 mile

143 **Town maps** of Chippenham and Trowbridge

144 **Index** of towns and villages

145 **Index** of streets, hospitals, industrial estates, railway stations, schools, shopping centres and universities

Digital Data

The exceptionally high-quality mapping found in this atlas is available as digital data in TIFF format, which is easily convertible to other bit mapped (raster) image formats.

The index is also available in digital form as a standard database table. It contains all the details found in the printed index together with the National Grid reference for the map square in which each entry is named.

For further information and to discuss your requirements, please contact Philip's on 020 7531 8439 or george.philip@philips-maps.co.uk

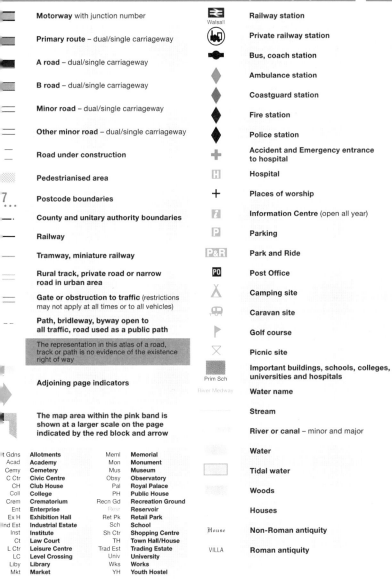

Motorway with junction number		Railway station	
Primary route – dual/single carriageway		Private railway station	
A road – dual/single carriageway		Bus, coach station	
B road – dual/single carriageway		Ambulance station	
Minor road – dual/single carriageway		Coastguard station	
Other minor road – dual/single carriageway		Fire station	
Road under construction		Police station	
Pedestrianised area		Accident and Emergency entrance to hospital	
Postcode boundaries		Hospital	
County and unitary authority boundaries		Places of worship	
Railway		Information Centre (open all year)	
Tramway, miniature railway		Parking	
Rural track, private road or narrow road in urban area		Park and Ride	
Gate or obstruction to traffic (restrictions may not apply at all times or to all vehicles)		Post Office	
Path, bridleway, byway open to all traffic, road used as a public path		Camping site	

The representation in this atlas of a road, track or path is no evidence of the existence right of way

Adjoining page indicators

The map area within the pink band is shown at a larger scale on the page indicated by the red block and arrow

Caravan site

Golf course

Picnic site

Prim Sch — Important buildings, schools, colleges, universities and hospitals

River Medway — Water name

Stream

River or canal – minor and major

Water

Tidal water

Woods

Houses

House — Non-Roman antiquity

VILLA — Roman antiquity

t Gdns	Allotments	Meml	Memorial
Acad	Academy	Mon	Monument
Cemy	Cemetery	Mus	Museum
C Ctr	Civic Centre	Obsy	Observatory
CH	Club House	Pal	Royal Palace
Coll	College	PH	Public House
Crem	Crematorium	Recn Gd	Recreation Ground
Ent	Enterprise	Resr	Reservoir
Ex H	Exhibition Hall	Ret Pk	Retail Park
Ind Est	Industrial Estate	Sch	School
Inst	Institute	Sh Ctr	Shopping Centre
Ct	Law Court	TH	Town Hall/House
L Ctr	Leisure Centre	Trad Est	Trading Estate
LC	Level Crossing	Univ	University
Liby	Library	Wks	Works
Mkt	Market	YH	Youth Hostel

k grey border on the inside edge of some pages indicates that the does not continue onto the adjacent page

■ The small numbers around the edges of the maps identify the 1 kilometre National Grid lines

cale of the maps is 3.92 cm to 1 km
ches to 1 mile 1: 25344

0	1/4	1/2	3/4	1 mile
0	250m 500m	750m	1 kilometre	

cale of the maps on pages numbered in red
cm to 1 km 5 inches to 1 mile 1: 12672

0	220 yards	440 yards	660 yards	1/2 mile
0	125m	250m	375m 1/2 kilometre	

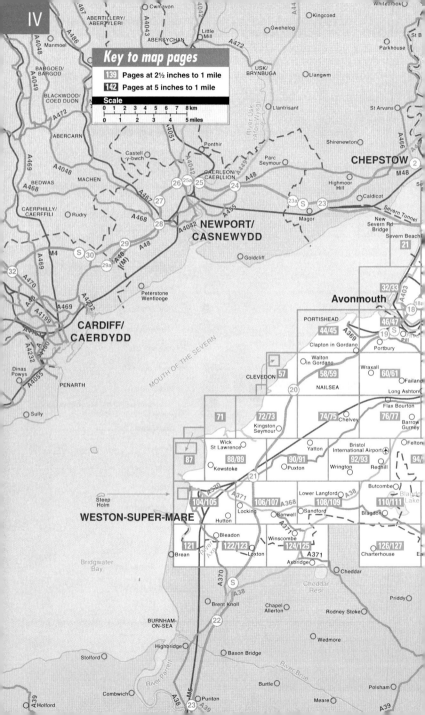

IV

Key to map pages

139 Pages at 2½ inches to 1 mile
142 Pages at 5 inches to 1 mile

Scale

0 1 2 3 4 5 6 7 8 km
0 1 2 3 4 5 miles

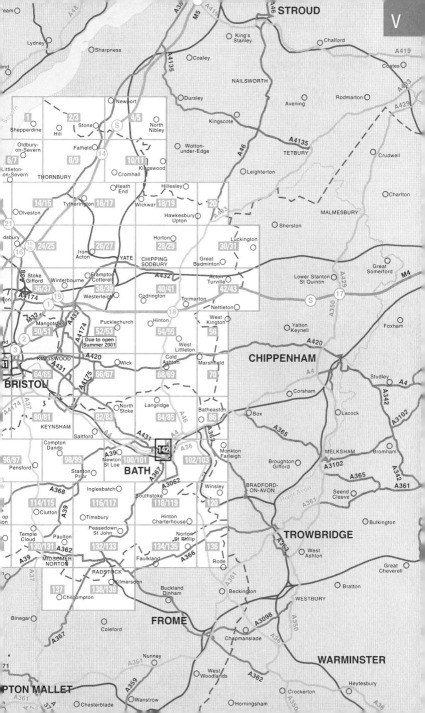

Route planning

Scale

| 0 | 1 | 2 | 3 | 4 | 5 | 6 | 7 | 8 km |
| 0 | 1 | 2 | 3 | 4 | 5 miles |

VIII

Major administrative and Postcode boundaries

County and unitary authority boundaries
Postcode boundaries
Area covered by this atlas

Scale
0   5   10   15 km
0   5   10 miles

Cardiff

Newport

Monmouthshire

Gloucestershire

Wiltshire

Somerset

City of Bristol

South Gloucestershire

Bath and North-East Somerset

North Somerset

SO
ST

SO
ST

Weston-super-Mare

Shepperdine
Severn Beach
Thornbury
Stone — GL13
North Nibley — GL11
GL12
Wickwar
Almondsbury
Stoke Gifford
Yate — BS37
GL9
Acton Turville
GL8
Marshfield
SN14
Batheaston
Monkton Farleigh — SN13
BA15
Bath — BA1
Sharpstone
BA2
BA14
BA11
BA3
Radstock
Midsomer Norton
Clutton
BA5
Axbridge — BS26
Blagdon
Sandford
Banwell — BS29
BS25
Locking
Wick St Lawrence — BS22
BS24
BS23
TA8
Yatton — BS49
BS40
Chew Magna
BS39
BS41
BS48
Nailsea
Clevedon — BS21
Portishead — BS20
Long Ashton
Failand
Lower
BS8
BS9
Westbury on Trym
BS11 — Avonmouth
BS10
Hallen
BS32
BS35
BS34
BS7
BS6
Bristol — BS1
BS2 — Kingswood
BS5
BS16
Mangotsfield
BS36 — Winterbourne
Lower Soundwell
BS15
BS30
Wick
BS3
Highridge — BS13
Stockwood
BS4
BS14
Keynsham — BS31
BS39
Sandford

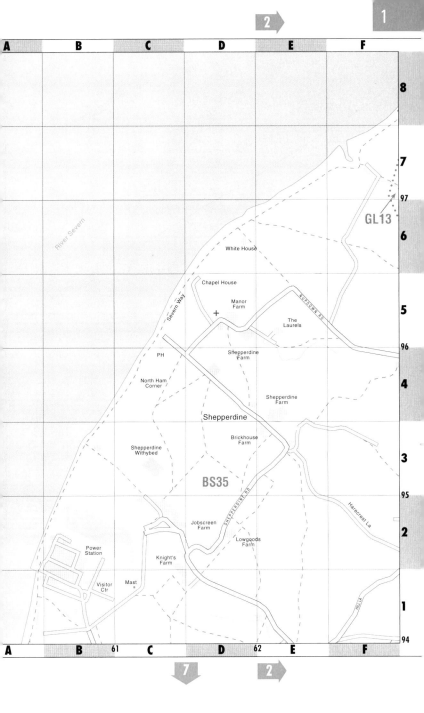

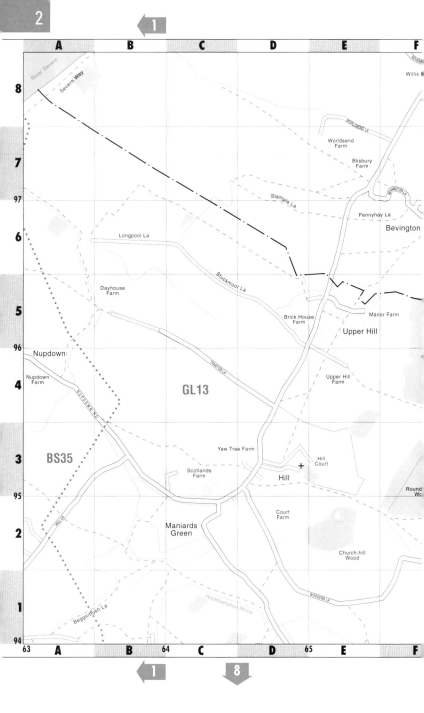

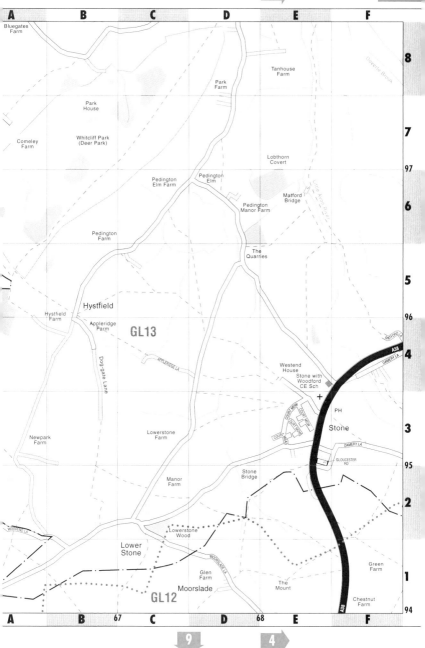

8

7

97

6

5

96

4

3

95

2

1

94

Bluegates Farm

Tanhouse Farm

Park Farm

Park House

Comeley Farm

Whitcliff Park (Deer Park)

Lobthorn Covert

Pedington Elm Farm

Pedington Elm

Matford Bridge

Pedington Manor Farm

Little Avon River

Doverte Brook

Pedington Farm

The Quarries

Hystfield

GL13

Hystfield Farm

Appleridge Farm

Appleridge La

Dog-gate Lane

Westend House

Stone with Woodford CE Sch

BETTON LA

A38

GAMERY LA

PH

Stone

Newpark Farm

Lowerstone Farm

COURT MDW

COURT VIEW

COURT ORCHD

DAMERY LA

GLOUCESTER RD

Manor Farm

Stone Bridge

Lowerstone Wood

Lower Stone

Glen Farm

MOORSLADE LA

WICKWAR LA

GL12

Moorslade

The Mount

Green Farm

Chestnut Farm

A38

67

68

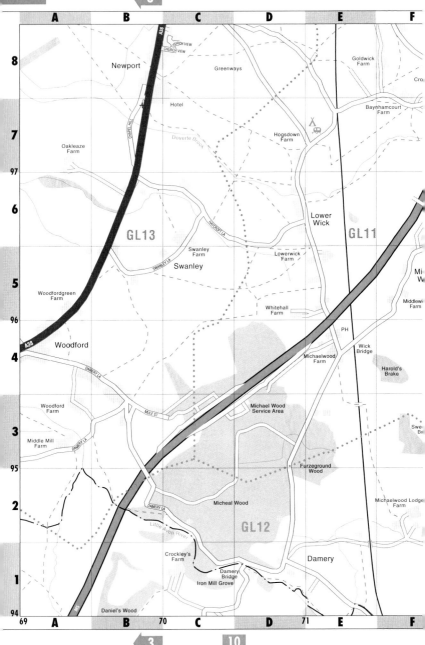

8

7

97

6

GL13

5

96

4

3

95

2

1

94

A38
CHURCH VIEW
CHURCH VIEW
Newport
Hotel
CHAPEL HILL
Doverte Brook
Greenways
Hogsdown Farm
Goldwick Farm
Baynhamcourt Farm
Cro
Oakleaze Farm
Lower Wick
GL11
Swanley Farm
Swanley
HACROFT LA
SWANLEY LA
Lowerwick Farm
Mi W
Woodfordgreen Farm
Middlewi
Whitehall Farm
PH
A38
Woodford
Michaelwood Farm
Wick Bridge
Harold's Brake
DAMERY LA
MILE ST
Michael Wood Service Area
Woodford Farm
Swe Br
Middle Mill Farm
DAMERY LA
Furzeground Wood
Micheal Wood
Michaelwood Lodge Farm
DAMERY LA
Little Avon River
GL12
Crockley's Farm
Damery Bridge
Iron Mill Grove
Damery
Daniel's Wood

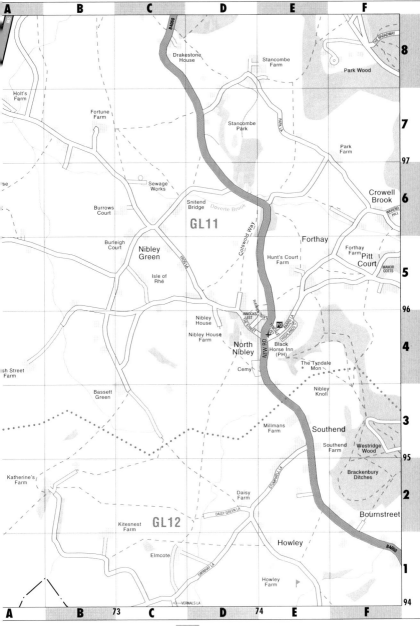

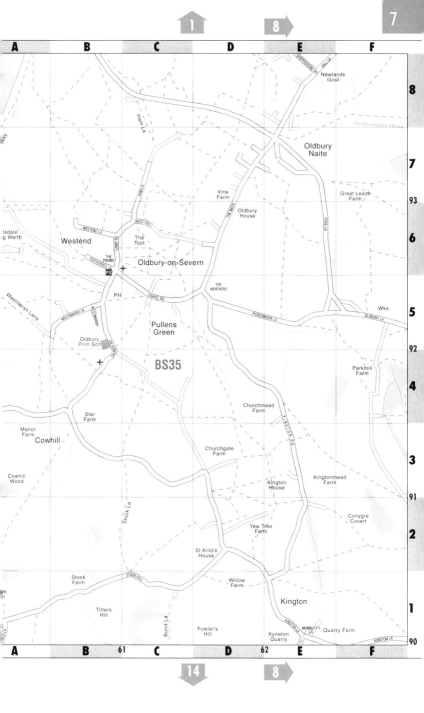

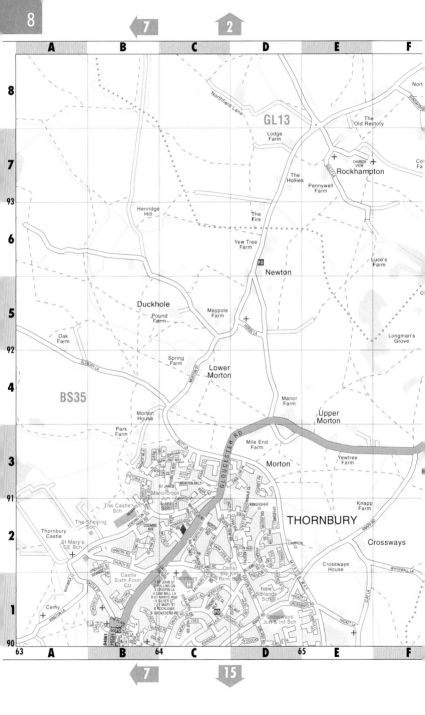

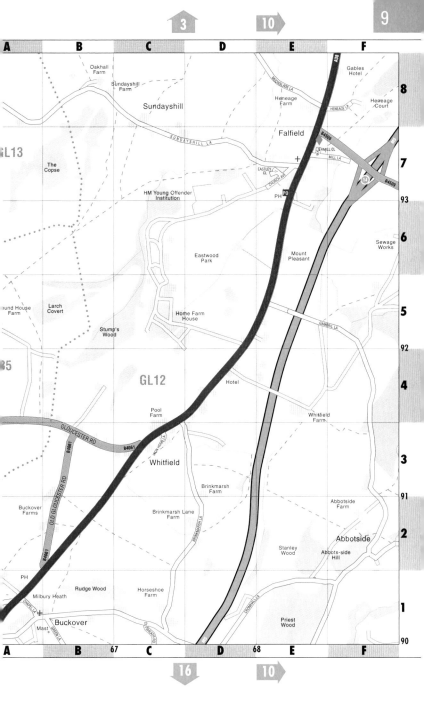

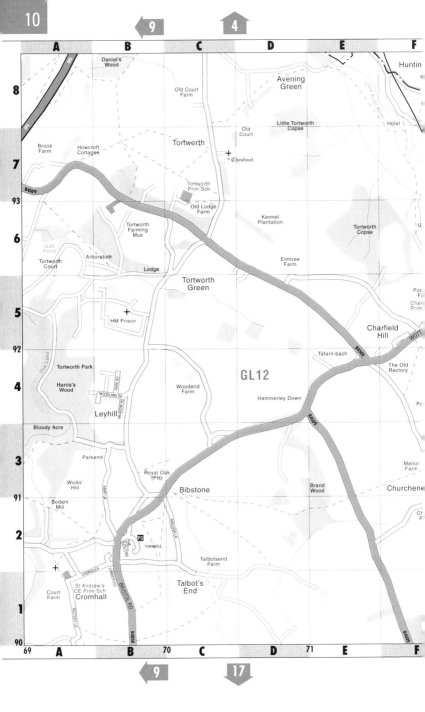

A **B** **C** **D** **E** **F**

8

Daniel's Wood

Old Court Farm

Avening Green

Little Tortworth Copse

Huntin

Hotel

Little Avon River

7

Brook Farm

Howcroft Cottages

Old Court

Tortworth

+ Chestnut

93

B4509

Tortworth Prim Sch

Old Lodge Farm

Kennel Plantation

U

6

Gall Pond

Tortworth Farming Mus

Tortworth Copse

Tortworth Court

Arboretum

Lodge

Tortworth Green

Elmtree Farm

5

+
HM Prison

Charfield Hill

WOTT

92

The Lake

Tortworth Park

Tafarn-bach

B4509

The Old Rectory

4

Harris's Wood

WOODLAND RD

PARK RD

MEADOW RD

Woodend Farm

GL12

Hammerley Down

B4509

Po

Leyhill

Bloody Acre

3

Parkend

Royal Oak (PH)

Manor Farm

Churchen

Wicks' Hill

URLEY LA

Bibstone

Brand Wood

91

Sodam Mill

Ch
F

2

THE BEALINGS

PO

TOWNWELL

FARLEIGH LA

Talbotsend Farm

CHINGILEA

LONGCROSS

BRISTOL RD

1

+

Court Farm

St Andrew's CE Prim Sch
Cromhall

RECTORY LA

Talbot's End

90

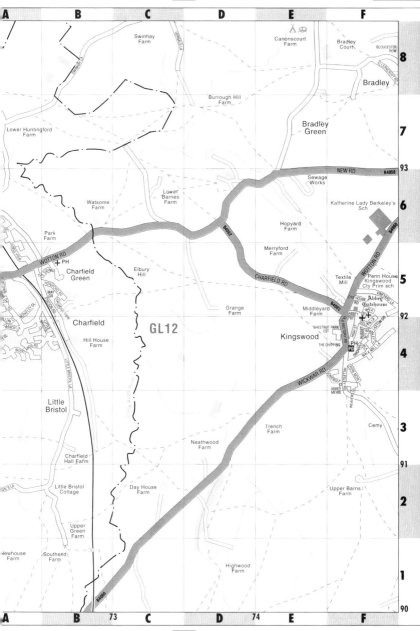

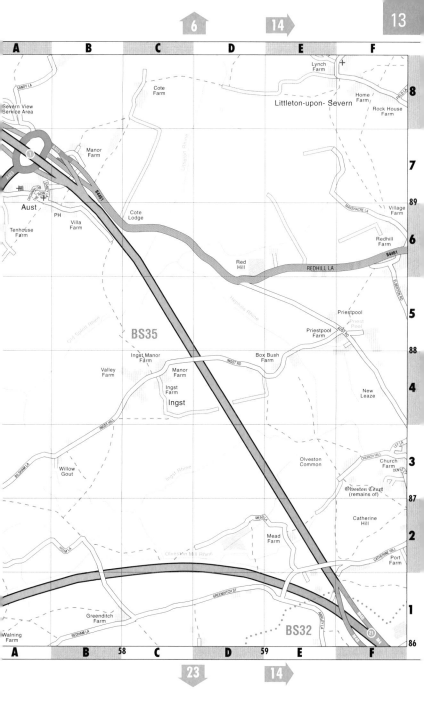

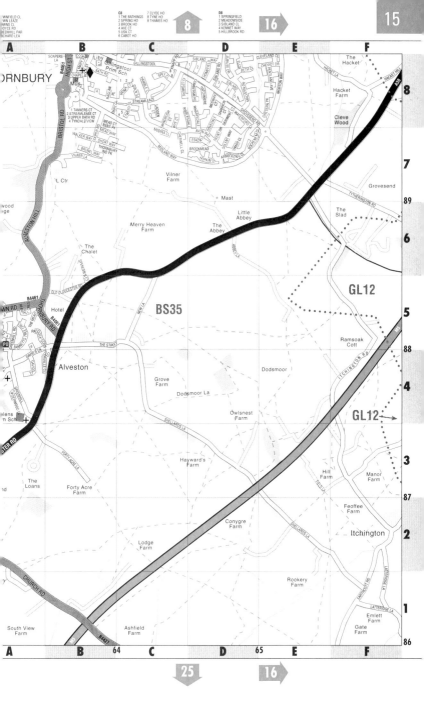

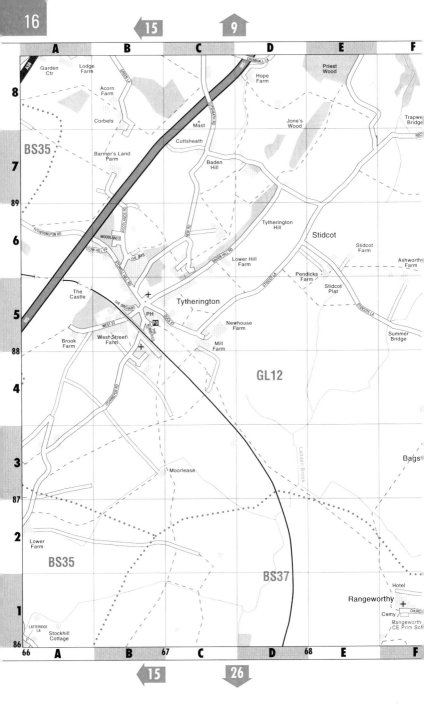

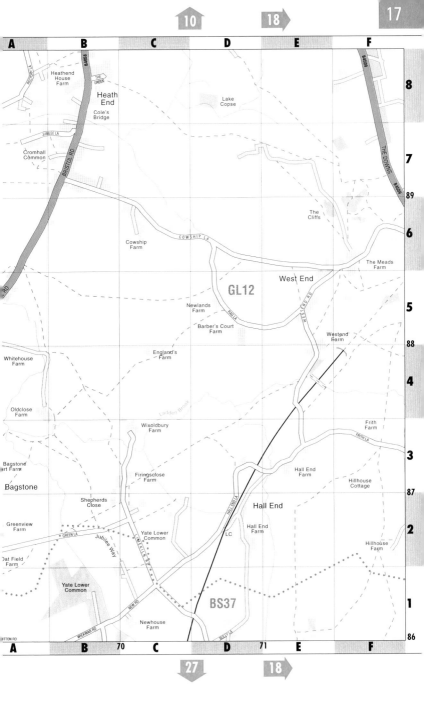

10
18

A B C D E F

8

Heathend House Farm

Heath End

Cole's Bridge

THE GREEN

B4059

BRISTOL RD

JUBILEE LA

Cromhall Common

Lake Copse

THE DOWNS

B4509

7

89

The Cliffs

6

Cowship Farm

COWSHIP LA

West End

The Meads Farm

GL12

Newlands Farm

Barber's Court Farm

WEST END RD

RAG LA

5

88

Westend Farm

England's Farm

Whitehouse Farm

Laddon Brook

4

Oldclose Farm

Frith Farm

Wixoldbury Farm

FRITH LA

Bagstone art Farm

3

Bagstone

Firingsclose Farm

Hall End Farm

Hillhouse Cottage

87

Shepherds Close

HALL END LA

Hall End

Greenview Farm

GREEN LA

JUBILEE WAY

Yate Lower Common

NEW RD

LC

Hall End Farm

2

Oat Field Farm

Hillhouse Farm

Yate Lower Common

NEW RD

Newhouse Farm

BS37

BULLY LA

1

86

HITTON RD

WICKWAR RD

A B C D E F

27
18

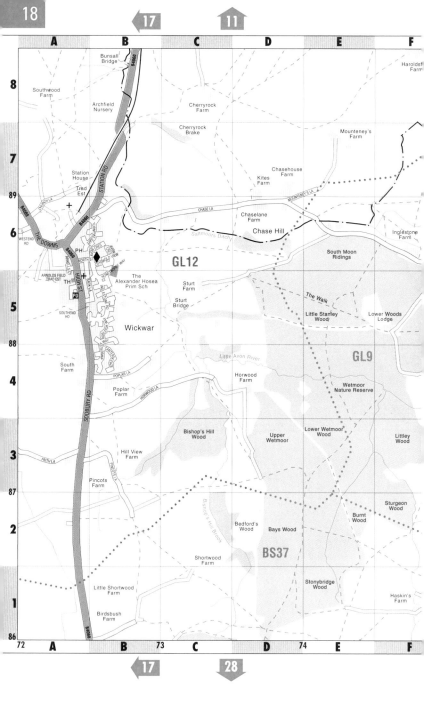

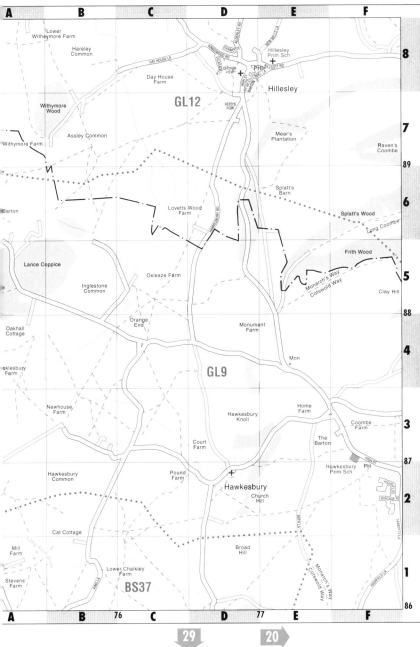

A B C D E F

Lower
Witheymore Farm

Hareley
Common

DAY HOUSE LA

Day House
Farm

KINGSWOOD RD

ALBERT ST RD

YARMOUTH

HIGH ST

CHURCH
VIEW

NEW MILL LA

Hillesley
Prim Sch

WALL CLOSE

ALLCOTT RD

PH

HIGH ST

MARTIN

Hillesley

GL12

REED'S
ROW

Withymore
Wood

Withymore Farm

Assley Common

Mear's
Plantation

Raven's
Coombe

Splatt's
Barn

Splatt's Wood

Barton

Lovetts Wood
Farm

HAWKESBURY RD

Long Coombe

Frith Wood

Lance Coppice

Oxleaze Farm

Monarch's Way
Cotswold Way

Clay Hill

Inglestone
Common

Orange
End

Monument
Farm

Oakhall
Cottage

GL9

Mon

cklesbury
Farm

Newhouse
Farm

Hawkesbury
Knoll

Home
Farm

Coombe
Farm

Court
Farm

The
Barton

HIGH ST

Hawkesbury
Common

Pound
Farm

Hawkesbury

Church
Hill

Hawkesbury
Prim Sch

PH

HIGHFIELDS

BURDAGE RD

SANDPITS LA

Little Avon River

Cat Cottage

BATH LA

Mill
Farm

Broad
Hill

Monarch's Way
Cotswold Way

HIGHFIELD LA

Stevens'
Farm

Lower Chalkley
Farm

KILN LA

BS37

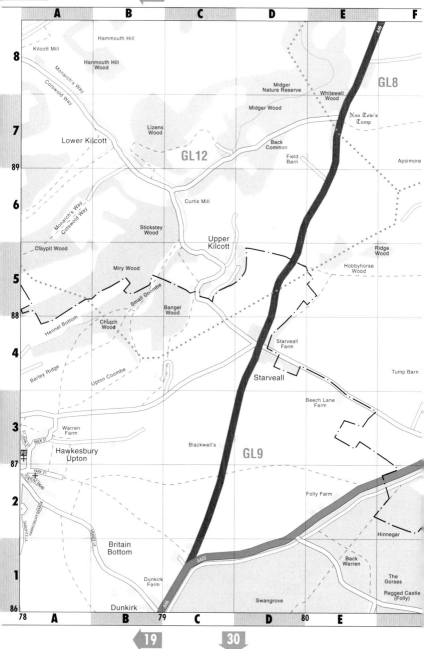

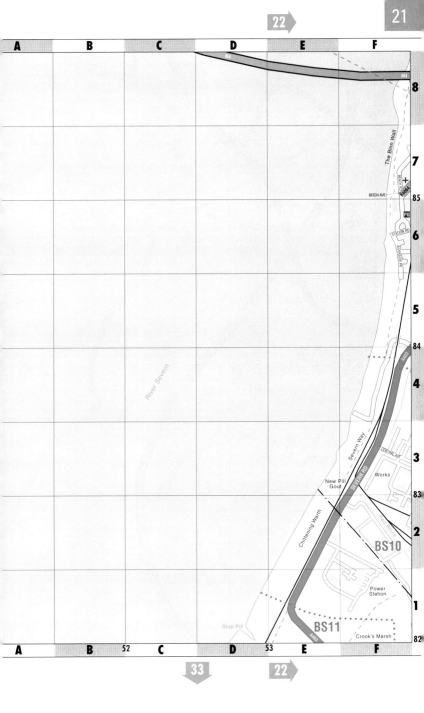

| A | B | C | D | E | F |

33
22

M4

The Binn Wall

8

7

BEECH AVE

85

PO

STATION RD

6

5

84

A403

4

Severn Way

CENTRAL AVE

3

New Pill
Gout

SEVERN RD

Works

83

Chittening Warth

2

BS10

Power
Station

1

Stup Pill

BS11

A403

Crook's Marsh

82

River Severn

52

53

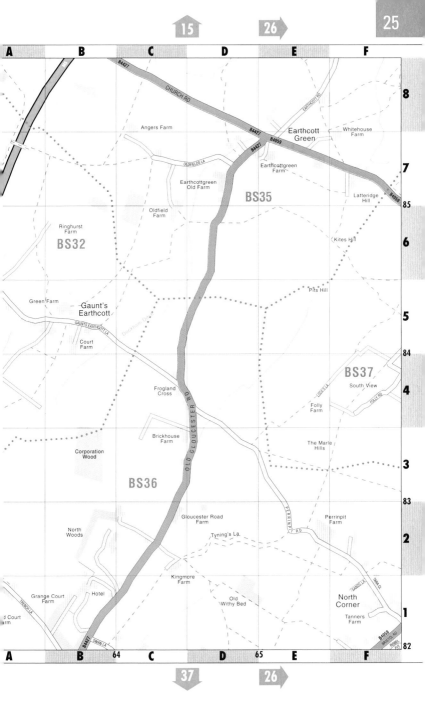

A   **B**   **C**   **D**   **E**   **F**

B4427

CHURCH RD

EMERSONS RD

8

Angers Farm

B4427

Earthcott
Green

Whitehouse
Farm

B4059

OLDFIELDS LA

B4427

Earthcottgreen
Farm

7

Earthcottgreen
Old Farm

BS35

Latteridge
Hill

B4058

85

Oldfield
Farm

Ringhurst
Farm

Kites Hill

6

BS32

Green Farm

Pits Hill

5

Gaunt's
Earthcott

GAUNTS EARTHCOTT LA

Drownham Gate

BS37

South View

84

Court
Farm

Frogland
Cross

LOCKS LA

FOLLY RD

4

OLD GLOUCESTER RD

Folly
Farm

Brickhouse
Farm

The Marle
Hills

Corporation
Wood

3

BS36

83

North
Woods

Gloucester Road
Farm

PERRINPIT RD

Perrinpit
Farm

2

Tyning's La.

TRINCLE LA

Kingmore
Farm

SWAN CL

Grange Court
Farm

Hotel

Old
Withy Bed

North
Corner

SANDS LA

1

d Court
arm

B4427

SWAN LA

Tanners
Farm

B4058

BRISTOL RD

ROBBS LA

82

A   **B**   64   **C**   **D**   65   **E**   **F**

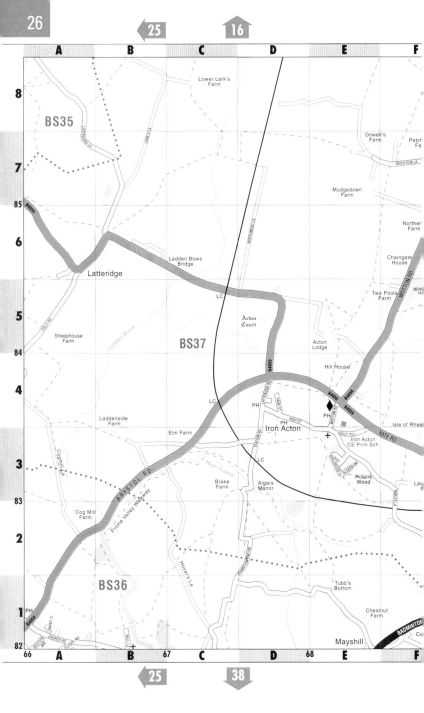

A B C D E F

8

Lower Lark's Farm

BS35

LATTERIDGE LA

LARK'S LA

7

PATCH ELM LA

Dowell's Farm

Patch Fa

85

B4058

6

Mudgedown Farm

Northern Farm

NORTHMEAD LA

Ladden Bows Bridge

Chaingate House

Latteridge

TOLL RD

WOTTON RD

BECKI FA

LC

5

Two Pools Farm

Acton Court

Acton Lodge

84

Sheephouse Farm

BS37

Hill House

Ladden Brook

B4059

4

Laddenside Farm

LC

PH

LATTERIDGE RD

B4058

B4059

PARK

B4059

Elm Farm

PH

HIGH ST

Isle of Rhee

Iron Acton

PH

YATE RD

Cogmill La

STATION RD

Iron Acton CE Prim Sch

HOLLY HILL

3

River Frome

Brake Farm

Algars Manor

LC

ACORN DR

NORTH RD

Robins Wood

Law

83

Cog Mill Farm

Frome Valley Walkway

BRISTOL RD

MILL LA

NIBLEY LA

2

BS36

Hover's La

FRAMPTON END RD

Tubb's Bottom

1

PH

B4058

Chestnut Farm

BADMINTON

82

HOLLY HILL

BRISTOL RD

JUNIPER CL

CHURCH RD

SCHOOL RD

MILL LA

Mayshill

Ce

66 A B 67 C D 68 E F

Rangeworthy

Southwood Farm

Leechpool

Mill

Bully La

Yate Court

Yate Court (remains of)

8

Tan House Farm

Hartstrow

7

Old Wood Colliery (dis)

TANHOUSE LA

Jubilee Way

85

Yate Rocks

The Barton Farm

6

Ford Farm

Greenlane Farm

Sunnyside Farm

Engine Common

BS37

5

Outdoor Sports Complex

The Rocks

84

North Road Prim Sch

Brimsham Green Sec Sch

Stone Mill

B4060

Hampshire Way

Tyler's Farm

4

GOOSE GREEN WAY

Goose Green

3

IRON ACTON WAY

1 OAKLAND BSN PK
2 ORCHARD CT

THE ALPHA CTR

Great Weston Bsns Pk

RAINBOW CT

Cranleigh Court Inf Sch

Fromebank Jun Sch

St Mary's CE Prim Sch

Schs

RIDGEWAY

83

The Laurels

NORTHRIDGE BSNS CTR

Yate

1 BADMINTON CT
2 THE BADMINTON CT

Superstore

2

Nibley

BADMINTON RD

STATION RD

Liby

STATION RD

Sh Ctr

1

KENNEDY WAY

Factory

Westerleigh Common

YATE

King Edmund Com Sch

82

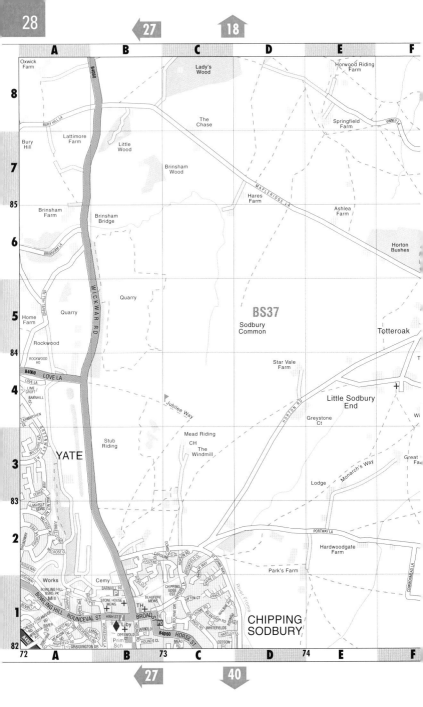

Oxwick Farm

Lady's Wood

Horwood Riding Farm

8

BURY HILL LA

The Chase

Springfield Farm

VINNEY LA

Bury Hill

Lattimore Farm

Little Wood

7

Brinsham Wood

MAPLERIDGE LA

85

Brinsham Farm

Brinsham Bridge

Hares Farm

Ashlea Farm

BRINSHAM LA

WICKWAR RD

6

Horton Bushes

Quarry

Quarry

BS37

5

Home Farm

GRAVEL HILL RD

Quarry

Sodbury Common

Totteroak

Rockwood

84

ROCKWOOD RD

Star Vale Farm

T

B4060

LOVE LA

LOVE LA

LIME CROFT

BARNHILL CL

HORTON RD

Little Sodbury End

4

Greystone Ct

Wi

CARMARTHEN CL

Jubilee Way

Stub Riding

Mead Riding

YATE

CH The Windmill

Monarch's Way

Great Fa

3

Lodge

BROADWAY

83

Hardwoodgate Farm

PORTWAY LA

2

MELROSE CL

CAROLINE CL

COUZENS CL

Park's Farm

River Frome

COMMONMEAD LA

Works

Cemy

BARNHILL RD

STONE HOUSE MEWS

CHIPPING EDGE EST.

BEAUFORT MEWS

CHIPPING SODBURY

1

BOWLING HILL

ROUNCEVAL ST

HIGH ST

BROAD ST

HORSE ST

B4060

Prim Sch

HOUNDS CL

MEAD RD

WHITEFIELDS

CLEESON CL

82

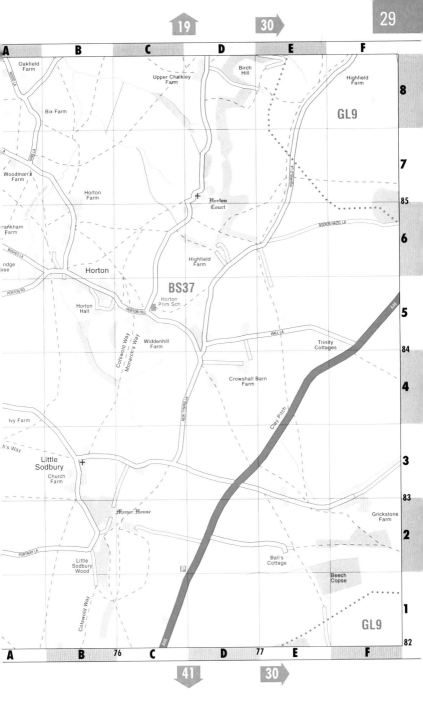

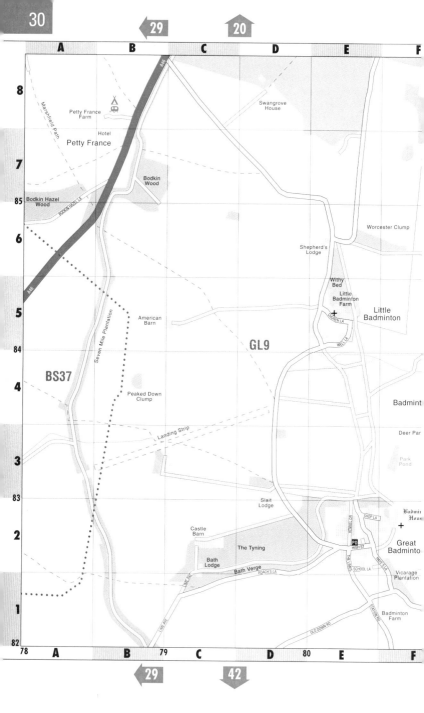

A **B** **C** **D** **E** **F**

8

Marshfield Path

Petty France
Farm

Hotel
Petty France

Swangrove
House

7

Bodkin
Wood

85

Bodkin Hazel
Wood

BODKIN HAZEL LA.

Worcester Clump

6

Shepherd's
Lodge

Withy
Bed

Little
Badminton
Farm

**Little
Badminton**

5

Seven Mile Plantation

American
Barn

CHURCH LA.

WELL LA.

GL9

84

BS37

4

Peaked Down
Clump

Badmint

Deer Par

Landing Strip

Park
Pond

3

Slait
Lodge

83

Badmin
Hous

Castle
Barn

The Tyning

2

SHOP LA.

PENNIE DR.

Great
Badminto

PO
HIGH ST

Bath
Lodge

THE SWAN

SCHOOL LA.

PIKE'S LA.

Vicarage
Plantation

LIME AVE.

Bath Verge

BGACH'S LA.

Badminton
Farm

OLD DOWN RD.

FROME RD.

1

82

A **B** **C** **D** **E** **F**

78   79   80

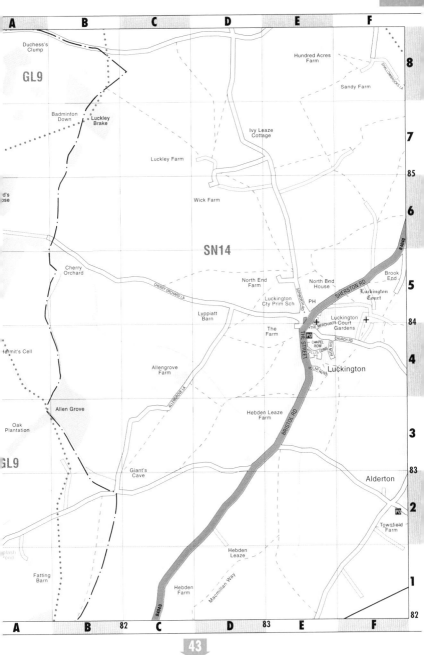

8

GL9

Duchess's Clump

Hundred Acres Farm

Sandy Farm

7

Badminton Down

Luckley Brake

Ivy Leaze Cottage

85

Luckley Farm

d's se

Wick Farm

6

SN14

Cherry Orchard

CHERRY ORCHARD LA

North End Farm

North End House

Brook End

5

Luckington Cty Prim Sch

PH

SHERSTON RD

Luckington Court

Lyppiatt Barn

Luckington Court Gardens

THE MERCHANTS

84

The Farm

THE STREET

PO

CHURCH RD

ermit's Cell

Allengrove Farm

CHAPEL ROW

4

ALLENGROVE LA

Luckington

POLAR MOUND

Allen Grove

Hebden Leaze Farm

BRISTOL RD

Oak Plantation

3

GL9

Giant's Cave

83

Alderton

PO

2

Townfield Farm

plash Pond

Hebden Leaze

Fatting Barn

Macmillan Way

1

Hebden Farm

B84040

82

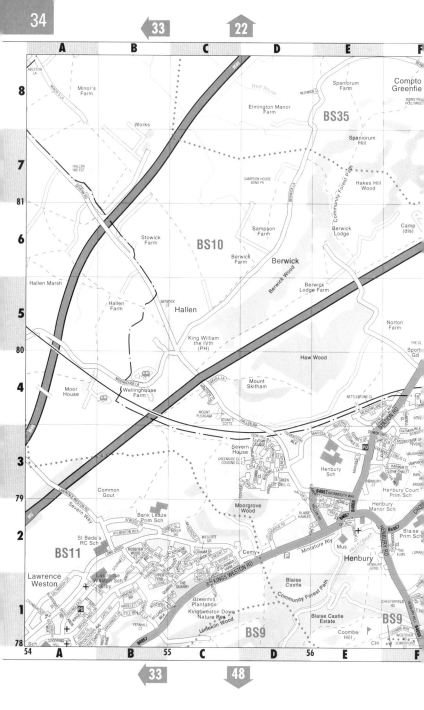

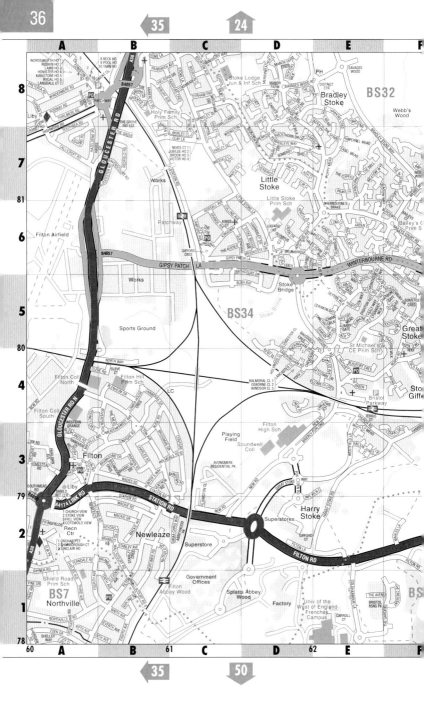

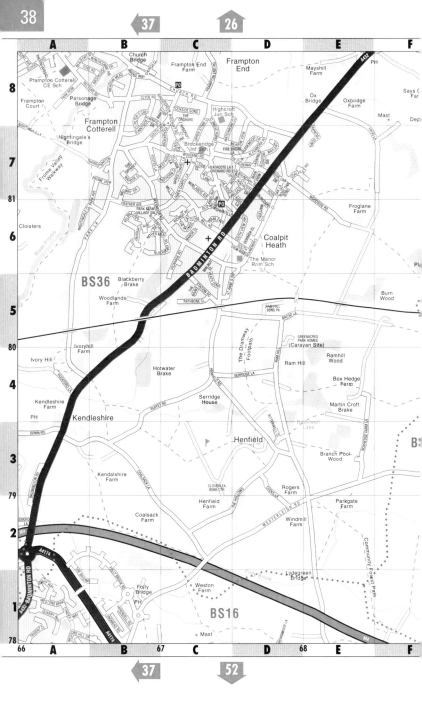

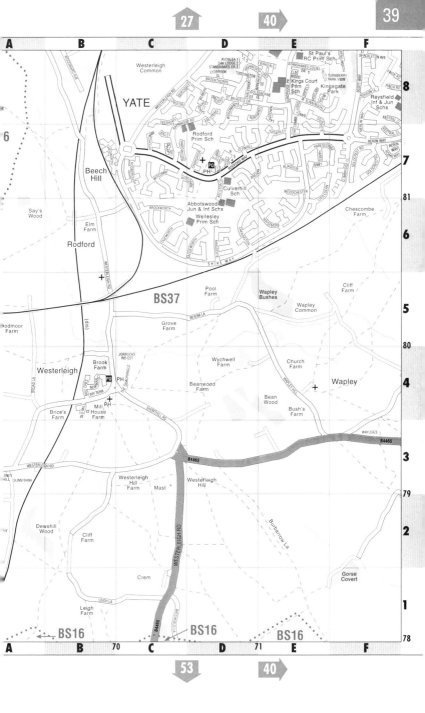

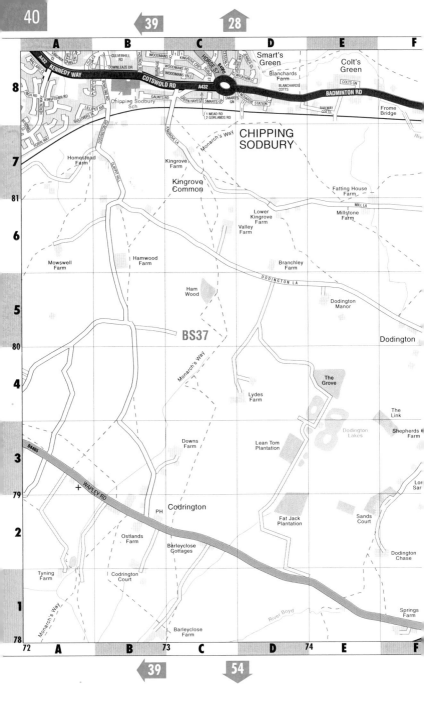

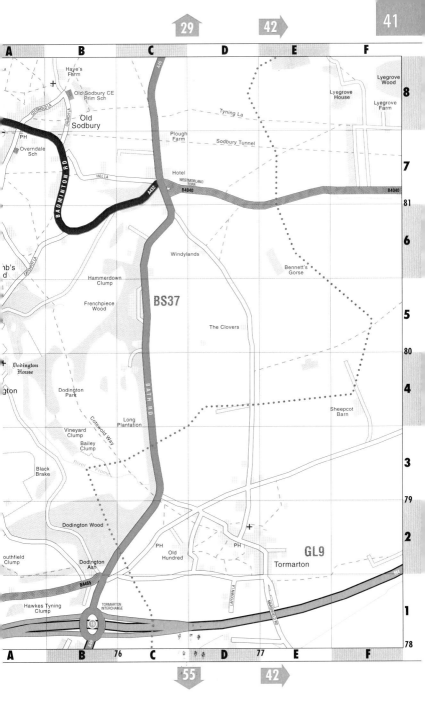

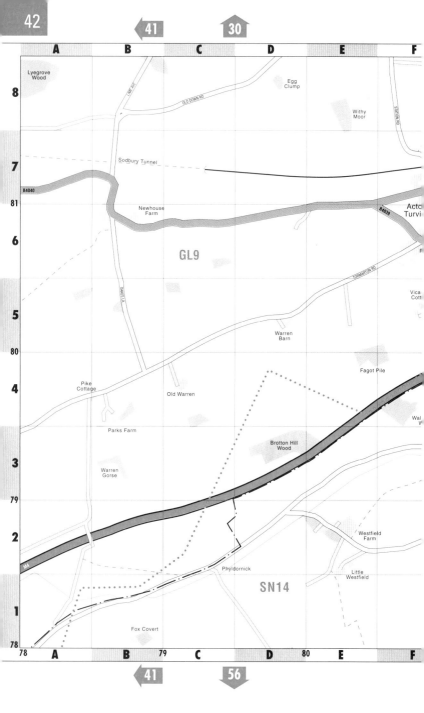

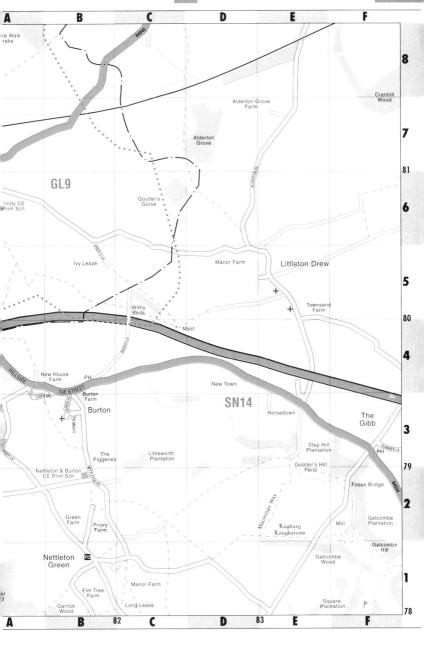

A B C D E F

8

Cranhill Wood

7

Alderton Grove Farm

81

GL9

Alderton Grove

6

Trinity CE Prim Sch

Goulter's Gorse

Ivy Leaze

Manor Farm

Littleton Drew

5

Withy Beds

Townsend Farm

80

Mast

4

HILLSIDE

New House Farm

PH

THE STREET

Burton Farm

New Town

SN14

Horsedown

The Gibb

3

DOWN WAY

Burton

The Piggeries

Littleworth Plantation

Step Hill Plantation

Goulter's Hill Farm

PH

79

Nettleton & Burton CE Prim Sch

Fosse Bridge

2

Green Farm

Priory Farm

Macmillan Way

Lugbury Longbarrow

Mill

Gatcombe Plantation

Gatcombe Hill

Nettleton Green

PO

Gatcombe Wood

1

Elm Tree Farm

Manor Farm

Square Plantation

Garrick Wood

Long Leaze

78

A B 82 C D 83 E F

Black
Nore

SEVERNMEADE

FEDDON
VILLAGE

Brackenwood
Gdns

Hang
Rock

Redcliff
Bay

Redcliffe
Bay

BS20

Charcombe
Bay

Charcombe
Wood

Mast

PH

Weston
Down

Weston
Lodge

Black
Strip

The
Ripple

The
Conygar

Culver
Cliff

WALTON BAY
HOUSE PARK
HOMES

TWO ACRES
CVN PK

BS21

Farley

Weston
Wood

Pigeon House
Bay

Signal
Station

Walton
Down

Common Hill
Wood

PH

Weston in
Gordano

Canon's
Wood

B3124

Walton
Bay

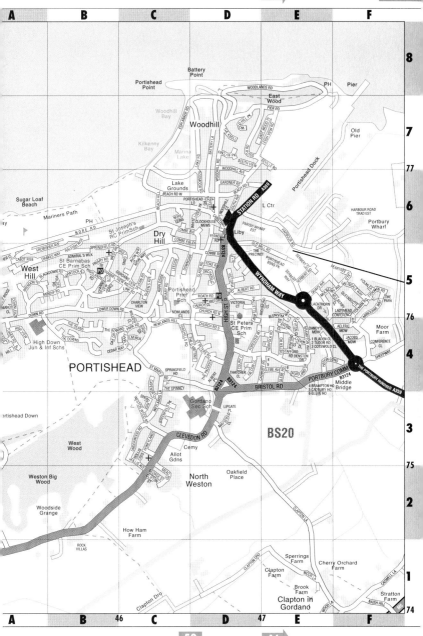

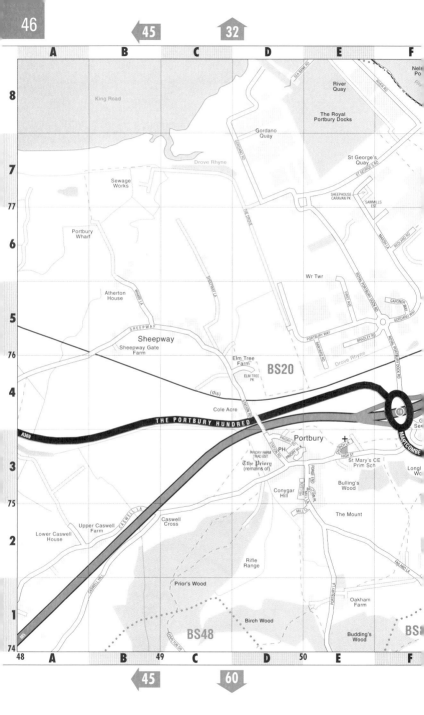

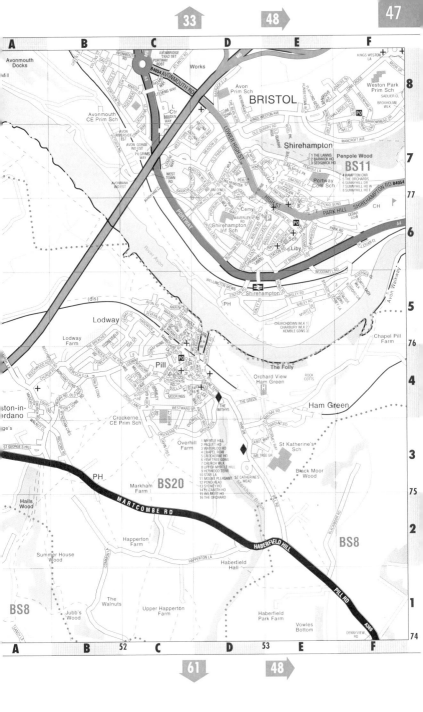

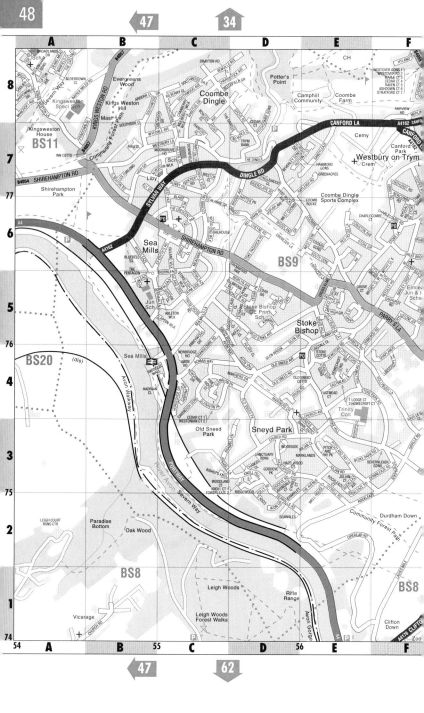

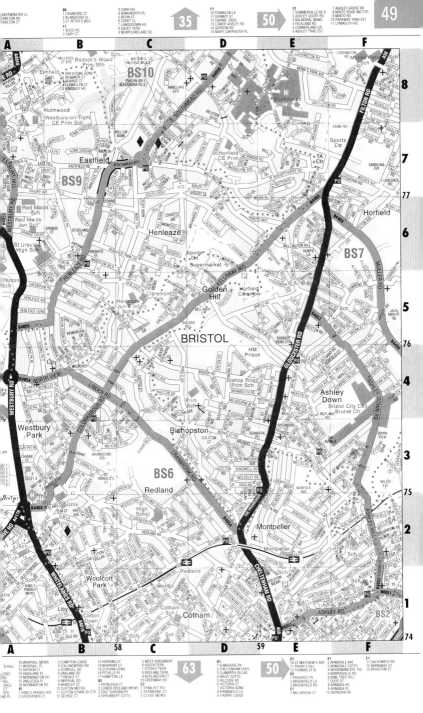

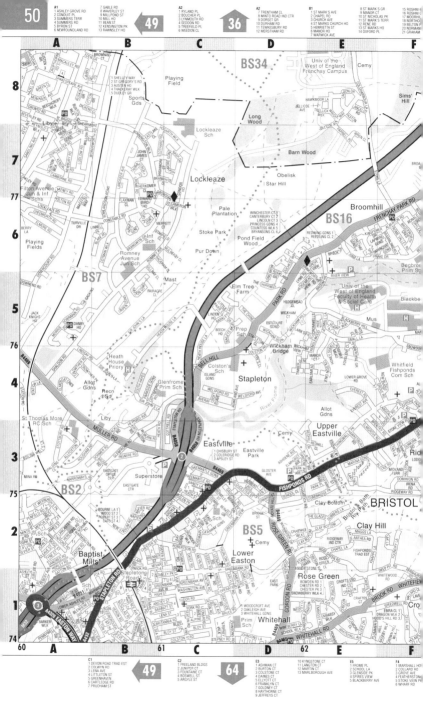

50

A1
1 ASHLEY GROVE RD
2 CONDUIT PL
3 SUMMERS TERR
4 SUMMERS RD
5 BYRON ST
6 NEWFOUNDLAND RD

7 GABLE RD
8 WAVERLEY ST
9 MILLPOND ST
10 MILL HO
11 BEAN ST
12 KENSINGTON PK
13 RAWNSLEY HO

49

A2
1 RYLAND PL
2 BOUCHER PL
3 LYNMOUTH RD
4 GEDDON RD
5 TREEFIELD PL
6 WEEDON CL

36

A2
7 TRENTHAM CL
8 MINTO ROAD IND CTR
9 DORSET GR
10 DURHAM RD
11 TEWKESBURY RD
12 MEERSTHAM RD

B1
1 ST MARK'S AVE
2 CHAPEL RD
3 CHURCH AVE
4 ST MARKS CHURCH HO
5 HENRIETTA ST
6 MANOR HO
7 WARWICK AVE

8 ST MARK'S GR
9 MANOR CT
10 ST NICHOLAS HO
11 ST MARK'S TERR
12 RENE RD
13 ST MARKS HO
14 OXFORD PL

15 ROSHNI 1
16 ROSHNI 2
17 MOORHILL
18 NORTHCOTE
19 FELTON PL
20 NORMANHU
21 GRAHAM

C1
1 DEVON ROAD TRAD EST
2 COLWYN RD
3 LENA AVE
4 LITTLETON ST
5 GREENHAVEN
6 CARTLEDGE RD
7 PRUDHAM ST

49

C2
1 FREELAND BLDGS
2 JUNIPER CT
3 FOUNTAINE CT
4 BOSWELL ST
5 ARGYLE ST

64

E3
1 ASHMAN CT
2 BURTON CT
3 COLSTONE CT
4 DAINES CT
5 ELLYOTT CT
6 FRANKLYN ST
7 GOLDNEY CT
8 HAYTHORNE CT
9 JEFFREYS CT

10 KYNGSTONE CT
11 LANGTON CT
12 MARTIN CT
13 MARLBOROUGH AVE

E5
1 FROME PL
2 SCHOOL LA
3 GLENSIDE PK
4 SPIRES VIEW
5 BLACKBERRY AVE

F4
1 MARSHALL HO
2 COLLARD HO
3 GROVE AVE
4 FEATHERSTON
5 STOKE VIEW HO
6 WHARF RD

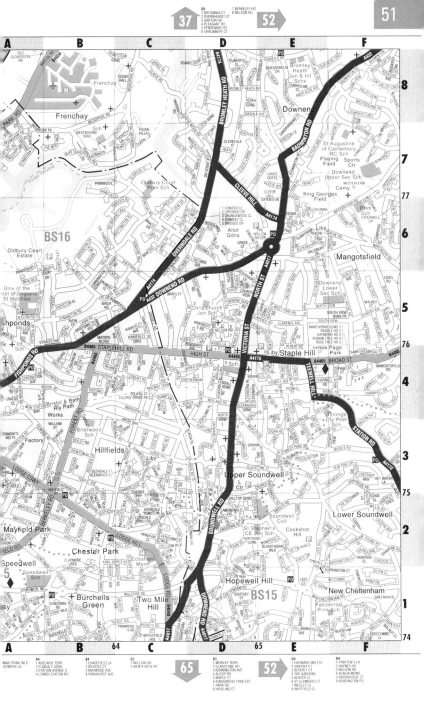

51

37 ◀ 52 ▶

D5
1 BRITANNIA CT
2 OVERNHURST CT
3 GARON HO
4 PLEASANT HO
5 PENDENNIS HO
6 SHRUBBERY CT

7 BERKELEY HO
8 NELSON HO

MAS PRING WLK
DOWERS LA

A4
1 ADELAIDE TERR
2 FLMDALF GDNS
3 STATION AVENUE S
4 LOWER STATION RD

B4
1 CHASEFIELD LA
2 BRIDGES CT
3 MAYWOOD AVE
4 PARKHURST AVE

C2
1 WILLOW GR
2 WENTFORTH DR

D1
1 MORLEY TERR
2 GLADSTONE RD
3 KENNINGTON AVE
4 ALSOP RD
5 MAPLE CT
6 KINGSWOOD TRAD EST
7 PARK RD
8 HICKLING CT

D3
1 HAYWARD IND EST
2 VINCENT CT
3 BEVERLY CT
4 THE GARDENS
5 BEAZER CL
6 ST CLEMENTS CT
7 WESLEY CL
8 WHITFIELD CL

D4
1 PRATTEN'S LA
2 HAYNES HO
3 NELSON RD
4 ACACIA MEWS
5 BROOKRIDGE CT
6 KENSINGTON RD

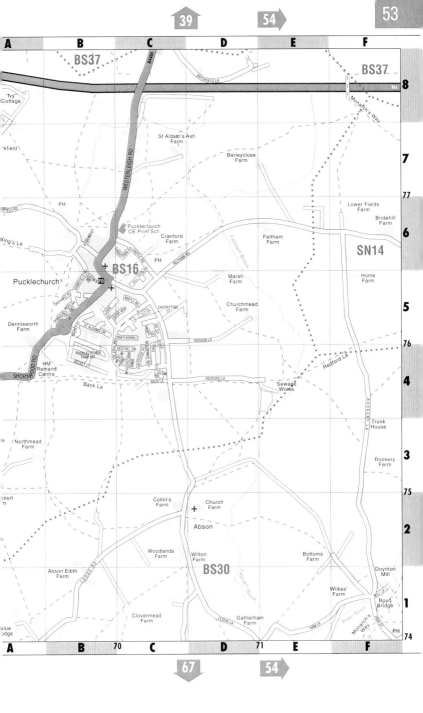

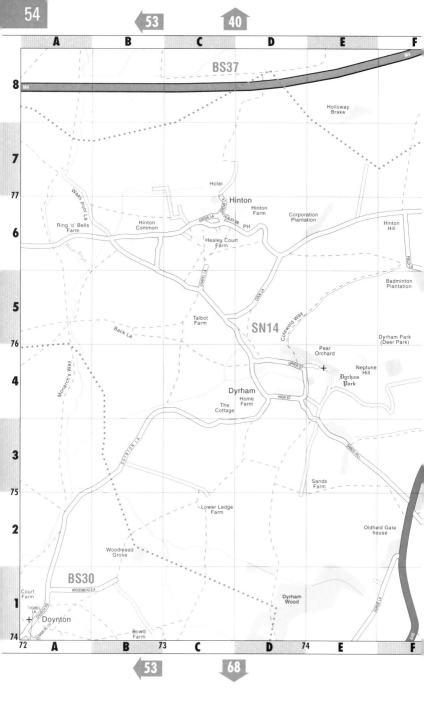

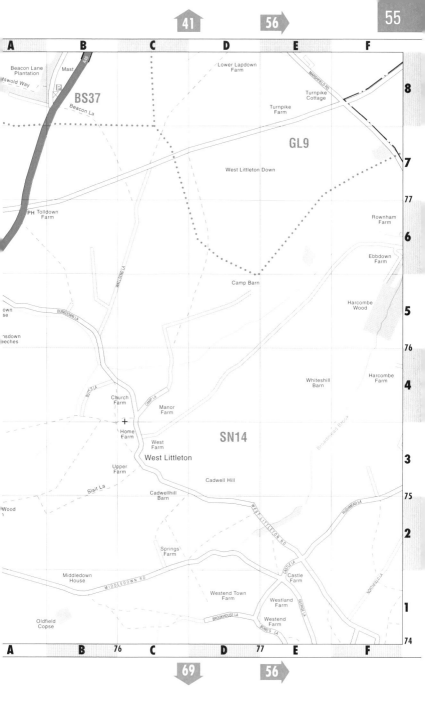

Beacon Lane
Plantation

Mast

Cotswold Way

BS37

Beacon La

Lower Lapdown
Farm

MARSHFIELD RD

Turnpike
Cottage

Turnpike
Farm

8

GL9

West Littleton Down

7

77

PH Tolldown
Farm

Rownham
Farm

6

Ebbdown
Farm

DUNSDOWN LA

WHITE END LA

own
se

nsdown
eeches

Camp Barn

Harcombe
Wood

5

76

BUTTS LA

CAMP LA

Church
Farm

Manor
Farm

Whiteshill
Barn

Harcombe
Farm

4

Home
Farm

West
Farm

SN14

Broadmead Brook

West Littleton

3

Upper
Farm

Cadwell Hill

Slait La

Cadwellhill
Barn

WEST LITTLETON RD

75

Wood

BUSHMEAD LA

2

Springs
Farm

CASTLE LA

Castle
Farm

NORTHFIELD LA

GORSE LA

Middledown
House

MIDDLEDOWN RD

Westend Town
Farm

Westland
Farm

1

Oldfield
Copse

BROOKHOUSE LA

BOND'S LA

Westend
Farm

74

A B 76 C D 77 E F

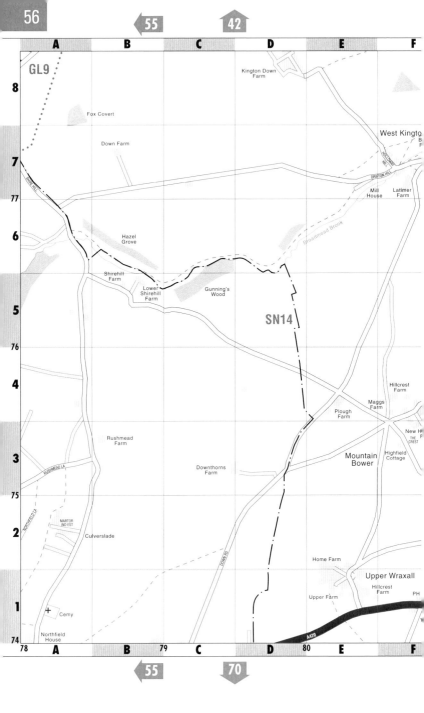

GL9

8

Fox Covert

Down Farm

Kington Down Farm

West Kingto
B
F

7

HOLT DRIVE

DRIFTON HILL

Mill House

Latimer Farm

77

Hazel Grove

Broadmead Brook

6

Shirehill Farm

Lower Shirehill Farm

Gunning's Wood

SN14

5

76

Hillcrest Farm

4

Maggs Farm

Plough Farm

New H
THE CREST
F

Rushmead Farm

Mountain Bower

Highfield Cottage

3

Downthorns Farm

75

RUSHMEAD LA

NORTHFIELD LA

MARTOR IND EST

Culverslade

2

DOWN RD

Home Farm

Upper Wraxall

Hillcrest Farm

PH

1

Upper Farm

Cemy

A429

Northfield House

74

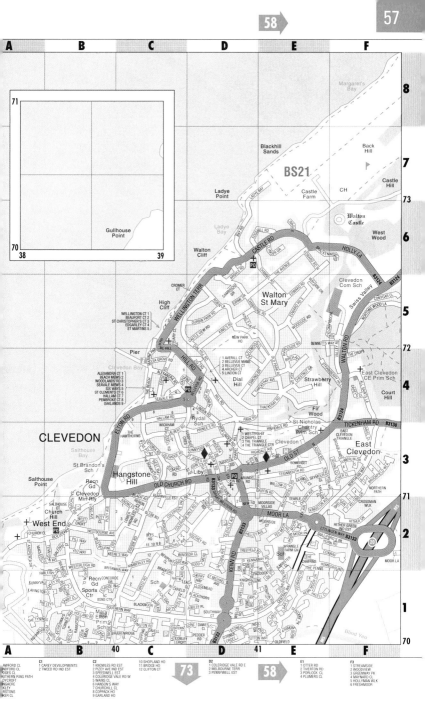

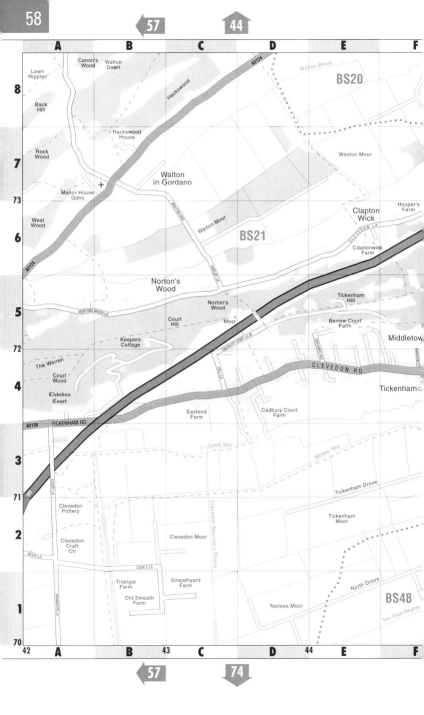

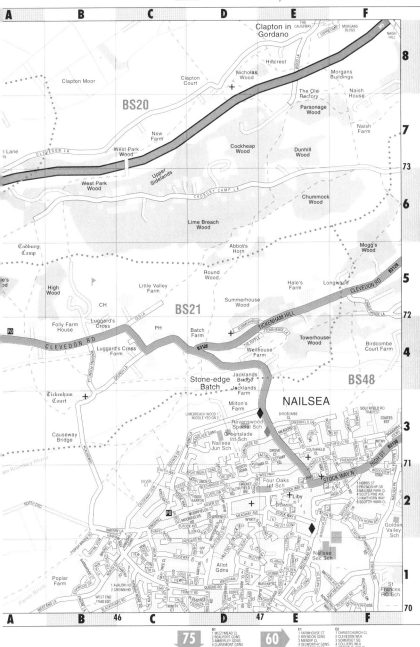

A B C D E F

Clapton in Gordano

THE CAUSEWAY
SWANSTAIL
MORGANS BLDGS
NAISH HILL

8

Hillcrest
Nicholas Cl
Clapton Wood
Clapton Court
Morgans Buildings
Naish House
The Old Rectory
Parsonage Wood

BS20

New Farm
Naish Farm

7

West Park Wood
CLEVEDON LA

Cockheap Wood
Dunhill Wood

West Park Wood
Upper Sidelands
CADBURY CAMP LA

73

Chummock Wood

6

Lime Breach Wood

Cadbury Camp
Abbot's Horn
Mogg's Wood

Round Wood

High Wood
Little Valley Farm
BS21
Summerhouse Wood
Hale's Farm
Longwood
CLEVEDON RD
B3128

5

CH
OLD LA

Folly Farm House
Luggard's Cross
PH
Batch Farm
SUMMERHOUSE LA
TICKENHAM HILL
STONEHENGE
THE TIPPLE
Towerhouse Wood
COURTHOUSE LA
Birdcombe Court Farm

72

P0
CLEVEDON RD
Luggard's Cross Farm
CHURCH LA
B3128
Wellhouse Farm

BS48

4

Stone-edge Batch
Jacklands Bridge
Jacklands Farm

Tickenham Court
Milton's Farm
NAILSEA
SOUTHFIELD RD TRADEST
COATES EST

Causeway Bridge
LIMEBREACH WOOD
MIDDLE YEO GN 2
Ravenswood Special Sch
Greenslade Inf Sch
BIRDCOMBE CL
GREENFIELD CL
WITHY CL
B3130

3

Nailsea Jun Sch
SOUTHFIELD RD
FRIENDSHIP RD
HIGH ST

71

NIGHTINGALE GDNS
WESTWAY
ABBOTS HORN
DROVE
STOCK WAY N
E1
1 HOBBS CT
2 FRIENDSHIP GR
3 NAILSEA PARK CL
4 SCOTS PINE AVE
5 HAWTHORN WAY
6 SCOTCH HGRN CL

2

SILVER CT
FRYTH WAY
FOSSE BARTON
SILVER ST
CRICKET
Four Oaks Inf Sch
STOCK WAY N
Liby
SYCAMORE
STOCK WAY S
GOLDEN VALLEY SCH

MOORFIELDS
MEADWAY AVE
VALLEY GDNS

WATERY LA
CHAPEL
LION CL
ORCHARD CL
IVY CL
MIZZY CL
CLARKEN
POLDEN
Nailsea Sec Sch

1

NORTH DRO
Parish Brook
YEW
YEW
RIDGEWAY
GOSS LA
TREE CL
Allot Gdns
COOMBE
St Frances RC Sch

Poplar Farm
WEST END TRAD EST
BLACKHAIRS RD
1 AVALON HO
2 CROWN HO
TRINITY CL
QUEENS RD
TRINITY CT
PLOUGHTAIL
CORFE
HATTERHOUSE

70

A B C D E F

D1
1 MIZZYMEAD CL
2 BRENDON GDNS
3 AMBERLEY GDNS
4 CLAREMONT GDNS
5 DOWNLAND CL
6 DORCHESTER CL

E1
1 FARMHOUSE CT
2 BRENDON GDNS
3 MENDIP CL
4 SELWORTHY GDNS
5 DUNSTER GDNS
6 BIDDISHAM CL

E2
1 CHRISTCHURCH CL
2 CLEVEDON WLK
3 SOMERSET SQ
4 COLLIERS WLK
5 CROWN GLASS PL
6 VALLEY CL
7 FARMHOUSE CL

| | A | B | C | D | E | F |

Naish
Hill

Charlton
Farm

The Downs
Scn

Windmill
Hill

8

Bullock's
Bottom

The
Cleaves

BS20

Racecourse
Farm

Old Hill

7

Moat House
Farm

Breach Wood

New Forest

CADBURY CAMP
LA

73

Moat
Cottages

Barn
Plantation

6

White
House

C L E V E D O N   R D

Higher
Farm

Limekiln
Cottages

Limekiln
Plantation

The
Ripple

Works

Court
Farm

BS48

5

West Hill

The
Warren

Sidelands
Cottages

Wraxall
Court

The Sidelands

72

Rectory

Ham Farm

HAM LA

Wraxall
CE Prim Sch

Home
Farm

Tyntesfield

4

C L E V E D O N   R D

BRISTOL RD

Truckle
Wood

Wraxall
House

Cradle
Bridge

Wraxall

PH

FRYTH
HO

Tyntesfield Park

NORTHAMPTON
HO

3

Hazel Farm

St John's
House

Holly
Cottage

Lower
Lodge

71

Orchard
Farm

2

NAILSEA

Brook Farm

Watercress
Farm

Gable
Farm

CLEVEDON RD

Watercress
Wood

1

East
End

1 KEMBLE CL
2 WOODFORD CL
3 SHERSTON CL
4 CRICKLADE CT
5 SUNNINGDALE CT
6 GLENEAGLES CL
7 ST ANDREWS CL
8 NOWHERE LA
9 CHELVEY RISE

BACKWELL ROW

BACKWELL COMM

Bathing Pond
Wood

BIRDLIP CL

70

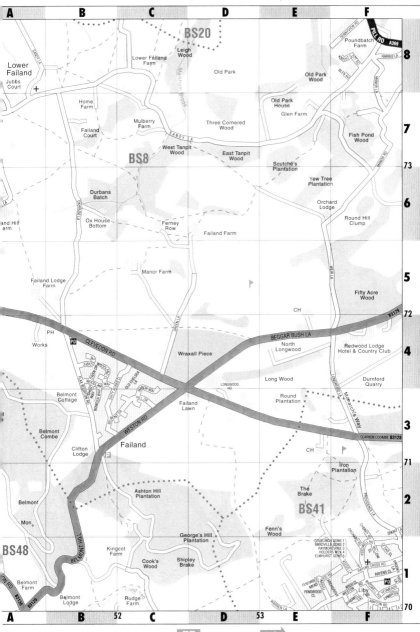

BS20

Leigh Wood

Lower Failand Farm

Lower Failand

Jubbs Court

Home Farm

Mulberry Farm

Failand Court

Failand Lodge Farm

Durbans Batch

Ox House Bottom

Ferney Row

Failand Farm

Manor Farm

BS8

West Tanpit Wood

East Tanpit Wood

Three Cornered Wood

Old Park

Old Park Wood

Old Park House

Glen Farm

Scutché's Plantation

Yew Tree Plantation

Fish Pond Wood

Orchard Lodge

Round Hill Clump

Poundbatch Farm

PILL RD   A369

HARRIS LA

DONKEY VIEW RD

KNIGHT CL

GLEN FM

8

7

73

6

Failand Lodge Farm

PH

Works

CLEVEDON RD

Wraxall Piece

Belmont Cottage

Belmont Combe

Clifton Lodge

Belmont

Mon

BS48

Belmont Farm

Belmont Lodge

Kingcot Farm

Cook's Wood

Rudge Farm

Failand

WESTON RD

OLD CRES

Failand Lawn

Ashton Hill Plantation

George's Hill Plantation

Shipley Brake

CH

Fifty Acre Wood

BEGGAR BUSH LA

North Longwood

Long Wood

LONGWOOD HO

Round Plantation

CH

Redwood Lodge Hotel & Country Club

Durnford Quarry

Iron Plantation

The Brake

BS41

Fenn's Wood

CLARKEN COOMBE B3128

MORTON'S WAY

BELMONT HILL

5

72

4

3

71

2

1

70

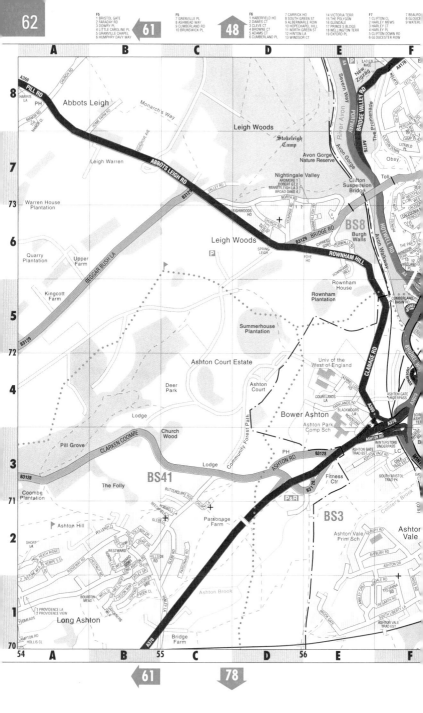

61

48

Abbots Leigh

Leigh Woods

Leigh Warren

BS8

Leigh Woods

Ashton Court Estate

Bower Ashton

BS41

Long Ashton

BS3

Ashton Vale

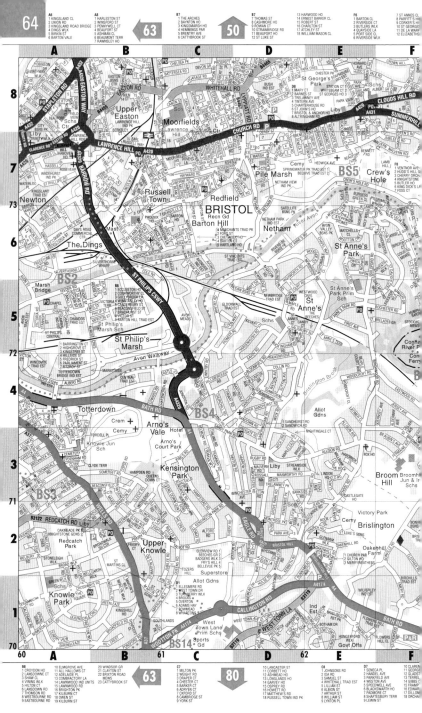

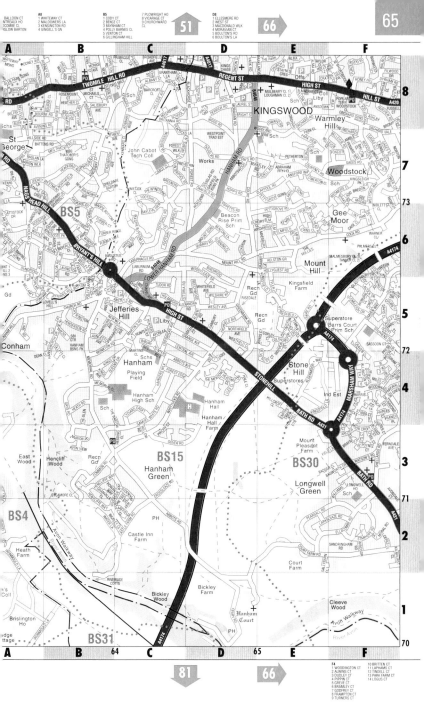

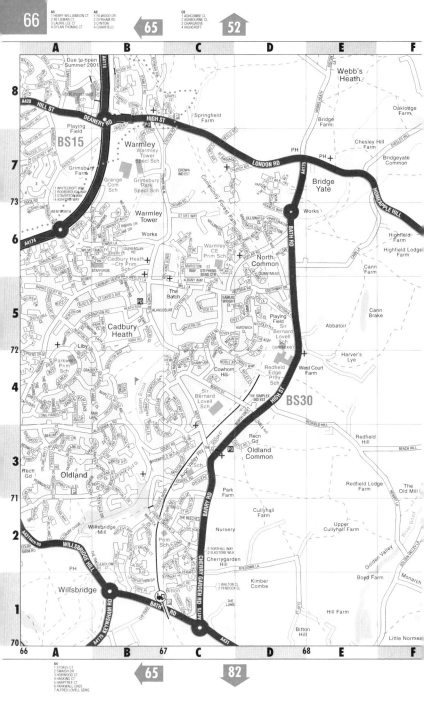

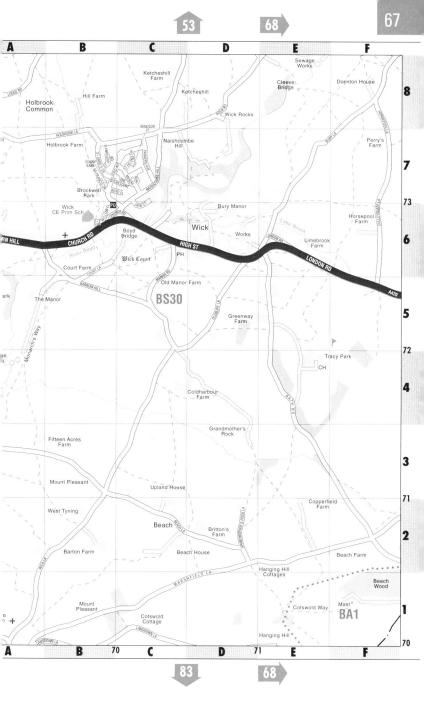

A B C D E F

8

Holbrook
Common

Hill Farm

Ketcheshill
Farm

Ketcheshill

Cleeve
Bridge

Sewage
Works

Doynton House

WINDSOR
CT

Wick Rocks

HOLBROOK LA

Holbrook Farm

Naishcombe
Hill

Perry's
Farm

7

Brockwell
Park

SUNNY
BANK

BOYD CL

73

Wick
CE Prim Sch

Bury Manor

Horsepool
Farm

Lime Brook

CHURCH RD

Boyd
Bridge

Wick

HIGH ST

Works

Limebrook
Farm

LONDON RD

6

RN HILL

River Boyd

Wick Court

PH

OLD
LONDON
RD

A420

Court Farm

COLBRT LA

Old Manor Farm

BARROW HILL

BS30

5

The Manor

Monarch's Way

Greenway
Farm

QUBRY LA

72

Tracy Park

CH

4

B.M. RD

Coldharbour
Farm

Grandmother's
Rock

Fifteen Acres
Farm

3

Mount Pleasant

Upland House

Copperfield
Farm

71

West Tyning

Beach

BEACH LA

Britton's
Farm

GRANDMOTHER'S ROCK LA

2

Barton Farm

Beach House

Beach Farm

WICK LA

MARSHFIELD LA

Hanging Hill
Cottages

Beach
Wood

Mount
Pleasant

Cotswold
Cottage

Cotswold Way

Mast

BA1

1

LANSDOWN LA

LANSDOWN LA

Hanging Hill

70

A B C D E F

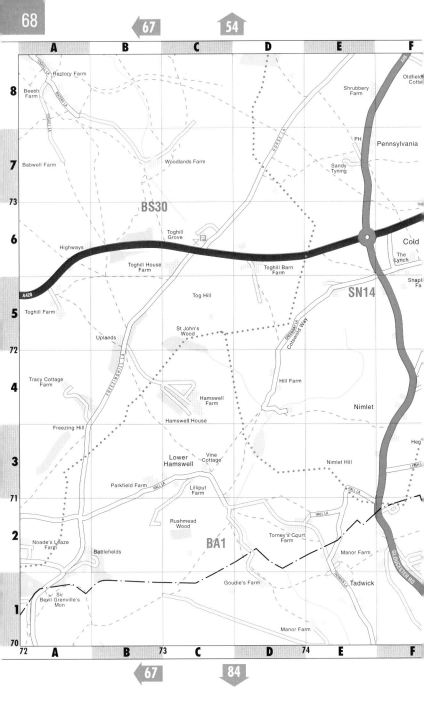

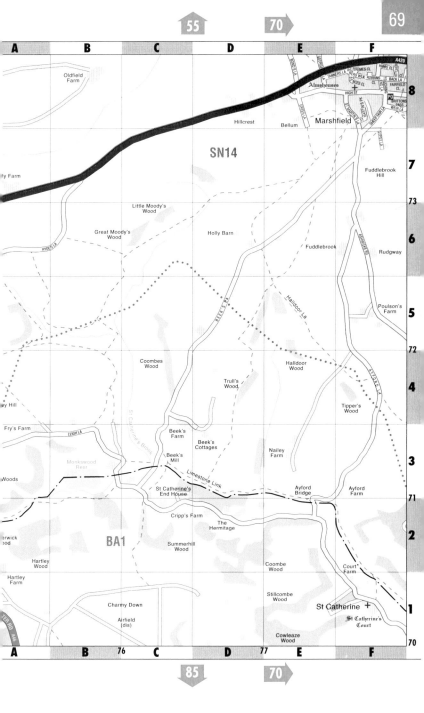

A B C D E F

A420

8 Greenview Farm
Garston Farm
Star Farm
Bell Sq HAY
HAYFIELD
CHIPPENHAM RD
HAY ST
MEAD RD
BARTON
CHURCH LA
TYTHE CT
BACK LA
Marshfield
CE Prim Sch
East End
Star La
Woodlands
Newleaze Wood

7 Ringswell
Ringswell Common
Doncombe Brook
Cloud Wood
Doncombe Scrubs
DONCOMBE HILL
Sewage Wks

73 Henleyhill Barn
Woodleaze Barn
Marshfield Wood

6 Henley Hill
Henleyhill Plantation
Colern

5 SN14
Raizes Plantation
Raizes Wood
Barracks

72 The Raizes
West Lodge
The Warren

4 Ashwicke Grange
International Sch of Choueifat
Centre Plantation
East Lodge
Colerne Airfield

3 Motcombe Farm
Ashwicke Home Farm
Pixtonsgreen
Clift Wood
ASHWICK RD
PH

71 Longley Wood
Cherry Wood
Diamond Wood

2 Motcombe Wood
Bandywell Wood
Hunters Hall
Abbotscombe Wood
Breach Wood
Dicknick Wood
OAKFORD LA
Orchard Wood
BATH RD

Oakleigh
The Rocks
Draught Wood

1 BA1
Limestone Link
Westwood Farm
West Wood

70 Oakford Farm
Three Shires Stone
ROAD HILL

78 A B 79 C D 80 E F

A B C D E F

St Thomas's
Head

Piers

Woodspring Bay

Wick Warth

Middle Hope
(Nature Reserve)

BS22

Twr

Woodspring
Priory

River Banwell

WARTH LA

Woodspring
Farm

71

	A	B	C	D	E	F

8

7

69

6

Dowlais Ditch

Kingston Pill

Hook's
Ear

Sea
Fa

Treble Hou
Farm

5

68

Sewa
Wor

4

Channel View
Farm

BS21

Broadstone Rhyne

MIDDLE LA

MIDDLE LA

3

67

Broadstone
Farm

BROADSTONE LA

Wharf
Farm

HAM LA

Ham
Farm

2

Ham Rhyne

P
F

1

Sewage
Works

Mendip View
Farm

YEO BANK LA

Yeo Bank
Farm

BS22

MIDDLE LA

Mill Leaze Rhyne

66

36	A	B	37	C	D	38	E	F

71

89

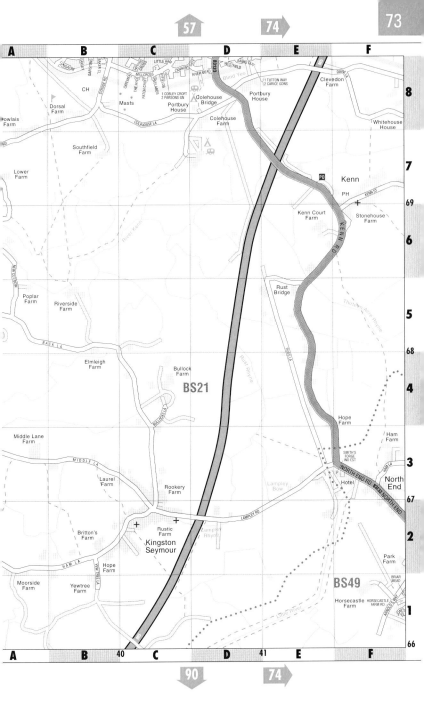

8

7

69

6

5

68

4

3

67

2

1

66

A

CH

Dorsal Farm

owlais Farm

Southfield Farm

Lower Farm

Poplar Farm

Riverside Farm

Elmleigh Farm

BACK LA

Middle Lane Farm

MIDDLE LA

Laurel Farm

Britton's Farm

Moorside Farm

HAM LA

Yewtree Farm

YEW TREE LA

Hope Farm

B

STRODE RD

GARSTONS

BAKER RD

LONGACRE

CARLINGH

CABSTAND

THE HYDE

PATCH CROFT

TREELANDS

MILLCROSS

LITTLE HAM

CANNONS GATE

COLEHOUSE LA

Masts

Bullock Farm

BULLOCKS LA

Rookery Farm

Rustic Farm

Kingston Seymour

C

Colehouse Bridge

Portbury House

RIVER MEAD

1 COBLEY CROFT
2 PARSONS GN

D

B3133

WESTFIELD

BANKS CL

Colehouse Farm

River Kenn

Reed Rhyne

LAMPLEY RD

Lampley Rhyne

Lampley Bow

BS21

E

Blind Yeo

Portbury House

1 TUTTON WAY
2 CARICE GDNS

KENN RD

Rust Bridge

Hope Farm

NORTH END RD

SMITH'S FORGE IND EST

Hotel

B3133 NORTH END

THE RHINE

F

Clevedon Farm

DAVID

Whitehouse House

Kenn

PO

PH

KENN ST

Kenn Court Farm

Stonehouse Farm

Thirteen Acre Rhyne

Ham Farm

North End

HAM LA

Park Farm

BRIAR MEAD

BS49

Horsecastle Farm

HORSECASTLE FARM RD

ARNOLDS WAY

DINGLE LA

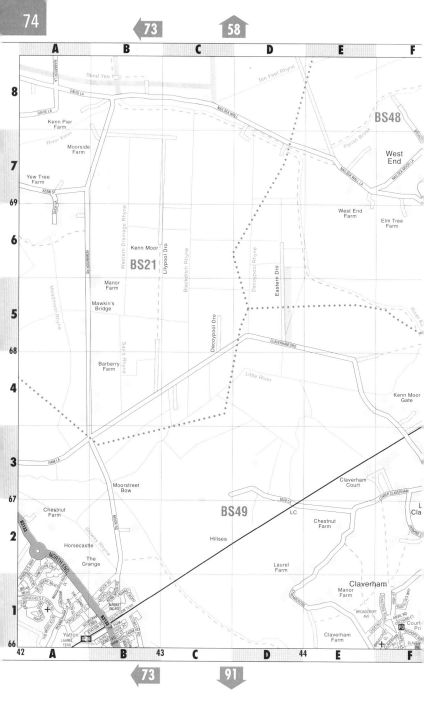

A **B** **C** **D** **E** **F**

8

ST. MONICK WK

Blind Yeo

DAVIS LA

NAILSEA WALL

Ten Feet Rhyne

BS48

Kenn Pier
Farm

River Kenn

Moorside
Farm

West
End

7

Yew Tree
Farm

KENN ST

NAILSEA WALL LA

NAILSEA MOOR LA

BELL

69

DUCK LA

West End
Farm

Elm Tree
Farm

6

Kenn Moor

BS21

Western Drainage Rhyne

Lilypool Dro

Blackditch Rhyne

Decoypool Rhyne

Eastern Dro

River Ax

KENNMOOR RD

Manor
Farm

Mawkin's
Bridge

5

Meadmoor Rhyne

Decoypool Dro

CLAVERHAM DRO

68

Say's Rhyne

Barberry
Farm

Little River

4

Kenn Moor
Gate

HAM LA

3

Moorstreet
Bow

Claverham
Court

67

MUD LA

LOWER CLAVERHAM

Chestnut
Farm

Cla

BS49

LC

B3133

Chestnut
Farm

Moor Rd

Shower Rhyne

2

Horsecastle

Hillsea

The
Grange

Laurel
Farm

Claverham

NORTH END

Manor
Farm

BROADCROFT
AVE

PO
Court
Pri

1

HORSECASTLE FARM RD

MARKET
IND EST

STATION RD

BISHOP'S RD

ORCHARD CT

AVRIL RD

FRAN

Yatton

LAUREL
TERR

Chestnut
Farm

Claverham
Farm

66

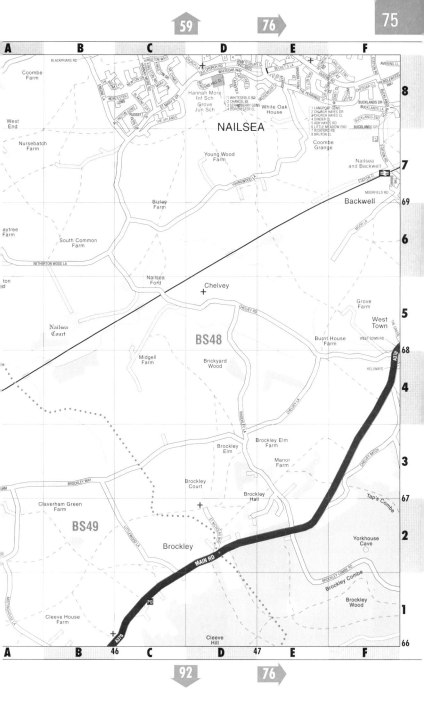

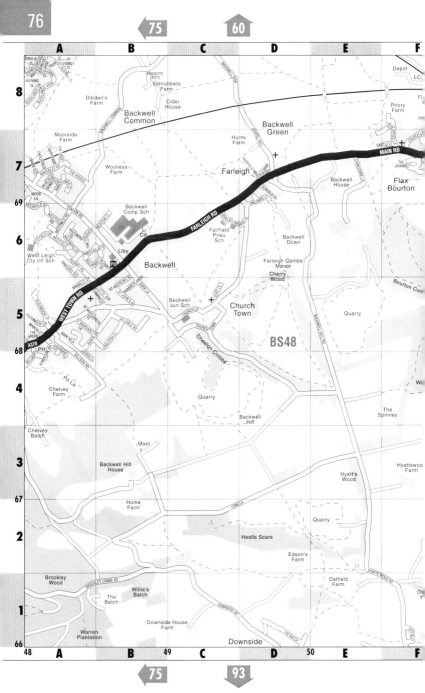

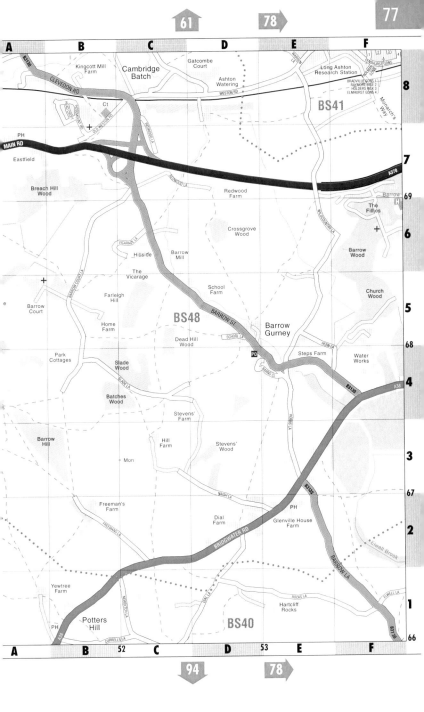

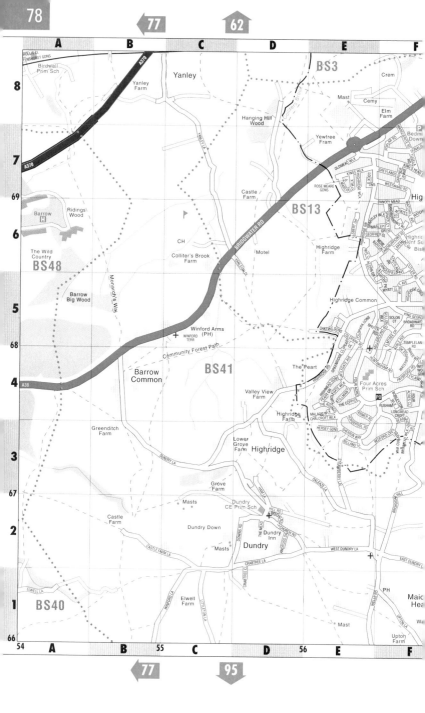

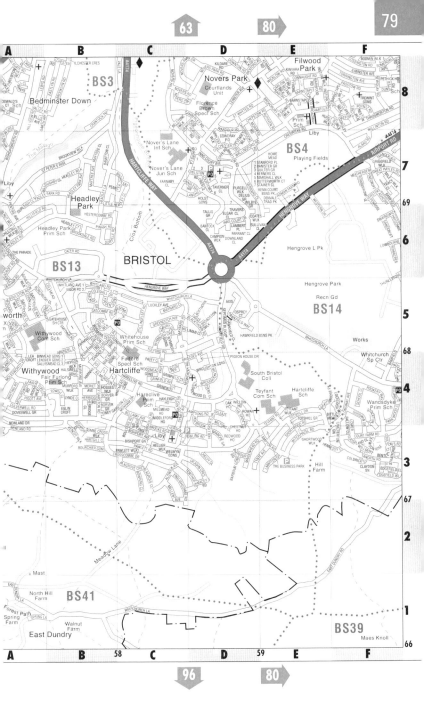

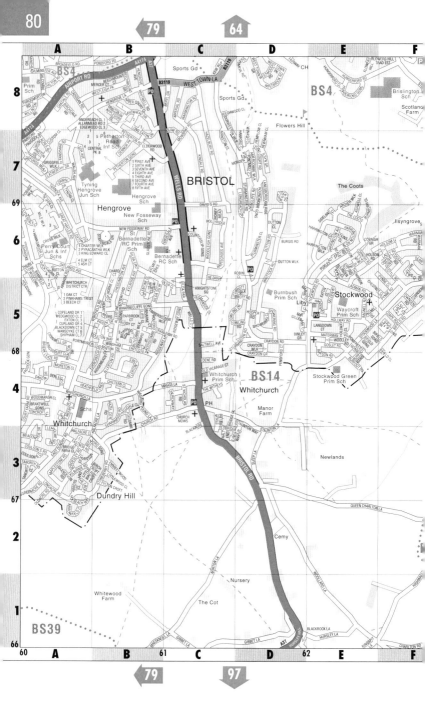

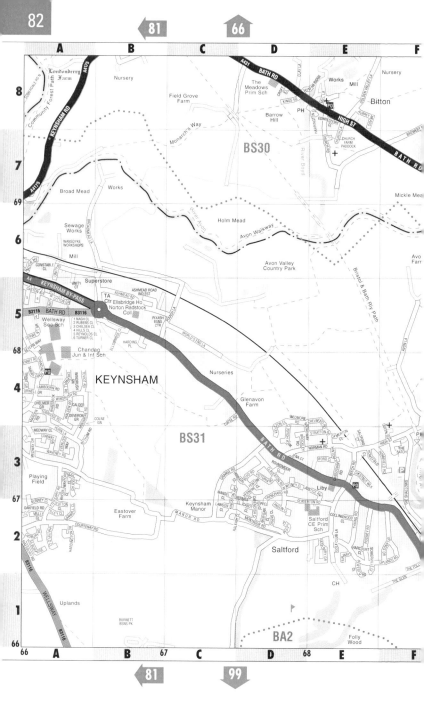

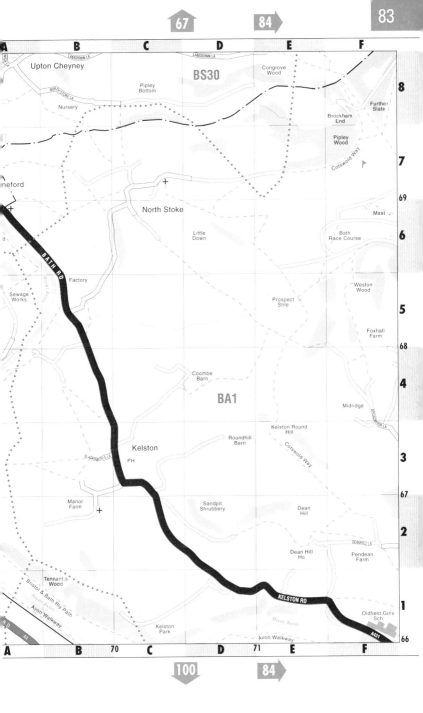

Upton Cheyney

BS30

Congrove Wood

LANSDOWN LA

LANSDOWN LA

Pipley Bottom

Nursery

NORTH STOKE LA

Further Slate

Brockham End

Pipley Wood

Cotswold Way

neford

North Stoke

Mast

Little Down

Bath Race Course

BATH RD

Factory

Sewage Works

River Avon

Prospect Stile

Weston Wood

Foxhall Farm

Coombe Barn

BA1

Midridge

Weston FOR LA

Kelston

PH

BLACKSMITH'S LA

Roundhill Barn

Kelston Round Hill

Cotswold Way

Manor Farm

Sandpit Shrubbery

Dean Hill

DEANHILL LA

Dean Hill Ho

Pendean Farm

Tennant's Wood

Bristol & Bath Rly Path

River Avon

Kelston Park

KELSTON RD

River Avon

Avon Walkway

Avon Walkway

Oldfield Girls Sch

A431

A4

A4

A   B   70   C   D   71   E   F

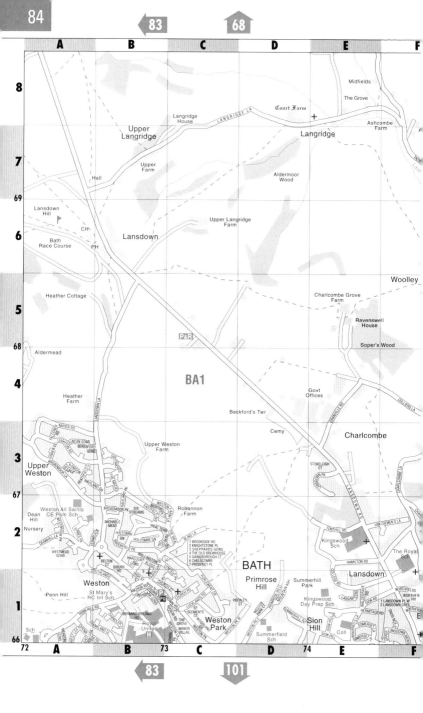

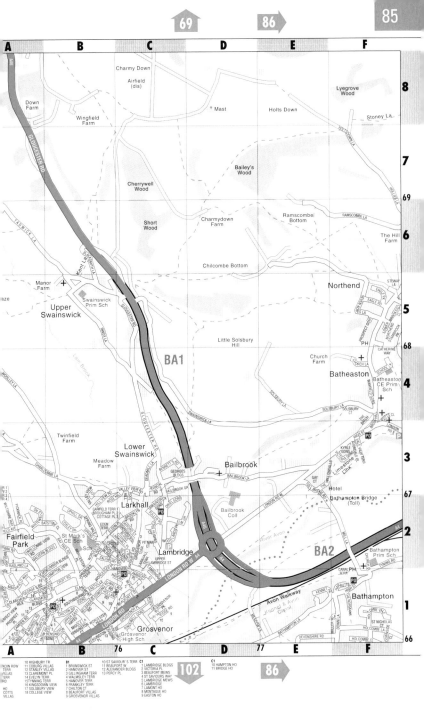

85

8

7

69

6

5

68

4

3

67

2

1

66

Charmy Down
Airfield
(dis)

Lyegrove
Wood

Down
Farm

Holts Down

Stoney La.

GLOUCESTER RD

Wingfield
Farm

Mast

Bailey's
Wood

HOLCOMBE LA

Cherrywell
Wood

Ramscombel
Bottom

RAMSCOMBE LA

TADWICK LA

Short
Wood

Charmydown
Farm

The Hill
Farm

Chilcombe Bottom

STIRWAY
LA

Manor
Farm

Northend

EAGLE RD

Swainswick
Prim Sch

Upper
Swainswick

Kentl

BLACKSMITHS

GLOUCESTER RD

Little Solsbury
Hill

Church
Farm

PH

CHURCH LA

CATHERINE
WAY

Batheaston

Batheaston
CE Prim
Sch

BA1

WARFIELD GDNS

SWAINSWICK LA

SOLSBURY LA

SOLSBURY

Lam Brook

MOSLEY LA

Twinfield
Farm

SOLSBURY LA

LONDON
RD

HIGH ST

Lower
Swainswick

Meadow
Farm

GLOUCESTER RD

Bailbrook

BAILBROOK LA

KYRLE
GDNS

Limestone
Link

Larkhall

GEORGES
BLDGS

BAILBROOK LA

GAY
CT

Hotel

Bathampton Bridge
(Toll)

Bailbrook
Coll

LONDON VIEW

FELL BRIDGE RD

Fairfield
Park

St Mark's
CE Sch

Sch

PITMAN
CT

WOOD

UPPER
LAMBRIDGE ST

Lambridge

River Avon

BA2

Bathampton
Prim Sch

HAMPTON ROW

LONDON RD W

Kennel & Avon Canal

CANAL
PH

EYNING RD

Bathampton

Grosvenor

Grosvenor
High Sch

Avon Walkway

Kennel & Avon Canal

ST NICHOLAS

DEVONSHIRE RD

HOLCOMBE LA

BATHAMPTON LA

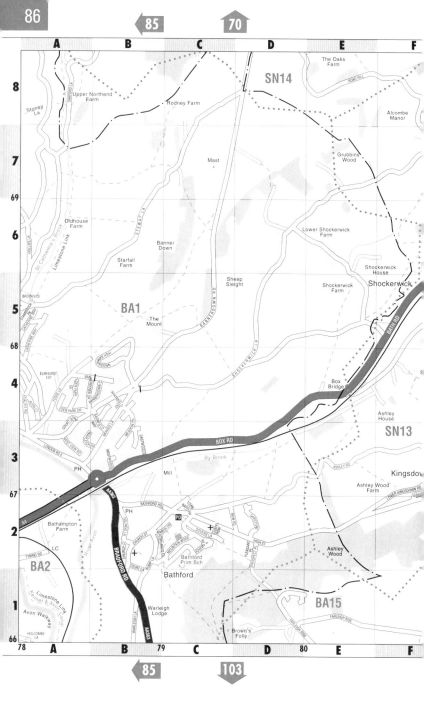

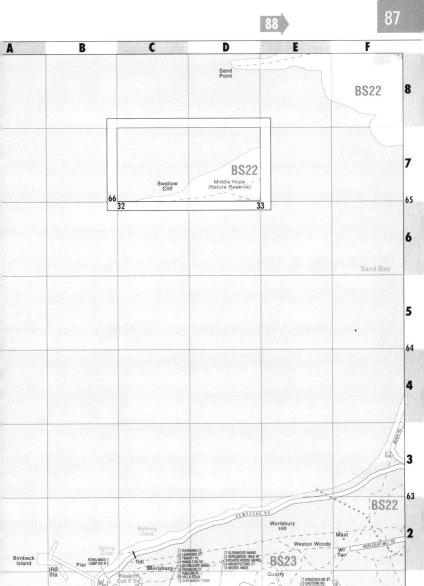

Sand
Point

BS22

8

BS22

7

Swallow
Cliff

Middle Hope
(Nature Reserve)

66

32   33

65

6

Sand Bay

5

64

4

3

BLACK RD

63

KEWSTOKE RD

BS22

Worlebury
Hill

Weston Woods

Mast

2

Bathing
Cove

Spring
Cove

FORELANDS 1
CAMP RD N 2

Toll

Westcliff
Coll F Ed

Worlebury

BS23

Quarry

Wr
Twr

WORLEBURY MILL RD

Birnbeck
Island

Pier

IRB
Sta

Anchor Head

1 RAINHAM CT.
2 LEAWOOD CT
3 TRINITY RD
4 HAMILTON RD
5 BOONEAZE MANS
6 PARAGON CT
7 RAGLAN PL
8 VILLA ROSA
9 SHRUBBERY TERR

1 GLENWOOD MANS
2 SHRUBBERY WLK W
3 COACH HOUSE MEWS
4 KNIGHTSTONE CT
5 WOODLANDS

1 KINGSHOLME CT
2 EASTERN RD
3 SYCAMORES

HIGHCROFT

EASTCOMBE
GDNS

SEDGEMOOR
RD

LB
Sta

MANILLA
CRES

KNIGHTSTONE CT
SHRUBBERY RD

SOUTH RD
ST MATTHEW'S RD

GROVE PARK RD

FR'S AVE

ALBANY

BRISTOL
ROAD LOWER

Cemy

62

ATLANTIC
CT

ATLANTIC RD S

ST JOHN'S RD

CHURCH RD

COOMBE RD

ST JOSEPH'S RD

TREWARTHA
PK

MONTPELIER E

STON-SUPER-MARE

8

7

65

6

5

64

4

3

63

2

1

62

A
B
C
D
E
F

BS21

Lower Wick Farm

Icelton Farm

Tutshill Ear

Yeo Bank Farm

Appleton Farm

Council Hos

East-town Farm

Icelton

Cypress Farm

Cedar Farm

Rose Court

Sluice Farm

Wick St Lawrence

Ebdon Court Farm

Hippisley's Farm

Ebdon

1 FOXGLOVE CL
2 LAVENDER CL
3 YARROW CT

Bourton

Manor Farm

nchmead Farm

Ebdon Lane Farm

Court Farm

Willow Farm

Manor Farm

BS22

KELSTON GDNS

PERRYMEAD

LANSDOWN GDNS

Prim Schr

THE FIELDS

WHEATFIELD

GILL AVE

New Ear La

WALLDROGE AVE

Brimbleworth Farm

COLLETT CL

HINCKLEY CL

GILBERYN DR MAGDALEN WAY

WESLEY DR

DEAN ST

COULSON DR

DUNEDIN WAY

St Georges

The Round Pond

The Lawns

A370

PURN WAY

CHRIST

DALEY CL

COURTENAY WLK

THE LAWNS

CABOT WAY

SPENCER DR

RUDHALL GDN

BRIMBLEWORTH

Grove Farm

QUEEN'S WAY

SUMMERFIELD

Priory Com Sch

LC

Haybow Farm

BS24

WORLINGTON CRES

VINE GDNS

Ind Est

PO

SATTON RD

TRELAWN CL

Doubleton Farm

Prim Sch

Superstores

APPLETREE MEWS

Bristol Road Bridge

ROSE COTTS

BRISTOL RD

PH

WILLOW CL

Rolstone Stuntree Farm

MARLBORO

NEW BRISTOL RD

BRISTOL RD

B3440

WEST BOURTON RD

Poplar Farm

Rolstone Farm

WORLE COURT

Worle Parkway

SOMERSET AVE

SCOT ELM DR

BLACKTHORN TERR

PARBURY WAY

Way Wick

HONEYSUCKLE

West Wick

WEST WICK

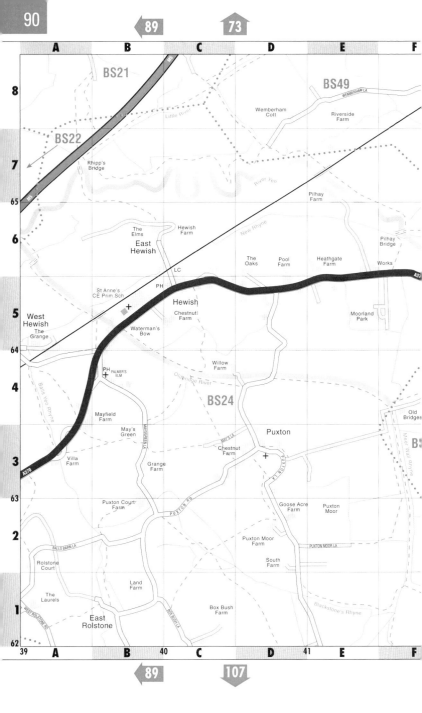

BS21

BS49

8

Wemberham Cott

Riverside Farm

WEMBERHAM LA

BS22

7

Rhipp's Bridge

River Yeo

65

Pilhay Farm

M5

6

The Elms

Hewish Farm

East Hewish

New Rhyne

The Oaks

Pool Farm

Heathgate Farm

Pilhay Bridge

Works

LC

St Anne's CE Prim Sch

PH

Hewish

A371

5

West Hewish

The Grange

Waterman's Bow

Chestnut Farm

Moorland Park

64

PH PALMER'S ELM

Willow Farm

Oldbridge River

4

Mayfield Farm

May's Green

BS24

Old Bridges

Balls Yeo Rhyne

MAYPOLE LA

MAY'S LA

Puxton

Chestnut Farm

PUXTON LA

Meer Wall Rhyne

B

3

Villa Farm

Grange Farm

PUXTON RD

Goose Acre Farm

Puxton Moor

A370

63

Puxton Court Farm

Blackstone's Rhyne

2

BALLS BARN LA

Puxton Moor Farm

PUXTON MOOR LA

Rolstone Court

South Farm

The Laurels

Land Farm

BOX BUSH LA

Box Bush Farm

1

WEST ROLSTONE RD

East Rolstone

62

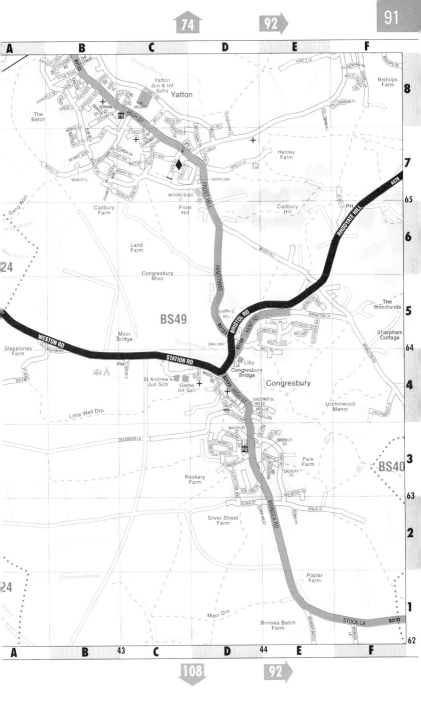

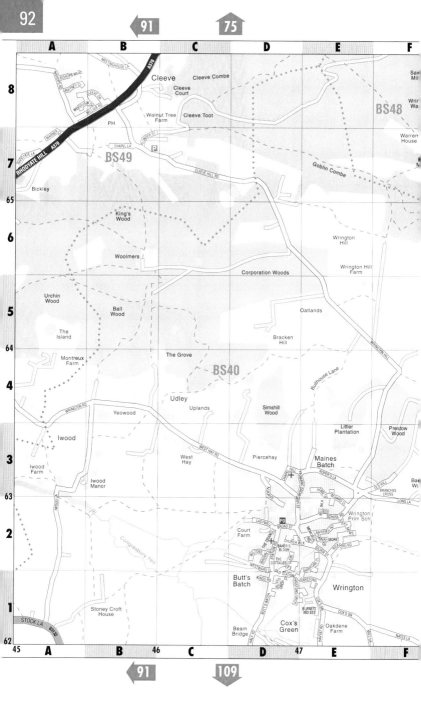

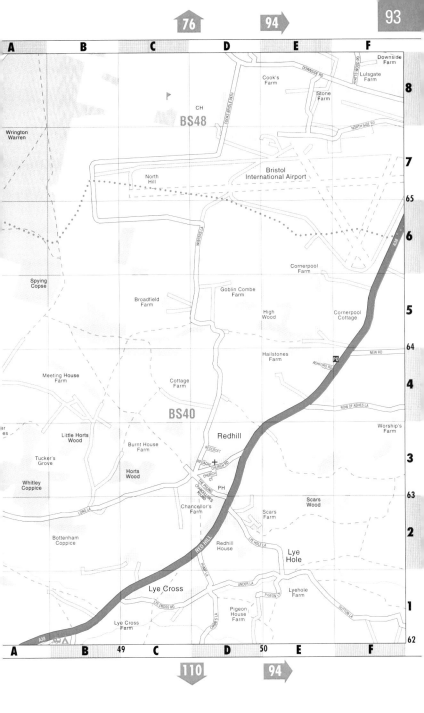

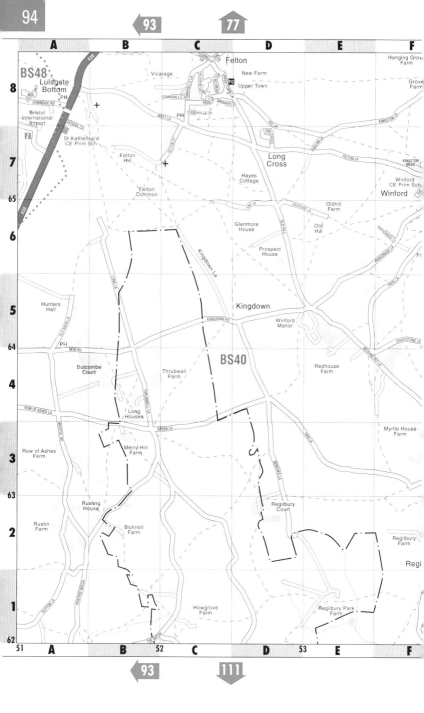

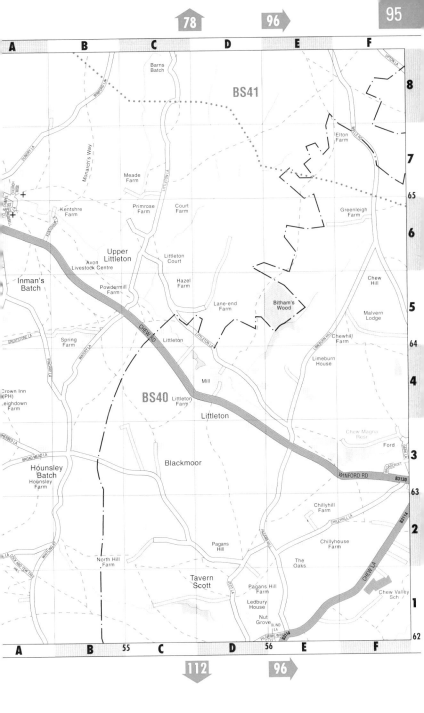

BS41

Barns
Batch

Elton
Farm

Monarch's Way

WINFORD LA

Meade
Farm

Greenleigh
Farm

Kentshre
Farm

Primrose
Farm

Court
Farm

Upper
Littleton

Littleton
Court

Chew
Hill

Avon
Livestock Centre

Inman's
Batch

Powdermill
Farm

Hazel
Farm

Malvern
Lodge

Lane-end
Farm

Bitham's
Wood

CHEW RD

LITTLETON LA

Chewhill
Farm

Greatstone La

Spring
Farm

Littleton

Limeburn
House

LIMEBURN HILL

Crown Inn
(PH)

Leighdown
Farm

WALNUT LA

Mill

BS40

Littleton
Farm

Littleton

Chew Magna
Resr

Ford

PRIORS LA

HERBED LA

BROAD MEAD LA

Hounsley
Batch

Blackmoor

WINFORD RD

B3130

Hounsley
Farm

Chillyhill
Farm

CHILLYHILL LA

B3114

Chillyhouse
Farm

NORTH HILL LA COTE LAND TOP TREE MILL LA

WHITE MEAD

North Hill
Farm

Pagans
Hill

PAGANS HILL

The
Oaks

Tavern
Scott

Pagans Hill
Farm

BURDS LA

CHEW LA

Chew Valley
Sch

Ledbury
House

Nut
Grove

BLIND
LA

PILGRIMS WALK B3114

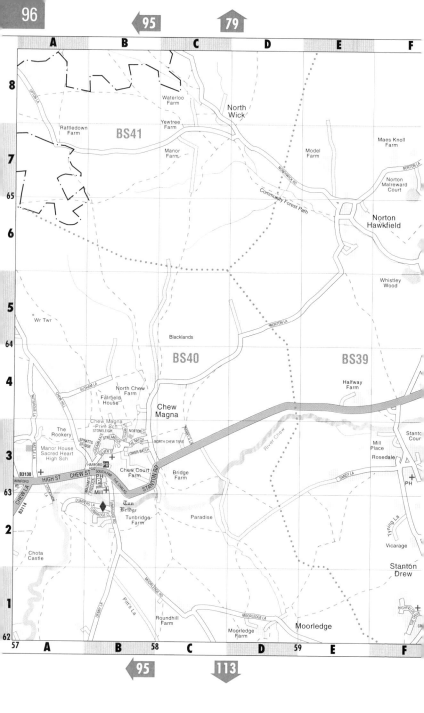

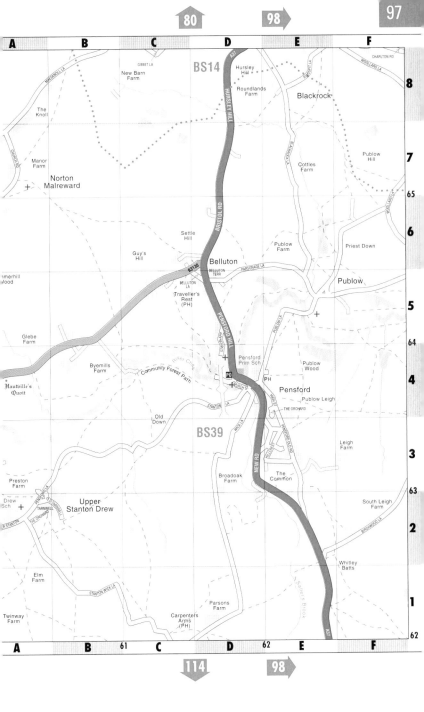

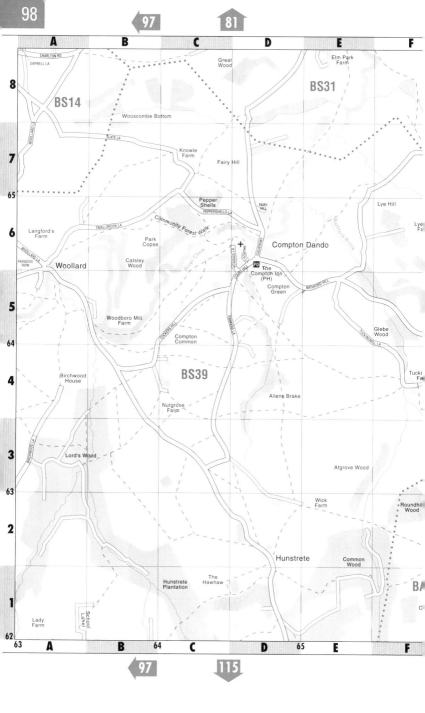

A B C D E F

8

7

65

6

5

64

4

3

63

2

1

62

A B C D E F

BS14

BS31

BS39

BA

CHARLTON RD
DAPWELL LA
WOOLLARD LA
WOOLLARD LA
PARADISE ROW
Langford's Farm
Woollard
SLATE LA
SMALLBROOK LA
Community Forest Walk
PEPPERSHELLS LA
Pepper Shells
Knowle Farm
Wooscombe Bottom
Great Wood
Elm Park Farm
Fairy Hill
Lye Hill
Lye Fa
Bathford Brook
FAIRY HILL
Compton Dando
Park Copse
Catsley Wood
River Chew
CLEVEWAY
THE STREET
COURT HILL
PO
The Compton Inn (PH)
Compton Green
BATHFORD HILL
Glebe Wood
TUCKINGMILL LA
Woodboro Mill Farm
COOKS HILL
Compton Common
RAMBLE LA
Tucki Fa
Birchwood House
Allens Brake
Atgrove Wood
Roundhill Wood
Nutgrove Farm
BIRCHWOOD LA
Lord's Wood
Wick Farm
Hunstrete
Common Wood
C
Hunstrete Plantation
The Hawhaw
Lady Farm
School Lane!

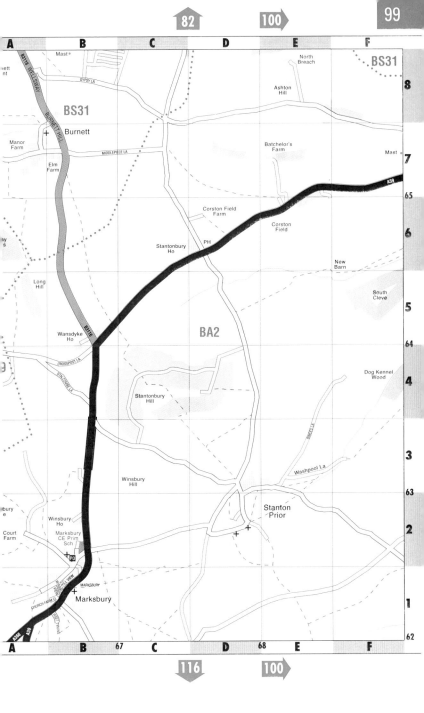

BS31

A B C D E F

Mast

GYPSY LA

North
Breach

8

Ashton
Hill

BS31

Manor
Farm

Burnett

BS31

BURNETT HILL

MIDDLEPIECE LA

Batchelor's
Farm

Mast

7

65

Elm
Farm

Corston Field
Farm

Corston
Field

6

Stantonbury
Ho

PH

New
Barn

Long
Hill

South
Cleve

5

Wansdyke
Ho

B3116

BA2

64

CROSSPOST LA

STARCROSS LA

Dog Kennel
Wood

4

Stantonbury
Hill

BRIDES LA

3

Washpool La

63

Winsbury
Hill

Stanton
Prior

2

Winsbury
Ho

Court
Farm

Marksbury
CE Prim
Sch

PO

BURNETT VIEW

MARKSBURY

Marksbury

CHURCH FARM CL

STREET FARM

1

A39

A39

62

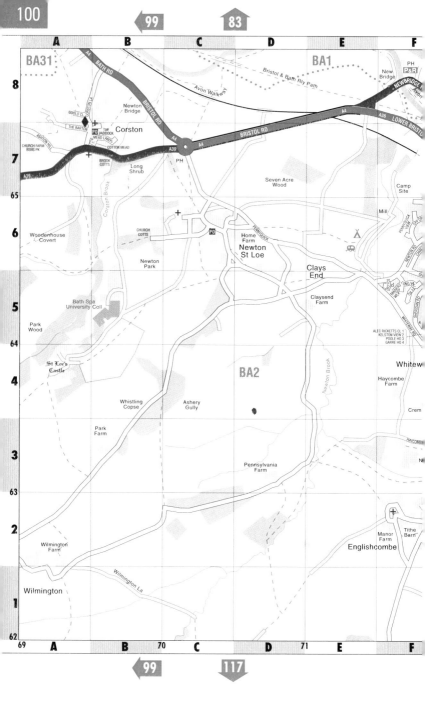

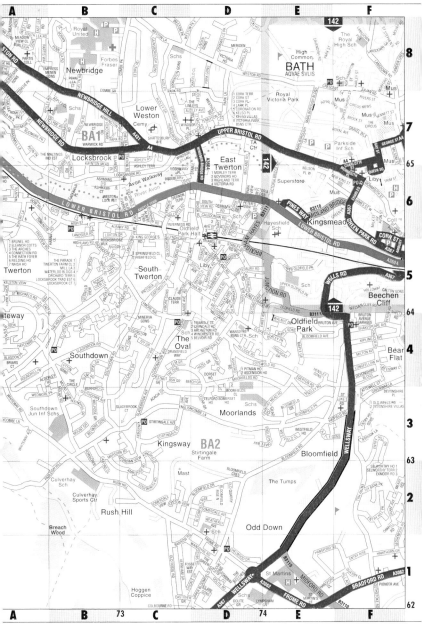

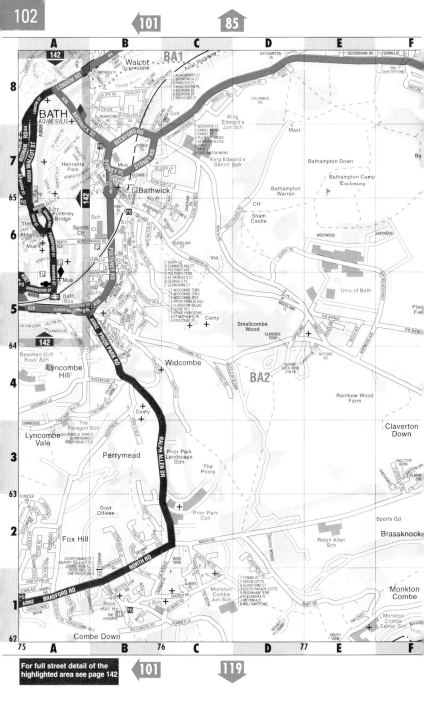

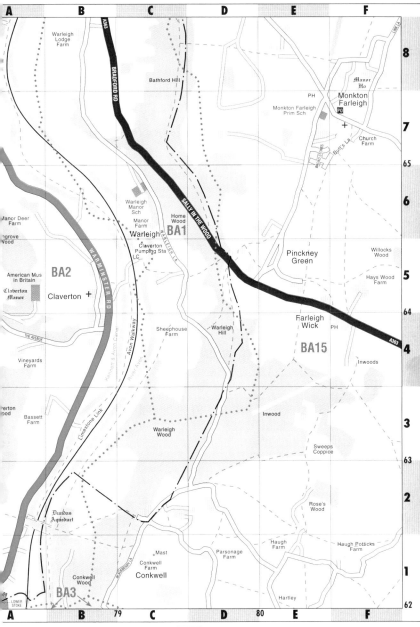

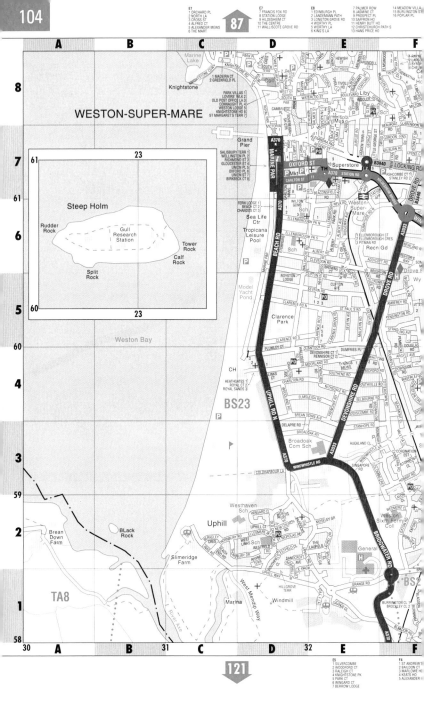

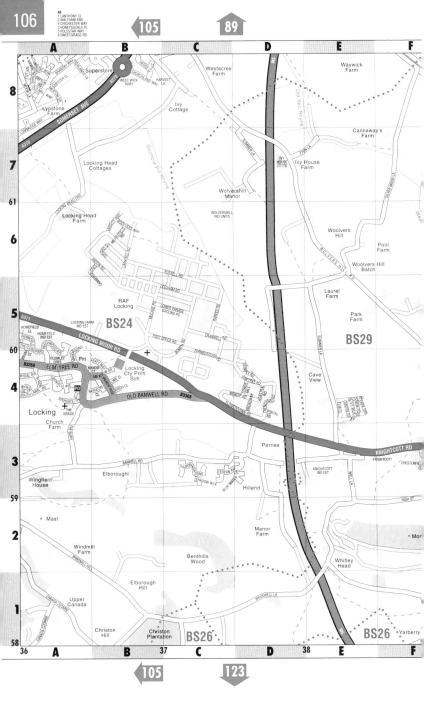

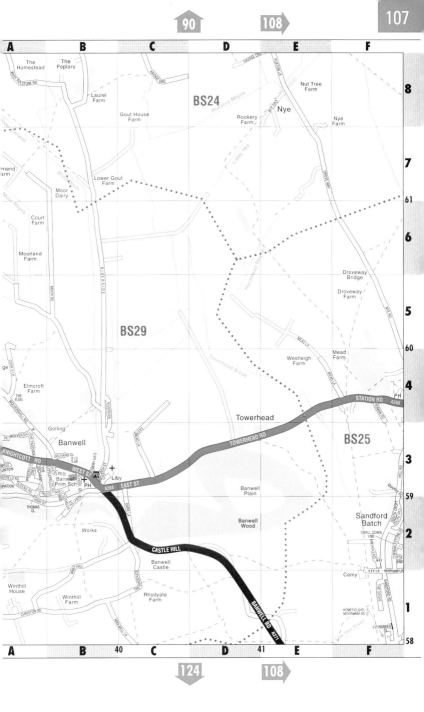

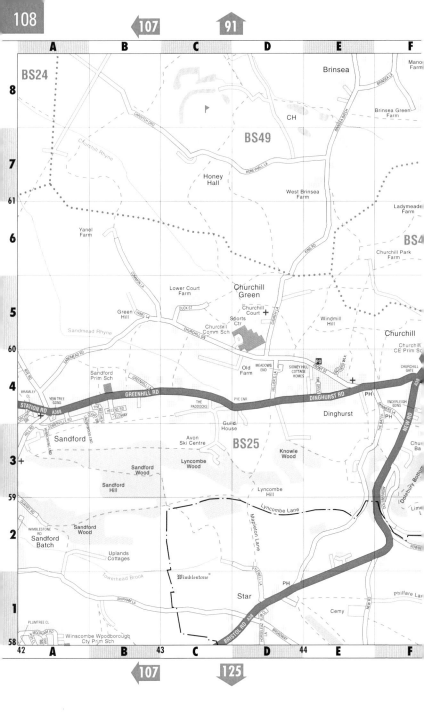

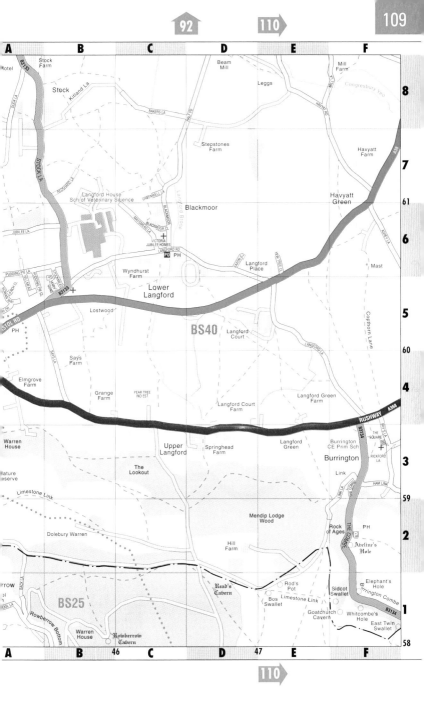

Hotel
Stock
Farm
Stock
Kittland La
Beam
Mill
Leggs
Mill
Farm
Congresbury Yeo

DEAN LA
STOCK LA

BAKERS LA

Stepstones
Farm

Havyatt
Farm

Langford House
Sch of Veterinary Science
GREENHILL LA
BLACKMOOR
Blackmoor
Havyatt
Green

JUBILEE LA
VICTORIA
JUBILEE HOMES
LANGFORD ROAD
PO PH
Langford
Place
Mast

PUDDING PIE LA
Wyndhurst
Farm
Lower
Langford
ASH TREE LA
YEW TREE LA

ST MARY'S
Lostwood
BS40
Langford
Court
COPHORN LANE

Elmgrove
Farm
Say's
Farm
Grange
Farm
PEAR TREE
IND EST
Langford Court
Farm
Langford Green
Farm

Warren
House
Upper
Langford
Springhead
Farm
Langford
Green
Burrington
CE Prim Sch
THE SQUARE
RICKFORD LA
Burrington

Nature
Reserve
The
Lookout
Link
HAM LINK

Limestone Link
Dolebury Warren
Mendip Lodge
Wood
Rock
of Ages
THE COOMBE
PH

BS25
Hill
Farm
Read's
Cavern
Rod's
Pot
Limestone Link
Sidcot
Swallet
Aveline's
Hole

Elephant's
Hole

Warren
House
Rowberrow Bottom
Rowberrow
Cavern
Bos
Swallet
Goatchurch
Cavern
Whitcombe's
Hole
East Twin
Swallet
B3134

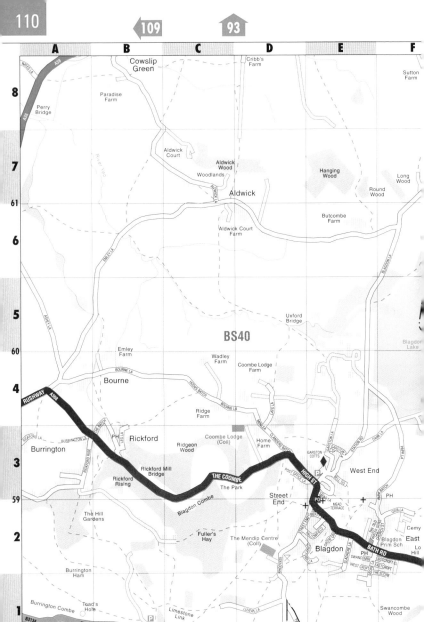

8

Cowslip
Green

Cribb's
Farm

Sutton
Farm

Paradise
Farm

Perry
Bridge

7

Aldwick
Court

Aldwick
Wood

Woodlands

Hanging
Wood

Long
Wood

61

Aldwick

Round
Wood

6

Aldwick Court
Farm

Butcombe
Farm

5

Uxford
Bridge

BS40

Blagdon
Lake

60

Emley
Farm

Wadley
Farm

Coombe Lodge
Farm

BOURNE LA

Bourne

4

RUSHWAY   A368

BOURNE LA

Ridge
Farm

Coombe Lodge
(Coll)

Home
Farm

West End

Burrington

PH

Rickford

Ridgeon
Wood

GARSTON
COTTS

3

Rickford Mill
Bridge

THE COOMBE

HIGH ST

Rickford
Rising

The Park

Street
End

MEAD
TERRACE

PH

59

Blagdon Combe

Blagdon
Prim Sch

Cemy

East

2

The Hill
Gardens

Fuller's
Hay

The Mendip Centre
(Coll)

Blagdon

Lo
Hill

Burrington
Ham

SWANCOMBE

WEST CROFT

Burrington
Combe

Toad's
Hole

Limestone
Link

Swancombe
Wood

1

B3134

THE COMBE

Lower Ellick
Wood

Lower Ellick
Farm

NEWFIELDS

Rhodyate Hill
Farm

58

B3134

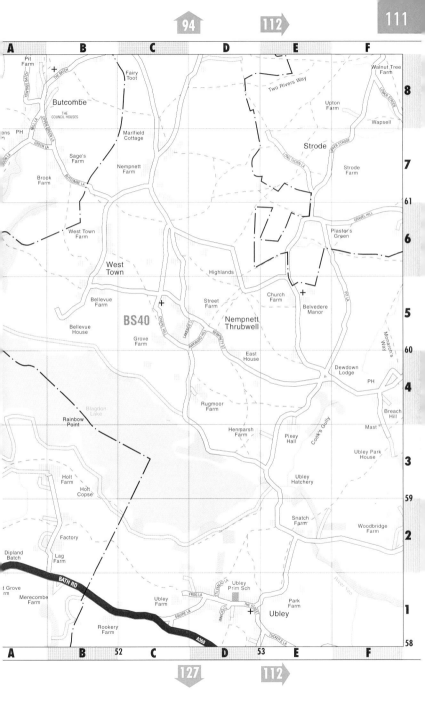

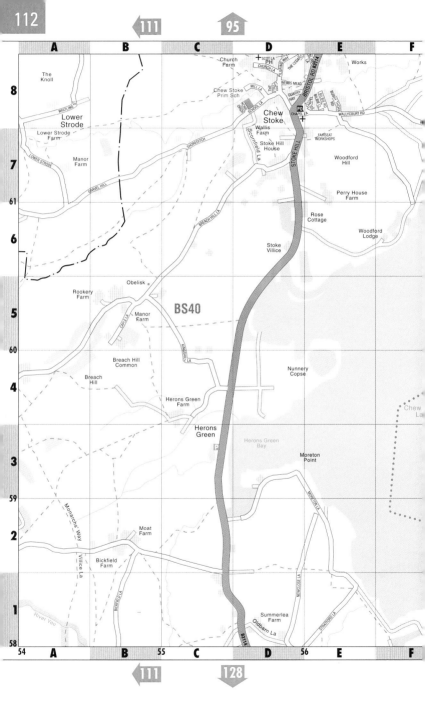

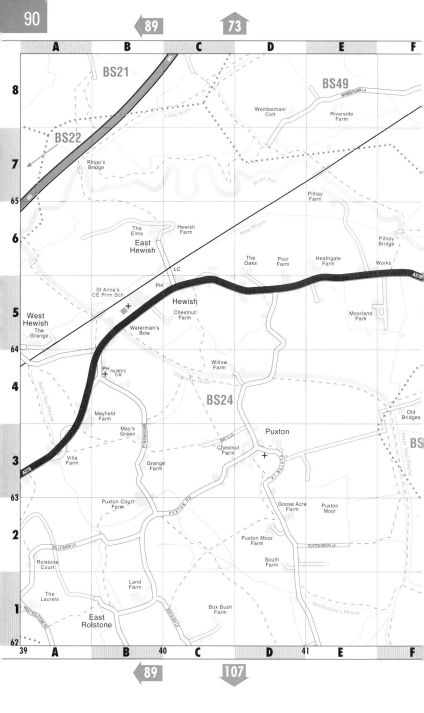

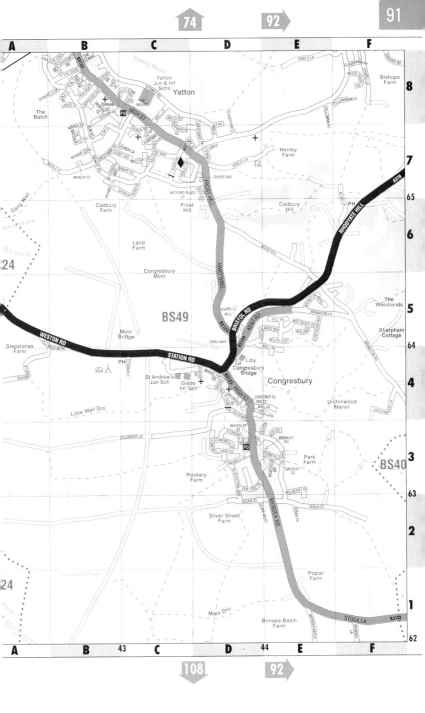

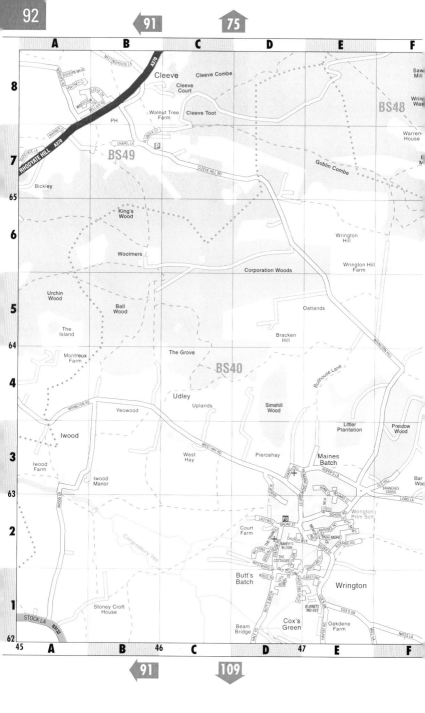

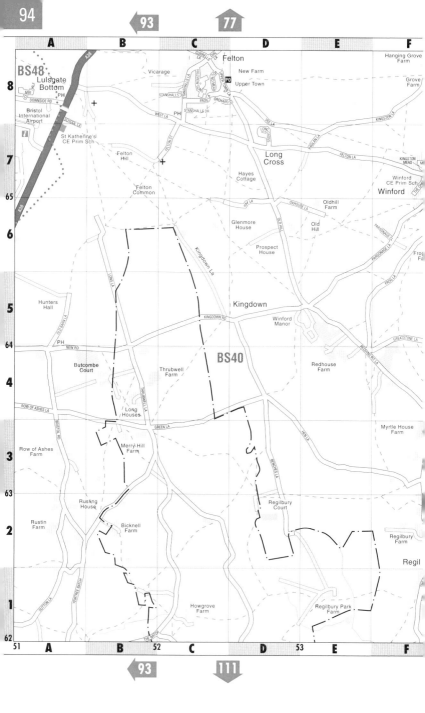

BS48
Lulsgate
Bottom

Bristol
International
Airport

St Katherine's
CE Prim Sch

Felton
Hill

Felton
Common

Vicarage

Felton

New Farm

Upper Town

WEST LA

PH

Hanging Grove
Farm

Grove
Farm

Long
Cross

Hayes
Cottage

Winford
CE Prim Sch

Winford

Oldhill
Farm

Glenmore
House

Old
Hill

Prospect
House

Kingdown La

Hunters
Hall

Kingdown

KINGDOWN RD

Winford
Manor

BS40

PH

NEW RD

Butcombe
Court

Thrubwell
Farm

Redhouse
Farm

Greatstone La

Row of Ashes La

Long
Houses

GREEN LA

Myrtle House
Farm

Row of Ashes
Farm

Merry Hill
Farm

Rustin
Farm

Rushng
House

Bicknell
Farm

Regilbury
Court

Regilbury
Farm

Regil

Howgrove
Farm

Regilbury Park
Farm

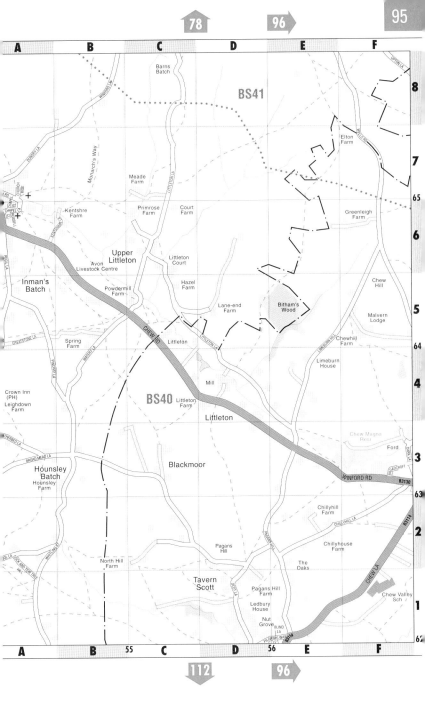

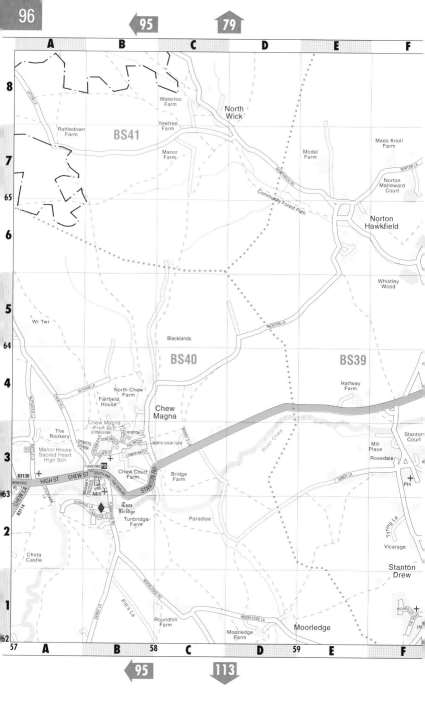

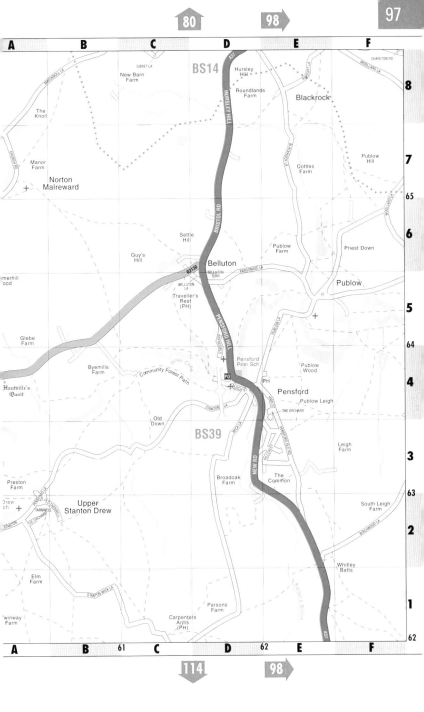

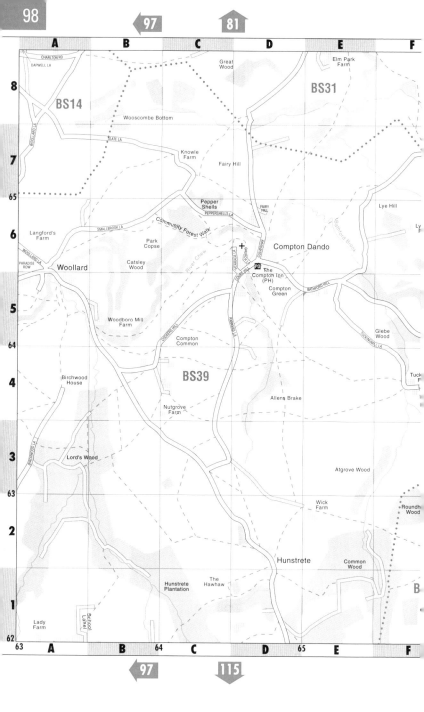

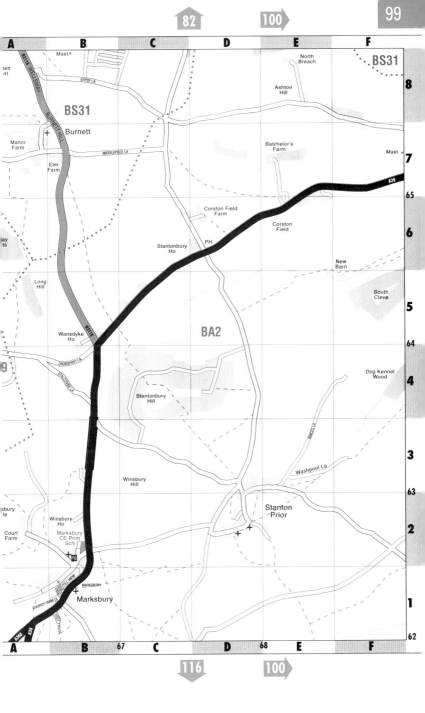

A　B　C　D　E　F

BS31

8

North Breach

Mast

GYPSY LA

BS31

BURNETT HILL

Burnett

Ashton Hill

Manor Farm

MIDDLEPIECE LA

Batchelor's Farm

Mast

7

65

Elm Farm

Corston Field Farm

Corston Field

6

Stantonbury Ho

PH

New Barn

Long Hill

South Cleve

5

Wansdyke Ho

BA2

64

CROSSPOST LA

Dog Kennel Wood

4

Stantonbury Hill

BINKS LA

3

Washpool La

Winsbury Hill

63

Winsbury Ho

Stanton Prior

2

Court Farm

Marksbury CE Prim Sch

PO

MARKSBURY

1

Marksbury

A39

A39

62

A　B　C　D　E　F

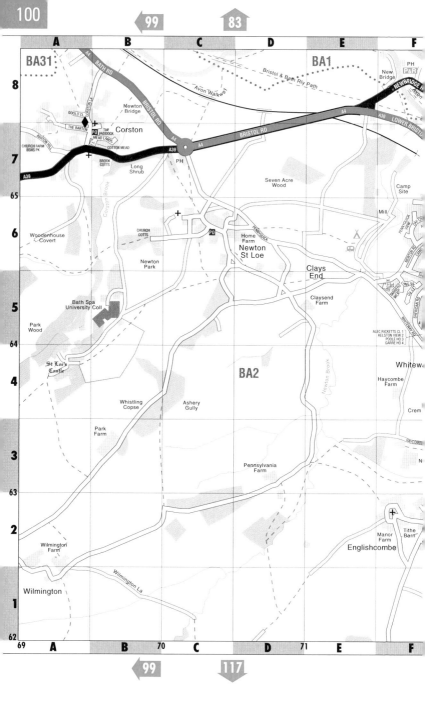

BA31

BA1

PH
P&R

New
Bridge

BATH RD

8

Newton
Bridge

BRISTOL RD

NEWBRIDGE H

GOOLD CL

CORSTON LA

THE BARTON

PO

Corston

MEAD LANE

THE PADDOCK

Avon Walkway

Bristol & Bath Rly Path

A4

A4

BRISTOL RD

A36

LOWER BRISTOL

7

CHURCH FARM
BSNS PK

ASHTON CL

COTTON MEAD

BROOK
COTTS

A39

A39

Long
Shrub

PH

A4

Seven Acre
Wood

Camp
Site

65

Mill

PENNYRIDGE

6

Woodenhouse
Covert

CHURCH
COTTS

PO

Home
Farm

Newton
St Loe

NEWTON RD

PENNYRIDGE

Newton
Park

Clays
End

BRY

LONG VW

MALTHOUSE

SHERIDAN RD

5

Bath Spa
University Coll

Claysend
Farm

ALEC RICKETTS CL 1
KELSTON VIEW 2
POOLE HO 3
GARRE HO 4

64

Park
Wood

Newton Brook

Whitew

4

St Loe's
Castle

BA2

Haycombe
Farm

Crem

Whistling
Copse

Ashery
Gully

HAYCOMB

3

Park
Farm

Pennsylvania
Farm

N

63

2

Wilmington
Farm

Manor
Farm

Tithe
Barn

Englishcombe

1

Wilmington

Wilmington La

62

69   A   B   70   C   D   71   E   F

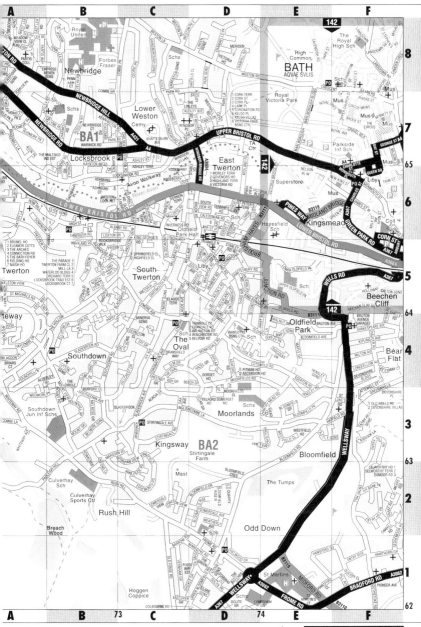

118 102

For full street detail of the highlighted area see page 142.

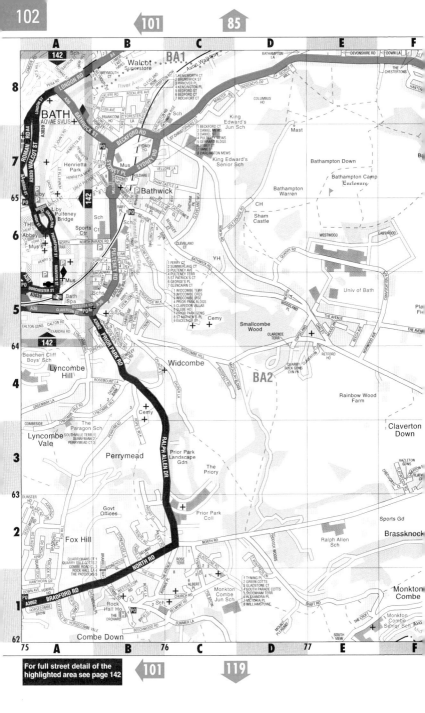

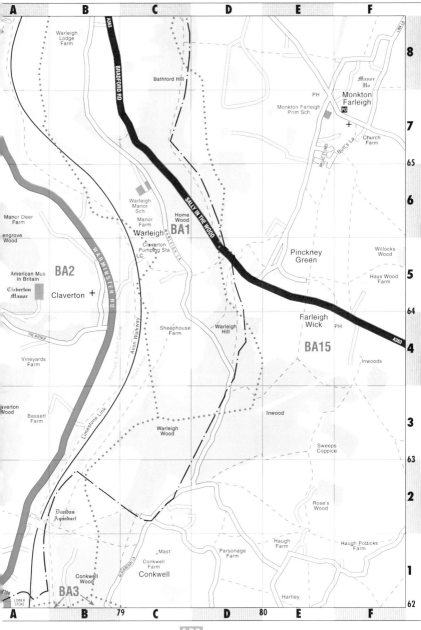

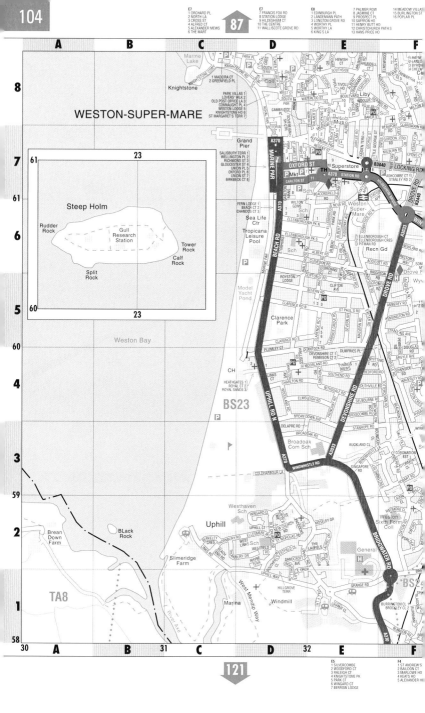

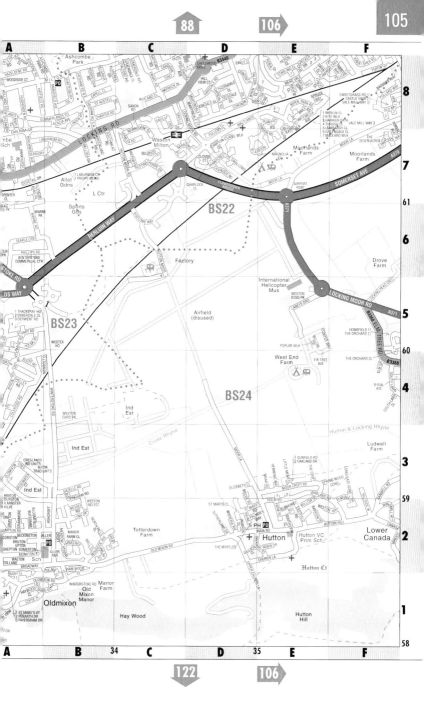

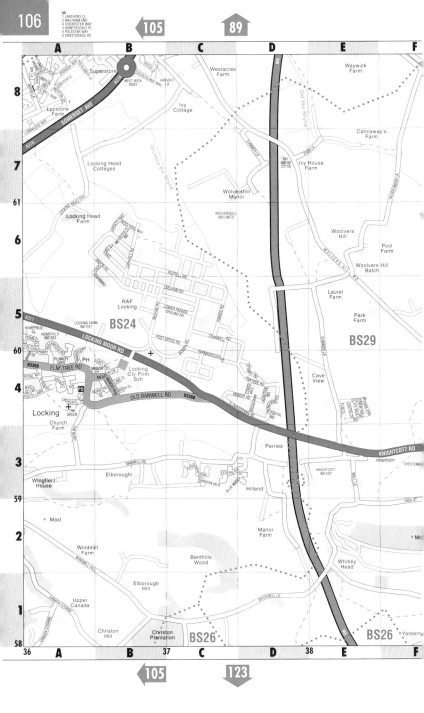

106

All
1 LANTHONY CL
2 WALTHAM END
3 CHICHESTER WAY
4 HONEYSUCKLE PL
5 POLESTAR WAY
6 SWEETGRASS RD

105

89

8

Superstore

Westacres
Farm

Waywick
Farm

Lypstone
Ave

WEST WICK
RDBT

CHURCHLAND WAY

HARVEST
LA

Ivy
Cottage

Old Yeo Rhyne

SOMERSET AVE

A370

Cannaway's
Farm

7

Locking Head
Cottages

Grumble Pill Rhyne

SUMMER LA

IVY
HOUSE
COTTS

Ivy House
Farm

TRIM LA

SILVER MOOR LA

61

Wolvershill
Manor

WOLVERSHILL
IND UNITS

Locking Head
Farm

Woolvers
Hill

Pool
Farm

6

WOLVERS HILL RD

Woolvers Hill
Batch

RUSSELL RD

LEEDHAM RD

Laurel
Farm

Park
Farm

5

A371

LOCKING MOOR RD

Locking Farm
Ind Est

RAF
Locking

LOWER PARADE
GROUND RD

BS24

CRANWELL RD

SUMMER LA

BS29

60

HOMEFIELD
CL

HOMEFIELD
IND EST

B3368

ELM TREE RD

PLUMLEY
CRES

PH

POST OFFICE RD

FARNBOROUGH RD

Cave
View

Locking
Cty Prim
Sch

MANOR CL

4

RYDAL AVE

PO

OLD BANWELL RD

B3368

Locking

Church
Farm

LYCHGATE
THE GREEN

MENDIP RD

BROADWAY

PORTAL
RD

THUNDERBOLT RD

3

BANWELL RD

Perries

KNIGHTCOTT RD

Elborough

KNIGHTCOTT
IND EST

KNIGHTCOTT

CHESTERFI

Wingfield
House

Hillend

BLUE WAITE

WELL LA

HIGH ST

59

2

• Mast

Windmill
Farm

Manor
Farm

Whitley
Head

Mc

Benthills
Wood

1

WINDMILL HILL

Elborough
Hill

BRIDEWELL LA

Upper
Canada

CANADA COOMBE

M5

Christon
Hill

Christon
Plantation

BS26

BS26

• Yarberry

58

90
108

A   **B**   **C**   **D**   **E**   **F**

8

The
Homestead

The
Poplars

Laurel
Farm

BS24

Rockers Rhyne

Nut Tree
Farm

NYE RD

Nye

Rookery
Farm

Nye
Farm

Gout House
Farm

7

61

Moor
Dairy

Lower Gout
Farm

Court
Farm

Blind Yeo

Hartlake Rhyne

DROVE WAY

Droveway
Bridge

Droveway
Farm

Moorland
Farm

BS29

MEAD LA

6

5

60

RIVERSIDE

MOOR RD

Libby Yeo

Towerhead Brook

Westleigh
Farm

MEAD LA

Mead
Farm

4

Elmcroft
Farm

THE
ELMS

Golling

Banwell

RIVERSIDE

STATION RD
A368

PH

HOWARD RD

BS25

NIGHTCOTT RD

WEST ST

P

Banwell
Prim Sch

PH

EAST ST
A368

Libby

TOWERHEAD RD

Towerhead

Banwell
Plain

QUARRY LA

Sandford
Batch

SMALL DOWN
END

3

59

ORCHARD CL

PARK LA

THOMAS
CL

Works

Banwell
Wood

COPSE
END

SHIPHAM LA

THE GROVE

SANDFORD RD

2

CASTLE HILL

Banwell
Castle

ILEX LA

Cemy

Winthill
House

Winthill
Farm

Rhodyate
Farm

BANWELL RD
A371

CHRISTON RD

HOMEFIELD CL
MOORHAM RD

EVERGREEN

1

58

Lox Yeo River

A   **B**   40   **C**   **D**   41   **E**   **F**

124
108

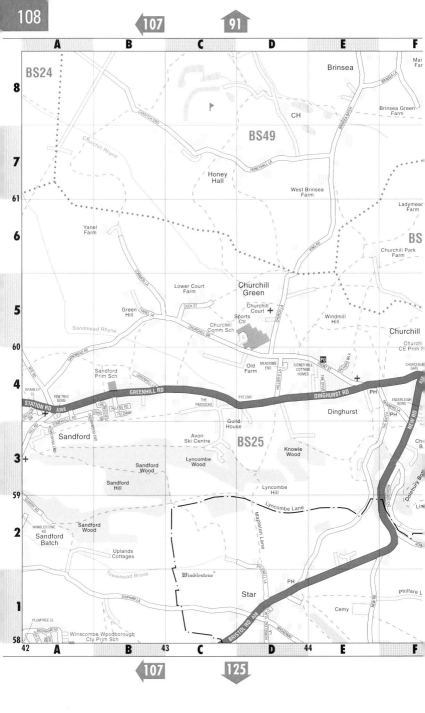

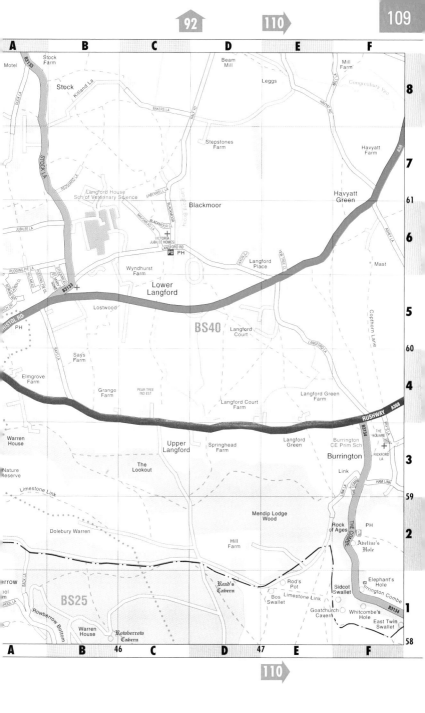

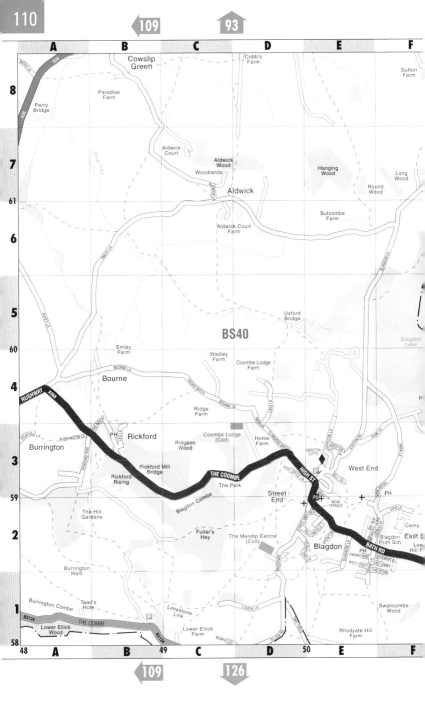

8

7

61

6

5

60

4

59

3

2

1

58

Perry
Bridge

Paradise
Farm

Cowslip
Green

Cribb's
Farm

Sutton
Farm

Aldwick
Court

Aldwick
Wood

Woodlands

Aldwick

Hanging
Wood

Long
Wood

Round
Wood

Butcombe
Farm

Aldwick Court
Farm

Uxford
Bridge

BS40

Blagdon
Lake

Emley
Farm

Wadley
Farm

Coombe Lodge
Farm

Bourne

RUSHWAY

Ridge
Farm

PH

Rickford

Ridgeon
Wood

Coombe Lodge
(Coll)

Home
Farm

GARSTON
COTTS

West End

Burrington

Rickford Mill
Bridge

THE COOMBE

HIGH ST

POST OFFICE LA

Rickford
Rising

The Park

Street
End

PO

MEAD
TERRACE

PH

Blagdon Combe

Blagdon
Prim Sch

East E
Low
Hill F

The Hill
Gardens

Fuller's
Hay

The Mendip Centre
(Coll)

Blagdon

BATH RD

Cemy

EASTCROFT CL

WEST CROFT

THE SQUARE

Burrington
Ham

Burrington Combe

Toad's
Hole

P

THE COOMBE

Limestone
Link

LUVERS LA

Lower Ellick
Farm

NEWFIELDS

Swancombe
Wood

Rhodyate Hill
Farm

B3134

Lower Ellick
Wood

B3134

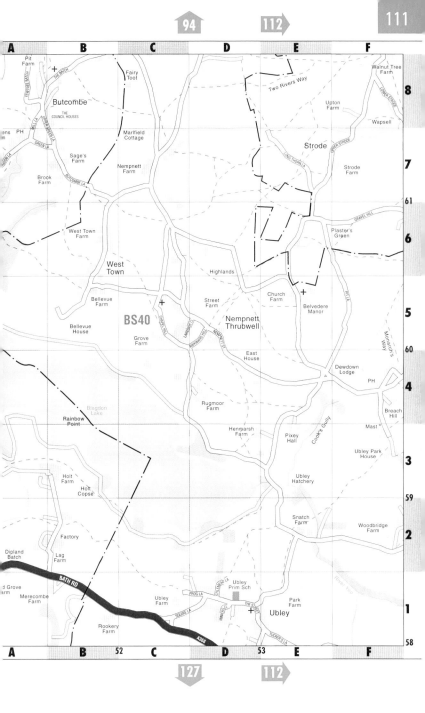

A   **B**   **C**   **D**   **E**   **F**

Pit Farm

THE BATCH

Butcombe

THE COUNCIL HOUSES

Fairy Toot

Walnut Tree Farm

Two Rivers Way

Upton Farm

Wapsell

8

MILL LA

UPPER SCHOLE LA

GREEN LA

PH

ans

in

Marlfield Cottage

Strode

LONG THORN LA

LOWER STRODE

UPPER STRODE

Strode Farm

7

Sage's Farm

Nempnett Farm

Brook Farm

BUTCOMBE LA

61

West Town Farm

Plaster's Green

GRAVEL HILL

6

West Town

Highlands

Church Farm

Belvedere Manor

Bellevue Farm

Street Farm

Nempnett Thrubwell

PIT LA

5

BS40

CHAPEL HILL

LANCE FIELD

AIRWAY FIELD

NEMPNETT ST

Bellevue House

Grove Farm

East House

Monarch's Way

60

Dewdown Lodge

PH

4

Blagdon Lake

Rainbow Point

Rugmoor Farm

Cook's Gully

Breach Hill

Mast

Henmarsh Farm

Pixey Hall

Ubley Park House

3

Ubley Hatchery

Holt Farm

Holt Copse

59

Snatch Farm

Woodbridge Farm

2

Factory

Dipland Batch

Lag Farm

BATH RD

d Grove arm

Merecombe Farm

Ubley Farm

SQUIRE LA

MEAD LA

FROG LA

TUCKWELL LA

INNOX LA

THE STREET

Ubley Prim Sch

Park Farm

Ubley

1

Rookery Farm

A368

TUCKER'S LA

58

A   **B**   52   **C**   **D**   53   **E**   **F**

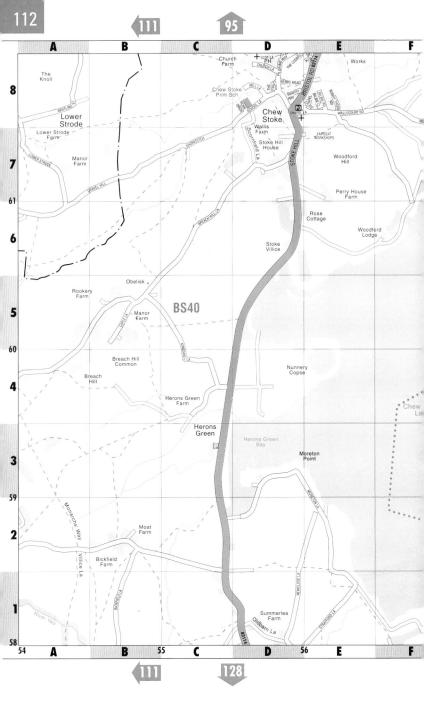

A   B   C   D   E   F

8

The Knoll

WHITLING

Lower Strode

Lower Strode Farm

LOWER STRODE

7

Manor Farm

GRAVEL HILL

61

BREACH HILL LA

6

Obelisk

Rookery Farm

5

BS40

Manor Farm

CROSS LA

60

Breach Hill Common

KING'S LA

Breach Hill

4

Herons Green Farm

Herons Green

59

Monarch's Way

3

Moat Farm

Villice La

2

Bickfield Farm

ROOKERY LA

River Yeo

1

58

Church Farm

Chew Stoke Prim Sch

SCHOOL LA

SHRODREDITCH

PH

SCOT LA

CHURCH LA

THE CROSS

WEBBS MEAD

MILL LA

THE BATCH

QUARRY HAY

BRISTOL RD B3114

Works

BRISTOL RD

WALLYCOURT RD

PO
Chapel La

Chew Stoke

Wallis Farm

Stoke Hill House

Scornfield La

STOKE HILL

FAIRSEAT WORKSHOPS

Woodford Hill

Perry House Farm

Rose Cottage

Woodford Lodge

Stoke Villice

Nunnery Copse

Herons Green Bay

Moreton Point

MORETON LA

Summerlea Farm

Oldbarn La

B3114

MEW LODGE LA

STRATFORD LA

Chew La

54   A   B   55   C   D   56   E   F

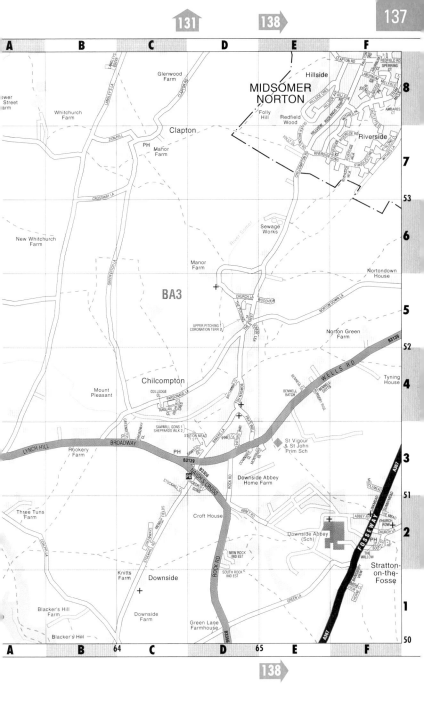

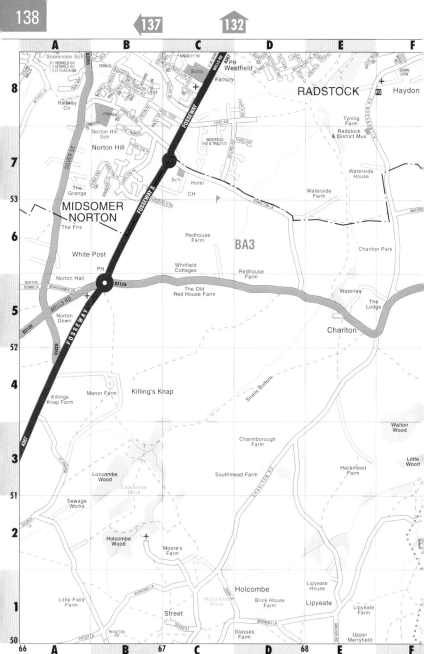

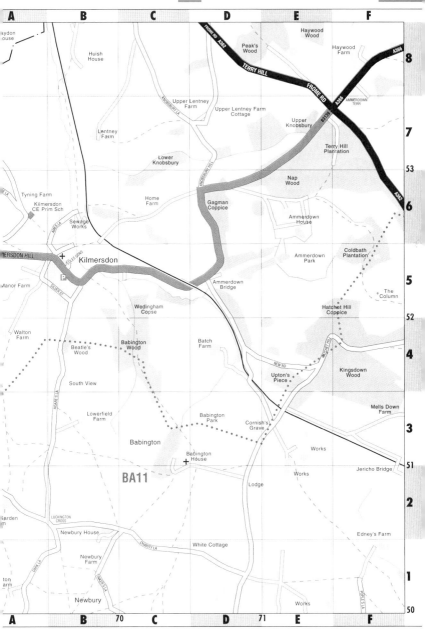

A B C D E F

8

FROME RD A362

Peak's Wood

Haywood Wood

Haywood Farm

A366

TERRY HILL

FROME RD

Huish House

Upper Lentney Farm

Upper Lentney Farm Cottage

Upper Knobsbury

B3139

AMMERDOWN TERR

7

KNOBSBURY LA

Lentney Farm

Lower Knobsbury

Terry Hill Plantation

53

KNOBSBURY HILL

Nap Wood

A362

Tyning Farm

Home Farm

Gagman Coppice

Ammerdown House

6

Kilmersdon CE Prim Sch

Sewage Works

AMES LA

Ammerdown Park

Coldbath Plantation

KILMERSDON HILL

Kilmersdon

EGLES LONG

Ammerdown Bridge

5

Manor Farm

P

SILVER ST

Wedingham Copse

Hatchet Hill Coppice

The Column

52

Walton Farm

Beatle's Wood

Babington Wood

Batch Farm

HATCHET HILL

Kingsdown Wood

4

HOARE S LA

South View

NEW RD

Upton's Piece

Lowerfield Farm

Babington Park

Cornish's Grave

Mells Down Farm

3

Babington

Babington House

Works

51

BA11

Lodge

Works

Jericho Bridge

2

LUCKINGTON CROSS

Newbury House

CHARITY LA

White Cottage

Edney's Farm

arden

Newbury Farm

AMES LA

DRACLA

ton arm

Newbury

Works

POL S LA

1

50

A B C 70 D 71 E F

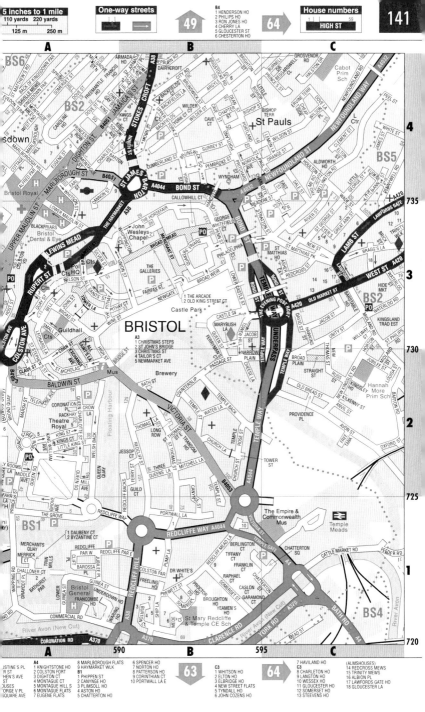

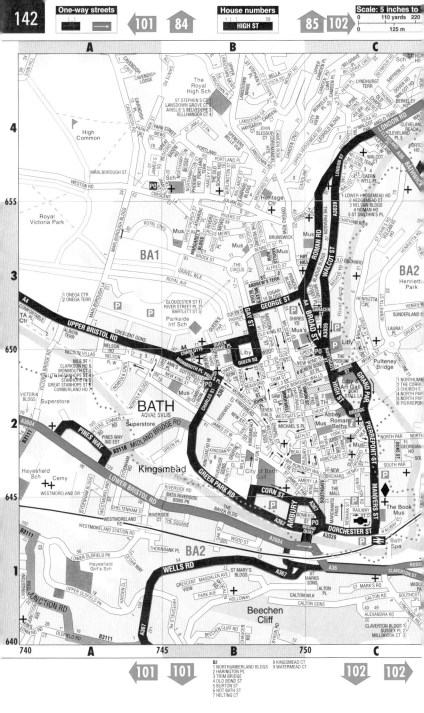

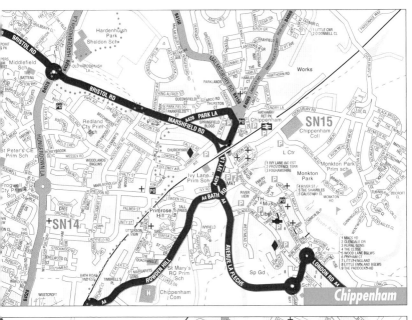

Chippenham

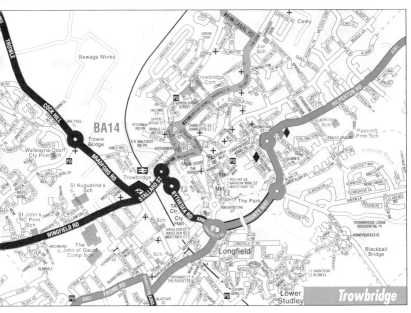

Trowbridge

Index

Street names are listed alphabetically and show the locality, the Postcode District, the page number and a reference to the square in which the name falls on the map page

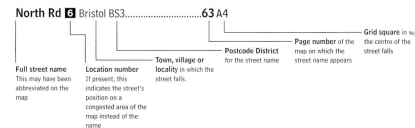

North Rd **6** Bristol BS3..............**63** A4

Grid square in which the centre of the street falls

Page number of the map on which the street name appears

Postcode District for the street name

Town, village or locality in which the street falls.

Location number If present, this indicates the street's position on a congested area of the map instead of the name

Full street name This may have been abbreviated on the map

Abbreviations used in the index

App **Approach**	Cl **Close**	Espl **Esplanade**	N **North**	S **South**
Arc **Arcade**	Comm **Common**	Est **Estate**	Orch **Orchard**	Sq **Square**
Ave **Avenue**	Cnr **Corner**	Gdns **Gardens**	Par **Parade**	Strs **Stairs**
Bvd **Boulevard**	Cotts **Cottages**	Gn **Green**	Pk **Park**	Stps **Steps**
Bldgs **Buildings**	Ct **Court**	Gr **Grove**	Pas **Passage**	St **Street, Saint**
Bsns Pk **Business Park**	Ctyd **Courtyard**	Hts **Heights**	Pl **Place**	Terr **Terrace**
Bsns Ctr **Business Centre**	Cres **Crescent**	Ind Est **Industrial**	Prec **Precinct**	Trad **Trading Est**
Bglws **Bungalows**	Dr **Drive**		Estate	Prom **Promenade**	Wlk **Walk**
Cswy **Causeway**	Dro **Drove**	Intc **Interchange**	Ret Pk **Retail Park**	W **West**
Ctr **Centre**	E **East**	Junc **Junction**	Rd **Road**	Yd **Yard**
Cir **Circus**	Emb **Embankment**	La **Lane**	Rdbt **Roundabout**	

Town and village index

Abbots Leigh 62 A8	Clapton In Gordano 45 E1	Hewish 90 A2	Newton St Loe 100 D7	Thornbury. . . . .
Acton Turville 42 F6	Claverham 74 F1	High Littleton 115 D1	North End 73 A3	Tickenham 5
Almondsbury 24 A4	Cleeve. 92 A8	Hillesley 19 C8	North Nibley 5 E4	Timsbury 11
Alveston 15 A5	Clevedon 57 B1	Hinton 54 C5	Norton St Philip 135 E4	Tockington 1
Aust 13 A7	Clutton 114 F3	Hinton Blewett 129 E4	Olveston 14 D3	Tormarton. 4
Avonmouth 33 C4	Coalpit Heath 38 D7	Hinton Charterhouse . . 119 E1	Paulton 131 D5	Tortworth 1
Axbridge. 125 A1	Codrington 40 B3	Holcombe 138 E1	Peasedown St John . . . 133 D8	Tytherington 1
Backwell. 76 A7	Cold Ashton 68 F6	Horton 29 A6	Pensford. 97 E7	Ubley 9
Badminton 30 D2	Colerne. 70 F6	Hutton 105 E2	Pill 47 D4	Upper Swainswick 8
Banwell 107 B3	Compton Bishop 124 B2	Iron Acton. 26 E3	Pilning 22 E6	Upton Cheyney 8
Barrow Gurney 77 E4	Compton Dando 98 E5	Kelston 83 B3	Pitt Court 5 F5	Wellow 11
Bath 101 C3	Compton Martin 128 A6	Kenn 73 A6	Portbury 46 E5	West Harptree 12
Bath 142 C3	Congresbury 91 F6	Keynsham. 81 C2	Portishead 45 B5	West Kington 5
Bathampton 85 E1	Corston. 100 A7	Kilmersdon. 139 B6	Priddy. 127 B7	Westerleigh 3
Batheaston 85 B2	Cromhall. 10 B2	Kingsdown 86 F5	Priston 117 A5	Weston 8
Bathford 86 E3	Doynton 54 A1	Kingston Seymour 73 A5	Publow 97 E7	Weston-Super-Mare . . 10
Bevington 2 F7	Dundry 78 A1	Kingswood 11 F4	Pucklechurch 53 D3	Westwood. 12
Bishop Sutton. 113 D4	Dunkerton 117 C4	Langford. 109 C8	Radstock 132 E1	Wickwar 1
Bitton 82 E8	Dyrham. 54 B3	Langridge 84 D8	Rangeworthy 27 A8	Wick 6
Blagdon 110 C7	East Harptree 128 C3	Leigh Woods 62 C7	Redhill 93 E4	Wick St Lawrence. 8
Bleadon 122 B6	Easter Compton 23 A1	Limpley Stoke. 120 A5	Rockhampton 8 E7	Wickwar 1
Brean 121 A2	Easton-In-Gordano 47 A4	Littleton-Upon-Severn. . 13 A8	Rode. 136 F1	Winford 9
Bristol. 63 A1	Elberton 14 D4	Litton 129 B1	Rowberrow 109 A1	Winscombe. 12
Bristol. 141 A1	Failand 61 B3	Locking 106 D4	Saltford. 82 D2	Winsley 12
Brockley 75 D4	Falfield. 9 D2	Long Ashton 62 A1	Severn Beach 22 A5	Winterbourne 3
Burrington 109 F3	Farmborough 116 A6	Loxton 123 A3	Shipham 125 D6	Woodford . . . .
Burton 43 D6	Farrington Gurney 130 B4	Luckington 31 D2	Shirehampton. 47 C7	Woolley 8
Camerton 132 F1	Faulkland 134 D2	Lympsham 122 A1	Shockerwick. 86 D4	Woolverton. 13
Charfield. 11 A1	Felton 94 D3	Marksbury 99 E3	Southstoke 118 F7	Wraxall 6
Charlcombe 84 F4	Flax Bourton. 76 F7	Marshfield 69 E8	Stanton Drew 96 F1	Wrington 9
Cheddar 125 F1	Frampton Cotterell. 38 C6	Midford. 119 C5	Star. 108 D1	Yate 2
Chew Magna. 96 B3	Freshford 120 A4	Midsomer Norton 132 B2	Stanton Easton 130 E1	Yatton 9
Chilcompton. 137 D2	Hallen. 34 E8	Monkton Combe 102 E8	Stone 3 C4	
Chipping Sodbury. 28 B1	Hambrook. 37 E2	Monkton Farleigh. 103 E7	Stratton On The Fosse . 137 F2	
Churchill. 108 F4	Hawkesbury Upton 20 A2	Nailsea 59 D2	Swainswick. 85 C3	
Churchill Green 108 B5	Henfield. 38 D2	Newport. 4 B7	Temple Cloud 114 E1	

5c B–Aug 145

Ctr BS21 57 B1
:l BS31 81 F6
:t Bath BA2 102 B7
3S4 64 F5
in BA1 142 C2
lo 5 BS37 39 D7
.a
Charterhouse BA3 120 A4
ry BS35 15 D6
lews GL12 11 F4
'k BS31 81 F6
td Bristol BS9 48 F7
pton BA3 137 D2
On The Fosse BA3 137 F2
t Bath BA1 142 C2
od GL12 11 F5
ew Bath BA2 102 B5
k BA3 133 A3
iew Gdns BA2 102 B5
ale BS36 37 E6
ate St BA1 142 C2
ood Dr BS9 48 C5
ood Pk BS34 36 C2
Cl BS22 89 A3
Ave BS15 65 C4
Cl BS14 80 A3
Horn BS48 59 D2
Leigh Rd BS8 62 C7
Rd BS15 65 C2
Way BS9 49 E6
bury Rd BS48 59 D1
ord Rd BS6 49 B1
wood Bristol BS15 65 D7
37 39 D7
wood Inf Sch BS37 39 D6
wood Jun Sch
39 D6
Rd BS35 22 A5
Farm Cl BS39 131 D5
en Rd BS6 140 B4
on Gdns BA2 118 D8
on Rd BS16 51 A3
La BS35 22 A5
Wlk BS9 48 C5
o BS9 48 C4
n Cl BS5 64 B8
n Fry Ho BS15 65 E7
Rd BS16 53 D3
Ave Bristol BS16 51 D4
-Super-Mare BS23 105 B8
Cl BS16 51 D3
Ct BS31 81 C4
Gr BA2 101 C3
Mews 4 BS16 51 D4
Rd Bristol BS16 51 D4
k BA3 132 E1
nodation Rd
121 E6
BS11 33 C4
Cl BS22 89 B5
Gr BS13 78 E6
n's Rd 7 BS3 63 C4
ush Cl BS13 79 A5
d BS16 51 A3
Cl BA2 133 D8
Ct 5 BS8 62 F6
Hay 6 BS4 64 D1
l Rd BS24 106 D4
Gate BS16 52 B7
t Rd BS23 104 E6
mbe Rd
BS14 80 B5
-Super-Mare BS23 104 E4
n Rd BS3 63 E3
e Pl
Fishponds BS16 50 F4
tol, Upper Easton BS5 64 B8
e Terr 1 BS16 51 A4
's Wlk BS20 45 B5
Ct 6 BS5 64 C7
Mdw BS20 45 F4
t BS3 63 B3
t BS5 64 B6
s Belvedere BA1 142 B4
Dr BS16 37 F1
oon Ct 1 BS5 65 A7
oon Hill
Inf Schs BS5 65 A7
oon Rd BS5 65 A7
Rd BS14 80 A8
Rdbt BS24 105 E7
ne Way BS22 105 C6
Way BS11 47 C8
urt BS30 66 B5
d BS4 79 F7
BS23 87 F1
Gate BS14 36 E5
Rd Bath BA2 101 C6
BS6 49 F1
St BS15 65 C8
Way BS30 66 C5
arle Row 9 BS8 62 F6
Ave
own St John BA2 133 C7
-Super-Mare BS23 104 E6
Cres BS2 64 B5
Ct BS23 104 E6
Gr BS5 64 F8
Par BS5 64 D8
Park Pl BS6 49 F1
Pk BS6 49 F1

Albert Pl Bath BA2 102 C1
1 Bristol, Bedminster BS3 63 C3
Bristol, Eastfield BS9 49 A7
Portishead BS20 45 D4
Albert Quadrant BS23 104 E8
Albert Rd Bristol BS15 65 D5
Bristol BS16 51 E4
Bristol BS2 64 A4
Clevedon BS21 57 C3
Keynsham BS31 81 E5
Portishead BS20 45 D5
Severn Beach BS35 22 A6
Weston-Super-Mare BS23 104 E6
Albert St BS5 64 C8
Albert Terr Bath BA2 101 C6
Bristol BS16 50 F4
Alberton Rd BS16 50 F6
Albion Cl BS16 51 F5
Albion Pl 16 BS2 141 C3
Albion Rd BS5 50 B1
Albion St 6 BS5 64 C8
Albion Terr Bath BA1 142 A3
Bristol BS34 24 B1
Alburys BS40 92 D3
Alcove Rd BS16 50 F3
Alder Dr BS5 50 E1
Alder Terr BA3 132 E2
Alder Way BA2 118 D8
Aldercombe Rd BS9 48 C8
Alderdown Cl BS11 48 A8
Alderley Rd Bath BA2 101 B4
Hillesley GL12 19 D8
Aldermoor Way BS30 65 E4
Aldernay Ave BS4 64 F4
Alders The BS16 37 B1
Alderton Rd Bristol BS7 49 E8
Burton SN14 43 D6
Aldwick Ave BS13 79 C3
Aldwick La BS40 110 C7
Aldworth Ho BS2 141 C4
Alec Ricketts Cl BA2 100 F5
Alexander Bldgs 12 BA1 85 B1
Alexander Ho 5 BS23 104 F4
Alexander Hosea
Prim Sch The GL12 18 B5
Alexander Mews BS23 104 E7
Alexander Pl BA3 120 C6
Alexander Way BS49 91 B7
Alexandra Cl BS16 51 D4
Alexandra Ct BS21 57 C4
Alexandra Gdns BS16 51 D4
Alexandra Par BS23 104 E7
Alexandra Park Ctr BS16 50 F4
Alexandra Pk Bristol BS16 50 F4
Bristol BS6 49 C2
Paulton BS39 131 E5
Alexandra Pl Bath BA2 102 C1
Bristol BS16 51 D4
Alexandra Rd Bath BA2 142 C1
Bristol BS10 49 C8
Bristol BS13 78 F7
Bristol BS15 65 D5
Bristol BS8 140 B4
Clevedon BS21 57 C4
Coalpit Heath BS36 38 D7
Alexandra Terr BS39 131 E5
Alexandra Way BS35 8 B3
Alford Rd BS4 64 C2
Alfred Ct BS23 104 E7
Alfred Hill BS2 141 A4
Alfred Lovell Gdns 7
BS30 66 A4
Alfred Par BS2 141 A4
Alfred Pl BS2 140 C4
Alfred Rd Bristol BS3 63 D3
Bristol BS6 49 A4
Alfred St Bath BA1 142 B3
Bristol BS2 64 A6
Bristol BS5 64 D8
Weston-Super-Mare BS23 104 E8
Algars Dr BS37 26 E3
Algiers St BS3 63 D3
Alison Gdns BS48 76 A7
All Hallows Ct 11 BS5 64 B8
All Hallows Rd BS5 64 B8
All Saints La BS21 57 F4
All Saints Rd BA1 142 B4
All Saints' La BS1 141 A2
All Saints' Rd Bristol BS8 140 A4
Weston-Super-Mare BS23 87 E1
All Saints' St BS1 141 A3
Allanmead Rd BS14 80 B8
Allengrove La SN14 31 C3
Allens La BS25 125 F8
Aller BS24 105 B2
Aller Par BS24 105 B2
Allerton Cres BS14 80 B4
Allerton Gdns BS14 80 B5
Allerton Rd BS14 80 B4
Allfoxton Rd BS7 50 A3
Allington Dr BS30 65 F4
Allington Gdns BS48 75 C8
Allington Rd BS3 140 C1
Allison Ave BS4 64 E4
Allison Rd BS4 64 E3
Alma Cl BS15 65 E8
Alma Ct BS8 49 B1
Alma Rd Bristol BS15 51 E1
Bristol BS8 140 B4
Alma Road Ave BS8 140 B4
Alma St Bristol BS8 49 B1
Weston-Super-Mare BS23 104 E7
Alma Vale Rd BS8 140 A4
Almeda Rd BS5 65 A6
Almond Cl BS22 89 A1
Almond Way BS16 51 F5
Almondsbury Bsns Ctr
BS32 24 D3

Almondsbury CE Prim Sch
BS32 24 A4
Almondsbury Intc BS32 24 D4
Almondsbury Rdbt BS32 24 B3
Almorah Rd BS3 63 E3
Almshouses
5 Bristol BS1 141 A2
Marshfield SN14 69 E8
Alpha Ctr The BS37 27 C3
Alpha Rd BS3 63 D4
Alpine Cl BS39 131 F4
Alpine Gdns BA1 142 C4
Alpine Rd Bristol BS5 50 C1
Paulton BS39 131 F4
Alsop Rd 4 BS15 51 D1
Alton Pl BA2 142 C1
Alton Rd BS7 49 F5
Altringham Rd 8 BS5 64 D8
Alverstoke BS14 79 F7
Alveston Hill BS35 15 A6
Alveston Rd BS32 14 D3
Alveston Wlk BS9 48 B7
Alwins Ct 2 BS30 65 F4
Ambares Ct BA3 137 F8
Amberey Rd BS23 104 F5
Amberlands Cl BS48 76 A7
Amberley Cl Bristol BS16 51 D7
Keynsham BS31 81 E4
Amberley Gdns 3 BS48 59 D1
Amberley House Sch BS8 49 A1
Amberley Rd Bristol BS16 51 D7
Bristol BS34 36 B8
Amberley Way GL12 18 B4
Amble Cl BS15 65 F7
Ambleside Ave BS10 35 B2
Ambleside Rd BA2 101 C2
Ambra Ct BS8 140 A2
Ambra Terr BS8 140 A2
Ambra Vale BS8 140 A2
Ambra Vale E BS8 140 A2
Ambra Vale S BS8 140 A2
Ambra Vale W BS8 140 A2
Ambrose Rd BS8 140 A2
Ambury BA1 142 B1
Amercombe Wlk BS14 80 D7
American Mus in Britain
BA2 103 A5
Amery La BA1 142 C2
Ames La BA3 139 B6
Amesbury Dr BS24 122 B6
Ammerdown Terr BA3 139 F7
Anchor Cl BS5 64 F6
Anchor Rd Bathford BA1 84 B1
Bristol BS1 140 C2
Bristol BS15 52 A2
Holcombe BA3 138 E1
Anchor Way BS20 47 D4
Ancliff Sq BA15 120 E4
Andereach Cl BS14 80 B8
Andover Rd BS4 63 F2
Andrew Millman Ct BS37 27 F1
Andruss Dr BS41 78 D2
Angels Gd BS4 64 F6
Angers Rd BS4 64 A4
Anglesea Pl 15 BS8 49 A2
Anglo Terr BA1 142 C4
Animal Farm & Ctry Pk
TA8 121 B2
Annandale Ave BS22 88 E1
Anson Cl BS31 82 D2
Anson Rd Locking BS24 106 B5
Weston-Super-Mare BS22 88 D4
Anstey St BS5 50 B1
Anstey's Rd BS15 65 C5
Ansteys Cl BS15 65 B5
Anthea Rd BS5 50 E2
Antona Ct BS11 47 D7
Antona Dr BS11 47 D7
Antrim Rd BS9 49 B6
Anvil Rd BS49 74 F1
Anvil St BS2 141 C2
Apex Ct BS32 24 D3
Apperley Cl BS37 39 E8
Apple Tree Dr BS25 125 A8
Appleby Wlk BS4 79 D7
Applecroft BA2 133 E6
Appledore 4 BS22 88 F2
Appledore Cl BS14 80 B8
Applegate BS10 35 B3
Appleridge La GL13 3 C4
Appletree Ct BS22 89 B2
Appletree Mews BS22 89 B2
Applin Gn BS16 52 C6
Appsley Cl BS22 88 C1
Apseleys Mead BS32 24 C2
Apsley Rd Bath BA1 101 A7
Bristol BS8 49 A1
Apsley St BS5 50 C3
Arbutus Dr BS9 48 C8
Arcade The 2 BS1 141 B3
Arch Cl BS41 61 F1
Archer Ct Bristol BS30 65 F3
Clevedon BS21 57 D4
Archer Wlk BS14 80 E6
Arches The Bath BA2 101 A6
1 Bristol BS5 64 B7
Archfield Ct BS6 49 C1
Archfield Rd BS6 49 C1
Archgrove BS41 61 F1
Archway St BA2 102 B5
Arden Cl Bristol BS32 36 E6
Weston-Super-Mare BS22 88 F3
Ardenton Wlk BS10 35 A3
Ardern Cl BS9 48 B8
Ardmore BS8 62 D7
Argus Ct BS3 63 C2
Argus Rd BS3 63 C3
Argyle Ave Bristol BS5 50 C2

Argyle Ave *continued*
Weston-Super-Mare BS23 104 F4
Argyle Dr BS37 27 E4
Argyle Pl BS8 140 A2
Argyle Rd Bristol BS16 51 B2
Bristol BS2 141 B4
Clevedon BS21 57 D6
Argyle St Bath BA2 142 C2
6 Bristol BS3 63 C4
5 Bristol BS5 50 C2
Argyle Terr BA2 101 C6
Arkells Ct GL12 18 A6
Arley Cotts 4 BS6 49 D1
Arley Hill BS6 49 D1
Arley Pk BS6 49 D1
Arley Terr BS5 50 E1
Arlingham Way BS34 23 F1
Arlington Mans BS8 140 B4
Arlington Rd Bath BA2 101 D5
Bristol BS4 64 D5
Arlington Villas BS8 140 B3
Armada Ho BS2 141 B4
Armada Pl BS1 141 B4
Armada Rd BS14 80 A6
Armes Ct BA2 142 C1
Armidale Ave 2 BS6 49 E1
Armidale Cotts 3 BS6 49 E1
Armoury Sq BS5 64 A8
Armstrong Cl BS35 15 D7
Armstrong Ct BS37 27 C3
Armstrong Dr BS30 66 B5
Armstrong Way BS37 27 B3
Arnall Dr BS10 34 F1
Arncliffe EPD BS10 49 C8
Arneside Rd BS10 35 C1
Arno's St BS4 64 A3
Arnold Ct BS37 28 B1
Arnold's Way BS49 74 A2
Arnolds Field Trad Est
GL12 18 A5
Arnolfini (Arts Ctr) BS1 141 A1
Arnor Cl BS22 89 A4
Arrowfield Cl BS14 80 A2
Artemesia Ave BS22 105 E8
Arthur Skemp Cl BS5 64 B7
Arthur St Bristol BS2 64 A5
7 Bristol BS5 64 C8
Arthurs Cl BS16 52 C6
Arthurswood Rd BS13 79 A4
Arundel Cl BS13 79 B5
Arundel Ct BS7 49 D3
Arundel Rd Bath BA1 85 A1
Bristol BS7 49 D3
Clevedon BS21 57 D3
Arundel Wlk BS31 81 D5
Arundell Ct BS23 104 E8
Arundell Rd BS23 87 E1
Ascension Ho BA2 101 D4
Ascot Cl BS16 37 F1
Ascot Rd BS10 35 E2
Ash Brook BS39 115 D1
Ash Cl Bristol BS16 51 C3
Bristol BS34 36 D7
Winscombe BS25 108 A1
Yate BS37 27 D3
Ash Ct BS14 80 A6
Ash Gr Bath BA2 101 C4
Bristol BS16 51 D3
Clevedon BS21 57 E4
Weston-Super-Mare BS23 104 E2
Ash Hayes Dr BS48 59 E1
Ash Hayes Rd BS48 59 F1
Ash La BS32 23 D2
Ash Rd Banwell BS29 106 E4
Bristol BS7 49 E5
Ash Ridge Rd BS32 24 B3
Ash Tree Cl BS24 122 C6
Ash Tree Ct BA3 132 E1
Ash Wlk BS10 35 B3
Ashbourne Cl 2 BS30 66 C6
Ashbrooke House Sch
BS23 104 D6
Ashburton Rd BS10 35 C1
Ashbury Dr BS22 88 B2
Ashcombe Cl 1 BS30 66 C6
Ashcombe Cres BS30 66 D6
Ashcombe Ct BS23 104 F7
Ashcombe Gdns BS23 105 A8
Ashcombe Park Rd BS23 88 A1
Ashcombe Prim Sch
BS23 105 A7
Ashcombe Rd BS23 104 F7
Ashcott BS14 79 F7
Ashcroft BS24 105 B2
Ashcroft Ave BS31 81 D5
Ashcroft Rd BS9 48 C7
Ashdene Ave BS5 50 D3
Ashdene Rd BS23 105 A8
Ashdown Ct BS9 48 F8
Ashdown Rd BS20 45 A6
Ashel's Batch BA3 129 C1
Asher La BS2 141 C3
Ashes La BA3 120 A4
Ashey La BS40 110 A5
Ashfield Pl BS6 49 F1
Ashfield Rd BS3 63 B3
Ashfield Terr 8 BS3 63 B3
Ashford Dr BS24 105 A1
Ashford Rd Bath BA2 101 D4
Bristol BS34 36 A7
Redhill BS40 93 E4
Ashford Way BS15 66 A7
Ashgrove
Peasedown St John BA2 133 D8
Thornbury BS35 8 C1
Ashgrove Ave
Abbots Leigh BS8 62 B7
Bristol BS7 49 F4

Ashgrove Cl BS7 49 F4
Ashgrove Ct BA2 133 D8
Ashgrove Rd Bristol BS3 63 B3
Bristol BS7 49 F4
Ashland Rd BS13 79 A4
Ashleigh Cl
Paulton BS39 131 E6
Weston-Super-Mare BS23 105 A8
Ashleigh Cres BS49 91 B8
Ashleigh Rd
Weston-Super-Mare BS23 105 A8
Yatton BS49 91 B8
Ashley BS15 65 F8
Ashley Ave BA1 101 C7
Ashley Cl Bristol BS7 49 F4
Winscombe BS25 125 A7
Ashley Court Rd 2 BS7 49 F2
Ashley Down Jun & Inf Schs
BS7 49 F5
Ashley Down Rd BS7 49 F4
Ashley Grove Rd
7 Bristol BS2 49 F2
1 Bristol BS2 50 A1
Ashley Hill BS6,BS7 49 F2
Ashley Ho BS34 23 F1
Ashley La BA15 120 F7
Ashley Par BS2 49 F2
Ashley Pk BS6 49 F3
Ashley Rd
Bathford BA1 86 E3
Bristol BS6 49 E1
Clevedon BS21 57 B1
Ashley St BS2 50 A1
Ashley Terr BA1 101 C7
Ashley Trad Est 6
BS2 49 F2
Ashman Cl 5 BS5 64 A8
Ashman Ct 1 BS16 50 E3
Ashmans Ct BA1 101 B6
Ashmans Gate BS39 131 E5
Ashmans Yd BA1 101 B6
Ashmead BS39 114 E1
Ashmead Ho 12 BS5 64 C7
Ashmead Rd BS31 82 B5
Ashmead Road Ind Est
BS31 82 B5
Ashmead Way 8 BS1 62 F5
Ashton BS16 37 C1
Ashton Ave BS1 140 A1
Ashton Cl BS21 57 B1
Ashton Court Est BS41 62 C4
Ashton Cres BS48 59 D1
Ashton Dr BS3 62 F2
Ashton Gate Prim Sch
BS3 63 A4
Ashton Gate Rd BS3 63 A4
Ashton Gate Terr 3 BS3 63 A4
Ashton Gate Trad Est
BS3 62 E3
Ashton Gate Underpass
BS3 62 F3
Ashton Hill BA2 100 A7
Ashton Rd
Bristol, Ashton Gate BS3 62 F4
Bristol, Bower Ashton BS3 62 D3
Ashton Vale Prim Sch BS3 62 F2
Ashton Vale Rd BS3 62 E3
Ashton Vale Trad Est
BS3 62 F1
Ashton Way BS31 81 E6
Ashvale Cl BS48 60 A2
Ashville Rd BS3 63 A4
Ashwell Cl BS14 80 E6
Ashwicke BS14 80 A6
Ashwicke Rd SN14 70 B3
Ashwood BS40 128 F4
Aspen Cl SN14 70 F6
Aspen Park Rd BS22 105 E8
Aspley Cl BA1 101 B7
Assembly Rooms La
BS1 141 A2
Aston Ho 4 BS1 141 B1
Astry Cl BS11 34 A1
At-Bristol BS1 140 C1
Atchley St 17 BS5 64 B7
Atherston BS30 66 D5
Athlone Wlk BS4 63 E1
Atholl Cl BS22 88 F3
Atkins Cl BS14 80 E6
Atlantic Ct BS23 87 C1
Atlantic Rd
Bristol BS11 47 C8
Weston-Super-Mare BS23 87 C1
Atlantic Rd S BS23 87 C1
Atlas Cl BS5 51 A2
Atlas Rd BS3 63 E3
Atlas St BS2 64 B5
Atlay Ct BS49 74 B1
Attewell Ct BA2 101 F4
Atwell Dr BS32 24 B1
Atwood Dr BS11 34 B2
Aubrey Ho 9 BS3 63 B3
Aubrey Meads BS30 82 E8
Aubrey Rd BS3 63 B3
Auburn Ave BS30 66 B3
Auburn Rd BS6 49 B1
Auckland Cl BS23 104 F3
Audley Ave BA1 101 D7
Audley Cl
Bath BA1 101 D7
Rangeworthy BS37 27 A8
Audley Gr BA1 101 C7
Audley Park Rd BA1 101 C7
Audley Wlk BS9 49 D7
Augustine's Cl BS20 44 E4

Augustus Ho BS15 .... 65 B6
Aust La BS9 .... 49 A8
Aust Rd Olveston BS35 ..... 13 F5
  Pilning BS35 .... 12 D3
Austen Dr BS22 .... 89 B4
Austen Gr BS7 .... 50 A8
Austen Ho BS7 .... 50 A8
Autumn Mews BS24 ..... 106 A8
Avalon Cl BS49 .... 74 A1
Avalon Ho BS48 .... 59 C1
Avalon Rd BS5 .... 65 B6
Avebury Rd BS3 .... 62 F2
Avening Cl BS48 .... 76 A8
Avening Rd BS15 .... 65 A8
Avenue Pl BA2 .... 102 B1
Avenue The Backwell BS48 .. 76 A7
  Bath, Claverton Down BA2 . 102 E5
  Bath, Combe Down BA2 ... 102 C1
  Bristol BS16 .... 36 E1
  Bristol BS5 .... 64 F8
  Bristol BS7 .... 49 E3
  Bristol BS8 .... 49 A1
  Bristol BS9 .... 48 E3
  Bristol BS9 .... 48 E3
  Bristol, Little Stoke BS34 ... 36 C6
  Bristol, Patchway BS34 .... 24 B2
  Clevedon BS21 .... 57 E6
  Keynsham BS31 .... 81 E6
  Timsbury BA3 .... 116 B2
  Winscombe BS25 .... 125 C8
  Yate BS37 .... 27 D1
  Yatton BS49 .... 91 B8
Averay Rd BS16 .... 50 C4
Averill Cl BS21 .... 57 D4
Avon & Somerset Pol HQ
  BS20 .... 44 F3
Avon Bsns Pk BS16 ...... 51 A3
Avon Cl Bristol BS5 ..... 64 F6
  Keynsham BS31 .... 81 F6
  Weston-super-Mare BS23 . 104 F7
Avon Cres Bristol BS1 ... 140 A1
  Wickwar GL12 .... 18 B6
Avon Ct Batheaston BA1 .. 86 A4
  Bristol BS16 .... 51 B5
Avon Gorge Ind Est BS11 . 47 C7
Avon Gorge
  Nature Reserve BS8 .... 62 E7
Avon Gr BS9 .... 48 D2
Avon Hts BA1 .... 120 C6
Avon La BS31 .... 82 F5
Avon Mdws BS22 .... 64 C5
Avon Mill La BS31 ...... 81 F6
Avon Pk Bath BA1 ...... 101 A7
  Bristol BS5 .... 64 D7
Avon Prim Sch BS11 .... 47 D8
Avon Rd Bristol BS13 .... 79 A6
  Charfield GL12 .... 11 A4
  Keynsham BS31 .... 81 F5
Avon Rise SN14 .... 31 E4
Avon Riverside Est BS11 . 47 C7
Avon Ski Ctr BS25 ..... 108 C3
Avon St Bath BA1 ...... 142 B2
  Bristol BS2 .... 141 C2
Avon Trad Est BS2 ..... 64 A5
Avon Vale BS9 .... 48 D4
Avon Valley Bsns Pk BS4 . 64 E6
Avon Valley Ctry Pk BS31 . 82 D6
Avon Valley Rly BS30 .... 66 C3
Avon View BS15 .... 65 B3
Avon Way Bristol BS10 .. 49 D7
  Bristol BS8 .... 48 C4
  Portishead BS20 .... 45 C5
  Thornbury BS35 .... 15 D2
Avonbank Ind Est BS11 .. 47 B7
Avonbridge Trad Est BS11 . 47 C8
Avoncliff Halt BA15 .... 120 F5
Avondale Bldgs BA1 .... 85 B2
Avondale Bsns Ctr BS15 . 51 C2
Avondale Ct Bristol BS30 . 65 F3
  Bristol BS9 .... 48 D3
Avondale Pl BA1 .... 85 F3
Avondown Cl BS10 ..... 35 D2
Avondown Ct BS3 ...... 63 C2
Avondowns Ct BS8 .... 140 A4
Avonlea Bristol BS15 ... 65 C5
  Yate BS37 .... 39 D8
Avonleaze BS9 .... 48 B5
Avonleigh Ct BA2 ...... 63 B2
Avonleigh Rd BS3 ...... 63 B2
Avonmouth CE Prim Sch
  BS11 .... 47 C8
Avonmouth Rd
  Avonmouth BS11 .... 33 D1
  Bristol BS11 .... 47 C8
Avonmouth Sta BS11 ... 33 D1
Avonmouth Way
  Avonmouth BS11 .... 33 D1
  Bristol BS11 .... 34 B1
Avonmouth Way W BS11 . 33 B1
Avonside Ind Est BS2 ... 64 C6
Avonside Rd BS2 .... 64 C6
Avonside Way BS4 ..... 64 D6
Avonsmere Residential Pk
  BS34 .... 36 C3
Avonvale Rd BS5 ...... 64 C7
Avonwood Cl BS11 ..... 47 E6
Awdelett Cl BS11 ...... 34 B8
Awkward Hill BS40 ..... 75 E8
Axbridge Cl BS48 ...... 75 E8
Axbridge First Sch BS26 . 125 C1
Axbridge Moor Dro BS26 . 125 C1
Axbridge Mus BS26 .... 125 C2
Axbridge Rd Bath BA2 .. 102 A2
  Bristol BS3 .... 63 F2

Axbridge Rd *continued*
  Cheddar BS27 .... 125 F2
Axe Cl BS23 .... 105 A5
Axe Ct ■ BS35 .... 15 C8
Axford Way BA2 .... 133 D8
Axis BS14 .... 79 D5
Aycote Cl BS22 .... 88 B3
Ayford La SN14 .... 69 F4
Aylesbury Cres BS3 ..... 63 B1
Aylesbury Rd BS3 ...... 63 B1
Aylmer Cres BS14 ...... 80 B6
Aylminton Wlk BS11 .... 34 B2
Ayr St BA2 .... 101 D6
Azalea Rd BS22 .... 89 A5
Aztec Ctr The BS32 .... 24 A2
Aztec W BS32 .... 24 A2

B

Back La Axbridge BS26 ... 125 C2
  Keynsham BS31 .... 81 E6
  Kingston Seymour BS21 .. 73 A5
  Litton BA3 .... 129 B1
  Litton BA3 .... 129 E2
  Marshfield SN14 .... 69 F8
  Pill BS20 .... 47 C5
  Pucklechurch BS16 ..... 53 C4
  Rowberrow BS25 ...... 109 A1
  Winscombe BS25 ...... 18 A5
Back Of Kingsdown Par
  BS6 .... 141 A4
Back St
  Hawkesbury Upton GL9 ... 20 A3
  Weston-super-Mare BS23 . 104 E7
Back Stoke La BS9 ...... 48 F6
Backfields BS2 .... 141 B4
Backfields Ct BS2 ...... 141 B4
Backfields La BS2 ...... 141 B4
Backwell Bow BS48 ..... 60 C1
Backwell Comm BS48 ... 76 B8
Backwell Comp Sch BS48 . 76 B6
Backwell Hill Rd BS48 .. 76 E5
Backwell Jun Sch BS48 .. 76 C5
Backwell Wlk BS13 ..... 78 F8
Baden Hill Rd GL12 .... 16 C6
Baden Ho BA1 .... 142 B4
Baden Rd Bristol BS15 .. 66 A7
  Bristol BS5 .... 64 C7
Badenham Gr BS11 ..... 47 F8
Bader Cl BS37 .... 27 D3
Badger Cl BS30 .... 65 F3
Badger Rise BS20 ...... 44 F3
Badger's La BS32 .... 23 C3
Badgers Cl BS32 .... 24 D3
Badgers Rise BS10 ..... 35 E4
Badgers Way BS24 ..... 105 F8
Badgers Wlk BS4 ...... 64 D2
Badgeworth BS37 ...... 39 D6
Badman Cl BS39 .... 131 D5
Badminton BS16 .... 37 C1
Badminton Ct BS37 .... 27 C2
Badminton Ctr The BS37 . 27 C2
Badminton Gdns BA1 .. 101 C8
Badminton Rd Bristol BS2 . 49 F1
  Bristol, Downend BS16 ... 51 E7
  Chipping Sodbury BS37 .. 41 B7
  Frampton
    Cotterell BS36,BS37 ... 38 C6
Badminton Road Trad Est
  BS37 .... 27 B1
Badminton Wlk BS16 ... 51 E7
Badock's Wood Prim Sch
  BS10 .... 35 B1
Baggridge Hill BA2 .... 134 F7
Baglyn Ave BS15 ...... 51 F3
Bagnell Cl BS14 ...... 80 E5
Bagnell Rd BS14 ...... 80 E5
Bagstone Rd
  Rangeworthy BS37, GL12 .. 16 F2
  Rangeworthy GL12 ...... 16 F4
Bagworth Dr BS30 ..... 65 F3
Bailbrook Coll BA1 ..... 85 D2
Bailbrook Gr BA1 ...... 85 C3
Bailbrook La BA1 ...... 85 D3
Baildon Cres BS23 ..... 105 A4
Baildon Ct ■ BS23 .... 104 F4
Baildon Rd BS23 ...... 105 A4
Bailey Cl BS22 .... 105 E8
Bailey's Court Prim Sch
  BS32 .... 36 F6
Baileys Court Rd BS32 .. 36 F6
Baileys Ct BS32 .... 36 F6
Baileys Mead Rd BS16 .. 50 C5
Bailiffs Cl BS26 .... 125 C1
Bailiffs' Wall BS26 .... 125 B1
Bainsbury View BA3 ... 137 F1
Baker Cl ■ BS21 .... 57 B1
Baker St ■ BS23 ...... 104 E8
Baker's Bldgs BS40 .... 92 D2
Bakers Ground BS34 ... 37 A5
Bakers La
  Chilcompton BA3 ...... 137 D3
  Englishbat BS40 .... 109 C8
Bakers Par BA3 .... 116 B2
Bakersfield BS30 ...... 66 B3
Balaclava Rd BS16 .... 50 F3
Baldwin St BS1 .... 141 A2
Balfour Rd BS3 .... 63 B3
Ballance St BA1 ...... 142 B4
Ballast La BS11 .... 33 E2
Balls Barn La BS24 .... 90 A2
Balmain St BS4 .... 64 A3
Balmoral Cl BS34 ..... 36 D4
Balmoral Ct BS16 ..... 52 A5

Balmoral Mans ■ BS7 ... 49 F2
Balmoral Rd Bristol BS30 . 65 F2
  Bristol BS7 .... 49 F2
  Keynsham BS31 .... 81 E4
Balmoral Way BS22 .... 88 D2
Baltic Pl BS20 .... 47 D4
Bamfield BS14 .... 80 A6
Bampton ■ BS22 ...... 88 F2
Bampton Cl Bristol BS13 . 79 B7
  Bristol BS16 .... 52 C6
Bampton Croft BS16 ... 52 C6
Bampton Dr BS16 ...... 37 D1
Banfield Cl BS11 ...... 48 A8
Bangor Gr BS4 .... 64 F5
Bangrove Wlk BS11 .... 47 E8
Banister Gr BS4 .... 79 D7
Bank Leaze Prim Sch
  BS11 .... 34 B2
Bank Pl BS20 .... 47 D4
Bank Rd Avonmouth BS11 . 33 D7
  Bristol BS15 .... 65 D8
  Pilning BS35 .... 22 E6
Banks Cl BS21 .... 73 D8
Bankside BS16 .... 51 F4
Bankside Rd BS4 ...... 64 D2
Banner Rd BS6 .... 49 E1
Bannerdown Cl BA1 .... 86 B4
Bannerdown Dr BA1 .... 86 A4
Bannerdown Rd BA1 ... 86 C5
Bannerleigh La BS8 .... 62 E6
Bannerleigh Rd BS8 .... 62 E6
Bannerman Rd BS5 .... 64 B8
Bannerman Road Prim Sch
  BS5 .... 50 B1
Bannetts Tree Cres BS35 . 15 A5
Bantock Cl BS4 .... 79 D6
Bantry Rd BS4 .... 79 E8
Banwell Cl Bristol BS13 . 79 A8
  Keynsham BS31 .... 82 A2
Banwell Cty Prim Sch
  BS29 .... 107 B3
Banwell Rd
  Banwell BS26,BS29 .... 123 E8
  Bath BA2 .... 118 D8
  Bristol BS3 .... 63 A3
  Locking BS24 .... 106 B3
  Winscombe BS25,BS29 .. 107 E1
Banyard Rd BS20 ...... 46 E5
Baptist St BS5 .... 50 A1
Barberry Farm Rd BS49 . 74 B1
Barbour Gdns BS13 .... 79 D3
Barbour Rd BS13 ...... 79 D3
Barcroft Cl BS15 ...... 65 C8
Barker Cl ■ BS5 ...... 64 F7
Barker Wlk BS5 .... 50 A1
Barkers Mead BS37 .... 27 F4
Barkleys Hill BS16 .... 50 C5
Barlands Ho BS10 ..... 34 F3
Barley Cl Bristol BS16 .. 52 A6
  Frampton Cotterell BS36 . 38 C8
Barley Close Prim Sch
  BS16 .... 52 A6
Barley Croft BS9 ...... 48 F5
Barley Cross BS22 ..... 89 A5
Barn Cl BS27 .... 80 E4
Barn End
  East Harptree BS40 .... 128 E3
  Marshfield SN14 ...... 70 A8
Barn Hill BA2 .... 133 F5
Barn La BS39 .... 115 A7
Barn Owl Way BS34 ... 36 F5
Barn Pool BS25 ...... 125 F8
Barnabas Cl BS26 ..... 125 D2
Barnabas St ■ BS2 .... 49 E1
Barnaby Cl BA3 ...... 132 B2
Barnack Trad Est BS3 .. 63 D1
Barnard Wlk BS31 ..... 81 D4
Barnard's Cl BS49 .... 91 C7
Barnes St ■ BS5 ...... 64 D8
Barnfield Way BA1 .... 86 B3
Barnhill Cl BS37 ..... 28 A4
Barnhill Rd BS37 ..... 28 B1
Barns Cl
  Barrow Gurney BS48 ... 77 E4
  Nailsea BS48 .... 59 E2
Barnstaple Ct BS4 .... 79 E8
Barnstaple Rd BS4 .... 79 F8
Barnstaple Wlk BS4 ... 79 F8
Barnwood Ct BS48 .... 59 B1
Barnwood Rd BS37 ... 39 C7
Barossa Pl BS1 ...... 141 A1
Barrack's La BS11 .... 47 D8
Barratt St BS5 .... 50 C1
Barrington Cl BS15 ... 51 F2
Barrington Ct
  Bristol BS15 .... 51 E1
  Bristol BS4 .... 64 A3
Barrow Court La BS19 .. 77 B5
Barrow Ct BS21 ...... 58 F4
Barrow Hill BS30 ..... 67 B5
Barrow Hill Cres BS11 . 47 C7
Barrow Hill Rd BS11 ... 47 D6
Barrow Hospl
  Barrow Gurney BS48 ... 77 F6
Barrow La BS40 ...... 111 E6
Barrow Rd Bath BA2 ... 101 C1
  Bristol BS2 .... 64 A7
  Hutton BS24 .... 105 E2
Barrow St BS48 ...... 77 D5
Barrowmead Dr BS11 .. 47 F7
Barrows The BS22 ..... 105 C2
Barrs Court Ave BS30 .. 66 A5
Barrs Court Prim Sch
  BS30 .... 66 A5
Barrs Ct BS30 .... 66 A5
Barrs La GL11 .... 5 E4
Barry Cl Bristol BS30 .. 66 C6
  Weston-super-Mare BS24 . 105 A1

Barry Rd BS30 .... 66 C2
Barstable Ho BS2 ..... 141 C3
Bartholomew Row BA3 . 116 B2
Bartlett St BA1 ...... 142 B3
Bartlett's Rd BS3 ..... 63 C2
Bartletts Way BS3 .... 63 C2
Barton Bldgs BA1 .... 142 B3
Barton Cl Alveston BS35 . 15 A5
  ■ Bristol BS4 .... 64 F6
  Winterbourne BS36 .... 37 E5
Barton Ct BS5 .... 64 C6
Barton Dro BS25 ..... 124 D5
Barton Gn BS5 .... 64 B7
Barton Hill Inf Sch BS5 . 64 B6
Barton Hill Prim Sch BS5 . 64 B6
Barton Hill Rd BS5 .... 64 B7
Barton Hill Trad Est ■
  BS5 .... 64 B6
Barton Ho BS5 .... 64 C6
Barton Manor BS2 .... 64 A6
Barton Rd Bristol BS2 . 141 C2
  Winscombe BS26 ..... 124 C6
Barton St Bath BA1 ... 142 B2
  Bristol BS1 .... 141 A4
Barton The Bleadon BS24 . 122 C6
  Bristol BS15 .... 65 C4
  Corston BA2 .... 100 A7
Barton Vale ■ BS2 .... 64 A6
Bartonia Gr BS4 ...... 64 D1
Barwick Ho BS11 ..... 47 F7
Barwood Cl BS15 ..... 65 F8
Batch Bsns Pk BS24 .. 121 F2
Batch La Clutton BS39 . 114 F3
  Lympsham BS24 ...... 121 F3
Batch The Backwell BS48 . 76 D1
  Beach The BS21 ...... 85 F3
  Blagdon BS40 .... 111 B8
  Burrington BS40 ...... 110 B3
  Chew Magna BS40 ..... 96 B3
  Churchgrove BS25 .... 108 F4
  Farmborough BA3 .... 116 A6
  Hinton Charterhouse BA3 . 119 E1
  Salford BS31 .... 82 F3
  Yatton BS49 .... 91 B7
Batchfield La BS16,BS37 . 53 D8
Bates Cl BS5 .... 64 A8
Bath Abbey BA1 ...... 142 C2
Bath Bldgs BS6 .... 49 E1
Bath Foyer The BA2 .. 101 A6
Bath Hill Keynsham BS31 . 81 F5
  Wellow BA2 .... 118 D2
Bath Ind Heritage
  Ctr BA1 .... 142 B4
Bath New Rd BA3 ..... 132 F4
Bath Old Rd BA3 ..... 132 F4
Bath Postal Mus BA1 . 142 C3
Bath Race Course BA1 . 83 F6
Bath Rd Bath BA1,BA2,BS30 . 82 F7
  Blagdon BS40 .... 111 B1
  Bristol BS2 .... 141 C1
  Bristol BS3 .... 64 D4
  Bristol BS31 .... 81 B8
  Bristol BS4,BS31 .... 64 F1
  Bristol,Longwell Green BS30 . 65 F3
  Bristol,North Common BS30 . 66 D6
  Bristol,Totterdown BS4,BS2 . 64 D3
  Bristol,Willsbridge BS30 . 66 C1
  Chipping Sodbury BS37,GL9 . 41 C4
  Churchill BS25 ...... 109 C4
  Colerne SN14 .... 70 E2
  Farmborough BA3 .... 115 E5
  Kingsdown SN13 ..... 86 F5
  Norton St Philip BA3 .. 135 E5
  Paulton BS39 .... 131 F6
  Peasedown St John BA2 . 133 C7
  Saltford BS31 .... 82 D3
  Thornbury BS35 .... 15 B8
  Wick BS30 .... 67 E4
Bath Riverside Bsns Pk
  BA2 .... 142 B1
Bath Small Sch BA1 ... 85 C2
Bath Spa Sta BA1 .... 142 C1
Bath Spa Univ Coll BA1 . 84 E1
Bath Spa University Coll
  BA2 .... 100 B5
Bath St Bath BA1 ..... 142 C2
  Bristol BS1 .... 141 B2
  Bristol BS16 .... 51 E4
  Bristol BS3 .... 63 A4
Bath View BA3 .... 137 F1
Bathampton La BA2 ... 85 E7
Bathampton Prim Sch
  BA2 .... 85 F2
Batheaston CE Prim Sch
  BA1 .... 85 F4
Bathford Hill Bathford BA1 . 86 B2
  Compton Dando BS39 . 98 E5
Bathford Prim Sch BA1 . 86 C2
Bathings The ■ BS35 .. 15 C8
Bathurst Par BS1 ..... 141 A1
Bathurst Rd BS22 .... 105 C8
Bathwell Rd BS4 ...... 64 A3
Bathwick Hill BA2 .... 102 C6
Bathwick Rise BA2 .... 102 B8
Bathwick St BA1,BA2 .. 142 C4
Batley Ct BS30 ...... 66 D4
Batstone Cl BA1 ..... 85 B2
Batten Ct BS37 ...... 28 C1
Batten's La BS5 ...... 65 A6
Battenburg Rd BS5 ... 65 A8
Battens Rd BS5 ...... 64 F8
Battersby Way BS10 .. 34 E2
Battersea Rd BS5 .... 64 C8
Battery La BS20 ..... 45 D6
Battle La BS40 ...... 96 A3
Battson Rd BS14 .... 80 E4

Baugh Gdns BS16
Baugh Rd BS16
Baxter Cl BS15
Bay Gdns BS5
Bay Rd BS21
Bay Tree Cl BS34
Bay Tree View BS22
Bayer Bldg The BA2
Bayham Rd BS4
Bayleys Dr BS15
Baynham Ct ■ BS15
Baynton Ho ■ BS5
Baynton Mdw BS16
Baynton Rd BS3
Bayswater Ave BS6
Bayswater Rd BS7
Baytree Ct BS22
Baytree Rd BS22
Baytree Sch BS22
Baytree View BS22
Beach Ct BS23
Beach Ford Rd BS23
Beach Hill Bristol BS30
  Portishead BS20
Beach La BS30
Beach Mews BS21
Beach Rd
  Severn Beach BS35
  Weston-Super-Mare BS23
  Weston-Super-Mare BS23
Beach Rd E BS20
Beach Rd W BS20
Beach The BS21
Beachgrove Gdns BS16
Beachgrove Rd BS16
Beachley Wlk BS11
Beacon Rd BA1
Beacon Rise Prim Sch
  BS15
Beaconlea BS15
Beaconsfield Rd
  Bristol BS30
  Bristol BS5
  Bristol BS8
  Clevedon BS21
  Weston-super-Mare BS23
Beaconsfield St ■ BS5
Beale Cl BS14
Beam St BS5
Bean Acre The BS11
Beanhill Cres BS35
Bearbridge Rd BS13
Beau St BA1
Beauchamp Rd BS7
Beauchamps Dr BS22
Beaufort BS16
Beaufort Ave
  Midsomer Norton BA3
  Yate BS37
Beaufort Bldgs ■ BS8
Beaufort Cres BS34
Beaufort Ct Bristol BS21
  Clevedon BS21
Beaufort E ■ BS5
Beaufort Gdns ■ BS48
Beaufort Ho ■ BS5
Beaufort Hts BS5
Beaufort Mews
  ■ Bath BA1
  Chipping Sodbury BS37
  Bristol BS5
Beaufort Rd Bristol BS15
  Bristol BS5
  Bristol,Kingswood BS15
  Bristol,Staple Hill BS16
  Bristol,Vinney Green BS16
  Frampton Cotterell BS36
  Weston-super-Mare BS23
  Yate BS37
Beaufort St Bristol BS3
  ■ Bristol BS5
Beaufort Villas ■ BA1
Beaufort Way BS10
Beauley Rd BS3
Beaumont Cl Bristol BS30
  Weston-super-Mare BS22
Beaumont St BS5
Beaumont Terr ■ BS5
Beaver Cl BS36
Beazer Cl ■ BS16
Beck Cl BS16
Beck Ho BS34
Becket Ct BS16
Becket Dr BS22
Becket Prim Sch BS22
Becket Rd BS22
Becket's La BS48
Beckford Farm BS37
Beckford Ct ■ BA2
Beckford Gdns Bath BA2
  Bristol BS14
Beckford Rd BA2
Beckhampton Rd BA2
Beckington BS24
Beckington Rd BS3

Bradley Rd continued
Portbury BS20 . . . . .46 E5
Bradley Stoke Way BS32 . . . .36 E7
Bradstone Rd BS36 . . . . . .37 D5
Bradville Gdns BS41 . . . . . .77 F8
Bradwell Gr BS10 . . . . .49 C8
Brae Rd BS25 . . . . .125 B8
Brae Rise BS25 . . . . .125 A8
Braemar Ave BS7 . . . . .35 F1
Braemar Cres BS7 . . . . . . .35 F1
Braemor Ct BS9 . . . . .49 A8
Bragg's La BS2 . . . . .141 C3
Braikenridge Cl BS21 . . . . .57 C1
Braikenridge Rd BS4 . . . . .64 D4
Brainsfield BS9 . . . . .48 F6
Brake Cl Bristol BS15 . . . . .65 F7
Bristol BS32 . . . . .36 E2
Brake The
Coalpit Heath BS36 . . . . . . .38 C5
Yate BS37 . . . . .27 E5
Brakewell Gdns BS14 . . . . .80 A4
Bramble Dr BS9 . . . . .48 D3
Bramble La BS9 . . . . .48 C3
Bramble Rd BS22 . . . . .88 E3
Bramble Way BA2 . . . . . . .102 B1
Brambles The
Hinton Charterhouse BA3 . .119 E1
Keynsham BS31 . . . . .81 D3
Bramblewood BS49 . . . . . .74 B1
Brambling Wlk BS16 . . . . . .50 F6
Bramley Cl Kingswood GL12 .11 F4
Locking BS24 . . . . .106 A5
Olveston BS35 . . . . .14 A3
Peasedown St John BA2 . . .133 D7
Pill BS20 . . . . .47 C4
Sandford BS25 . . . . .108 A4
Yatton BS49 . . . . .91 B7
Bramley Ct ⁸ BS30 . . . . . . .65 F4
Bramley Rd BS4 . . . . .76 A5
Bramleys The BS48 . . . . . . .75 B8
Brampton Ho BS20 . . . . . . .45 E4
Brampton Way BS20 . . . . . .45 E4
Bramshill Dr BS22 . . . . .88 F3
Branch Rd BA3 . . . . .119 F2
Branche Gr BS13 . . . . .79 D3
Branches Cross BS40 . . . . .92 E3
Brandash Rd BS37 . . . . . . .28 C1
Brandon Ho BS8 . . . . .140 B2
Brandon St BS1 . . . . .140 C2
Brandon Steep BS1 . . . . . .140 C2
Brangwyn Gr BS7 . . . . .50 B6
Brangwyn Sq BS22 . . . . . . .88 F2
Branksome Cres BS34 . . . . .36 B3
Branksome Dr Bristol BS34 .36 B3
Winterbourne BS36 . . . . . . .37 E6
Branksome Rd BS6 . . . . . . .49 B3
Bransby Way BS24 . . . . . .106 A8
Branscombe Ct BS3 . . . . . .63 D2
Branscombe Rd BS9 . . . . . .48 C4
Branscombe Wlk BS20 . . . .44 F3
Branwhite Cl BS7 . . . . .50 B7
Brassknocker Hill BA2 . . . .102 F2
Brassmill Ent Ctr BA1 . . . .101 A7
Brassmill La BA1 . . . . .101 A7
Brassmill Lane Trad Est
BA1 . . . . .101 A7
Bratton Rd BS4 . . . . .79 D7
Braunton Rd BS3 . . . . .63 C3
Braydon Ave BS32 . . . . . . .36 D7
Brayne Ct BS30 . . . . .65 F3
Braysdown Cl BA2 . . . . . . .133 B6
Braysdown La BA2 . . . . . .133 C7
Breach Hill La BS40 . . . . .112 C6
Breach La BS48 . . . . .74 F7
Breach Rd BS3 . . . . .63 A3
Breaches Gate BS32 . . . . . .36 F6
Breaches The BS20 . . . . . . .47 B5
Brean Down Ave
BS9 . . . . .49 B5
Weston-Super-Mare BS23 . .104 E4
Brean Rd BS24 . . . . .121 F1
Brecknock Rd BS4 . . . . . . .64 A3
Brecon Cl BS9 . . . . .49 B6
Brecon Rd BS9 . . . . .49 B6
Brecon View BS24 . . . . . . .105 A1
Bredon BS37 . . . . .39 D7
Bredon Cl BS15 . . . . .65 F7
Bredon Nook Rd BS10 . . . . .49 C7
Bree Cl BS22 . . . . .89 A4
Brendon Ave BS23 . . . . . . .104 F8
Brendon Cl BS30 . . . . .66 C4
Brendon Gdns
BS48 . . . . .59 E1
Brendon Rd Bristol BS3 . . . .63 D3
Portishead BS20 . . . . .45 A5
Brenner St BS5 . . . . .50 B2
Brent Cl BS24 . . . . .105 B2
Brent Rd BS7 . . . . .49 F5
Brentry Ave ⁶ BS5 . . . . . . .64 B7
Brentry Hospl BS10 . . . . . . .35 D2
Brentry La BS10 . . . . .35 B3
Brentry Lo BS10 . . . . .35 A4
Brentry Prim Sch BS10 . . . .35 A4
Brentry Rd BS16 . . . . .50 F3
Brereton Way BS30 . . . . . . .66 B4
Brewerton Cl BS10 . . . . . . .35 C3
Brewery Hill BS30 . . . . .82 F7
Brewery La BA3 . . . . .138 D1
Briar Cl Nailsea BS48 . . . . .60 A2
Radstock BA3 . . . . .138 D8
Briar Ct BS20 . . . . .47 C4
Briar Mead BS49 . . . . .74 A1
Briar Rd BS24 . . . . .105 E3
Briar Way BS16 . . . . .51 C3
Briar Wlk BS16 . . . . .51 C3

Briarfield Ave BS15 . . . . . . .65 C5
Briarleaze BS35 . . . . .14 F2
Briars Ct BA2 . . . . .101 A4
Briars The BS48 . . . . .75 F7
Briarside Ho BS10 . . . . .35 D3
Briarside Rd BS10 . . . . .35 D3
Briarwood BS9 . . . . .48 F6
Briarwood Sch BS16 . . . . . .51 B3
Briary Rd BS20 . . . . .45 C5
Bravels Gr BS6 . . . . .49 F2
Brick Cotts BS35 . . . . .6 E1
Brick St BS2 . . . . .141 C3
Bridewell La Bath BA1 . . . .142 B2
Hutton BS24, BS25, BS29 . .106 D1
Bridewell St BS1 . . . . .141 A3
Bridge Bldgs BS39 . . . . . .131 B3
Bridge Cl BS14 . . . . .80 C4
Bridge Farm Cl BS14 . . . . . .80 A3
Bridge Farm Inf Sch BS14 .80 A4
Bridge Farm Jun Sch
BS14 . . . . .80 A4
Bridge Farm Sq BS49 . . . . .91 D4
Bridge Gdns BA3 . . . . .116 A6
Bridge Ho ⁴ Bath BA1 . . . . .85 C1
⁴ Clevedon BS21 . . . . .57 C2
Weston-Super-Mare BS23 . .104 E5
Bridge Place Rd BA3 . . . . .132 E8
Bridge Rd Bath BA2 . . . . . .101 C5
Bleadon BS24 . . . . .122 B5
Bristol BS15 . . . . .52 A3
Bristol BS16 . . . . .50 B3
Bristol BS5 . . . . .50 B3
Leigh Woods BS8 . . . . .62 E6
Weston-Super-Mare BS23 . .104 F5
Yate BS37 . . . . .27 A2
Bridge Sr Bath BA2 . . . . . .142 C2
Bridge St Bristol BS1 . . . . .141 A2
Bristol BS5 . . . . .50 D2
Bridge Valley Rd BS8 . . . . .62 E8
Bridge Way BS36 . . . . .38 B8
Bridge Wlk BS7 . . . . .50 A8
Bridgeleap Rd BS16 . . . . . .51 F8
Bridges Ct ⑤ BS16 . . . . . . .51 B4
Bridges Dr BS16 . . . . .51 C6
Bridgeman Rd BS34 . . . . . .36 B3
Bridgwater Ct BS24 . . . . . .105 A3
Bridgwater Rd
Dundry BS41,BS13,BS48 . . .78 D6
Lympsham BS24 . . . . .122 C5
Weston-Super-Mare BS23,BS24
BS23,BS24 . . . . .104 C2
Winscombe BS25 . . . . .125 A5
Bridle Way BS35 . . . . .14 F4
Briercliffe Rd BS9 . . . . .48 D7
Brierly Furlong BS34 . . . . . .36 D3
Briery Leaze Rd BS14 . . . . .80 A4
Bright St Bristol BS15 . . . . .65 D8
Bristol BS5 . . . . .64 B7
Brighton Cres BS3 . . . . .63 B2
Brighton Mews BS8 . . . . . .140 B4
Brighton Pk ⑧ BS5 . . . . . . .64 B8
Brighton Pl BS15 . . . . .51 D1
Brighton Rd Bristol BS34 . . .35 F8
Bristol BS6 . . . . .49 C1
Weston-Super-Mare BS23 . .104 E6
Brighton St ⁶ BS2 . . . . .49 E1
Brighton Terr ⑤ BS3 . . . . . .63 B2
Brigstocke Rd BS2 . . . . . . .141 B4
Brimbles BS7 . . . . .36 B2
Brimbleworth La BS22 . . . . .89 C3
Brimridge Rd BS25 . . . . . .125 A8
Brimsham Green Sec Sch
BS37 . . . . .27 D4
Brinkmarsh La GL12 . . . . . . .9 D2
Brinkworthy Rd BS16 . . . . . .50 E6
Brinmead Wlk BS13 . . . . . .78 F3
Brins Cl BS34 . . . . .36 F4
Brinsea Batch BS49 . . . . . .108 E8
Brinsea La BS49 . . . . .108 F8
Brinsea Rd BS49 . . . . .91 E2
Brinsham La BS37 . . . . .28 A6
Briscoes Ave BS13 . . . . .79 D4
Brislington Hill BS4 . . . . . . .64 E2
Brislington Ret Pk BS4 . . . . .64 E1
Brislington Sch BS4 . . . . . . .80 F8
Brislington Trad Est BS4 . . .64 F2
Bristol & Anchor Ho ⁷
BS5 . . . . .64 D8
Bristol Bsns Pk BS16 . . . . . .36 E1
Bristol Cathedral Sch
BS1 . . . . .140 C2
Bristol City Coll
Brunel Ctr BS7 . . . . .49 F4
Bristol City Fball Gd BS3 . . .62 F3
Bristol Dental Hospl BS1 . .141 A3
Bristol Eye Hospl BS1 . . . .141 A3
Bristol Gate ⁸ BS8 . . . . . . .62 F5
Bristol General Hospl
BS1 . . . . .141 A1
Bristol Gram Sch BS8 . . . .140 C3
Bristol Harbour Rly BS1 . . .140 C1
Bristol Ind Mus BS1 . . . . . .141 A1
Bristol Old Vic Theatre Sch
BS8 . . . . .49 A1
Bristol Parkway N BS34 . . . .37 A5
Bristol Parkway Sta BS34 . .36 F4
Bristol Rd Bristol BS16 . . . . .37 C2
Chew Stoke BS40 . . . . .112 E8
Churchill BS25 . . . . .109 A5
Congresbury BS49 . . . . .91 D5
Cromhall GL12 . . . . .17 B7
Farrington Gurney BS39 . . .132 B5
Frampton Cotterell BS36 . . .26 B3
Keynsham BS31 . . . . .81 F6
Luckington SN14 . . . . .31 E3

Bristol Rd continued
Newton St Loe BA2 . . . . . .100 D7
Paulton BS39 . . . . .131 E7
Pensford BS39 . . . . .97 D6
Thornbury BS20 . . . . .45 E4
Radstock BA3 . . . . .132 F3
Redhill BS40 . . . . .94 A3
Thornbury BS35 . . . . .15 B8
Weston-Super-Mare BS22 . . .89 C2
Whitchurch BS14 . . . . .80 D3
Winscombe BS25 . . . . .125 C8
Winterbourne BS16 . . . . . . .37 D4
Wraxall BS48 . . . . .60 A3
Bristol Rd Lower BS23 . . . . .87 F1
Bristol Road-Lower BS23 . .87 E1
Bristol Royal Infmy BS2 . . .141 A4
Bristol Vale Ctr For Ind
BS3 . . . . .63 D1
Bristol View BA2 . . . . .118 C8
Bristol Waldorf Sch BS8 . .140 B3
Bristol Zoo Gdns BS8 . . . . .48 F1
Bristow Broadway BS11 . . .33 C1
Bristowe Ho BS16 . . . . .51 B5
Bristowe Rd BS16 . . . . .51 B5
Britannia Cl BS16 . . . . .51 F5
Britannia Cres BS34 . . . . . .36 D5
Britannia Ct ⑧ BS16 . . . . . .51 D5
Britannia Rd Bristol BS15 . . .65 C8
Bristol BS34 . . . . .35 E7
Bristol BS5 . . . . .50 D3
Britannia Way BS21 . . . . . . .57 C1
British Rd BS3 . . . . .63 C3
Brittan Pl BS20 . . . . .46 E3
Brittania Bldgs BS8 . . . . . .140 A1
Britten's Cl BS39 . . . . .65 F4
Britten's Ct BS39 . . . . .131 F6
Britten's Hill BS39 . . . . . . .131 F6
Brittons Pass SN14 . . . . . . .69 F8
Brixham Rd BS3 . . . . .63 C2
Brixton Rd BS5 . . . . .64 B8
Brixton Road Mews ㉒
BS5 . . . . .64 B8
Broad Croft BS32 . . . . .24 C2
Broad La Coalpit Heath BS36 .38 D5
Westerleigh BS37 . . . . .39 A4
Yate BS37 . . . . .27 C4
Broad Mead La BS40 . . . . . .95 A3
Broad Oak Rd BS13 . . . . . . .78 F4
Broad Oaks BS8 . . . . .62 E6
Broad Plain BS2 . . . . .141 C2
Broad Quay Bath BA1 . . . . .142 C1
Bristol BS1 . . . . .141 A2
Broad Rd Blagdon BS40 . . .126 D8
Bristol BS15 . . . . .51 C1
Broad St Bath BA1 . . . . . . .142 C3
Bristol BS1 . . . . .141 A3
Bristol BS16 . . . . .51 F4
Chipping Sodbury BS37 . . . .28 B1
Congresbury BS49 . . . . .91 D4
Wrington BS40 . . . . .92 D2
Broad Stones BA15 . . . . . .103 E7
Broad Street Pl BA1 . . . . . .142 C3
Broad Weir BS1 . . . . .141 B3
Broad Wlk BS4 . . . . .64 A2
Broadbury Rd BS4 . . . . .79 E8
Broadcroft BS40 . . . . .95 F3
Broadcroft Ave BS49 . . . . . .74 F1
Broadcroft Cl BS49 . . . . . . .74 F1
Broadfield Ave BS15 . . . . . .51 C1
Broadfield Rd BS4 . . . . .64 A2
Broadlands BS21 . . . . .57 F3
Broadlands Ave BS31 . . . . .81 D6
Broadlands Dr BS11 . . . . . . .34 A1
Broadleas BS13 . . . . .79 C7
Broadleaze BS11 . . . . .47 E7
Broadleaze Way BS25 . . . .107 F2
Broadleys Ave BS9 . . . . . . .49 C7
Broadmead BS1 . . . . .141 B3
Broadmead La BS31 . . . . . .82 A6
Broadmoor La BA1 . . . . . . .84 A3
Broadmoor Vale BA1 . . . . . .84 A3
Broadoak Com Sch BS23 . .104 E3
Broadoak Hill BS41 . . . . . . .78 F2
Broadoak Rd
Langford BS40 . . . . .109 A5
Weston-Super-Mare BS23 . .104 D3
Broadoak Wlk BS16 . . . . . . .51 B4
Broadstone La BS31 . . . . . .72 F3
Broadstone Wlk BS13 . . . . .79 D5
Broadwalk Sh Ctr BS4 . . . . .64 A2
Broadway Bath BA2 . . . . . .102 B6
Chilcompton BA3 . . . . .137 C3
Locking BS24 . . . . .106 D4
Saltford BS31 . . . . .82 D3
Shipham BS25 . . . . .125 E8
Weston-Super-Mare BS24 . .105 A2
Yate BS37 . . . . .27 F2
Broadway Ave BS9 . . . . .49 C6
Broadway Cl BA3 . . . . .137 C3
Broadway Inf Sch BS37 . . . .27 F2
Broadway La BA2 . . . . .132 B6
Broadway Rd Bristol BS13 . .78 F5
Bristol BS7 . . . . .49 F5
Broadway The BS16 . . . . . . .50 F7
Brock End BS20 . . . . .44 F3
Brock St BA1 . . . . .142 B3
Brockeridge Inf Sch BS36 . .38 C7
Brockhurst Gdns BS15 . . . . .65 A8
Brockhurst Rd BS15 . . . . . .65 A8
Brockley Cl Bristol BS34 . . . .36 C7
Nailsea BS48 . . . . .59 D1
Weston-Super-Mare BS24 . .104 F1
Brockley Combe Rd BS48 . .76 B1
Brockley Cres BS24 . . . . . .104 F1
Brockley La BS48 . . . . .75 D4
Brockley Mini Farm BS48 . .92 F7

Brockley Rd BS31 . . . . .82 D3
Brockley Way BS49 . . . . . . .75 B3
Brockley Wlk BS13 . . . . .79 A8
Brockridge La BS36 . . . . . . .38 C7
Brocks Rd BS13 . . . . .79 C3
Brocks Rd BS13 . . . . .79 C3
Brockway BS48 . . . . .59 F2
Brockworth BS37 . . . . .39 C6
Brockworth Cres BS16 . . . . .50 F6
Bromfield Wlk BS16 . . . . . . .52 B7
Bromley Dr BS16 . . . . .51 D8
Bromley Heath Ave BS16 . . .51 D8
Bromley Heath
Jun & Inf Schs BS16 . . . . . .51 E8
Bromley Heath Rd BS16 . . . .51 D8
Bromley Rd Bristol BS7 . . . . .49 F5
Stanton Drew BS39 . . . . . . .96 F1
Bromley Sq BS49 . . . . .91 E3
Brompton Cl BS15 . . . . .66 A8
Brompton Rd BS24 . . . . . . .105 A2
Broncksea Rd BS7 . . . . .35 F1
Brook Cl BS41 . . . . .62 B1
Brook Cotts BA2 . . . . .100 B7
Brook Gate BS3 . . . . .62 E1
Brook Hill BS6 . . . . .49 F1
Brook Ho Bristol BS34 . . . . .36 C8
⑧ Thornbury BS35 . . . . .15 C8
Brook La Bristol BS16 . . . . . .50 E6
Bristol BS6 . . . . .49 F1
Brook Lintons BS4 . . . . .64 D3
Brook Rd Bath BA2 . . . . . . .101 D6
Bristol BS15 . . . . .66 B8
Bristol BS3 . . . . .63 D4
Bristol BS5 . . . . .50 C1
Bristol BS6 . . . . .49 F1
Bristol,Hillfields BS16 . . . . . .51 B4
Bristol,Mangotsfield BS16 . .51 F3
Brook St Bristol BS5 . . . . . . .64 C7
Chipping Sodbury BS37 . . . .40 A8
Brook Way BS32 . . . . .36 D8
Brookcote Dr BS34 . . . . .36 D6
Brookdale Rd BS13 . . . . .79 B6
Brookfield Ave BS7 . . . . .49 D3
Brookfield Cl BS37 . . . . .28 C2
Brookfield La ② BS6 . . . . . . .49 D2
Brookfield Pk BA1 . . . . .84 B2
Brookfield Rd Bristol BS34 . .36 B8
⑧ Bristol BS6 . . . . .49 D2
Brookfield Wlk
Bristol BS30 . . . . .79 B8
Clevedon BS21 . . . . .57 F3
Brookhouse La SN14 . . . . . .55 D1
Brookland Rd Bristol BS6 . . .49 D3
Weston-Super-Mare BS22 . .105 B7
Brooklands BA2 . . . . .117 D3
Brooklea BS30 . . . . .66 B3
Brookleaze BS9 . . . . .48 B5
Brookleaze Bldgs BA1 . . . . .85 B2
Brooklyn BS40 . . . . .92 D2
Brooklyn Rd Bath BA1 . . . . .85 C2
Bristol BS13 . . . . .79 B8
Brookmead BS35 . . . . .15 D8
Brookridge Ct ⑤ BS16 . . . . .51 D4
Brookridge Ho BS10 . . . . . . .34 F3
Brooks La BS41 . . . . .62 L1
Brookside Paulton BS39 . . .131 E6
Pill BS20 . . . . .47 D3
Brookside Cl
Batheaston BA1 . . . . .85 F5
Paulton BS39 . . . . .131 E6
Brookside Dr
Farmborough BA3 . . . . .84 B1
Frampton Cotterell BS36 . . .38 B8
Brookside Ho BA1 . . . . .84 B1
Brookside Rd BS4 . . . . .64 D2
Brookthorpe BS37 . . . . .39 D8
Brookthorpe Ave BS11 . . . . .34 A1
Brookview Wlk BS13 . . . . . . .79 B7
Broom Farm Cl BS48 . . . . . .75 E8
Broom Hill BS16 . . . . .50 E5
Broom Hill La BS39 . . . . . .131 E8
Broomground BA15 . . . . . .120 E7
Broomhill Jun & Inf Schs
BS4 . . . . .64 F3
Broomhill La BS39 . . . . . . .114 C3
Broomhill Rd BS4 . . . . .65 A2
Brooms The BS16 . . . . .38 A1
Brotherswood Ct BS32 . . . . .24 D4
Brougham Hayes BA2 . . . .101 D6
Brougham Pl BA1 . . . . .85 B2
Broughton Ho BS1 . . . . . . .141 B1
Brow Hill BA2 . . . . .85 F3
Brow The Bath BA2 . . . . . .101 B5
Bath BA2,Monkton Combe .102 C1
Browne Ct ④ BS8 . . . . .62 F6
Browning Ct BS7 . . . . .50 B8
Brownlow Rd BS23 . . . . . . .104 E4
Browns Ct BS23 . . . . .104 E6
Broxholme Wlk BS11 . . . . . .47 E7
Bruce Ave BS5 . . . . .50 C1
Bruce Rd BS5 . . . . .50 C1
Brue Cl BS23 . . . . .105 A5
Brummel Way BS39 . . . . . .131 C6
Brunel Cl Bristol BS30 . . . . .66 A4
Weston-Super-Mare BS24 . .104 F1
Brunel Ct BS37 . . . . .27 C2
Brunel Ho BA2 . . . . .101 A6
Brunel Lock Rd BS1 . . . . . . .62 F5
Brunel Rd Bristol BS13 . . . . .79 A8
Nailsea BS48 . . . . .59 B1
Brunel Way Bristol BS1, BS3 .62 F4
Brunswick Pl Bath BA1 . . . .142 B3
⑩ Bristol BS1 . . . . .62 F5
Brunswick Sq BS2 . . . . . . .141 B4
Brunswick St ① Bath BA1 . . .85 B1
Bristol BS2 . . . . .141 B4

Brunswick St continued
Bristol BS5 . . . . .64 B7
Bruton BS24 . . . . .66 A1
Bruton Ave Bath BA2 . . . . .101 E4
Portishead BS20 . . . . .45 A5
Bruton Avenue Garages
Bruton Cl Bristol BS5 . . . . . .64 F8
⑦ Nailsea BS48 . . . . .59 D1
Bruton Pl BS8 . . . . .140 B3
Bryansons Cl BS16 . . . . .50 D6
Bryant Ave BA3 . . . . .138 C1
Bryant Gdns BS21 . . . . .57 C1
Bryant's Hill BS5 . . . . .65 B6
Bryants Cl BS16 . . . . .37 D1
Brynland Ave BS7 . . . . .49 F4
Buckingham Dr BS32 . . . . . .36 E8
Buckingham Dr BS34 . . . . . .36 F4
Buckingham Gdns BS16 . . . .51 E4
Buckingham Ho BS34 . . . . . .36 F4
Buckingham Pl
Bristol BS16 . . . . .51 E4
Bristol BS8 . . . . .140 A3
Buckingham Rd
Bristol BS4 . . . . .64 B3
Weston-Super-Mare BS24 . .105 A2
Buckingham St BS3 . . . . . . .63 C3
Buckingham Vale BS8 . . . . .140 A4
Buckland Gn BS22 . . . . .88 F4
Bucklands Batch BS48 . . . . .75 F8
Bucklands Dr BS48 . . . . .76 A7
Bucklands End BS48 . . . . . . .75 F8
Bucklands Gr BS48 . . . . .75 F8
Bucklands La BS48 . . . . .75 F8
Bucklands View BS48 . . . . . .76 A8
Bud Ho ② BS2 . . . . .141 C3
Bude Ave BS5 . . . . .64 F8
Bude Cl BS48 . . . . .59 E1
Bude Rd BS34 . . . . .36 B8
Building of Bath Mus
BA1 . . . . .142 C4
Bull La Bristol BS5 . . . . .64 F6
Pill BS20 . . . . .47 C5
Bull's Hill BA2 . . . . .116 B2
Bullens Cl BS32 . . . . .24 D1
Buller Rd BS4 . . . . .64 D2
Bullocks La BS21 . . . . .73 A6
Bully La BS37 . . . . .38 B4
Bumper's Batch BA2 . . . . .118 C8
Bungalows The BS26 . . . . .125 C2
Bungay's Hill BA3,BS39 . . .133 B8
Bunting Ct BS22 . . . . .88 F1
Burbank Cl BS30 . . . . .66 A4
Burchells Ave BS15 . . . . . . .51 C1
Burchells Green Cl BS15 . . .51 C1
Burchells Green Rd BS15 . . .51 C1
Burchill Cl BS39 . . . . .131 E5
Burcombe Cl BS36 . . . . .38 D7
Burcott Rd BS11 . . . . .33 F5
Burden Cl BS32 . . . . .36 F6
Burford Rd BS14 . . . . .80 A4
Burfoote Gdns BS14 . . . . . . .80 E4
Burfoote Rd BS14 . . . . .80 E4
Burford Cl Bath BA2 . . . . . .101 B5
Portishead BS20 . . . . .45 A5
Burford Gr BS11 . . . . .47 F5
Burgage Cl BS37 . . . . .28 C1
Burgess Green Cl BS4 . . . . .64 F6
Burghill Rd BS10 . . . . .35 B2
Burghley Ct BS36 . . . . .37 E6
Burghley Rd BS6 . . . . .49 E3
Burgis Rd BS14 . . . . .80 D6
Burleigh Gdns BA1 . . . . .84 A2
Burleigh Way GL12 . . . . .18 B5
Burley Ave BS16 . . . . .52 A5
Burley Crest BS16 . . . . .52 A5
Burley Gr BS16 . . . . .52 A5
Burlington Rd Bristol BS6 . . .49 B2
Portishead BS20 . . . . .45 D5
Burlington St Bath BA1 . . . . .85 B1
⑤ Weston-Super-Mare
BS23 . . . . .104 E8
Burnbush Cl BS14 . . . . .80 E6
Burnbush Prim Sch BS14 . . .80 E6
Burnell Dr BS2 . . . . .141 C4
Burneside Cl BS10 . . . . .35 D2
Burnett Bsns Pk BS31 . . . . .81 E3
Burnett Hill BS31 . . . . .81 D2
Burnett Ind Est BS40 . . . . . .92 E1
Burney Way BS30 . . . . .66 A3
Burnham Cl Bristol BS15 . . .51 F1
Weston-Super-Mare BS24 . .104 F1
Burnham Dr Bristol BS15 . . .51 F1
Weston-Super-Mare BS24 . .104 F1
Burnham Rd Bath BA2 . . . .101 B6
Bristol BS11 . . . . .47 E7
Weston-Super-Mare BS24 . .104 F1
Burns Cl BS23 . . . . .105 B2
Burrington Cl Nailsea BS48 .75 F8
Weston-Super-Mare BS24 . .104 F1
Burrington Combe BS40 . . .110 C2
Burrington La BS40 . . . . . .109 F3
Burrington Wlk BS13 . . . . . .79 A8
Burrough Way BS36 . . . . . . .37 E6
Burrows La BA3 . . . . .138 D3
Burton Cl BS1 . . . . .141 B1
Burton Ct ② Bristol BS16 . . .51 D4
Bristol BS8 . . . . .140 B3
Burton St ⑤ Bath BA1 . . . .142 B3
Burton St ⑤ BS1 . . . . .141 B1
Burwalls Rd BS8 . . . . .62 E6
Bury Hill BS36 . . . . .26 B1
Bury Hill La BS37 . . . . .39 D4
Bury Hill View BS16 . . . . . . .52 A6

BS30 . . . . .67 F7
e BS24 . . . . .106 A3
art Cl BS11 . . . . .34 A1
ere BS34 . . . . .36 D5
. Alveston BS32 . . . . .14 F5
ld BS37 . . . . .34 A3
d BS1 . . . . .35 E1
ld Est BS5 . . . . .64 D8
ld BS37 . . . . .29 A6
lo BS2 . . . . .63 F3
k BS4 . . . . .63 F3
horn Rd BS40 . . . . .112 E8
ss Park The BS13 . . .79 E3
e BS24 . . . . .105 A2
abe La BS40 . . . . . .111 B7
abe Wlk BS14 . . . . . .80 B5
La
agna BS40 . . . . .96 A4
agna Rd BS39 . . . . . .96 B3
Cl BS39 . . . . .115 D1
 BS55 . . . . .64 F8
 BS55 . . . . .64 F7
Wlk 3 BS5 . . . . .64 F6
 BS5 . . . . .8 C3
atch BS40 . . . . .92 D1
La BS4 . . . . .59 A3
iffe BS40 BS41 . . . . . .62 C3
eld Cl BS10 . . . . .49 E7
eld Pk BS21 . . . . .57 C2
eld Rd BS1 . . . . .49 E7
eld Cl BS36 . . . . .38 B6
here Rd BS23 . . . . . .105 A4
rth Ct BS4 . . . . .79 D7
Cl BS14 . . . . .80 A6
atch BS26 . . . . .124 B3
rch BS40 . . . . .92 D1
Wlk BS7 . . . . .50 A8
BA2 . . . . .52 B8
BS21 . . . . .73 C8
t BS20 . . . . .104 A4
t BS23 . . . . .104 F8
l Bristol BS16 . . . . . . .51 E4
BS8 . . . . .140 B3
d Bath BA2 . . . . .101 F4
BS24 . . . . .106 A4
-Super-Mare BS23 . .105 A4
le 5 Bristol BS2 . . . . .55 A4
0
ne Ct BS1 . . . . .141 A1

Camberley Wlk BS22 . . . . .105 E8
Camborne Rd BS7 . . . . .50 A7
Cambrian Dr BS37 . . . . .27 E3
Cambridge Cres BS39 . . . . . .49 A7
Cambridge Gr BS21 . . . . .57 D5
Cambridge Pk BS6 . . . . .49 B3
Cambridge Pl BS21 . . . . . . .104 D8
Cambridge Rd Bristol BS7 . . .49 E4
  Clevedon BS21 . . . . .57 D5
Cambridge St Bristol BS3 . . . .63 F4
8 Bristol BS5 . . . . .64 B8
Cambridge Terr BA2 . . . . . . 102 B5
Cambrook Ho BS39 . . . . . . .130 F8
Camden Cres BA1 . . . . .142 B4
Camden Cl BA1 . . . . .142 B4
Camden Rd Bath BA1 . . . . . .85 A1
  Bristol BS3 . . . . .140 B1
Camden Row BA1 . . . . .142 B4
Camden Terr Bristol BS8 . . .140 A2
Cameley CE Prim Sch
  Weston-Super-Mare BS23 . .114 E6
Cameley CE Prim Sch
  BS39 . . . . .114 C1
Cameley La BS39 . . . . .130 E8
Cameley Gn BA2 . . . . .100 F6
Cameley Rd BS39 . . . . .130 C8
Camelford Rd BS5 . . . . .50 D1
Cameron Wlk BS7 . . . . .50 C6
Cameroons Cl BS31 . . . . .81 F4
Camerton CE Prim Sch
  BA2 . . . . .132 E8
Camerton Cl BS31 . . . . .82 E3
Camerton Hill BA2 . . . . . . .132 E8
Camerton Rd Bristol BS5 . . . .50 D1
  Timsbury BA3 . . . . .116 C1
Camp La SN14 . . . . .55 C4
Camp Rd Bristol BS8 . . . . . . .62 F7
  Thornbury BS35 . . . . .7 B6
  Weston-Super-Mare BS23 . .87 D1
Camp Rd N BS21 . . . . .87 B1
Camp View Nailsea BS48 . . . .59 D2
  Winterbourne BS36 . . . . . . .37 E4
Campbell Ct BS11 . . . . .33 F1
Campbell Farm BS11 . . . . . . .33 F1
Campbell Farm Dr BS11 . . . . .33 F1
Campbell St BS2 . . . . .49 E1
Campion Cl Thornbury BS35 . . .8 D2
  Weston-Super-Mare BS22 . .105 D7
Campion Dr BS32 . . . . .24 D2
Campion Wlk BS4 . . . . .79 D6
Camplins BS21 . . . . .57 C1
Camvale BA2 . . . . .133 B8
Camview BS39 . . . . .131 D6
Camwal Ind Est BS2 . . . . . . .64 A5
Camwal Rd BS2 . . . . .64 A5
Canada Coombe BS24 . . . . .106 A1
Canada Way BS1 . . . . .140 B1
Canal Terr BA2 . . . . .85 F1
Canberra Cres BS24 . . . . . .106 B6
Canberra Gr BS34 . . . . .36 B4
Canberra Rd BS23 . . . . .104 F3
Candy Ct BS4 . . . . .64 D5
Canford La BS9 . . . . .48 E8
Canford Rd BS9 . . . . .48 F8
Cann La BS30 . . . . .66 E6
Cannans Cl BS36 . . . . .37 E7
Cannon St Bristol BS1 . . . . .141 A4
  Bristol BS3 . . . . .63 C4
Cannons Gate BS21 . . . . .73 C8
Canon St BS5 . . . . .64 C8
Canon's Rd BS1 . . . . .140 C1
Canon's Wlk BS15 . . . . .51 F2
Canons Cl BA2 . . . . .101 B2
Canons Rd BS1 . . . . .140 C2
Canons Way BS1 . . . . .140 C1
Canons Wlk BS27 . . . . .88 D2
Canowie Rd BS6 . . . . .49 B3
Cantell Gr BS14 . . . . .80 E5
Canterbury Cl
  Weston-Super-Mare BS22 . .89 B3
  Yate BS37 . . . . .27 E3
Canterbury Ct BS16 . . . . .50 E6
Canterbury Rd BA2 . . . . . . .101 D5
Canterbury St 11 BS5 . . . . . .64 B6
Canters Leaze GL12 . . . . .18 B4
Cantock's Cl BS8 . . . . .140 C3
Canvey Cl BS10 . . . . .49 E7
Canynge Ho 2 BS1 . . . . . . .141 B1
Canynge Rd BS8 . . . . .62 F8
Canynge Sq BS8 . . . . .62 F8
Canynge St BS1 . . . . .141 B2
Capel Cl BS15 . . . . .66 B8
Capel Rd BS11 . . . . .34 B1
Capell Cl BS22 . . . . .105 B8
Capenor Cl BS20 . . . . .45 C4
Capgrave Cl BS4 . . . . .65 A3
Capgrave Cres BS4 . . . . .65 A3
Caple La BS40 . . . . .112 B5
Caraway Gdns BS5 . . . . .50 C2
Cardigan Cres BS22 . . . . . . .105 C8
Cardigan Rd BS9 . . . . .49 B6
Cardill Cl BS13 . . . . .79 A8
Cardinal Cl BA2 . . . . .118 D8
Carditch Dro BS49 . . . . . . .108 B8
Carey Developments 1
  BS21 . . . . .57 F4
Carey's Cl BS21 . . . . .57 F4
Carfax Ct BS6 . . . . .49 A3
Carice Gdns BS21 . . . . .73 D8
Carisbrooke Rd BS4 . . . . .79 D7
Carlingford Terr BA3 . . . . . .133 A2
Carlingford Terrace Rd
  BA3 . . . . .133 A2
Carlow Rd BS4 . . . . .79 E8
Carlton Cl BS39 . . . . .114 F3
Carlton Ct 2 BS9 . . . . .49 A7
Carlton Ho 2 BS9 . . . . .49 A7
Carlton Mans BS23 . . . . . . .104 C8
Carlton Pk BS5 . . . . .64 C8

Carlton St BS23 . . . . .104 D7
Carlyle Rd BS5 . . . . .50 C1
Carmarthen Cl BS37 . . . . . . .27 F4
Carmarthen Gr BS30 . . . . . . .66 B1
Carmarthen Rd BS9 . . . . .49 A5
Carnarvon Rd BS6 . . . . .49 D2
Caroline Bldgs BA2 . . . . . . .102 B5
Caroline Cl
  Chipping Sodbury BS37 . . . .28 B2
  Keynsham BS31 . . . . .81 C4
Caroline Ho BS2 . . . . .141 A4
Caroline Pl BA1 . . . . .142 B4
Carpenter Cl BS23 . . . . .105 A7
Carpenters La BS31 . . . . .81 E5
Carr Ho Bath BA2 . . . . .101 A6
8 Bristol BS2 . . . . .49 F1
Carre Gdns BS22 . . . . .88 F4
Carrick Ho 7 BS8 . . . . .62 F6
Carrington Rd BS3 . . . . .63 A3
Carroll Ct BS16 . . . . .36 E1
Carsons Rd BS16 . . . . .52 B2
Carter Rd BS39 . . . . .131 D5
Carter Wlk BS32 . . . . .36 D8
Carters Way BA3 . . . . .137 D3
Cartledge Rd 6 BS5 . . . . .50 B1
Cary Ct 8 BS2 . . . . .49 F1
Cashmore Ho 6 BS5 . . . . .64 C7
Casion Ct BS1 . . . . .141 B1
Cassell Rd BS16 . . . . .51 C5
Cassey Bottom La BS5 . . . . . .65 A7
Casson Dr BS16 . . . . .50 E8
Castle Batch Prim Sch
  BS22 . . . . .89 A5
Castle Cl Bristol BS10 . . . . . . .34 E2
  Flax Bourton BS48 . . . . .76 F7
Castle Coombe BS35 . . . . .8 C1
Castle Ct Bristol BS4 . . . . . . .64 C4
  Thornbury BS35 . . . . .8 B1
Castle Farm La BS41 . . . . . . .78 B2
Castle Farm Rd BS15 . . . . . . .65 C2
Castle Gdns BA2 . . . . .101 E3
Castle Hill BS29 . . . . .107 C2
Castle La SN14 . . . . .55 C2
Castle Prim Sch BS31 . . . . . . .81 D4
Castle Rd Bristol BS15 . . . . . .51 D2
  Bristol BS30 . . . . .66 C6
  Clevedon BS21 . . . . .57 C6
  Pucklechurch BS16 . . . . . . .53 C6
  Weston-Super-Mare BS22 . .88 E3
Castle Sch The BS35 . . . . .8 B2
Castle Sixth Form Ctr BS35 . . .8 B1
Castle St Bristol BS1 . . . . . . .141 B3
  Thornbury BS35 . . . . .8 B1
Castle View BS24 . . . . .105 F8
Castle View Rd BS21 . . . . . . .57 D5
Castlegate Ho BS4 . . . . .64 E1
Castlewood Cl BS21 . . . . .57 D4
Caswell Hill BS20 . . . . .46 B1
Caswell La BS20 . . . . .46 B2
Catbrain Hill BS10 . . . . .35 B6
Catbrain La BS10 . . . . .35 B6
Catchpot La BS37 . . . . .41 A6
Catemead BS21 . . . . .73 C8
Cater Rd BS13 . . . . .79 B6
Cathay La BA1 . . . . .142 B3
Cathcart Ho BA1 . . . . .142 C4
Cathedral Church of the
  Holy & Undivided Trinity
  BS1 . . . . .140 C2
Cathedral Gram Sch BS1 . . .140 C2
Cathedral Mead SE BS3 . . . . .63 D4
Catherine Mead St BS3 . . . . .63 D4
Catherine St BS11 . . . . .47 C8
Catherine Way BA1 . . . . .86 A5
Catley Gr BS41 . . . . .62 B2
Cato St BS5 . . . . .50 B2
Catstock Dr BS5 . . . . .65 A6
Cattle Market Rd BS1 . . . . . .141 C1
Cattybrook Rd BS16 . . . . .52 D5
Cattybrook St
  6 Bristol BS5 . . . . .64 B7
  2 Bristol BS5 . . . . .64 B8
Caulfield Rd BS22 . . . . .89 B4
Causeway BS48 . . . . .59 B3
Causeway The
  Coalpit Heath BS36 . . . . . . .38 D7
  Congresbury BS49 . . . . .91 D4
  Nailsea BS20 . . . . .59 F8
  Yatton BS49 . . . . .91 C7
Causeway View BS48 . . . . . . .59 C2
Causley Dr BS30 . . . . .66 A5
Cautletts Cl BA3 . . . . .137 E4
Cavan Wlk BS4 . . . . .63 D1
Cave Ct BS2 . . . . .141 B4
Cave Dr BS16 . . . . .51 D6
Cave Gr BS16 . . . . .52 B7
Cave St BS2 . . . . .141 B4
Cavell Ct BS21 . . . . .57 C1
Cavendish Cl BS31 . . . . .82 D2
Cavendish Cres BA1 . . . . . . .142 A4
Cavendish Gdns BS9 . . . . . . .48 C4
Cavendish Lodge BA1 . . . . . .142 A4
Cavendish Pl BA1 . . . . .142 A4
Cavendish Rd Bath BA1 . . . .142 A4
  Bristol BS34 . . . . .35 F8
  Bristol BS9 . . . . .49 A5
Caveners Ct BS22 . . . . .88 B1
Caversham Dr BS48 . . . . .60 A2
Caves Cotts BS16 . . . . .52 A6
Cecil Ave BS5 . . . . .51 A1
Cecil Rd Bristol BS15 . . . . . . .65 D8
  Bristol BS8 . . . . .62 F7
  Weston-Super-Mare BS23 . .87 E1
Cedar Ave BS22 . . . . .88 C1
Cedar Cl Bristol BS30 . . . . . . .66 B4
  Bristol BS34 . . . . .35 F7
  Long Ashton BS41 . . . . .61 F1
Cedar Ct Bristol BS16 . . . . . . .51 E6

Cedar Ct continued
  Bristol BS9 . . . . .48 F8
  Bristol,Combe Dingle BS9 . .48 D7
  Bristol,Sneyd Park BS9 . . . .48 C4
Cedar Dr BS31 . . . . .81 D4
Cedar Gr Bath BA2 . . . . .101 D3
  Bristol BS9 . . . . .48 D5
Cedar Hall BS16 . . . . .51 C8
Cedar Pk BS9 . . . . .48 D5
Cedar Row BS11 . . . . .47 F6
Cedar Terr BA3 . . . . .132 D1
Cedar Way Bath BA2 . . . . . .142 A1
  Nailsea BS48 . . . . .60 A2
  Portishead BS20 . . . . .45 C4
  Pucklechurch BS16 . . . . . . .53 C5
  Weston-Super-Mare BS23 . .37 D5
Cedarhurst Rd BS20 . . . . .44 E4
Cedarn Ct BS22 . . . . .88 A4
Cedars The BS40 . . . . .112 D8
Cedern Ave BS24 . . . . .106 C3
Cedric Rd BA1 . . . . .101 C8
Celandine Cl BS35 . . . . .8 D2
Celestine Rd BS37 . . . . .27 C3
Celia Terr BS4 . . . . .64 F6
Celtic Way BS24 . . . . .122 B7
Cemetery Rd BS4 . . . . .64 A3
Cennick Ave BS15 . . . . .51 E1
Centaurus Rd BS34 . . . . .35 D7
Central Ave Bristol BS15 . . . . .65 C5
  Severn Beach BS10 . . . . . . .22 A3
Central Pk BS14 . . . . .80 B7
Central Trad Est BS4 . . . . . . .64 E4
Central Way Bristol BS10 . . . .49 E8
  Clevedon BS21 . . . . .57 E1
Centre The Keynsham BS31 . .81 F5
  Weston-Super-Mare BS23 . 104 E7
Ceres Cl BS30 . . . . .65 F2
Cerimon Gate BS34 . . . . .36 E5
Cerney Gdns BS48 . . . . .60 A2
Cerney La BS11 . . . . .47 E5
Cesson Cl BS37 . . . . .40 C8
Chadleigh Gr BS4 . . . . .79 D7
Chaffinch Dr BA3 . . . . .138 B8
Chaffins The BS21 . . . . .57 E2
Chaingate La BS37 . . . . .27 A6
Chakeshill Cl BS10 . . . . .35 C3
Chakeshill Dr BS10 . . . . .35 C4
Chalcombe Cl BS34 . . . . .36 C8
Chalcroft Ho 1 BS34 . . . . . . .63 A4
Chalcroft Wlk BS13 . . . . .78 E4
Chalet The BS10 . . . . .34 E3
Chalfield Cl BS31 . . . . .82 A2
Chalfont Rd BS22 . . . . .105 C8
Chalford Cl BS37 . . . . .39 D8
Chalk Farm Cl BS39 . . . . .97 A7
Chalks Rd BS5 . . . . .64 D8
Chalks The BS40 . . . . .96 B3
Challender Ave BS10 . . . . . . .34 F2
Challoner Ct BS1 . . . . .141 A1
Challow Dr BS22 . . . . .88 A4
Champion Rd BS15 . . . . .52 A2
Champneys Ave BS10 . . . . . . .34 F3
Chancel Cl Bristol BS9 . . . . . .48 D3
  Nailsea BS48 . . . . .59 D1
Chancellor's Pound BS40 . . . .93 D3
Chancery St BS5 . . . . .64 B7
Chandag Inf Sch BS31 . . . . . .82 A4
Chandag Jun Sch BS31 . . . . . .82 A4
Chandag Rd BS31 . . . . .82 A4
Chandler Cl BA1 . . . . .84 B1
Chandos Cl BS23 . . . . .104 D6
Chandos Rd Bristol BS6 . . . . .49 C1
  Keynsham BS31 . . . . .81 E7
Chandos Trad Est BS2 . . . . . .64 A5
Channel Cl BS22 . . . . .88 B3
Channel Ho BS9 . . . . .48 C4
Channel Rd BS21 . . . . .57 E5
Channel View Cres BS20 . . . .45 C4
Channel View Rd BS20 . . . . . .45 B5
Channell's Hill BS9 . . . . .49 A8
Channon's Hill BS16 . . . . .50 F4
Chantry Cl BS48 . . . . .59 C1
Chantry Dr BS22 . . . . .89 A4
Chantry La BS16 . . . . .37 F1
Chantry Mead Rd BA2 . . . . .101 E3
Chantry Rd Bristol BS8 . . . . . .49 B1
  Thornbury BS35 . . . . .8 B2
Chapel Barton
  7 Bristol BS3 . . . . .63 B2
  Nailsea BS48 . . . . .59 C2
Chapel Cl Bristol BS15 . . . . . .66 A8
  Chew Stoke BS40 . . . . . . .112 E8
  Farrington Gurney BS39 . . .130 E4
  Nailsea BS48 . . . . .59 E2
Chapel Gdns BS10 . . . . .35 A6
Chapel Green La BS6 . . . . . . .49 A3
Chapel Hill Backwell BS48 . . .76 D7
  Clevedon BS21 . . . . .57 D3
  Newport GL13 . . . . .4 B7
  Ubley BS40 . . . . .111 C5
  Wrington BS40 . . . . .92 C3
Chapel La Acton Turville GL9 . .43 A6
  Bristol BS11 . . . . .34 C2
  Bristol BS16 . . . . .50 E2
  Bristol BS5 . . . . .50 E2
  Bristol,Frenchay BS16 . . . . .51 A4
  Bristol,Fishponds BS16 . . . .51 A4
  Chew Stoke BS40 . . . . . . .112 D8
  Chipping Sodbury BS37 . . . .41 A7

Bur–Cha 149

Chapel La continued
  Claverham BS49 . . . . .91 F8
  Cleeve BS49 . . . . .92 B7
  Hillesley GL12 . . . . .19 E8
  Hinton SN14 . . . . .54 C5
  Thornbury BS35 . . . . .9 A1
  Winford BS40 . . . . .95 A6
Chapel Lawns BA3 . . . . .132 C4
Chapel Rd Bristol BS13 . . . . .79 A6
  Bristol BS15 . . . . .65 C5
  2 Bristol BS5 . . . . .50 B1
  Bristol BS34 . . . . .132 E4
  Radstock BA3 . . . . .132 E4
  Thornbury BS35 . . . . .7 C5
Chapel Row Bath BA1 . . . . . .142 B2
  Bathford BA1 . . . . .86 C2
  Luckington SN14 . . . . .31 E4
  Pill BS20 . . . . .47 C4
Chapel St Bristol BS2 . . . . . . .64 A5
  Thornbury BS35 . . . . .15 B8
Chapel Way BS4 . . . . .64 E6
Chaplin Rd BS5 . . . . .50 B1
Chapter St BS2 . . . . .141 B4
Charbon Gate BS34 . . . . .36 F5
Charborough Ct BS34 . . . . . . .36 A2
Charborough Rd BS34 . . . . . .35 F2
Charborough Road
  Prim Sch BS34 . . . . .35 F2
Charbury Wlk BS11 . . . . .47 E5
Chard Cl BS48 . . . . .75 F8
Chard Ct BS14 . . . . .80 B6
Chard Rd BS21 . . . . .57 E1
Chardstock Ave BS9 . . . . .48 D8
Chardyke Dr BS39 . . . . .114 E1
Charfield 4 BS15 . . . . .66 A8
Charfield Prim Sch GL12 . . . .10 F5
Charfield Rd Bristol BS10 . . . .35 D1
  Kingswood GL12 . . . . .11 E5
Chargrove 3 Bristol BS30 . . . .66 C6
  Yate BS37 . . . . .39 D7
Charis Ave BS10 . . . . .49 C7
Charity La BA3 . . . . .139 C1
Charlcombe La BA1 . . . . .84 F3
Charlcombe Rise BA1 . . . . . . .84 F2
Charlcombe View Rd BA1 . . .85 A2
Charlcombe Way BA1 . . . . . . .84 F2
Charlecombe Ct BS9 . . . . .48 F6
Charlecombe Rd BS9 . . . . . . .48 F6
Charles Ave BS34 . . . . .36 F4
Charles Cl BS35 . . . . .8 B3
Charles England Ho BS34 . . . .35 F7
Charles Pl BS8 . . . . .140 A2
Charles Rd BS34 . . . . .36 B3
Charles St Bath BA1 . . . . . . .142 B2
  Bristol BS1 . . . . .141 A4
Charleton Ho 8 BS2 . . . . . . .141 C3
Charlock Cl BS22 . . . . .105 D7
Charlock Rd BS22 . . . . .105 D7
Charlotte St Bath BA1 . . . . . .142 B2
  Bristol BS1 . . . . .140 C3
  Bristol BS1 . . . . .140 C3
Charlotte St S BS1 . . . . .140 C2
Charlton Ave Bristol BS34 . . .35 F2
  Weston-Super-Mare BS23 . .104 D4
Charlton Cl BS34 . . . . .23 F1
Charlton Dr BS48 . . . . .60 C7
Charlton Gdns BS10 . . . . .35 A3
Charlton La Bristol BS10 . . . . .35 A3
  Radstock BA3 . . . . .138 D6
Charlton Mead Ct BS10 . . . . .35 B3
Charlton Mead Dr BS10 . . . . .35 B3
Charlton Pk
  Keynsham BS31 . . . . .81 D5
  Midsomer Norton BA3 . . . .138 B7
Charlton Pl BS10 . . . . .35 A3
Charlton Rd Bristol BS10 . . . .35 A3
  Bristol BS15 . . . . .51 B1
  Holcombe BA3 . . . . .138 D3
  Keynsham BS31,BS14 . . . . .81 C3
  Midsomer Norton BA3 . . . .138 B8
  Weston-Super-Mare BS23 . .104 D4
Charlton St 11 BS5 . . . . .64 B8
Charlton View BS20 . . . . .45 C5
Charminster Rd BS16 . . . . . . .51 B3
Charmouth Ct BA1 . . . . .63 D1
Charmouth Rd BA1 . . . . .101 B8
Charnell Rd BS16 . . . . .51 E4
Charnhill Brow BS16 . . . . .52 A4
Charnhill Cres BS16 . . . . .51 F4
Charnhill Dr BS16 . . . . .51 F4
Charnhill Ridge BS16 . . . . . . .52 A4
Charnhill Vale BS16 . . . . .51 F4
Charnwood BS16 . . . . .52 A4
Charnwood Rd BS14 . . . . .80 B4
Charter Rd BS22 . . . . .105 B8
Charter Wlk BS14 . . . . .79 F6
Charterhouse Cl BS48 . . . . . . .59 F1
Charterhouse Rd 6 BS5 . . . . .64 D8
Chartley BS9 . . . . .48 D2
Chase La BS12 . . . . .18 C6
Chase Rd BS15 . . . . .51 D2
Chase The BS16 . . . . .51 C3
Chasefield La 1 BS16 . . . . . . .51 B4
Chatcombe BS37 . . . . .39 E7
Chatham Pk BA2 . . . . .102 C6
Chatham Row BA1 . . . . .142 C3
Chatley Furlong BA2 . . . . . . .135 F3
Chatsworth Pk BS35 . . . . .8 B3
Chatsworth Rd Bristol BS16 . .51 B3
  Bristol BS4 . . . . .64 C4
Chatterton Gn BS14 . . . . .79 F3
Chatterton Ho 5 BS1 . . . . . .141 B1
Chatterton Rd BS37 . . . . .27 C1
Chatterton Sq BS1 . . . . .141 C1

Chatterton St BS1 .....141 C1
Chaucer Rd Bath BA2 ...101 F4
  Midsomer Norton BA3 ...138 B8
  Weston-Super-Mare BS23 ..105 A4
Chaundey Gr BS13 ....79 B5
Chavenage BS15 ....52 A1
Cheap St BA1 ....142 C2
Cheapside BS2 ....141 C4
Cheapside St **6** BS3 .....63 F4
Cheddar Cl BS48 ....75 F8
Cheddar Gr BS13 ....79 A8
Cheddar Grove Sch BS13 .79 A8
Cheddar Rd BS26 ....125 E2
Chedworth Bristol BS15 .51 F3
  Yate BS37 ....39 B7
Chedworth Cl BA2 ......102 F3
Chedworth Rd BS7 ......50 A6
Cheese La BS2 ....141 B2
Chelford Gr BS34 ....36 B8
Chelmer Gr BS31 ....81 F4
Chelmsford Wlk BS4 ....64 F5
Chelscombe BA1 ....84 B1
Chelsea Cl BS31 ....82 A5
Chelsea Pk BS5 ....64 C8
Chelsea Rd Bath BA1 ...101 C7
  Bristol BS5 ....50 B1
Chelsfield BS48 ....76 A7
Chelston Rd BS4 ....79 D7
Chelswood Ave BS22 ...105 C8
Chelswood Gdns BS22 ..105 D8
Cheltenham Cres **2** BS6 .49 F1
Cheltenham La BS6 .....49 F1
Cheltenham Rd BS6 .....49 F1
Cheltenham St BA2 .....142 A1
Chelvey Batch BS48 .....75 F3
Chelvey La BS48 ....75 E4
Chelvey Rd BS48 ....75 D5
Chelvey Rise BS48 ......60 A1
Chelvy Cl BS13 ....79 D3
Chelwood BS23 ....104 F8
Chelwood Dr BA2 ....101 D1
Chelwood Rd Bristol BS11 .47 D7
  Saltford BS31 ....82 E4
Chelwood Rdbt BS39 ..114 E8
Chepstow Pk BS16 ......37 F1
Chepstow Rd BS4 ....79 D8
Chepstow Wlk BS31 .....81 D5
Chequers Cl BS30 ....66 C3
Chequers Ct BS34 ......37 A6
Cherington Bristol BS15 .65 B5
  Yate BS37 ....39 D6
Cherington Rd Bristol BS10 .49 D7
Nailsea BS48 ....60 A2
Cheriton Pl Bristol BS10 .66 C6
  Bristol BS9 ....49 B7
Cherry Ave BS31 ....57 E2
Cherry Cl BS49 ....91 B8
Cherry Garden La BS30 .66 B2
Cherry Garden Prim Sch
  BS30 ....66 C2
Cherry Garden Rd BS30 .66 C1
Cherry Gdns BS30 ......66 C1
Cherry Gr Bristol BS16 ..52 A6
  Yate BS49 ....91 B8
Cherry Hay BS21 ....57 D1
Cherry La **4** BS1 ....141 B4
Cherry Orchard La
  3 Bristol BS5 ....64 F8
  Luckington SN14 ......31 C5
Cherry Rd
  Chipping Sodbury BS37 ..28 A1
  Long Ashton BS41 ......61 F1
  Nailsea BS48 ....59 D1
Cherry Tree Cl Bristol BS16 .51 C2
  Keynsham BS31 ....81 C4
  Radstock BA3 ....132 E1
Cherry Wood BS30 .....66 B2
Cherrytree Cres BS16 ...51 C2
Cherrytree Ct BS16 .....53 C5
Cherrytree Rd BS16 .....51 C2
Cherrywood Rd BS22 ...88 E2
Cherrywood Rise BS22 ..88 F2
Chertsey Rd BS6 ....49 B1
Cherwell Cl BS35 ....15 C7
Cherwell Rd BS31 ....82 A4
Chescombe Rd BS49 ....91 B7
Chesham Rd N BS22 ...105 B8
Chesham Rd S BS22 ....105 B8
Cheshar Way BS15 .....51 D1
Cheshire Cl BS37 ....27 E3
Chesle Cl BS20 ....44 E3
Chesle Way BS20 ......44 E3
Cheslefield BS20 ....44 E3
Chesley Hill BS30 ....66 F7
Chessel Cl BS32 ....24 C2
Chessel Ct **3** BS3 ......63 B2
Chessel St BS3 ....63 A3
Chessell Ave BS35 .....22 C7
Chessington Ave BS14 ..80 B5
Chester Cl BS24 ....106 A8
Chester Ct **3** BS5 ......64 C7
Chester Park
  Jun & Inf Schs BS16 ...51 A3
Chester Park Rd BS16 ..51 A2
Chester Pk BS5 ....50 E1
Chester Rd BS5 ....50 E1
Chester St BS5 ....50 E2
Chesterfield Ave BS6 ...49 E2
Chesterfield Cl BS29 ..106 F3
Chesterfield Ho BA3 ...132 B1
Chesterfield Hospl BS8 .140 A2
Chesterfield Rd
  Bristol BS16 ....51 E5
  Bristol BS6 ....49 E2
Chestermaster Cl BS32 .24 A5

Chesters BS30 ....66 A4
Chesterton Dr BS48 ....60 A2
Chesterton Ho **6** BS2 ..141 B4
Chestertons The BA2 ..102 F8
Chestnut Ave
  Axbridge BS26 ....125 C2
  Weston-Super-Mare BS22 .89 A1
Chestnut Chase BS48 ..60 A3
Chestnut Cl Banwell BS29 .107 A3
  Bristol BS14 ....80 F5
  Chipping Sodbury BS49 ...91 D4
  Paulton BS39 ....131 E6
  Radstock BA3 ....132 E1
  Thornbury BS35 ....8 C1
Chestnut Ct Bristol BS16 .52 A5
Chestnut Dr
  Chipping Sodbury BS37 ..28 A1
  Claverham BS49 ....74 F1
  Thornbury BS35 ....8 C1
Chestnut Gr Bath BA2 ..101 C4
  Clevedon BS21 ....57 E4
  Westwood BA15 ....120 F4
Chestnut Ho BS13 ......79 D3
Chestnut La BS24 .....122 B7
Chestnut Park Est GL12 .11 F4
Chestnut Rd Bristol BS15 .51 F3
  Bristol BS6 ....51 D6
  Long Ashton BS41 .....62 B2
Chestnut Way BS15 ....51 F3
Chestnut Wlk Bristol BS13 .79 A6
  Saltford BS31 ....82 E3
Chestnuts The BS25 ...125 A7
Chetwode Cl BS10 ......35 D3
Chetwood Ho BS5 ......64 C6
Chevening Cl BS34 .....36 D4
Chever's La BA3 ....135 E5
Cheviot Dr BS35 ....15 E8
Cheviot Way BS30 ......66 C5
Chew Cotts BS31 ....81 F5
Chew Ct BS40 ....113 D4
Chew Hill BS40 ....96 A4
Chew La BS40 ....95 F1
Chew Magna Prim Sch
  BS40 ....96 B3
Chew Rd BS40 ....95 C5
Chew St BS40 ....96 A3
Chew Stoke Prim Sch
  BS40 ....112 D8
Chew Valley Sch BS40 ..95 F1
Chewton Cl BS16 ....51 E3
Chewton Rd BS31 ......81 F2
Cheyne Rd BS9 ....48 D6
Chichester Ho BS4 .....64 F6
Chichester Pl BA3 .....133 A2
Chichester Way
  3 Weston-Super-Mare BS24 .106 A8
  Yate BS37 ....27 D3
Chickwell La BA3 ......135 A1
Chilcompton Rd BA3 ..137 E7
Chillington Ct BS34 ....23 E1
Chillwood Cl BS37 .....26 E3
Chillyhill La BS40 ......95 F2
Chiltern Cl Bristol BS14 .80 B4
  Bristol BS30 ....66 C5
Chiltern Pk BS35 ......15 E8
Chilton Rd Bath BA1 ...85 B1
  Bristol BS4 ....80 A8
Chilwood Cl BS37 ......26 E3
Chimes The BS48 ......75 C8
Chine The BS16 ....50 D8
Chine View BS16 ....51 F8
Chiphouse Rd BS15 ....51 F3
Chippenham Rd SN14 ..70 A8
Chipperfield Dr BS15 ..51 F1
Chipping Cross BS21 ...73 C8
Chipping Edge Est BS37 ..28 C1
Chipping Sodbury Sch
  BS37 ....40 B8
Chipping The GL12 ....11 F4
Chippings The BS16 ....50 D5
Chisbury St BS5 ....50 D3
Chittening Rd BS11 ....33 E7
Chock La BS9 ....49 A7
Christ Church CE Inf Sch
  BS16 ....51 D5
Christ Church CE Prim Sch
  BS8 ....140 B3
  Weston-Super-Mare BS23 .104 E8
Christ the King Prim Sch
  BS35 ....8 D1
Christchurch Ave BS16 ..51 D5
Christchurch CE Prim Sch
  BS15 ....65 B4
Christchurch Cl BS48 ..59 E2
Christchurch Jun Sch
  BS16 ....51 D5
Christchurch La BS16 ..51 D5
Christchurch Path S **12**
  BS23 ....104 E8
Christchurch Rd BS8 ..140 A3
Christian Cl BS22 ......89 A3
Christina Terr BS8 ....140 A1
Christmas St **3** BS1 ...141 A3
Christmas Stps **1** BS1 .141 A3
Christmas Tree BS34 ..24 B8
Christon Rd Banwell BS29 .107 A1
  Loxton BS26 ....123 C6
Christon Terr BS23 ...104 F2
Chubb Cl BS30 ....65 F5
Church Ave Bristol BS30 ..66 D7
  3 Bristol BS5 ....50 B1
  Bristol BS9 ....48 E4
  Falfield GL12 ....9 E7
Church Cl Bathampton BA2 .85 F2
  Bathford BA1 ....86 B2
  Bristol BS10 ....34 D2
  Clevedon BS21 ....57 A2
  Frampton Cotterell BS36 ..38 B8

Church Cl continued
  Portishead BS20 ....45 D5
  Yatton BS49 ....91 C7
Church Cotts
  Monkton Combe BA2 ..119 E8
  Newton St Loe BA2 ...100 B6
Church Ct
  Midsomer Norton BA3 ..132 A1
  Redhill BS40 ....93 D3
Church Dr Bristol BS5 ..64 E8
  Congresbury BS49 .....91 D4
Church Farm Bsns Pk
  BA2 ....100 A7
Church Farm Cl **2** BS15 .65 F8
Church Farm Paddock
  BS30 ....82 E7
Church Farm Rd BS16 ..52 C6
Church Hayes Cl **2** BS48 .75 E8
Church Hayes Dr **2** BS48 .75 E8
Church Hill Bristol BS4 ..64 E2
  Burton SN14 ....43 B3
  Freshford BA3 ....120 B5
  Olveston BS35 ....13 F3
  Radstock BA3 ....133 C1
  Timsbury BA3 ....116 B2
Church La Axbridge BS26 .125 C2
  Backwell BS48 ....76 C5
  Badminton GL9 ....30 E5
  Bath BA2 ....102 C4
  Batheaston BA1 ....85 F4
  Bishop Sutton BS39 ..113 D4
  Bitton BS30 ....82 E7
  Bristol BS1 ....141 B2
  Bristol BS10 ....34 E2
  Bristol BS16 ....37 F1
  Bristol BS3 ....63 D3
  Bristol BS8 ....140 B2
  Chew Stoke BS40 .....112 D8
  Chilcompton BA3 .....137 D5
  Chipping Sodbury BS37 ..41 A8
  Churchill BS25 ....108 D5
  Clutton BS39 ....114 E3
  Coalpit Heath BS36 ....38 C6
  Compton Bishop BS26 .124 B8
  Compton Dando BS39 ..98 D6
  Cromhall GL12 ....10 A1
  East Harptree BS40 ..128 E4
  Farmborough BA3 ....116 A6
  Farrington Gurney BS39 .131 A4
  Flax Bourton BS48 .....76 F7
  Hambrook BS16 ....37 E2
  Hutton BS24 ....105 E2
  Limpley Stoke BA3 ...120 A5
  Long Ashton BS41 .....62 C2
  Loxton BS26 ....123 D4
  Lympsham BS24 ......122 B1
  Marshfield SN14 ....70 A8
  Midsomer Norton BA3 ..132 A1
  Nailsea BS21 ....59 C4
  Paulton BS39 ....131 E6
  Portbury BS20 ....59 B3
  Rangeworthy BS37 .....16 F1
  Stratton On The Fosse BA3 .137 F2
  Timsbury BA3 ....116 B2
  Winscombe BS25 .....124 E6
  Winterbourne BS16 ....37 C6
  Yatton BS49 ....91 C7
Church La End BS48 ....76 F8
Church Leaze BS11 ....47 D6
Church Mdws BS14 ....80 C4
Church Par BS4 ....64 E2
Church Pl BS20 ....47 C4
Church Rd Abbots Leigh BS8 .62 A8
  Almondsbury BS32 .....24 A5
  Alveston BS35 ....15 A1
  Bath BA1 ....142 C4
  Bath BA2 ....102 C1
  Bitton BS30 ....82 E7
  Bristol BS13 ....79 A6
  Bristol BS15 ....65 E8
  Bristol BS15 ....65 E8
  Bristol BS3 ....63 A3
  Bristol BS34 ....36 A3
  Bristol BS5 ....64 D8
  Bristol BS7 ....49 E5
  Bristol, Frenchay BS16 .51 C7
  Bristol, Sneyd Park BS9 .48 D3
  Bristol, Upper Soundwell
    BS16 ....51 E3
  Bristol, Westbury-on-Trym
    BS9 ....49 A7
  Doynton BS30 ....54 A1
  Dundry BS41 ....78 D2
  Easter Compton BS35 .23 A1
  Easton-In-Gordano BS20 .47 A4
  Frampton Cotterell BS36 .38 C8
  Leigh Woods BS8 ......62 D6
  Luckington SN14 ....31 F4
  Lympsham BS24 ......122 A1
  Peasedown St John BA2 .133 B8
  Pensford BS39 ....97 A7
  Pilning BS35 ....22 B7
  Redhill BS40 ....93 D3
  Severn Beach BS35 ....22 A6
  Thornbury BS35 ....7 B5
  Weston-Super-Mare BS22 .88 E2
  Whitchurch BS14 ......80 B4
  Wick BS30 ....67 B6
  Winford BA2 ....95 A7
  Winscombe BS25 .....124 E7
  Winterbourne BS36 ....37 E4
  Yate, Goose Green BS37 .27 E3

Church Rd continued
  Yatton BS49 ....91 C7
Church Rd N BS20 ......45 D5
Church Rd S BS20 ......45 D4
Church Rise BS40 ......95 A7
Church Row BS40 .....137 F2
  Midsomer Norton BA3 ..132 A1
Church St Banwell BS29 .107 B3
  Bath BA1 ....142 C2
  Bath BA1 ....84 B1
  Bath BA2 ....102 B4
  Bathford BA1 ....86 B2
  Blagdon BS40 ....110 F2
  Bristol BS1 ....141 B2
  Bristol BS5 ....50 B1
  Bristol BS5 ....64 B6
  Norton St Philip BA11 ..135 E4
  Bristol BS5 ....50 B1
  Pensford BS39 ....97 D4
  Radstock BA3 ....132 F2
  Woolley BA1 ....84 F6
Church Town BS48 ......76 C5
Church View
  Almondsbury BS32 .....23 F4
  Bristol BS16 ....51 D5
  Bristol BS34 ....36 A3
  Hillesley GL12 ....19 D8
  Newport GL13 ....4 C8
  Paulton BS39 ....131 E6
  Wraxall BS48 ....60 B2
Church Wlk Pill BS20 ...47 C4
  Wrington BS40 ....92 D2
Churchdown Wlk BS11 ..47 E5
Churchend La GL12 ....10 F3
Churchfarm Cl BS37 ...27 F3
Churchill CE Prim Sch
  BS25 ....108 F4
Churchill Cl Bristol BS30 ..66 A5
  4 Clevedon BS21 ......57 C2
Churchill Comm Sch
  BS25 ....108 D5
Churchill Dr BS9 ....48 D7
Churchill Gate BS25 ..108 F4
Churchill Gn BS25 ....108 C5
Churchill Rd Bristol BS4 ..64 C4
  Weston-Super-Mare BS23 .105 A7
Churchland Way BS24 .106 B8
Churchpath Rd BS20 ...47 C4
Churchside BS16 ....51 B7
Churchward Cl **4** BS15 .65 B5
Churchward Rd
  Weston-Super-Mare BS22 .89 B3
  Yate BS37 ....27 B3
Churchway BA3 ....134 D1
Churchways BS14 ......80 C4
Churchways Ave BS7 ...49 E6
Churchways Cres BS7 ..49 E6
Churclands Rd **6** BS53 .63 B2
Churston Cl BS14 ......80 A3
Circle The BA2 ....101 B3
Circuit 32 BS5 ....64 B8
Circular Rd BS9 ....48 E2
Circus Mews BA1 .....142 B3
Circus Pl BA1 ....142 B3
Circus The BA1 ....142 B3
City Bsns Pk BS5 ......64 A8
City Mus & Art Gal BS8 .140 C3
City of Bristol Coll BA1 .142 B2
City of Bristol Coll
  South Bristol Ctr
    at Bedminster BS3 ....63 E2
City Rd BS2 ....141 B4
City View BA1 ....142 C4
Clamp The BS30 ....66 C3
Clanage Rd BS3 ....62 E4
Clanders Batch BS40 ..110 D3
Clandown CE Prim Sch
  BA3 ....132 E4
Clandown Rd BS39 ...133 D1
Clapton Dro BS20 ......45 D1
Clapton La BS20 ....45 E2
Clapton Rd BA3 ....131 D1
Clapton Wlk BS9 ......48 B5
Clare Ave BS7 ....49 C3
Clare Gdns BA2 ....101 D1
Clare Rd Bristol BS15 ..51 C2
  Bristol BS5 ....50 B2
  Bristol BS6 ....49 D1
Clare St Bristol BS1 ..141 A2
  Bristol BS5 ....64 B6
Clare Wlk BS35 ....8 B3
Claredon Villas BA2 ..102 B5
Claremont Ave BS7 ....49 D3
Claremont Cres BS23 ..87 B1
Claremont Ct BS9 .....49 C5
Claremont Gdns
  Clevedon BS21 ....57 E1
  Paulton BS39 ....131 B7
  4 Nailsea BS48 ....59 D1
Claremont Pl **1** BA1 ...85 B1
Claremont Rd Bath BA1 .85 B1
  Bristol BS7 ....49 D3
Claremont Specl Sch BS9 .49 C5
Claremont St BS5 ......50 B1
Claremont Terr **10** BS5 .64 D7
Claremont Wlk BA1 ....85 A1
Clarence Ave BS16 .....51 E5
Clarence Gdns BS16 ...51 E5
Clarence Grove Rd BS23 .104 E5
Clarence Pl Bath BA1 ..101 B8
  Bristol BS2 ....141 C4
Clarence Rd Bristol BS1 .141 B1
  Bristol BS15 ....51 E5
  Bristol BS2 ....64 A7

Clarence Rd E BS23 ...
Clarence Rd N BS23 ...
Clarence Rd S BS23 ...
Clarence St BA1 ....
Clarence Terr BA2 .....
Clarendon Rd Bath BA2 .
  Bristol BS6 ....
  Weston-Super-Mare BS23 ..
Clark Cl BS48 ....
Clark Dr BS16 ....
Clark St BS5 ....
Clarke St BS3 ....
Clarken Cl BS48 ....
Clarken Coombe BS41 ..
Clarkson Ave BS22 ....
Clarkson Ho BA1 ......
Clatworthy Dr BS14 ...
Claude Ave BA2 ....
Claude Terr BA2 ......
Clavell Rd BS10 ....
Claverham Cl BS49 ....
Claverham Dro BS49 ...
Claverham Pk BS49 ...
Claverham Rd Bristol BS16 .
  Yatton BS49 ....
Claverton Bldgs BA2 ..
Claverton Ct BA2 .....
Claverton Down Rd BA2 ..
Claverton Dr BA2 .....
Claverton Pumping Sta
  BA2 ....
Claverton Rd BS31 ....
Claverton Rd W BS31 ..
Claverton St BA2 .....
Clay Bottom BS5 ......
Clay Hill BS5 ....
Clay La Bitton BS30 ...
  Bristol BS30 ....
  Bristol BS34 ....
  Thornbury BS35 ....
Clay Pit Rd BS6 ....
Claydon Gn BS14 .....
Clayfield BS37 ....
Clayfield Rd BS4 ......
Claypiece Rd BS13 ....
Clayton Cl BS20 ......
Clayton St Avonmouth BS11 .
  3 Bristol BS5 ....
Cleave St BS2 ....
Cleeve Ave BS16 ......
Cleeve Dr BS49 ....
Cleeve Gn BA2 ....
Cleeve Gr BS31 ....
Cleeve Hill Bristol BS16 .
  Compton Martin BS40 ..
Cleeve Hill Extension
  BS16 ....
Cleeve Hill Rd BS40 ...
Cleeve La BS30 ....
Cleeve Lawns BS16 ...
Cleeve Lodge Cl BS16 .
Cleeve Lodge Rd BS16 .
Cleeve Park Rd BS16 ..
Cleeve Pl BS48 ....
Cleeve Rd Bristol BS4 ..
  Bristol, Frenchay BS16 .
  Bristol, Mangotsfield BS16 ..
  Yate BS37 ....
Cleeve Wood Rd BS16 ..
Cleevedale Rd BA2 ....
Clement St BS2 ....
Cleve Ct Bristol BS34 ..
  3 Bristol BS8 ....
Cleve House Sch BS4 ..
Cleve Rd BS34 ....
Clevedale BS16 ....
Clevedale Ct BS16 ....
Clevedon Com Sch BS21 .
Clevedon Craft Ctr BS21 .
Clevedon Cl BS21 .....
Clevedon Hospl BS21 ..
Clevedon La BS21 .....
Clevedon Min Rly BS21 .
Clevedon Pier BS21 ...
Clevedon Rd Bristol BS7 .
  Midsomer Norton BA3 ..
  Nailsea BS21 ....
  Nailsea BS48 ....
  Portishead BS20 ......
  Weston-Super-Mare BS23 ..
  Wraxall BS48 ....
  Wraxall BS48 ....
  Wraxall, Flax Bourton BS48 ..
Clevedon Terr BS6 ....
Clevedon Wlk **2** BS48 ..
Cleveland Cl BS35 ....
Cleveland Ct BA2 .....
Cleveland Gdns BA2 ...
Cleveland Mews BA1 ..
Cleveland Pl E BA1 ...
Cleveland Pl W BA1 ...
Cleveland Reach BA1 ..
Cleveland Row BA1 ...
Cleveland Terr BA1 ...
Cleveland Wlk BA1 ....
Cliff Court Dr BS16 ...
Cliff Rd
  Cheddar BA5, BS27, BS40 ..
  Weston-Super-Mare BS22 ..
Cliffe Dr BA3 ....
Clifford Gdns BS11 ...
Clifford Rd BS16 .....
Clift House Rd BS3 ...
Clift House Spur BS3 ..
Clift Pl BS1 ....

3 .... 63 A4
e BS23 .... 104 E5
BS8 .... 62 F7
all BS8 .... 140 A4
llege Prep Sch ... 48 F1
BS21 .... 57 C2
wn BS4 .... 62 F7
wn Rd BS8 .... 140 A3
wn Sh Ctr 11 ... 49 B1
wn Sta BS8 ... 49 B1
BS9 .... 48 E5
gh Sch BS8 ... 140 A4
l BS8 .... 140 A2
etro 10 BS8 .. 49 B1
ark Rd BS8 ... 62 F8
BS8 .... 140 A3
BS5 .... 64 A8
Bristol BS8 ... 140 A2
er-Mare BS23 . 104 E5
Bristol BS3 ... 63 C3
... 64 A8
I BS20 .... 45 C2
spension Bridge ... 62 E7
le BS8 .... 140 A2
le CI BS8 ..... 140 A2
ew 1 BS3 ..... 63 F4
ood CI BS8 .... 140 B2
ood Rd BS4 ... 140 B2
ood Cres BS8 .. 140 B2
ood Terr BS8 .. 140 A2
BS3 .... 63 C2
... 64 A8
d BS20 .... 45 C2
se Mews BS20 . 45 D6
Rd BS36 ...... 37 F6
d BS4 .... 63 D1
Bristol BS10 .. 35 A5
l BS3 .... 51 D3
BS20 .... 24 C1
4 .... 36 C6
ath BS20 ..... 38 C6
BS20 .... 44 F1
BS4 .... 57 D1
d BS4 .... 64 F2
I Ind Est BS39 131 A8
BS22 .... 105 D7
ound BS9 ..... 49 B7
ace BS22 ..... 36 D6
BS22 .... 89 A6
e Dr BS30 .... 66 A3
Bsns Ctr BS36 . 38 C3
BS20 .... 66 C5
ity Prim Sch ... 114 E3
h BS39 .... 115 B4
I BS1 .... 81 F4
2 BS3 .... 63 C2
s Bath BA2 ... 101 B6
5 .... 65 B6
7 BS35 .... 35 F2
7 BS35 .... 15 C8
aws 3 BS6 .... 49 C2
Bristol BS4 ... 64 A3
4 .... 49 B2
Cotterill BS36 . 38 B8
3 Bristol BS3 . 63 C3
... 64 A3
e CI BS14 ..... 80 A6
er BS21 ...... 57 E6
BS5 .... 50 C1
use Mews BS23 . 87 D1
e CI BS22 ..... 88 F2
d BS11 .... 47 D5
t BA3 .... 137 A2
BA1 .... 86 A4
La BS36 ...... 38 B3
Rd BS36 ...... 38 D7
BS14 .... 80 F5
t BS48 .... 59 F3
BS4 .... 60 A2
lk BS4 .... 79 D6
one Mews BS8 . 140 A4
BS5 .... 64 C7
5 .... 65 C6
Dr BS13 ...... 78 F4
oft BS21 ..... 73 C8
e BS36 .... 49 F2
Way BS49 .... 91 E5
illas 11 BA1 . 85 A1
ew Tree Hill ... 95 A2
S14 .... 54 D5
BS22 .... 104 D3
our Rd BS36 . 49 B4
Gdns BS1 .... 142 A2
BS13 .... 78 E5

Coldrick CI BS14 .... 79 F3
Cole Rd BS2 .... 64 B6
Colebrook Rd BS15 ...... 65 C8
Coleford Rd BS10 .... 35 D1
Colehouse La BS21 ...... 73 C8
Colemead BS13 .... 79 B5
Coleridge Ho BS34 ...... 24 A1
Coleridge Rd Bristol BS5 . 50 C2
 Clevedon BS21 .... 57 C3
 Weston-Super-Mare BS23 105 A4
Coleridge Vale Rd E 1 BS21 .. 57 D2
Coleridge Vale Rd N BS21 . 57 D2
Coleridge Vale Rd W 4 BS21 . 57 C2
Coles Gdns BA3 .... 139 B5
Colesborne CI BS37 ..... 39 E8
Coleshill Dr BS13 ...... 79 B5
Coley Rd BS40 .... 129 B4
Colin CI BS35 .... 8 D1
Coll of St Matthias Inf Sch BS16 .. 51 A5
Collard Ho 2 BS16 ...... 50 F4
Colledge CI BA3 .... 137 C4
College Ave BS16 ...... 51 A5
College CI BS16 .... 51 A5
College Fields BS8 ..... 62 F8
College Gn BS1 .... 140 C2
College Park Dr BS10 ... 34 F1
College Rd Bath BA1 .... 84 E1
 Bristol BS16 .... 51 A5
 Bristol BS8 .... 62 F8
College Sq 8 BS1 ...... 49 A7
College Sq BS1 .... 140 C2
College St BS1 .... 140 C2
College View 10 BA1 ... 85 A1
Collett CI BS15 .... 65 F5
 Weston-Super-Mare BS23 . 89 C4
Collett Way BS37 ...... 27 C3
Colliers Break BS16 .... 52 B5
Colliers CI BA3 ...... 132 D8
Colliers La BA1 ...... 84 F4
Colliers Wlk 4 BS48 ... 59 E2
Collin Rd BS4 .... 64 D4
Collingwood Ave BS15 .. 51 E1
Collingwood CI
 Saltford BS31 .... 82 E2
 Weston-Super-Mare BS22 . 88 E4
Collingwood Rd 4 BS6 .. 49 B1
Collins Ave BS34 ...... 36 D3
Collins St BS11 .... 47 B8
Collinson Rd BS13 ..... 79 B5
Colliter Cres BS3 ..... 63 B2
Collum La BS22 .... 88 E6
Coln Sq BS35 .... 15 D8
Colne Gn BS31 .... 82 A4
Colombo Cres BS23 .... 104 E3
Colston Ave BS1 ...... 141 A2
Colston CI Bristol BS16 . 51 D3
 Winterbourne BS36 .... 37 E4
Colston Cl BS7 .... 35 C7
Colston Dale BS16 .... 50 E4
Colston Fort 2 BS2 ... 141 A4
Colston Hill BS16 .... 50 D4
Colston Mews BS6 .... 49 B1
Colston Par BS1 ..... 141 B1
Colston Rd BS5 ...... 50 C1
Colston St Bristol BS1 . 141 A3
 Bristol BS16 .... 50 D4
Colston Yd BS1 ...... 141 A3
Colston's Girls Sch BS6 . 49 B1
Colston's Prep Sch BS16 . 50 D5
Colston's Prim Sch BS1 . 49 D1
Colston's Sch BS16 ... 50 C4
Colstone Ct 3 BS16 ... 50 E3
Colthurst Dr BS15 .... 65 E5
Colts Gn BS37 .... 40 E8
Columbus Ho BA2 .... 102 D8
Colwyn Rd 2 BS5 ..... 50 C1
Colyton 11 BS22 ..... 89 A2
Colyton Ct BS3 ...... 63 D3
Comb Paddock BS9 ... 49 B7
Combe Ave BS20 ..... 45 C6
Combe Cross Wlk BS13 . 79 B3
Combe Down Prim Sch BA2 .. 102 B1
Combe Fields BS20 ... 45 C6
Combe Gr BA1 .... 101 B8
Combe Hay La BA2 ... 118 B6
Combe La BS39 ...... 131 B6
Combe Pk BA1 ...... 101 C8
Combe Rd Bath BA2 .. 102 B1
 Portishead BS20 ..... 45 C6
Combe Road Ct BA2 .. 102 B1
Combe Side BS48 .... 76 A7
Combe The BS40 .... 109 F2
Combermere BS35 ... 15 D8
Combeside BA2 ..... 102 A3
Combfactory La 18 BS5 . 64 B8
Comfortable Pl BA1 .. 142 A3
Commercial Rd BS1 .. 141 A1
Common (East) The BS32 . 24 C1
Common La
 Churchill Green BS25 . 108 B5
 Easton-In-Gordano BS20 . 47 B2
Common Mead La BS16 . 37 A1
Common Rd Bristol BS15 . 65 B3
 Winterbourne BS36 ... 37 F7
Common The Bristol BS16 . 51 C7
 Bristol BS32 .... 24 C1
Commonfield Rd BS11 . 34 B1
Commonmead La BS37 . 40 F8
Compton Br BS9 ..... 48 D5
Compton Gn BS31 ... 81 E4
Compton Lodge 3 BS6 . 49 B1
Compton St BS5 .... 64 C7
Comrade Ave BS25 .. 125 E8

Comyn Wlk BS16 .... 51 A5
Concorde Dr Bristol BS10 . 35 B1
 Clevedon BS21 .... 57 B1
Concorde Rd BS34 ..... 35 E7
Condor CI BS22 .... 105 D8
Condor Ho BS7 .... 50 C7
Condover Rd BS4 ..... 65 A3
Conduit PI 2 BS2 ..... 50 A1
Conduit Rd BS2 ...... 50 A1
Cone The BS10, BS34 .. 35 C6
Coneygree BS13 ...... 78 F6
Conference Ave BS20 .. 45 F5
Conference CI BS20 ... 45 F4
Congleton Rd BS5 .... 64 C8
Conham Hill BS15 .... 65 A5
Conham Rd BS4,BS5,BS15 . 64 F5
Conham Vale BS15 .... 65 A5
Conifer CI Bristol BS16 . 51 D6
 Frampton Cotterell BS36 . 26 D1
Conifer Way BS24 .... 105 E5
Coniston Ave BS9 .... 48 E6
Coniston CI BS30 .... 66 D6
Coniston Cres BS23 .. 104 F4
Coniston Prim Sch BS34 . 23 F1
Connaught PI BS23 .. 104 D8
Connaught Rd BS4 ... 79 E8
Connection Rd BA2 .. 101 A6
Constable CI BS31 ... 81 F6
Constable Dr BS22 ... 88 F3
Constable Rd BS7 ... 50 B6
Constantine Ave BS36 . 36 E5
Constitution Hill BS8 . 140 B2
Convent CI BS10 .... 34 D3
Convocation Ave BA2 . 102 F5
Conway Gn BS31 .... 82 A3
Conway Rd BS4 ..... 64 C4
Conygar CI BS21 .... 57 F5
Conygre Gn BA3 .... 116 B2
Conygre Gr BS34 ... 36 A3
Conygre Rd BS34 ... 36 B3
Conygre Rise BA3 .. 115 F6
Cook CI BS30 ...... 66 C4
Cook St BS11 ...... 47 C8
Cook's Folly Rd BS9 . 48 C3
Cook's La Banwell BS29 . 107 A4
 Clevedon BS21 ..... 58 B2
Cooke's Dr BS35 ... 23 A1
Cooks Bridle Path BS48 . 93 D8
Cooks CI BS32 ..... 24 D3
Cooks Gdns BS48 ... 60 A2
Cooks La BS36 ..... 38 D2
Cooksley Rd BS5 ... 64 C8
Cookworthy CI 2 BS5 . 64 B6
Coomb End BA3 .... 132 F3
Coomb Rocke BS9 .. 48 D5
Coomband Ho BA3 .. 132 F3
Coombe Ave BS35 ... 8 B2
Coombe Bridge Ave BS9 . 48 D6
Coombe CI BS10 ... 34 D3
Coombe Dale
 Backwell BS48 ..... 94 A8
 Bristol BS9 .... 48 C6
Coombe Gdns BS9 .. 48 E6
Coombe La Bristol BS9 . 48 E6
 Compton Bishop BS26 . 124 A6
 East Harptree BS40 .. 128 E4
 Easton-In-Gordano BS20 . 47 A1
Coombe Lodge (Coll) BS40 .. 110 D3
Coombe Rd Bristol BS5 . 50 C2
 Nailsea BS48 ...... 59 D1
 Weston-Super-Mare BS23 . 87 E1
Coombe The
 Blagdon BS40 ..... 110 C3
 Compton Martin BS40 . 128 A6
 Nailsea BS48 ...... 34 F1
Coombes Way BS30 . 66 D4
Cooper Rd Bristol BS9 . 48 F7
 Thornbury BS35 ... 15 B7
Cooperage La BS3 .. 140 B1
Cooperage Rd BS5 . 64 D7
Coopers Dr BS37 ... 27 F5
Coots The BS14 ... 80 E6
Cope Pk BS32 .... 24 C5
Copeland Dr BS14 . 80 B5
Copford La BS41 .. 62 B1
Copley Ct BS15 ... 65 E5
Copley Gdns Bristol BS7 . 50 B6
 Weston-Super-Mare BS22 . 88 F2
Coppack Ho 8 BS21 . 57 C2
Copperfield Dr BS22 . 88 E3
Coppice End Cnr BS24 . 122 C2
Coppice The Bristol BS13 . 78 E4
 Bristol BS32 ...... 36 F2
Copse CI BS24 .... 105 A1
Copse Gr BS24 .... 122 B1
Copse End BS25 .. 107 F2
Copse Rd Bristol BS4 . 64 B3
 Clevedon BS21 .... 57 C4
 Keynsham BS31 ... 82 C4
Copseland BA2 ... 102 D5
Copthorne CI BS14 . 80 B5
Corbet CI BS11 ... 34 C2
Corbett Ho 11 BS5 . 64 C7
Cordwell Wlk BS10 . 49 D7
Corey CI BS5 .... 49 E1
Corfe CI BS48 ... 59 D1
Corfe Cres BS31 . 81 E4
Corfe PI BS30 ... 66 B1
Corfe Rd BS4 ... 79 D7
Coriander Dr BS34 . 37 A7
Coriander Wlk BS5 . 50 C1
Corinthian Ct 9 BS1 . 141 B1
Cork PI BA1 ..... 101 D7
Cork St BA1 .... 101 D7
Cork Terr BA1 .. 101 D7

Corker's Hill 9 BS5 ...... 64 F6
Cormorant CI BS22 ..... 88 F1
Corn St Bath BA1 ...... 142 B2
 Bristol BS1 .... 141 A3
Corner Croft BS21 .... 57 D1
Cornfield CI BS32 .... 24 C1
Cornfields The BS22 .. 88 F5
Cornhill Dr BS14 .... 80 A7
Cornish Gr BS14 .... 80 E6
Cornish Rd BS14 .... 80 E6
Cornish Wlk BS14 ... 80 E6
Cornleaze BS13 .... 79 A5
Cornwall Cres BS37 . 27 F3
Cornwall Rd BS7 ... 49 D4
Cornwallis Ave
 Bristol BS8 .... 140 A2
 Weston-Super-Mare BS22 . 88 F4
Cornwallis Cres BS8 . 62 F6
Cornwallis Gr BS8 .. 140 A2
Coromandel Hts BA1 . 142 B4
Coronation Ave Bath BA2 . 101 C4
 Bristol BS16 ...... 51 A4
 Keynsham BS31 ... 81 D4
Coronation CI BS30 . 66 A5
Coronation Est BS23 . 104 F3
Coronation PI BS1 .. 141 A2
Coronation Rd
 Banwell BS29 ..... 107 A3
 Bath BA1 .... 101 D7
 Bleadon BS24 .... 122 C6
 Bristol BS15 ..... 66 A7
 Bristol BS3 ...... 63 E5
 Bristol BS3 ...... 140 B1
 Bristol BS30 ..... 66 B5
 Weston-Super-Mare BS22 . 88 F2
Coronation Terr BA3 . 137 D5
Corondale Rd BS22 . 105 D8
Corpus Christi
 RC Prim Sch BS23 . 104 D6
Corridor The BA1 ... 142 C2
Corsley Wlk BS4 ... 79 F8
Corston BA2 ..... 100 A8
Corston La BA2 ... 100 C2
Corston View BA2 . 101 C2
Cossham St BS16 .. 52 B5
Cossham Wlk BS5 .. 51 A1
Cossington Rd BS4 . 79 F8
Cossins Rd BS6 ... 49 B3
Costers CI BS35 .. 15 A5
Costiland Dr BS13 . 78 F6
Cote Dr BS9 ..... 49 A5
Cote House La BS9 . 49 A5
Cote La BS9 .... 49 A5
Cote Lea Pk BS9 .. 49 B7
Cote Paddock BS9 . 48 F5
Cote Pk BS9 .... 48 E6
Cote Rd BS9 .... 49 A4
Cotham Brow BS6 . 49 D1
Cotham Gdns 12 BS6 . 49 B1
Cotham Gr BS6 ... 49 D1
Cotham Gram Sch BS6 . 49 C1
Cotham Gram Sch
 Charnwood Annexe BS6 . 49 C1
Cotham Hill BS6 .. 140 C4
Cotham Lawn Ho BS6 . 140 C4
Cotham Lawn Rd BS6 . 140 C4
Cotham Pk BS6 ... 49 C1
Cotham Pk N BS6 . 49 C1
Cotham PI BS6 ... 140 C4
Cotham Rd BS6 ... 140 C4
Cotham Rd S BS6 . 141 A4
Cotham Side BS6 . 49 D1
Cotham Vale BS6 . 49 C1
Cotham Wlk Bristol BS7 . 50 B6
 1 Weston-Super-Mare BS22 88 F2
Cotrith Gr BS10 .. 34 E3
Cotswold CI BS20 . 45 E4
Cotswold La BS37 . 28 B1
Cotswold Rd Bath BA2 . 101 E4
 Bristol BS3 ...... 63 D3
 Chipping Sodbury BS37 . 40 B8
Cotswold View Bath BA2 . 101 B5
 Bristol BS35 ..... 51 D2
 Charfield GL12 .... 11 B5
 Wickwar GL12 .... 18 B6
Cottage PI Bath BA1 . 85 C2
 Bristol BS2 ...... 141 A4
Cottages The BS40 . 92 D2
Cotterell Ct BA1 .. 142 B2
Cottington Ct BS15 . 65 E5
Cottisford Rd BS5 . 50 B4
Cottle Gdns BS14 . 80 F6
Cottle Rd BS14 .. 80 F6
Cottles La BA15 . 120 F6
Cotton Mead BA2 . 100 B7
Cottonwood Dr BS30 . 66 A3
Cottrell Ave BS15 . 51 E1
Cottrell Rd BS5 .. 50 C3
Coulson Dr BS22 . 89 B3
Coulson Wlk BS15 . 51 C2
Coulson's CI BS14 . 80 A3
Coulson's Rd BS14 . 80 A3
Council Hos BS22 . 89 B8
Council Houses The
 Blagdon BS40 .... 111 B8
 Hinton Blewett BS39 . 129 E6
Counterpool Rd BS15 . 65 C7
Countership BS1 .. 141 B2
Countership Gdns BS14 . 80 B6
Countess Wlk BS16 . 50 D6

County St BS4 .... 64 A4
Court Ave Bristol BS34 . 36 F5
 Yatton BS49 .... 91 C7
Court CI Backwell BS48 . 76 C5
 Bristol BS7 .... 49 E7
 Portishead BS20 ... 45 D4
Court Dr BS25 .... 108 B4
Court Farm BS29 . 106 F5
Court Farm Rd Bristol BS14 79 F3
 Bristol BS30 ..... 65 E2
Court Gdns BA1 .. 86 A4
Court Hill BS39 .. 98 D5
Court La Bathford BA1 . 86 B2
 Clevedon BS21 ... 58 A3
 Shipham BS25 ... 125 F8
 Wick BS30 ...... 67 B6
Court Mdw GL13 .. 3 E3
Court Mead GL13 . 3 E3
Court PI BS22 ... 88 F2
Court Rd Bristol BS15 . 65 D7
 Bristol BS30 .... 66 C3
 Bristol BS7 ..... 49 E7
 Frampton Cotterell BS36 . 37 F8
 Weston-Super-Mare BS22 . 88 A5
Court View CI BS32 . 24 A5
Court-de-Wyck Prim Sch BS49 .. 74 F1
Courtenay Rd BS31 . 82 B2
Courtenay Wlk BS22 . 89 A3
Courteney Cres BS4 . 79 D7
Courtfield Gr BS16 . 51 A4
Courtlands Bristol BS32 . 24 E1
 Keynsham BS31 ... 81 E5
Courtlands La BS3 . 62 E4
Courtlands Unit BS34 . 79 D8
Courtmead BA2 ... 118 F7
Courtney Prim Sch BS15 . 65 F7
Courtney Rd BS15 . 65 F7
Courtney Way BS15 . 66 A7
Courtside Mews BS6 . 49 C1
Courtyard The BS40 . 128 E6
Courville CI BS35 . 10 D4
Cousins CI BS10 .. 34 D3
Cousins La BS5 .. 64 F8
Cousins Mews BS4 . 64 F6
Cousins Way BS16 . 52 B8
Couzens CI BS37 . 28 A2
Couzens PI BS34 . 36 F5
Coventry Wlk BS4 . 64 F6
Cowdray Rd BS4 . 79 D7
Cowhorn Hill BS30 . 66 C4
Cowleaze La BS40 . 128 C6
Cowler Wlk BS13 . 78 F4
Cowling Dr BS14 . 80 C5
Cowling Rd BS14 . 80 D5
Cowper Rd BS6 .. 49 C1
Cowper St BS5 .. 64 C7
Cowship La GL12 . 12 D1
Cowslip La BS26 . 123 D3
Cox Ct BS30 .... 65 F4
Cox's Gn BS40 ... 92 F1
Coxgrove Hill BS16 . 52 F7
Coxley Dr BA1 ... 85 C3
Cozens BS21 .... 57 F2
Crabtree CI BS41 . 78 D1
Crabtree La BS41 . 78 D2
Crabtree Wlk BS5 . 50 D2
Cradock CI BS30 . 66 C6
Crafts CI BS5 ... 50 E1
Cranberry Wlk BS9 . 48 C8
Cranbourne Chase BS16 . 88 A1
Cranbourne Rd BS34 . 35 F7
Cranbrook Rd BS6 . 49 A2
Crandale Rd BA2 . 101 D5
Crandell CI BS10 . 34 F4
Crane CI BS15 .. 66 B8
Cranford CI BS22 . 88 D1
Cranford Ct BS9 . 49 B6
Cranham BS37 .. 39 F7
Cranham CI BS15 . 51 F2
Cranham Dr BS34 . 24 C1
Cranham Rd BS10 . 49 C8
Cranhill Rd BA1 . 101 D8
Cranleigh BA2 .. 118 F7
Cranleigh Court Inf Sch BS37 .. 27 D3
Cranleigh Court Rd BS37 . 27 D2
Cranleigh Gdns BS9 . 48 E4
Cranleigh Rd BS14 . 80 B5
Cranmoor Gn BS35 . 22 D7
Cranmore BS24 .. 105 A2
Cranmore Ave BS31 . 81 E6
Cranmore Cres BS10 . 35 D1
Cranmore PI BA2 . 118 E8
Cranside Ave BS6 . 49 C4
Cransley Cres BS9 . 49 C7
Crantock Ave BS13 . 79 B8
Crantock Dr BS32 . 24 B5
Crantock Rd BS37 . 27 D1
Cranwell CI BS14 . 80 A5
Cranwell Gr BS14 . 80 A5
Cranwell Rd BS24 . 106 C5
Cranwells Pk BA1 . 101 D8
Crates CI BS15 .. 65 E8
Craven CI BS30 .. 65 F3
Craven Way BS30 . 65 F5
Crawford CI 1 BS21 . 57 B1
Crawl La BA3 ... 132 C4
Craydon Gr BS14 . 80 D4
Craydon Rd BS14 . 80 C4
Craydon Wlk BS14 . 80 D5
Crediton 8 BS22 . 89 A2
Crediton Cres BS4 . 63 F1
Crescent Gdns BA1 . 142 A3
Crescent La BA1 . 142 B4
Crescent Rd BS16 . 51 C6

Crescent The
Backwell BS48 .... 76 A6
Bristol BS16 .... 36 F1
Bristol BS16 .... 51 D3
Bristol, Henleaze BS9 .. 49 C6
Bristol, Sea Mills BS9 . 48 C6
Farmington Gurney BS39 131 B3
Lympsham BS24 .... 122 C5
Olveston BS35 .... 14 D4
Stanton Drew BS39 ...... 96 F1
Weston-Super-Mare BS22 . 88 B1
Wick BS30 .... 67 C7
Crescent View BA2 ..... 142 B1
Crescent View Ct BS22 .. 88 B1
Creslands Ind Units BS24 105 A3
Cresswell Cl BS22 ..... 89 A2
Crest The Bristol BS4 .. 64 C2
West Kington SN14 ..... 56 F3
Creswicke Ave BS15 .... 65 C5
Creswicke Rd BS4 ...... 79 E7
Crew's Hole Rd BS5 .... 64 E8
Crewkerne Cl BS48 ..... 60 B1
Cribb's La BS40 .... 93 D1
Cribbs Causeway Ctr BS34 35 A6
Cribbs Cswy BS10 ...... 35 A6
Crickback La BS40 ..... 96 A3
Cricket Field Gn BS48 .. 59 D2
Cricklade Ct BS48 ..... 60 A1
Cricklade Rd BS7 ...... 49 E4
Cripps Rd BS3 .... 63 C3
Crispin La BS35 .... 8 B1
Crispin Way BS15 ...... 51 F2
Crockerne CE Prim Sch
BS20 .... 47 C4
Crockerne Dr BS20 ..... 47 C3
Crockerne Ho BS20 ..... 47 C4
Crocombe BA3 .... 116 C3
Crocombe La BA3 .... 116 C3
Croft Ave BS16 .... 50 C4
Croft Cl BS30 .... 82 D8
Croft Rd BA1 .... 96 A4
Croft The Backwell BS48 76 A7
Bath BA2 .... 102 E1
Bristol BS16 .... 51 F5
Bristol BS30 .... 66 C6
Clevedon BS21 .... 57 F4
Hutton BS24 .... 105 E3
Westwood BA15 .... 120 F3
Croft View BS9 .... 49 C6
Crofters Wlk BS32 ..... 36 D8
Crofton Ave BS7 .... 49 F6
Crofton Fields BS36 ... 37 E6
Crofts End Ind Est BS5 . 50 E1
Crofts End Rd BS5 ..... 50 E1
Crokeswood Wlk BS11 ... 34 A1
Crome Rd BS7 .... 50 B7
Cromer Ct BS21 .... 57 D2
Cromer Rd Bristol BS5 .. 50 C2
Weston-Super-Mare BS23 104 E5
Cromhall La GL12 ...... 9 D1
Cromwell Ct BS15 ...... 65 E5
Cromwell Dr BS22 ...... 89 A4
Cromwell Rd Bristol BS6 65 A8
Bristol BS6 .... 49 E2
Cromwell St BS3 .... 63 C3
Cromwell View BS6 ..... 49 E2
Cromwells Hide BS16 ... 50 E5
Crook's La BS22 .... 88 A4
Croomes Hill BS16 ..... 51 D6
Cropthorne Rd BS7 ..... 36 A1
Cropthorne Rd S BS7 ... 50 A8
Crosby Row BS8 .... 140 A2
Cross Elms La BS9 ..... 48 E5
Cross Hands Rd BS35 ... 22 D7
Cross La BS26 .... 125 A2
Cross Lanes BS20 ...... 47 C4
Cross Moor Dr BS26 .... 125 B1
Cross Moor Dro BS26 ... 124 E1
Cross Moor Rd BS26 .... 125 B1
Cross St Bristol BS15 .. 51 D1
Keynsham BS31 .... 81 F7
Weston-Super-Mare BS23 104 E7
Cross The BS40 .... 128 F4
Cross Tree Gr BS32 .... 36 D8
Cross Wlk BS14 .... 80 A6
Crosscombe Dr BS13 ... 79 C3
Crossfield Rd BS16 .... 51 E3
Crossleaze Rd BS15 .... 65 C3
Crossley Cl BS36 ...... 37 F7
Crossman Ave BS36 .... 37 E5
Crossman Wlk BS21 .... 57 F2
Crosspost La BA2 ...... 99 B4
Crossway La BA3 .... 137 B2
Crossways Jun & Inf Sch
BS35 .... 8 D1
Crossways Rd Bristol BS4 64 A1
Thornbury BS35 .... 8 D1
Crow La Bristol BS1 ... 141 A2
Henbury BS10 .... 34 F2
Crow Mdw GL12 .... 11 F4
Crowe Hill BA3 .... 120 B5
Crowe La BA3 .... 120 B5
Crowley Way BS11 ...... 33 B1
Crown Gdns BS30 .... 66 B7
Crown Glass Pl 6 BS48 . 59 E2
Crown Hill Bath BA1 ... 84 C1
Bristol BS5 .... 64 F8
Winford BS40 .... 95 A5
Crown Hill Wlk BS5 .... 50 F1
Crown Ho BS48 .... 59 F3
Crown Ind Est BS30 .... 66 C7
Crown La BS16 .... 51 D4
Crown Rd Bath BA1 ..... 84 B1
Bristol BS15 .... 51 D2
Bristol BS30 .... 66 C6

Crowndale Rd BS4 ...... 64 A3
Crownleaze BS16 .... 51 D3
Crows Gr BS32 .... 24 D3
Crowther Pk BS7 .... 50 A4
Crowther Rd BS7 .... 50 A4
Crowther St 4 BS3 .... 63 B3
Crowthers Ave BS37 ... 27 E3
Croydon Ho 1 BS5 .... 64 B8
Croydon St BS5 .... 64 B8
Crunnis The BS32 ..... 36 E6
Crusty La BS20 .... 47 C5
Cuck Hill BS25 .... 125 E7
Cuckoo La
High Littleton BS39 ... 115 B3
Winterbourne BS36 ..... 37 F3
Wraxall BS48 .... 60 A6
Cuffington Ave BS4 .... 64 D4
Culleysgate La BS30 ... 67 F6
Culvert Cl BS32 ...... 128 F3
Culver St BS1 .... 140 C2
Culverhay BS39 .... 98 D6
Culverhay Sch BA2 .... 101 B2
Culverhill BS37 ...... 28 A1
Culverhill Sch BS37 .. 39 D7
Culvers Rd BS31 ...... 81 E6
Culvert The BS32 .... 36 D8
Culverwell Rd BS13 ... 79 A4
Cumberland Basin Rd BS8 62 F5
Cumberland Cl BS1 .... 140 A1
Cumberland Gr 6 BS6 .. 49 F2
Cumberland Ho BA1 .... 142 A2
Cumberland Pl 6 BS8 .. 62 F6
Cumberland Rd BS1 .... 140 A1
Cumberland Row BA1 ... 142 B2
Cumberland St BS2 .... 141 B4
Cumbria Cl BS35 ...... 8 E1
Cunningham Gdns BS16 . 51 B5
Curland Gr BS14 ...... 80 B5
Curlew Cl BS16 .... 50 F6
Curlew Gdns BS22 ..... 88 F1
Currells La BS40 ..... 77 B1
Curtis La BS34 .... 37 A4
Cuom Cl BS14 .... 80 A7
Cutler Rd BS13 .... 78 F6
Cutters Brook Jun Sch
BS22 .... 50 A2
Cutsheath Rd GL12 .... 16 C8
Cutters Row BS3 ...... 63 E4
Cygnet Cres BS22 ..... 88 F1
Cylde Pk BS6 .... 49 B2
Cynder Way BS16 ...... 38 A1
Cynthia Rd BA2 .... 101 D5
Cypress Ct BS9 .... 48 D3
Cypress Gdns BS8 ..... 62 E6
Cypress Gr BS9 .... 49 C6
Cypress Terr BA3 ..... 132 D1
Cyprus Wlk SN14 ...... 70 F6
Cyrus Ct BS16 .... 52 B7

D

Dafford St BA1 .... 85 C2
Dafford's Bldgs BA1 .. 85 C2
Daglands The BA3 ..... 132 E8
Daines Ct 8 BS16 .... 50 E3
Dairy Hill BA2 .... 134 B5
Dairycroft BS2 .... 141 B4
Daisy Green La GL12 .. 5 D2
Daisy Rd BS5 .... 50 D2
Dakin Cl BS4 .... 63 E1
Dakota Dr BS14 .... 80 A4
Dalby Ave BS3 .... 63 D4
Daldry Gdns BS35 ..... 14 A3
Dale St Bristol BS2 .. 141 C4
Bristol BS5 .... 64 F8
Daley Cl BS22 .... 89 B3
Dalkeith Ave BS15 .... 51 C1
Dalrymple Rd 11 BS2 . 49 E1
Dalston Rd BS3 .... 63 A4
Dalton Sq BS2 .... 141 B4
Dalwood 2 BS22 ...... 89 A2
Dame Court Cl BS22 .. 88 F4
Damery La Stone GL13 . 3 F3
Woodford GL13 .... 4 A4
Woodford GL13 .... 4 B2
Dampier Rd BS3 .... 63 A3
Damson Rd BS22 ...... 105 E7
Danbury Cres BS10 ... 35 C1
Danbury Wlk BS10 .... 35 C1
Danby Ho BS7 .... 50 A5
Dancey Mead BS13 .... 78 F6
Dandy's Mdw BS21 .... 68 E4
Dane Cl BA15 .... 120 E7
Dane Rise BA15 ...... 120 E7
Danecare Rd BS4 ..... 133 A3
Dangerfield Ave BS13 . 78 F6
Daniel Cl BS21 .... 57 F3
Daniel Mews BA2 ..... 102 B7
Daniel St BA2 .... 102 B7
Dane View Gdns BS20 . 45 C5
Dapps Hill BS31 ...... 81 F5
Dapwell La BS14, BS31 81 A3
Dark La Backwell BS48 . 76 F8
Banwell BS29 .... 107 C2
Blagdon BS40 .... 110 E3
Chew Magna BS40 ..... 95 F3
Freshford BA3 .... 120 B5
Holcombe BA3 .... 138 C1
Kilmersdon BA3 .... 139 A1
Darley Cl BS10 .... 34 D3
Darlington Mews BA2 . 102 B7
Darlington Pl BA2 ... 102 B6
Darlington Rd BA2 ... 102 B8
Darlington St BA2 ... 102 B7
Darmead BS24 .... 89 B1
Darnley Ave BS7 ..... 49 F7

Dart Cl BS35 .... 15 B8
Dart Rd BS21 .... 57 D1
Dartmoor St BS3 ..... 63 B3
Dartmouth Ave BA2 ... 101 C5
Dartmouth Cl BS22 ... 89 A2
Dartmouth Wlk BS31 .. 81 D4
Daubeny Cl BS16 ..... 51 B5
Daubeny Sch BS22 .... 141 A1
Daventry Rd BS4 ..... 63 F1
Davey St BS2 .... 49 F1
Davey Terr 3 BS2 .... 49 F1
David St BS2 .... 141 C3
David's Rd BS13 ..... 79 C5
Davids Cl BS35 ...... 15 A4
Davies Dr BS4 .... 64 F5
David's Rd BS14 ..... 80 C6
Davin Cres BS20 ..... 47 C3
Davis Cl BS30 .... 65 F5
Davis Ct BS35 .... 8 C2
Davis La BS21 .... 73 F8
Davis St BS11 .... 47 B8
Davron Ct BS3 .... 63 A3
Dawes Cl BS21 .... 57 D1
Dawes Ct 2 BS8 ..... 62 F6
Dawley Cl BS30 ...... 37 E7
Dawlish Rd BS3 ...... 63 D2
Dawn Rise BS15 ...... 52 A1
Daws Ct BS16 .... 51 B4
Day Cres BA2 .... 100 F6
Day House La GL12 ... 19 C8
Day's Rd BS2 .... 64 A4
Days Road Commercial Ctr
BS2 .... 64 A7
De Clifford Rd BS11 . 34 C2
De La Warre Ct BS4 .. 64 F6
De Verose Ct BS15 ... 65 E4
Deacon Cl BS35 ...... 37 E5
Deacon Cl BS22 ...... 88 C1
Deacons Ct BS22 ..... 88 C1
Deadmill La BA1 ..... 85 C3
Dean Ave BS35 .... 8 C2
Dean Cl Bristol BS15 . 65 B4
Weston-Super-Mare BS22 89 B3
Dean Cres 6 Bristol BS3 63 C4
1 Bristol BS3 .... 63 D4
Dean Cl BS37 .... 27 C3
Dean La BS3 .... 63 C3
Dean Rd Avonmouth BS11 33 C5
Yate BS37 .... 27 C3
Dean St Bristol BS2 . 141 B4
Bristol BS3 .... 63 C4
Deanery Cl Bristol BS15 66 B8
Bristol BS15 .... 66 B8
Deanery Rd Bristol BS1 140 C2
Bristol BS15 .... 66 B8
Deanery Wlk BA3 ..... 120 C6
Deanhill La BA1 ..... 84 A3
Deanna Ct BS16 ...... 51 E6
Deans Mead BS11 .... 48 A8
Deans The BS20 ...... 45 B4
Debecca's La BS20 ... 47 B5
Deep Coombe Rd BS3 . 63 A2
Deep Pit Rd BS5 ..... 50 F1
Deer Mead BS21 ...... 57 B1
Deerhurst Bristol BS15 51 E3
Yate BS37 .... 39 C8
Deering Cl BS11 ..... 34 B1
Deerleap BS25 .... 125 F8
Deers Wood Cty Prim Sch
BS15 .... 52 A2
Delabere Ave BS16 ... 51 C6
Delapre Rd BS23 ..... 104 D3
Delius Gr BS4 .... 79 D7
Dell The Bristol BS10 . 35 B2
Bristol BS32 .... 36 E7
Bristol BS9 .... 48 F5
Nailsea BS48 .... 59 D2
Weston-Super-Mare BS22 88 E4
Delvin Rd BS10 ...... 49 C8
Denbigh St BS2 ...... 49 F1
Dene Cl BS31 .... 81 F3
Dene Rd BS14 .... 80 D4
Denleigh Cl BS14 .... 80 A4
Denmark Ave BS1 ..... 140 C2
Denmark Pl BS7 ...... 49 E3
Denmark Rd BA2 ...... 101 D6
Denmark St BS1 ...... 140 C2
Dennington La BS22 .. 89 B4
Dennor Pk BS14 ...... 80 B7
Denny Cl BS20 .... 45 A5
Denny Isle Dr BS35 .. 22 C6
Denny La BS40 .... 96 N1
Denny View BS20 ..... 45 A5
Dennyview Rd BS8 .... 61 C8
Denston Dr BS20 ..... 45 E4
Denston Wlk BS13 .... 79 A7
Denton Patch BS16 ... 52 B7
Dentwood Gr BS9 .... 48 B8
Denvale Trad Pk BS4 . 79 E7
Denys Ct BS35 .... 14 A3
Derby Rd BS7 .... 49 F3
Derby St BS5 .... 64 D8
Derham Cl BS49 ..... 91 B8
Derham Pk BS49 ..... 91 B8
Derham Rd BS13 ..... 79 A5
Dermot St 11 BS2 ... 49 F1
Derrick Rd BS15 ..... 65 D8
Derricke Rd BS14 .... 80 F6
Derry Rd BS3 .... 63 B2
Derwent Cl BS34 ..... 36 A8
Derwent Ct BS35 ..... 15 D8
Derwent Gr BS31 ..... 82 A5
Derwent Rd Bristol BS5 51 A1
Weston-Super-Mare BS23 105 A5

Devaney Cl BS4 ...... 64 F5
Deveron Gr BS31 .... 82 A4
Devil's La GL12 ..... 11 A2
Devon Gr BS5 .... 64 C8
Devon Rd BS5 .... 50 C1
Devon Road Trad Est 1
.... 50 C1
Devonshire Bldgs
Bath BA2 .... 101 F4
Bristol BS3 .... 63 E4
Devonshire Ct BS23 .. 104 E4
Devonshire Dr BS20 . 44 F5
Devonshire Pl BA2 .. 101 F4
Devonshire Rd
Bathampton BA2 ...... 85 E1
Bristol BS6 .... 49 B3
Weston-Super-Mare BS23 104 E4
Devonshire Villas BA2 101 F3
Devralls Dr BS22 .... 24 D1
Dial Hill Rd BS21 ... 57 D4
Dial La Bristol BS16 . 51 D6
Felton BS40 .... 77 D1
Diamond Batch BS24 . 89 B1
Diamond Rd BS5 ..... 64 F7
Diamond St BS3 ..... 63 C3
Diamonite Ind Pk BS16 51 A3
Diana Gdns BS34 .... 36 E8
Dibden Cl BS16 ..... 52 A8
Dibden La BS16 ..... 52 B7
Dibden Rd BS16 ..... 52 A8
Dickens Cl BS7 ..... 50 A8
Dickenson Rd BS23 .. 104 E6
Dickenson's Gr BS49 91 E3
Didsbury Cl BS10 ... 34 F1
Dighton Ct 1 BS2 .. 141 A4
Dighton Gate BS34 .. 36 E5
Dighton St BS2 ..... 141 A4
Dillon Ct 17 BS5 ... 64 B8
Dinder Cl 4 BS48 ... 75 E8
Dinghurst Rd BS25 .. 108 E4
Dingle Cl BS9 ...... 48 C6
Dingle Ct BS13 ..... 78 F7
Dingle The BS9 ..... 48 D7
Dingle The Bristol BS9 48 D7
Winterbourne BS36 ... 37 F3
Dingle Vale BS9 .... 48 C6
Dinglewood Cl BS9 .. 48 D7
Dings Wlk 4 BS2 .... 64 A6
Dipland Gr BS40 .... 110 E2
District Ctr BS32 ... 36 E8
Dixon Gdns BA1 ..... 84 F1
Dixon Rd BS4 .... 64 F2
Dock Gate La BS8 ... 140 A1
Docks Ind Est BS11 . 33 E7
Doddington La BS37 . 40 D5
Dodington Rd BS37 .. 40 B7
Dodham Wlk BS16 .... 51 B6
Doleberrow BS25 .... 108 F3
Dolemoor La
Congresbury BS49 .... 91 A4
Congresbury BS49 .... 91 C3
Dolman Cl BS10 ..... 34 F3
Dominion Rd Bath BA2 101 A6
Bristol BS16 .... 50 F3
Donald Rd BS13 ..... 78 F7
Doncaster Rd BS10 .. 49 D8
Doncombe Hill SN14 . 70 F7
Doncombe La SN14 ... 70 F7
Donegal Rd BS4 ..... 63 D1
Dongola Ave BS7 .... 49 E4
Dongola Rd BS7 ..... 49 E4
Donnington Wlk BS31 81 D4
Doone Rd BS7 .... 49 F8
Dorcas Ave BS34 .... 36 F5
Dorchester Cl 8 BS48 59 D1
Dorchester Rd BS7 .. 50 A7
Dorchester St BA1 .. 142 C1
Dorester Cl BS10 ... 35 C4
Dorian Cl BS7 ...... 49 E7
Dorian Way BS7 ..... 49 E8
Dormer Cl BS36 ..... 38 D6
Dormer Rd BS5 ...... 50 B3
Dorset Cl BA2 ...... 101 D6
Dorset Gr 9 BS2 .... 50 A2
Dorset Ho BA2 ...... 101 D3
Dorset Rd Bristol BS15 51 D1
Bristol BS9 .... 48 F4
Dorset St Bath BA2 . 101 D6
6 Bristol BS3 .... 63 B3
Dorset Way BS37 .... 28 A3
Douglas Ct 3 BS23 .. 104 F5
Douglas Rd Bristol BS15 65 D7
Bristol BS7 .... 49 F7
Weston-Super-Mare BS23 104 F5
Doulton Way BS14 ... 80 B5
Dove La Bristol BS2 . 141 C4
Bristol BS5 .... 64 B7
Dovecote BS37 ...... 39 F7
Dovedale BS35 ...... 8 B3
Dover Ho BA1 .... 142 C4
Dover Pl 6 Bath BA1 85 A1
Bristol BS8 .... 140 B3
Dovercourt Rd BS7 .. 50 A4
Dovers La BA1 ...... 86 C2
Dovers Pk BA1 ...... 86 C2
Doveswell Gr BS13 .. 79 A4
Dovetail Dr BS23 ... 105 A7
Doveton St 8 BS3 .. 63 D4
Dovey Ct BS30 ...... 66 D5
Dowdeswell Cl BS10 . 34 F3
Dowding Rd BA1 ..... 85 B1
Dowland 18 BS22 ... 89 A2
Dowling Rd BS13 .... 79 D3

Down Ave BA2
Down Cl BS20
Down Farm Ho BS34
Down La BA2
Down Leaze 2 BS35
Down Rd Alveston BS35
Marshfield SN14
Portishead BS20
Winterbourne BS36
Down The Alveston BS35
Tockington BS32
Down View Bristol BS7
Radstock BA3
Downend Lower Sec Sch
BS16
Downend Park Rd BS16
Downend Pk BS7
Downend Rd Bristol BS15
Bristol BS7
Bristol BS7
Downend Upper Sec Sch
BS16
Downfield Bristol BS9
Keynsham BS31
Downfield Cl 1 BS35
Downfield Dr BS36
Downfield Lodge BS8
Downfield Rd BS8
Downland Cl Bristol BS13
6 Nailsea BS48
Downleaze Bristol BS16
Bristol BS20
Portishead BS20
Downleaze Dr BS37
Downleaze Rd BS9
Downman Rd BS7
Downs Cl 3 Alveston BS35
Weston-Super-Mare BS22
Downs Cote Ave BS9
Downs Cote Dr BS9
Downs Cote Gdns BS9
Downs Cote Pk BS9
Downs Cote View BS9
Downs Ct BS9
Downs Pk E BS6
Downs Pk W BS6
Downs Rd Bristol BS9
Dundry BS41
Downs Sch The BS48
Downs The Portishead BS20
Wickwar GL12
Downside BS20
Downside Abbey (Sch)
BA3
Downside Cl
Bathampton BA2
Bristol BS30
Chilcompton BA3
Downside Rd
Backwell BS48
Bristol BS8
Weston-Super-Mare BS23
Downsview Ct BS8
Downsway BS39
Downton Rd BS4
Dowry Pl 8 BS8
Dowry Rd BS8
Dowry Sq BS8
Doynton La SN14
Dr White's Cl BS1
Dragon Ct BS5
Dragon Rd BS34
Dragon Wlk BS5
Dragons Hill Cl BS31
Dragons Hill Ct BS31
Dragons Hill Gdns BS31
Dragonswell Rd BS10
Drake Ave BA2
Drake Cl Saltford BS31
Weston-Super-Mare BS22
Drake Rd BS3
Drakes Way BS20
Dransfield Way BA2
Draper Ct 3 BS5
Draycot Pl BS1
Draycott Rd BS7
Draydon Rd BS4
Drayton BS24
Drayton Cl BS14
Drayton Rd BS9
Drifton Hill SN14
Dring The BA3
Drive The Bristol BS14
Bristol BS9
Churchill BS25
Shipham BS25
Staverton BA3
Stanton Drew BS39
Weston-Super-Mare BS23
Drove Ct BS48
Drove Rd BS23
Drove Road Hospl BS23
Drove The BS20
Drove Way BS24, BS25
Druetts Cl BS10
Druid Cl BS9
Druid Hill BS9
Druid Rd BS9
Druid Stoke Ave BS9
Druid Woods BS9
Drumhead Way The
BS25
Drummond Ct BS30
Drummond Rd Bristol BS2
Bristol BS2
Dryleaze Keynsham BS31
Yate BS37
Dryleaze Rd BS16
Drysdale Cl BS22

.a BS5 .....50 E2
es BS9 .....49 B6
St BS8 .....49 A1
Way BS16 .....50 D6
BA3 .....132 E5
BA3 .....132 E5
Bristol BS16 .....51 E5
.....64 B7
enn BS21 .....74 A6
BS4 .....109 A8
hurchill BS25 .....108 C5
on GL12 .....16 C5
r Rd BS3 .....63 A3
BS31 .....81 E4
3 BS30 .....65 F4
Rd BS6 .....49 C3
.a 142 C2
Rd BS7 .....49 D4
East BS4 .....36 E5
Pl BS23 .....104 E5
a BS40 .....96 B2
n BA1 .....84 A3
le BS15 .....51 B2
ve BS15 .....51 B1
Rd BS15 .....51 B1
Rd BS10 .....34 E2
Rd BS6 .....49 B8
e Gdns BS5 .....65 A6
le BS5 .....65 A6
Prim Sch BS41 .....78 D2
BS15 .....65 D6
la Dundry BS41 .....78 C3
BS4 .....95 A7
ew BS4 .....64 A1
BA2 .....89 C4
Rd BS3 .....63 D3
ve BS34 .....35 F2
Rd BS3 .....63 D3
n Hill BA2 .....117 E4
Cl BS8 .....59 E1
Cl BS23 .....87 F1
Rd BS6 .....50 F3
Prim Sch BS10 .....35 C2
Rd BS10 .....35 C2
St 3 BS2 .....64 A3
la SN14 .....55 B5
Pl BA2 .....102 B6
res BS24 .....105 A2
t BS25 .....125 A8
dns Bristol BS30 .....66 B2
BS48 .....59 E1
o BA2 .....102 A2
d Bristol BS4 .....77 B5
BS3 .....81 E4
Rd BS49 .....74 F1
St BS34 .....35 F8
e Way 74 B1
ark Rd BS21 .....57 D5
BS5 .....64 A8
BA3 .....132 D8
Ho BS6 .....49 A3
Pk BS6 .....49 A3
r BS31 .....81 E4
r BS30 Bristol BS2 .....50 A2
GL12 .....11 A5
Cl BS13 .....79 A7
l BS31 .....81 C7
BS31 .....81 D2
BA2 .....101 E4
Ave BS3 .....63 A4
St BS3 .....63 A4
S40 .....127 F7
l BS37 .....27 E1
BS24 .....105 A2
S24 .....105 A2
d BS13 .....79 B6
n Wlk BS4 .....80 C8
BS14 .....80 D6
Rd BS6 .....80 D6
e Rd GL12 .....11 F5
BS37 .....27 A4
S13 .....79 D4
mas Ct 4 BS4 .....64 A4
ave BA3 .....131 F1
Cl BA3 .....131 F1
Gdns BA3 .....131 F1
The BA3 .....131 C7
S16 .....37 C1
l Bristol BS15 .....65 F8
9 .....49 D6
ar BS34 .....36 C8
ark (Deer Park)
BS15 .....65 F5
BS49 .....91 B8
S22 .....105 D8
s BS16 .....53 C5
BS34 .....35 C6
BA1 .....85 F5
Batheaston BA1 .....85 F5
4 .....64 D2
e BS9 .....91 B8
ood Bsns Pk
.....24 C3
ell Way BS5 .....64 C7
4 .....141 A4
d BS48 .....59 C1
Gr BS23 .....105 A7
d BS30 .....66 A4
Cres BS30 .....49 E8

Earthcott Rd BS35 .....15 F1
Easedale Cl BS10 .....35 D2
East Cl BA2 .....101 A5
East Clevedon
  CE Prim Sch BS21 .....57 F4
East Clevedon Triangle
  BS21 .....57 F3
East Croft BS9 .....49 C7
East Ct BS3 .....62 F3
East Dundry La BS41 .....79 A1
East Dundry Rd BS13, BS13 .....79 F2
East Gr BS6 .....49 F1
East Harptree Prim Sch
  BS40 .....128 F4
East Hill BS9 .....49 B7
East Lea Rd BA1 .....101 A8
East Mead BA3 .....132 B2
East Par BS9 .....48 C6
East Park Dr BS5 .....50 C2
East Pk BS5 .....50 C2
East Priory Cl BS9 .....50 D1
East Ridge Dr BS3 .....78 F5
East Shrubbery 3 BS6 .....49 B2
East St Avonmouth BS11 .....33 A1
  Banwell BS29 .....107 C3
  Bristol BS2 .....141 C4
  Bristol BS3 .....63 D4
East View BS16 .....51 F6
East Way BA2 .....101 A5
East Wlk BS37 .....27 F1
East Wood Pl BS20 .....45 E7
Eastbourne Rd 9 BS5 .....64 B8
Eastbury Cl BS23 .....87 C1
Eastbury Rd Bristol BS16 .....51 A4
  Thornbury BS35 .....8 C1
Eastcombe Gdns BS23 .....87 F1
Eastcombe Rd BS23 .....87 F1
Eastcote Pk BS14 .....80 B5
Eastcourt Rd BS39 .....132 D6
Eastcroft BS40 .....110 E2
Eastcroft Cl BS40 .....110 E2
Eastdown Rd BA3 .....132 D5
Eastern Ho BS23 .....87 E1
Eastertown BS24 .....122 D1
Eastfield BS9 .....49 B7
Eastfield Ave BA1 .....84 B2
Eastfield BS37 .....27 E4
Eastfield Gdns BS37 .....87 F1
Eastfield Pk BS23 .....87 F1
Eastfield Rd Bristol BS6 .....49 D2
  Bristol BS9 .....49 A7
  Bristol, Eastfield BS9 .....49 A7
  Hutton BS24 .....105 E2
Eastfield Terr BS9 .....49 B6
Eastgate Ctr BS5 .....64 B6
Eastgate Office Ctr BS5 .....64 B6
Eastlake Cl BS7 .....50 B7
Eastland Ave BS35 .....8 C2
Eastland Rd BS35 .....8 C2
Eastlea BS21 .....57 B1
Eastleigh Cl BS16 .....51 E4
Eastleigh Rd Bristol BS10 .....35 B1
  Bristol BS16 .....51 E3
Eastley Cl GL12 .....9 E7
Eastlyn Rd BS13 .....79 B8
Eastmead Ct BS9 .....48 E4
Eastmead La
  Banwell BS29 .....107 C3
  Bristol BS9 .....48 E4
Eastnor Rd BS14 .....80 A3
Easton Bsns Ctr BS5 .....64 A7
Easton CE Prim Sch BS5 .....64 A8
Easton Ct BA3 .....130 E1
Easton Hill Rd BS35 .....8 D1
Easton Ho 7 BA1 .....85 C1
Easton Rd Bristol BS5 .....64 B8
  Pill BS20 .....47 C4
Easton Way BS5 .....64 A8
Eastover Cl BS9 .....49 A8
Eastover Gr BA2 .....101 C1
Eastover Rd BS39 .....113 D1
Eastville BS48 .....59 E3
Eastway BS48 .....59 E3
Eastway Cl BS48 .....59 D2
Eastway Sq BS48 .....59 E3
Eastwood Rd BA2 .....102 F6
Eastwood Cl BS39 .....115 C1
Eastwood Cres BS4 .....64 F4
Eastwood Rd BS4 .....64 F4
Eastwoods BA1 .....86 B3
Eaton Cl Bristol BS14 .....80 E5
  Bristol BS16 .....51 B4
Eaton Cres BS8 .....140 A4
Eaton St 14 BA3 .....63 C3
Ebden Lo 18 BS22 .....89 A2
Ebdon Rd BS22 .....88 D2
Ebenezer La BS9 .....48 E5
Ebenezer St BS5 .....64 D7
Eccleston Ho 1 BS5 .....64 B6
Eckweek Gdns BA2 .....133 D8
Eckweek La BA2 .....133 E8
Eckweek Rd BA2 .....133 D8
Eclipse Ct BS16 .....51 D4
Eclipse Office Pk BS16 .....51 C4
Eden Gr BS7 .....36 A1
Eden Park Cl BA1 .....86 A4
Eden Park Dr BA1 .....86 A4
Edgar Bldgs BA1 .....142 B3
Edgarley Ct BS21 .....57 C5
Edgecombe Ave BS22 .....88 D2
Edgecombe Cl BS15 .....51 F1
Edgecumbe Rd BS6 .....49 B3
Edgecumbe La SN14 .....43 A3
Edgecumbe Rd BS6 .....49 B3
Edgefield Cl BS14 .....79 F3
Edgefield Rd BS14 .....79 F3

Edgehill Rd BS21 .....57 D6
Edgeware Rd Bristol BS16 .....51 D4
  Bristol BS3 .....63 C4
Edgewood Cl Bristol BS14 .....80 B8
  Bristol BS30 .....66 C3
Edgeworth BS37 .....39 C6
Edgeworth Rd BA2 .....101 C2
Edinburgh Pl 1 BS23 .....104 E8
Edinburgh Rd BA1 .....81 E4
Edington Gr BS10 .....35 A2
Edmund Cl BS16 .....51 D6
Edmund Ct BS16 .....53 B6
Edna Ave BS4 .....64 E3
Edward Bird Ho BS7 .....50 B6
Edward Ct BS31 .....81 F4
Edward Rd Bristol BS15 .....65 C8
  Bristol BS4 .....64 B4
  Clevedon BS21 .....57 E5
Edward Rd S BS21 .....57 E5
Edward Rd W BS21 .....57 E6
Edward St Bath BA1 .....102 B7
  Bath BA2 .....102 B7
  Bristol BS5 .....50 D2
  Bristol BS5 .....64 C7
Edwards Ct 16 BS5 .....64 D7
Edwin Short Cl BS30 .....82 F8
Effingham Rd BS6 .....49 E2
Egerton Brow BS7 .....49 D4
Egerton Rd Bath BA2 .....101 E4
  Bristol BS7 .....49 D4
Eggshill La BS37 .....39 C1
Eglin Croft BS13 .....79 B4
Eighth Ave Bristol BS14 .....80 A7
  Bristol BS7 .....36 B1
Eirene Terr BS20 .....47 D4
Elberton BS35 .....66 A8
Elberton Rd Bristol BS11 .....34 B1
  Bristol BS35 .....13 F5
Elborough Ave BS49 .....91 B8
Elborough Gdns BS24 .....106 C3
Elbridge Ho 3 BS2 .....141 C3
Elbury Ave BS15 .....51 C2
Elderberry Wlk
  Bristol BS10 .....35 C3
  Weston-Super-Mare BS22 .....88 F1
Elderwood Dr BS30 .....66 A3
Elderwood Rd BS14 .....80 B7
Eldon Pl BA1 .....85 B2
Eldon Terr BS3 .....63 D3
Eldon Way BS4 .....64 C5
Eldonwall Trad Est BS4 .....64 C5
Eldred Cl BS9 .....48 D5
Eleanor Cl BA2 .....101 A5
Eleanor Cotts BA2 .....101 A6
Eleventh Ave BS7 .....36 B1
Elfin Rd BS16 .....51 A5
Elgar Cl Bristol BS4 .....79 D6
  Clevedon BS21 .....57 E1
Elgin Ave BS7 .....49 F8
Elgin Pk BS6 .....49 B2
Elgin Rd BS16 .....51 B2
Eliot Cl Bristol BS7 .....36 A1
  Weston-Super-Mare BS23 .....105 A3
Elizabeth Cl Hutton BS24 .....105 D3
  Thornbury BS35 .....15 D8
Elizabeth Cres BS34 .....36 E4
Elizabeth Ho BS20 .....47 D4
Elizabeth Way BS16 .....52 B3
Elizabeths Mews 17 BS5 .....64 F6
Elkstone Wlk BS30 .....66 C2
Ellacombe Rd BS30 .....65 F2
Ellan Hay Rd BS34 .....37 A6
Ellbridge Cl BS9 .....48 D4
Ellen Ho BA2 .....101 A5
Ellenborough Cres BS23 .....104 E6
Ellenborough Ct BS23 .....104 E6
Ellenborough Ho BS8 .....140 A2
Ellenborough Park Rd
  BS23 .....104 E6
Ellenborough Pk N BS23 .....104 E6
Ellenborough Pk S BS23 .....104 E6
Ellencroft Rd GL12 .....11 F8
Ellesmere BS15 .....15 C8
Ellesmere Rd
  Bristol BS4 .....65 D1
  Weston-Super-Mare BS23 .....104 D4
Ellfield Cl BS13 .....78 F6
Ellick Rd BS40 .....110 D1
Ellicks Cl BS32 .....24 E2
Ellicott Rd BS7 .....49 F5
Ellinghurst Cl BS10 .....35 A2
Elliott Ave BS16 .....37 C1
Ellis Ave BS13 .....79 A8
Ellis Pk BS22 .....89 C4
Elliston Dr BA2 .....101 B4
Elliston La BS6 .....49 C2
Elliston Rd BS6 .....49 C2
Elm Cl Banwell BS29 .....107 B3
  Bristol BS34 .....36 D7
  Chipping Sodbury BS37 .....28 A1
  Nailsea BS48 .....59 C1
  Star BS25 .....108 D1
  Yatton BS49 .....91 B7
Elm Ct Bristol BS14 .....80 A6
  Bristol BS6 .....49 A4
  Keynsham BS31 .....81 C4
Elm Farm BS48 .....60 A2
Elm Gr Bath BA1 .....85 A1
  Locking BS24 .....105 C2
  Swainswick BA1 .....85 C3
Elm Hayes BS13 .....78 F6
Elm La BS6 .....49 A4

Elm Lodge Rd BS48 .....60 B2
Elm Park Prim Sch BS36 .....37 E6
Elm Pk BS34 .....36 A2
Elm Rd Bristol BS15 .....65 E6
  Bristol BS7 .....49 E4
  Paulton BS39 .....131 E5
Elm Terr BA3 .....138 C8
Elm Tree Ave Bristol BS16 .....52 A7
  Radstock BA3 .....132 D1
Elm Tree Pk BS20 .....46 D3
Elm Tree Rd Clevedon BS21 .....57 D2
  Locking BS24 .....106 A4
Elm View
  Midsomer Norton BA3 .....132 B1
  Temple Cloud BS39 .....114 E1
Elm Wlk Portishead BS20 .....45 D4
  Yatton BS49 .....91 B7
Elm Wood BS37 .....39 E8
ElmCroft Cres BS7 .....50 A4
Elmdale Cres BS35 .....8 C1
Elmdale Gdns 2 BS16 .....51 A4
Elmdale Rd Bristol BS3 .....63 B2
  Bristol BS8 .....140 B3
Elmfield BS15 .....65 E6
Elmfield Cl BS15 .....65 E6
Elmfield Rd BS9 .....49 A8
Elmfield Sch for Deaf
  Children BS10 .....49 B8
Elmgrove Ave 10 BS5 .....64 B8
Elmgrove Dr BS37 .....27 F2
Elmgrove Pk 1 BS6 .....49 E2
Elmgrove Rd Bristol BS16 .....50 E3
  Bristol BS6 .....49 D1
Elmham Way BS24 .....89 B1
Elmhirst Gdns BS37 .....28 A2
Elmhurst Ave BS5 .....50 E4
Elmhurst Est BA1 .....86 A4
Elmhurst Gdns BS41 .....77 F8
Elmhurst Rd BS24 .....105 E2
Elmhurst Est BS23 .....104 F8
Elming Down Cl BS32 .....36 D6
Elmlea Ave BS9 .....48 F5
Elmlea Jun & Inf Schs
  BS9 .....48 F5
Elmleigh Ave BS16 .....52 B5
Elmleigh Cl BS16 .....52 B5
Elmleigh Rd BS16 .....52 B5
Elmore Bristol BS15 .....51 F2
  Yate BS37 .....39 D8
Elmore Rd Bristol BS34 .....23 F1
  Bristol BS7 .....50 A6
Elms The BS34 .....37 C1
Elms The Banwell BS29 .....107 A4
  Bristol BS34 .....34 F2
Elmsleigh Rd BS23 .....104 E4
Elmsley La BS22 .....88 C5
Elmswood BS23 .....104 F8
Elmtree Cl BS15 .....51 D1
Elmtree Dr BS13 .....78 F5
Elmtree Way BS15 .....51 D1
Elmvale Dr BS24 .....105 F3
Elsbert Dr BS13 .....78 E5
Elstree Rd BS5 .....50 E1
Elton Ho 2 BS2 .....141 C3
Elton La BS7 .....49 D2
Elton Rd Bristol BS15 .....51 C1
  Bristol BS7 .....49 D2
  Bristol BS8 .....140 C3
  Clevedon BS21 .....57 C3
  Weston-Super-Mare BS22 .....89 A4
Elton St BS2 .....141 C4
Elvard Cl BS13 .....79 A4
Elvard Rd BS13 .....79 A4
Elvaston Rd BS3 .....63 E3
Elwell La BS40, BS41 .....78 A1
Ely Gr BS9 .....48 B7
Embassy Rd BS5 .....50 E1
Embassy Wlk BS5 .....50 E1
Embercourt Dr BS48 .....76 A6
Embleton Prim Sch BS10 .....35 C2
Embleton Rd BS10 .....35 C2
Emerson Green Prim Sch
  BS16 .....52 B7
Emerson Sq BS7 .....50 A8
Emersons Green La BS16 .....52 B6
Emersons Way BS16 .....52 C7
Emery Gate BS29 .....107 B3
Emery Rd BS4 .....64 F2
Emet Gr BS16 .....52 B6
Emet La BS16 .....52 B6
Emley La BS40 .....110 B6
Emlyn Cl 6 BS22 .....89 B4
Emlyn Rd BS5 .....50 C3
Emma-Chris Way BS34 .....36 C2
Emmanuel Ct BS8 .....140 A4
Emmett Wood BS14 .....80 B3
Empire & Commonwealth
  Mus The
  BS1 .....141 C1
Empire Cres BS15 .....65 E4
Empress Menen Gdns
  BA1 .....101 A8
Enderleigh Gdns BS25 .....108 F4
Enfield Rd BS16 .....51 A3
Engine Common La BS37 .....27 C5
Engine La BS48 .....75 B8
England's Cres BS36 .....37 E7
Englishcombe La BA2 .....101 D3
Englishcombe Rd BS13 .....79 C3
Englishcombe Way BA2 .....101 E4
Enmore BS24 .....105 A2
Ennerdale Cl BS23 .....105 A5
Ennerdale Rd BS10 .....35 D2
Enterprise Ctr The BS24 .....105 A3
Entry Hill BA2 .....101 F2
Entry Hill Dr BA2 .....101 F3

Entry Hill Gdns BA2 .....101 F3
Entry Hill Pk BA2 .....101 F2
Entry Rise BA2 .....101 F1
Epney Cl BS34 .....23 F1
Epsom Cl BS16 .....37 F1
Epworth Rd BS10 .....35 A3
Equinox BS32 .....24 C3
Erin Wlk BS4 .....79 D8
Ermine Way BS11 .....47 C8
Ermleet Rd 3 BS6 .....49 C2
Ernest Barker Cl 14 BS5 .....64 B7
Ernestville Rd BS16 .....50 F3
Ervine Terr BS2 .....141 C4
Esgar Rise BS22 .....88 E3
Eskdale BS15 .....15 D7
Eskdale Cl BS22 .....105 D8
Esmond Gr BS21 .....57 D4
Esplanade Rd BS20 .....45 C7
Essery Rd BS5 .....50 C3
Esson Rd BS15 .....51 B1
Estcourt Gdns BS16 .....50 D5
Estoril BS37 .....27 F1
Estune Wlk BS41 .....62 A2
Etloe Rd BS6 .....49 A4
Eton La BS29 .....106 E7
Eton Rd BS4 .....64 D3
Etonhurst BS23 .....104 D6
Ettlingen Way BS21 .....57 F2
Ettricke Dr BS16 .....51 B5
Eugene Flats 7 BS2 .....141 A4
Eugene St Bristol BS2 .....141 A4
  Bristol BS2, BS5 .....141 C4
Evans Cl BS4 .....64 F5
Evans Rd BS6 .....49 A2
Eve Rd BS5 .....50 B1
Evelyn Rd Bath BA1 .....101 B8
  Bristol BS10 .....49 C7
Evelyn Terr 14 BA1 .....85 A1
Evening Post Rdbt The
  BS2 .....141 C3
Evenlode Gdns BS11 .....47 F5
Evenlode Way BS31 .....82 A3
Evercreech Rd BS14 .....80 B4
Everest Ave BS16 .....50 E4
Everest Rd BS16 .....50 E4
Evergreen Cl BS25 .....107 F1
Ewart Rd BS22 .....105 C8
Exbourne 10 BS22 .....89 A2
Excelsior St BA2 .....102 B5
Excelsior Terr BA3 .....132 B1
Exchange Ave BS1 .....141 A2
Exeter Bldgs BS6 .....49 B2
Exeter Rd Bristol BS3 .....63 B4
  Portishead BS20 .....45 E4
  Weston-Super-Mare BS23 .....104 E5
Exford Cl BS23 .....104 F2
Exley Cl BS30 .....66 D5
Exmoor Rd BA2 .....101 F2
Exmoor St BS3 .....63 B3
Exmouth Rd BS4 .....63 F1
Exton BS24 .....105 A2
Exton Cl BS14 .....80 B5
Eyer's La BS2 .....141 C3

F

Faber Gr BS13 .....79 C4
Fabian Dr BS34 .....36 E5
Factory Rd BS36 .....37 F7
Failand Cres BS9 .....48 C5
Failand La BS20 .....46 F2
Failand Wlk BS9 .....48 C6
Fair Cl BA3 .....135 E4
Fair Furlong BS13 .....79 A4
Fair Furlong Prim Sch
  BS13 .....79 B4
Fair Hill BS25 .....125 E8
Fair Lawn BS30 .....66 B4
Fair View Dr BS6 .....49 C2
Fairacre Cl Bristol BS7 .....50 B8
  Locking BS24 .....106 B4
Fairacres Cl BS31 .....81 F5
Fairfax St BS1 .....141 B3
Fairfield Ave BA1 .....136 F1
Fairfield Cl Backwell BS48 .....76 D7
  Marshfield SN14 .....70 A8
  Weston-Super-Mare BS22 .....88 B1
Fairfield High Sch BS3 .....49 F2
Fairfield Mead BS48 .....76 D7
Fairfield Park Rd BA1 .....85 A2
Fairfield Pl BS3 .....63 B4
Fairfield Pneu Sch BS48 .....76 C6
Fairfield Rd Bath BA1 .....85 B1
  Bristol BS3 .....63 B4
  Bristol BS6 .....49 F2
Fairfield Terr Bath BA1 .....85 A1
  Peasedown St John BA2 .....133 C7
Fairfield View BA1 .....85 A2
Fairfield Way BS48 .....76 D7
Fairfoot Rd BS4 .....64 A3
Fairford Cl BS15 .....51 F2
Fairford Cres BS34 .....36 C8
Fairford Rd BS11 .....47 D7
Fairhaven BS37 .....27 E1
Fairhaven Rd BS6 .....49 C4
Fairlawn Ave BS34 .....36 A3
Fairlawn Rd BS6 .....49 F2
Fairlyn Dr BS15 .....51 F3
Fairoaks BS30 .....66 A3
Fairsear Workshops
  BS40 .....112 C2
Fairview BS22 .....88 F4
Fairview Ho BS9 .....48 F8

Fairview Rd BS15 ....65 F8
Fairway BS4 ....64 D1
Fairway Cl Bristol BS30 ...66 B4
  Weston-Super-Mare BS22 .88 B2
Fairway Ind Ctr BS34 .....35 F3
Fairways BS31 ....82 E2
Fairy Hill BS39 ....98 D6
Falcon Cl Bristol BS34 ....35 E5
  Bristol BS9 ....48 F8
  Portishead BS20 ....45 D4
Falcon Cres BS22 ....105 D8
Falcon Ct BS9 ....49 A7
Falcon Dr BS34 ....35 E8
Falcon Way BS35 ....8 D2
Falcon Wlk BS34 ....23 E1
Falcondale Rd BS9 ....48 F7
Falcondale Wlk BS9 ....49 A8
Falconer Rd BA1 ....84 A3
Falconridge Prim Sch BS15 .51 F1
Falfield Rd BS4 ....64 C3
Falfield Wlk BS10 ....49 C8
Falkland Rd 4 BS6 ....49 F2
Fallodon Ct BS9 ....49 B5
Fallodon Way BS9 ....49 B5
Fallowfield Blagdon BS40 .110 E2
  Bristol BS30 ....66 D5
  Weston-Super-Mare BS22 .88 F3
Falmouth Cl BS48 ....60 A1
Falmouth Rd BS7 ....49 E4
Fane Cl BS10 ....35 A3
Fanshawe Rd BS14 ....80 A7
Far Handstones BS30 ......66 A4
Faraday Rd 2 BS8 ....62 F5
Farendell Rd BS16 ....38 E1
Farington Rd BS10 ....49 D7
Farleigh Castle BA3 .....136 E8
Farleigh Coll BA3 ....136 D6
Farleigh La GL12 ....10 C2
Farleigh Rd Backwell BS48 ..76 C6
  Clevedon BS21 ....57 B1
  Keynsham BS31 ....81 D4
  Norton St Philip BA3 .....135 F5
Farleigh Rise BA15 ....86 E1
Farleigh View BA15 ......120 F3
Farleigh Wlk BS13 ....79 A8
Farler's End BS48 ....75 F8
Farley Cl BS34 ....36 C7
Farm Cl BS16 ....52 B6
Farm Ct BS16 ....51 E7
Farm La
  Easter Compton BS35 .....22 E2
  Wellow BA2 ....118 E1
Farm Lees GL12 ....11 A6
Farm Rd Bristol BS16 .....51 E7
  Hutton BS24 ....105 E2
  Weston-Super-Mare BS22 .88 B1
Farmborough Prim Sch
  BA3 ....115 F6
Farmcote GL12 ....119 D8
Farmer Rd BS13 ....78 E4
Farmhouse Cl 7 BS48 ....59 E2
Farmhouse Ct 1 BS48 ....59 E1
Farmwell Cl BS13 ....79 B5
Farnaby Cl BS4 ....79 C7
Farnborough Rd BS24 ...106 C4
Farndale BS5 ....65 A6
Farndale Rd BS22 ....105 D8
Farne Cl BS9 ....49 B5
Farr St BS11 ....47 B8
Farr's La BS1 ....141 A2
Farrant Cl BS4 ....79 D6
Farrington Fields BS39 ..131 C3
Farrington Gurney
  CE Prim Sch BS39 ....131 A4
Farrington Rd BS39 ....131 C4
Farrington Way BS39 .....131 A3
Farrs La BA2 ....102 B2
Farthing Combe BS26 ....125 D2
Farthing Row BA3 ....136 E1
Faukland View BA2 ......123 C7
Faulkland La BA2,BA3 ....134 C4
Faulkland Rd BA2 ....101 D5
Faversham Dr BS24 ......105 A1
Fawkes Cl BS15 ....66 B8
Fearnville Est BS21 ....57 C2
Featherbed La
  Chew Stoke BS40 ....95 A3
  Clutton BS39 ....114 C6
  Thornbury BS35 ....7 B6
Featherstone Rd 4 BS16 .50 F4
Feddon Village BS21 ......44 F5
Feeder Rd BS2 ....64 A5
Felix Rd BS5 ....64 B8
Felstead Rd BS10 ....35 E1
Feltham Rd BS16 ....53 C6
Felton Gr BS13 ....78 F7
Felton La BS40 ....94 E7
Felton St BS40 ....94 C7
Fenbrook Cl BS16 ....37 B1
Feniton 6 BS22 ....89 A2
Fennel Dr BS34 ....37 A7
Fennel La BS26 ....125 B2
Fennell Gr BS10 ....35 A2
Fenners BS22 ....89 A4
Fenshurst Gdns BS41 .....77 F8
Fenswood Cl BS41 ....61 C1
Fenswood Mead BS41 .....61 C1
Fenswood Rd BS41 ....61 C1
Fenton Cl BS31 ....82 D3
Fenton Rd BS7 ....49 D4
Ferenberge Cl BA3 ......116 A6
Fermaine Ave BS4 ....64 F3
Fern Cl Bristol BS10 ......35 B3
  Midsomer Norton BA3 ...132 B1
Fern Gr Bristol BS32 ......36 D8

Fern Gr continued
  Nailsea BS48 ....75 C8
Fern Lea BS24 ....122 B6
Fern Lodge BS23 ....104 D6
Fern Rd BS16 ....51 D5
Fern St BS2 ....49 F1
Fernbank Ct 2 BS6 ....49 C2
Fernbank Rd BS6 ....49 C2
Fernbrook Cl BS16 ....37 B1
Ferndale Ave BS30 ......66 A3
Ferndale Cl BS32 ....24 D7
Ferndale Rd Bath BA1 ....85 C3
  Bristol BS34 ....36 A2
  Portishead BS20 ....45 D6
Ferndene BS32 ....24 C2
Ferndown BS37 ....27 E1
Ferndown Cl BS11 ....48 A7
Fernhill BS32 ....24 C7
Fernhill Ct
  Almondsbury BS32 ....24 C7
  Bristol BS11 ....34 B1
Fernhill La BS11 ....34 B1
Fernhurst Rd BS5 ....50 F1
Fernlea Gdns BS20 ....47 B4
Fernlea Rd BS22 ....105 C7
Fernleaze BS36 ....38 C7
Fernleigh Ct 1 BS6 ....49 B2
Fernside BS48 ....76 A7
Fernsteed Rd BS13 ....78 F6
Ferry Cl BA2 ....102 B6
Ferry La BA2 ....102 B6
Ferry Rd BS15 ....65 D1
Ferry St BS1 ....141 B2
Ferry Steps Ind Est BS2 ..64 A4
Ferryman's Ct BS2 ......141 B2
Fiddes Rd BS6 ....49 C4
Field Farm Cl BS34 ....36 F4
Field La Bristol BS30 ......65 F3
  Dyrham SN14 ....54 F6
  Littleton-Upon-Severn BS35 .14 A8
  Litton BA3 ....130 A1
  Tytherington BS35 ....15 E3
Field Rd BS15 ....51 C1
Field View BS5 ....64 A8
Field View Dr BS16 ....51 C6
Fielders The BS22 ....89 B4
Fieldgardens Rd BS39 ...114 F1
Fielding Ho BA2 ....101 A6
Fielding's Rd BA2 ....101 C6
Fieldings BA15 ....120 E7
Fieldway BS25 ....108 B4
Fiennes Cl BS16 ....51 E4
Fifth Ave Bristol BS14 ....80 B7
  Bristol BS7 ....36 A1
Fifth Way BS11 ....33 E2
Filby Dr BS34 ....36 C8
Filer Cl BA2 ....133 D8
Filton Abbey Wood Sta
  BS7 ....36 B1
Filton Ave Bristol BS7 ....49 E6
  Bristol BS7,BS34 ....50 A7
Filton Avenue
  Jun & Inf Schs BS7 ....50 A7
Filton Coll N BS34 ....36 A4
Filton Coll S BS34 ....36 A4
Filton Gr BS7 ....49 F6
Filton High Sch BS34 .....36 A3
Filton Hill Prim Sch BS34 ..36 B4
Filton La BS34 ....36 D2
Filton Park Sch BS34 .....35 F2
Filton Rd Bristol BS16 ....36 F2
  Bristol BS34 ....36 D2
  Bristol BS7 ....49 F8
  Bristol,Frenchay BS16 ....37 B1
Filwood Broadway BS4 ...79 E8
Filwood Ct BS16 ....51 B3
Filwood Dr BS15 ....65 F8
Filwood Rd BS16 ....51 B3
Finch Cl Thornbury BS35 ....8 C2
  Weston-Super-Mare BS22 .105 E8
Finch Rd BS37 ....40 A8
Finmere Gdns BS22 ......89 A4
Fir La BS40 ....126 B8
Fir Lea BS48 ....59 B1
Fir Rd SN14 ....70 F6
Fir Tree Ave BS24 ....105 E4
Fir Tree Cl BS34 ....35 F7
Fir Tree La BS5 ....65 A7
Fircliff Pk BS20 ....45 D7
Fire Engine La BS36 ......38 D7
Fire Station La BS11 ......33 B2
Firework Cl BS15 ....66 B8
Firfield St BS4 ....64 A4
Firgrove Cres BS37 ......28 A2
Firgrove La BA2 ....117 B1
Firs Ct BS31 ....81 C4
Firs The Bath BA2 ....102 B1
  Bristol BS16 ....51 C6
  Limpley Stoke BA3 ......120 A5
First Ave Bath BA2 ....101 E4
  Bristol BS4 ....80 A7
  Bristol BS4 ....64 E5
  Portbury BS20 ....46 E5
  Radstock BA3 ....133 E8
First Way BS11 ....33 C1
Firtree Ave BS16 ....131 F4
Fisher Ave BS15 ....52 A1
Fisher Rd BS15 ....52 A1
Fishponds Rd BS5 ....50 D3
Fishponds Trad Est BS5 ..50 E2
Fishpool Hill BS10 ....35 B4
Fitchett Wlk BS10 ....34 F3
Fitzgerald Rd BS3 ....63 F3
Fitzharding Rd BS20 .....47 E3
Fitzroy Rd BS16 ....51 B2
Fitzroy St BS4 ....64 A4
Fitzroy Terr 7 BS6 ....49 B2
Five Acre Dr BS16 ....51 A7

Five Arches Cl BA3 ....132 D2
Flagstaff Rd BS26 ....123 D7
Flamingo Cres BS22 .....105 E8
Flat The BS39 ....114 D5
Flatwoods Cres BA2 .....102 F3
Flatwoods Rd BA2 ....102 F3
Flax Bourton Prim Sch
  BS48 ....76 F8
Flax Bourton Rd BS8 ......61 B3
Flaxman Cl BS7 ....50 B6
Flaxpits La BS36 ....37 E5
Florence Brown Specl Sch
  BS4 ....79 D8
Florence Gr BS22 ....105 B8
Florence Pk
  Almondsbury BS32 ....24 C5
  Bristol BS6 ....49 B4
Florence Rd BS16 ....51 E3
Florida Terr BA3 ....132 C2
Flowerdown Bridge
  BS22 ....105 D7
Flowerdown Rd BS34 ....106 D4
Flowers Hill BS4 ....64 E1
Flowers Hill Cl BS4 ....64 E1
Flowers Hill Trad Est BS4 ..64 E1
Flowerwell Rd BS13 ......79 B5
Folleigh Cl BS41 ....62 B2
Folleigh Dr BS41 ....62 B2
Folleigh La BS41 ....62 B2
Folliot Cl BS16 ....51 A7
Folly Bridge Cl BS37 .....27 D2
Folly Brook Rd BS16 .....38 B1
Folly Cl BA3 ....137 E7
Folly La Bristol BS2 ......64 A6
  Shipham BS25 ....125 E7
  Weston-Super-Mare BA3 .104 E1
Folly Rd BS37 ....26 A5
Folly The Bristol BS16 ....51 F7
  Cold Ashton SN14 ....68 F6
  Paulton BS39 ....131 F6
  Saltford BS31 ....82 F2
Fontana Cl BS30 ....66 B3
Fonthill Prim Sch BS10 ...35 E2
Fonthill Rd Bath BA1 .....84 E2
  Bristol BS10 ....35 D2
Fontmell Ct BS14 ....80 D7
Fontwell Dr BS16 ....37 F1
Footes La BS36 ....38 B7
Footshill Cl BS15 ....65 C6
Footshill Dr BS15 ....65 C7
Footshill Rd BS15 ....65 C6
Forbes Fraser Hospl BA1 .101 B8
Ford La Bristol BS16 ......52 B6
  Litton BA3 ....129 C1
Ford Rd
  Peasedown St John BA2 ..133 D8
  Wellow BA2 ....118 F1
Fords St BS5 ....64 C6
Forde Cl BS30 ....65 F5
Fordell Pl BS4 ....64 A3
Forefield Pl BA2 ....142 C1
Forefield Rise BA2 ......102 B4
Forehills Rd BS20 ....45 C4
Forelands BS23 ....87 B1
Forest Ave BS16 ....51 B3
Forest Dr Brentry BS10 ...35 C3
  Weston-Super-Mare BS23 .88 A1
Forest Edge BS15 ....65 C4
Forest Hills BS32 ....24 B5
Forest Rd Bristol BS15 ...65 D7
  Bristol BS16 ....51 B4
Forest Wlk Bristol BS15 ..65 C7
  Bristol BS16 ....51 B2
Forester Ave BA2 ....102 B8
Forester Ct BA2 ....142 C4
Forester La BA2 ....102 B8
Forester Rd Bath BA2 ...102 B8
  Portishead BS20 ....45 D4
Forge End BS20 ....46 E3
Forgotten World Mus
  BS26 ....123 D4
Fortescue Rd BA3 ....132 F2
Fortfield Rd BS14 ....80 B5
Forthill Way BS30 ....66 C2
Forty Acre La BS35 ....15 B3
Foss Cl 7 BS5 ....7 E6
Fosse Barton BS48 ....59 D2
Fosse Cl BS48 ....59 C2
Fosse Gdns BA2 ....118 D8
Fosse Gn BA3 ....132 E4
Fosse La Batheaston BA1 ..86 A4
  Nailsea BS48 ....59 D2
  Radstock BA3 ....132 D3
Fosse Way BS48 ....59 C2
Fosse Way Cotts BA3 ...132 D2
Fosse Way Est BA2 ......101 D1
Fossedale Ave BS14 .....80 C6
Fosseway BS8 ....142 A3
Fosseway Cl BS8 ....142 A3
Fosseway Ct BS8 ....142 A3
Fosseway Gdns BA3 ....132 D1
Fosseway Inf Sch BA2 ...101 E1
Fosseway Jun Sch BA2 ..101 D1
Fosseway S BS48 ....59 C1
Foster St 7 BS5 ....50 B1
Foundry Cotts BA3 ......116 B4
Foundry La BS5 ....50 F2
Fountain Ct Bristol BS32 ..36 D7
  2 Yate BS37 ....39 D7
Fountain La BS25 ....125 B7
Fountaine Ct 3 BS5 ......50 C2
Fountains Dr BS30 ....65 F6

Four Acre Ave BS16 ......51 E8
Four Acre Cres BS16 .....37 E1
Four Acre Rd BS16 ....51 E8
Four Acres BS13 ....78 E4
Four Acres Cl Bristol BS13 .78 F4
  Nailsea BS48 ....75 E8
Four Acres Prim Sch BS13 .78 E4
Four Oaks Inf Sch BS48 ...59 E2
Four Seasons Sq BS37 ...27 E1
Fourth Ave Bristol BS14 ..80 B7
  Bristol BS7 ....36 A1
Fourth Way BS11 ....33 E1
Fowey Cl BS48 ....76 A8
Fowey Rd BS22 ....89 A4
Fox & Hounds La BS31 ...81 F5
Fox Ave BS37 ....27 D2
Fox Cl BS4 ....64 F5
Fox Ct BS30 ....65 F3
Fox Den Rd BS34 ....36 D3
Fox Hill BA2 ....102 A1
Fox Rd BS5 ....50 B1
Foxborough Gdns BS32 ..24 D2
Foxcombe Rd Bath BA1 ..101 B7
  Bristol BS14 ....80 B4
Foxcote BS15 ....65 F7
Foxcote Rd BS3 ....63 A3
Foxcroft Cl BS32 ....36 F6
Foxcroft Rd BS5 ....64 D8
Foxe Rd BS36 ....38 B8
Foxfield Ave BS32 ....24 D3
Foxglove Cl Bristol BS16 ..50 E5
  Thornbury BS35 ....8 D2
Foxholes La BS32 ....14 C4
Foye Ho BS8 ....62 E6
Fraley Rd BS9 ....49 A7
Frampton Cotterell CE Sch
  BS36 ....38 A8
Frampton Cres BS16 .....51 C4
Frampton Ct
  8 Bristol BS30 ....65 F4
  19 Bristol BS5 ....64 D7
Frampton End Rd BS37 ...26 D2
France La GL9 ....22 C4
Frances Greeves Ct BS10 .34 F1
Francis Ct BS5 ....64 F7
Francis Fox Rd BS23 ....104 E7
Francis Ho BS2 ....141 A4
Francis Pl BS30 ....65 E6
Francis Rd Bristol BS10 ...49 C8
  Bristol BS3 ....63 C2
Francis Way BS30 ....66 D6
Francombe Gr BS10 ......49 E6
Francombe Ho BS1 ......141 A1
Frankcom Ho BA2 ....102 B7
Frankland Cl BA1 ....84 B1
Frankley Bldgs BA1 ....85 B1
Frankley Terr 6 BA1 .....85 B1
Franklins Cl BS35 ....141 B1
Franklin's Way BS49 .....74 F1
Franklyn Ct 5 BS16 ......50 E3
Franklyn La 10 BS2 ......49 F1
Franklyn St BS2 ....49 F1
Fraser Cl BS22 ....88 E4
Fraser St BS3 ....63 D3
Frayne Rd BS3 ....63 A4
Frederick Ave BA2 ......133 C7
Frederick Pl BS8 ....140 B3
Fredrick St BS4 ....64 A4
Free Tank BS2 ....141 C2
Freeland Bldgs 1 BS5 ....50 C2
Freeland Pl BS8 ....62 F6
Freelands BS21 ....73 C8
Freeling Ho BS1 ....141 B1
Freemans La BS48 ....77 B2
Freemantle Gdns BS5 ...50 C3
Freemantle Ho BS2 .....141 A4
Freemantle Rd BS5 ......50 C3
Freestone Rd BS2 ....64 A6
Freeview Rd BA2 ....101 A6
Freezinghill La BS30 ......68 B4
Fremantle La 8 BS6 ......49 D1
Fremantle Rd BS6 ....49 D1
Fremantle Sq BS6 ....49 D1
French Cl Nailsea BS48 ...59 F3
  Peasedown St John BA2 .133 D7
Frenchay CE Prim Sch
  BS16 ....51 B7
Frenchay Cl BS16 ....51 B7
Frenchay Hill BS16 ....51 C7
Frenchay Hospl BS16 ....50 F6
Frenchay Park Rd BS16 ..50 E6
Frenchay Rd Bristol BS16 .51 C6
  Weston-Super-Mare BS23 .104 E4
Frenchfield Rd BA2 .....133 D7
Freshford CE Prim Sch
  BA3 ....120 B5
Freshford La BA3 ....120 A4
Freshford Sta BA3 ......120 C5
Freshland Way BS15 .....65 B8
Freshmoor 4 BS21 ....57 H3
Friar Ave BS22 ....88 E3
Friars Ho 4 BS37 ....39 D7
Friary Cl Clevedon BS21 ...57 C5
  Westwood BA15 ....120 E4
Friary Grange Pk BS36 ...38 A8
Friary Rd Bristol BS7 .....49 D4
  Portishead BS20 ....45 B5
Friendly Row BS20 ....47 C5
Friendship Gr 8 BS48 ....59 F2
Friendship Rd Bristol BS4 .64 A3
  Nailsea BS48 ....59 F3
Friezewood Rd BS3 ......63 A4
Fripp Cl BS5 ....64 B6
Frith La GL12 ....17 F3

Frobisher Ave BS20 .....
Frobisher Cl
  Portishead BS20 ....
  Weston-Super-Mare BS22
Frobisher Rd BS3 ....
Frog La Bristol BS1 ......
  Coalpit Heath BS36 ......
Felton BS40 ....
North Nibley GL11 ....
Ubley BS40 ....
Winford BS40 ....
Frogmore St BS1 ....
Frome Ct BS35 ....
Frome Glen BS36 ....
Frome Old Rd BA3 ......
Frome Pl 1 BS16 ....
Frome Rd Bath BA2 .....
  Chipping Sodbury BS37 ..
  Norton St Philip BA3 ....
Frome St BS2 ....
Frome Valley Rd BS16 ...
Frome View BS36 ....
Frome Villas BS16 ......
Frome Way BS36 ....
Fromebank Jun Sch BS37
Fromeside Pk BS16 ......
Front St BS25 ....
Froomshaw Rd BS16 ....
Frost Hill BS49 ....
Fry Ct 2 BS3 ....
Fry's Cl BS16 ....
Fry's Hill BS4 ....
Fry's La BS40 ....
Fry's Well BA3 ....
Frys Hill BS13 ....
Fryth Ho BS48 ....
Fryth Way BS48 ....
Fulford Rd BS13 ....
Fulford Specl Sch BS13 .
Fulford Wlk BS13 ....
Fullens Cl BS22 ....
Fuller Rd BA1 ....
Fullers La BS25 ....
Fullers Way BA2 ....
Fullwell Cl BA3 ....
Fulmar Cl BS35 ....
Fulmar Rd BS22 ....
Fulwell La BA3 ....
Furber Ct BS5 ....
Furber Rd BS5 ....
Furber Ridge BS5 ......
Furber Vale BS5 ....
Furland Rd BS22 ......
Furlong Cl BA3 ....
Furlong The BS6 ....
Furnleaze BS39 ....
Furnwood BS5 ....
Furze Cl BS22 ....
Furze Rd Bristol BS16 ...
  Weston-Super-Mare BS22
Furzewood Rd BS15 ....
Fussell Ct BS15 ....
Fylton Croft BS14 .....

G

Gable Cl BS35 ....
Gable Rd 7 BS5 ....
Gables Cl BS29 ....
Gadshill Dr BS34 ......
Gadshill Rd BS5 ....
Gages Cl BS15 ....
Gages Rd BS15 ....
Gainsborough Cl BA1 ...
Gainsborough Dr BS22 .
Gainsborough Gdns BA1
Gainsborough Rd BS31 .
Gainsborough Sq BS7 ..
Galingale Way BS20 ...
Galleries The BS1 ......
Gallivan Cl BS34 ....
Galway Rd BS4 ....
Gambril La GL12 ......
Gander Cl BS13 ....
Ganges Cl Bristol BS9 ..
Peasedown St John BA2 .133 D7
  Weston-Super-Mare BS22
Garden Cl BS8 ....
Gardeners Wlk BS41 ...
Gardens Rd BS21 ......
Gardens The Bristol BS16
  4 Bristol, Upper Soundwe...
  BS16 ....
Gardner Ave BS13 .....
Gardner Rd BS20 ......
Garfield Ct BS5 ....
Garfield Terr BA1 .....
Garland Ho 9 BS21 ....
Garner Ct 4 BS22 .....
Garnet St BS3 ....
Garnett Pl BS16 ....
Garonor Way BS20 ....
Garre Ho BA2 ....
Garrett Dr BS32 ......
Garrick Rd BA2 ....
Garsdale Rd BS22 ....
Garston Cotts BS40 ...
Garston La BS40 ......
Garstons Bathford BA1 ..
  Clevedon BS21 ....
Garstons Cl BS48 .....
Garstons Orch BS40 ...
Garstons The BS20 ....
Garth Rd BS13 ....

on Ho 14 BS16 .....51 D5
ey Ho 14 BS5 ....64 C7
La BS2 ....64 A6
erry Rd BS1 ....140 B1
ions The BS7 ....50 A5
ions The BS11 ....81 F6
ions The BS11 ....48 A8
ombe Dr BS34 ....36 E4
ombe Rd BS13 ....79 B5
house La BS3 ....79 A5
house Cl BS13 ....79 A5
house Ct BS13 ....79 B5
house La BS13 ....79 B5
house Sh Ctr BS13 ....79 B5
house Way BS13 ....79 A5
sby Mead BS34 ....36 E5
orne Rd BS3 ....63 B4
on Rd BS2 ....50 A1
nt's La BS1 ....140 C2
nts Cl BS13 ....44 F4
nts Earthcott La BS32 ....25 B5
nts BS37 ....40 B8
ale BS73 ....85 F3
Elms Prim Sch BS13 ....79 A4
Elms Rd BS13 ....79 A4
St BA1 ....142 B3
ss Hill BA1 ....142 C4
er Rd BS7 ....36 A1
Rd BS15 ....65 B4
horne Cres BS37 ....27 D2
wood Ho 7 BS3 ....63 B3
elle Rd BS24 ....105 B3
shead BS20 ....45 C2
uton-Super-Mare BS23 ....104 E7
ange Whitefield Ct 141 B3
ge's Pl BA2 ....102 B6
ge's Rd BA1 ....85 A1
ges Bldgs BA1 ....85 C3
gian Ho BA2 ....142 C2
gian House (Mus) 140 C2
gian View BA2 ....101 C2
ald Rd BS3 ....63 A3
ard Rd BS23 ....104 F8
ard Bldgs BA2 ....102 B7
ard Cl BS4 ....79 D7
ish Ave Bristol BS16 ....51 F5
 Bristol BS16 ....64 C8
et La BS14 ....80 D1
s Ct 14 BS5 ....64 D7
sfold Rd BS13 ....79 C4
Rd BS56 ....49 D1
rd Ho BS34 ....36 D6
rd Ct BS37 ....27 A8
ard Ct BS34 ....36 D2
rd Rd BS10 ....34 F4
rds Pl BS13 ....79 A7
ck Rd BS48 ....59 C2
ert Rd Bristol BS1 ....51 D1
 BS5 ....64 C8
eryn Dr BS22 ....89 A3
el Cl BS14 ....80 C5
a Cres BS4 ....80 B6
t La BS24 ....80 B8
a Sq W BS14 ....80 B5
Ave BS16 ....51 B6
Mews BS22 ....89 A4
rd Cl BS15 ....65 B8
rd Rd BS13 ....78 A5
bank Cl BS14 ....80 D5
ngham Hill 6 BS5 ....65 B5
ngham Terr 3 BA1 ....85 B1
ngstool BS35 ....15 C8
ngstool Prim Sch 15 B8
ore Cl BS22 ....88 D1
Rd BS22 ....88 D1
ay Cl BS7 ....50 B6
on Cl BS34 ....105 D2
n Cl BS15 ....51 D1
ol Cl BS30 ....66 B3
ake Ave BS10 ....35 B3
n Ho BS4 ....64 E2
le Rd BS22 ....89 B4
ell's Gn BS15 ....65 A8
ne Patch La BS34 ....36 C6
ane The BS5 ....50 E2
stone Cl BA2 ....102 C2
stone La BS16 ....51 E3
stone La BS36 ....38 D7
stone Rd Bath BA2 ....102 C2
tol BS14 ....80 B6
 Bristol BS5 ....51 D1
stone St Bristol BS16 ....51 D1
ol BS5 ....64 D7
hwood Rd BS34 ....132 B3
sdale Rd BS16 ....51 A5
ville Dr BS39 ....129 E6
ville Gdns BS15 ....65 C2
s House La BS2 ....64 B5
tonbury Cl Bristol BS30 ....60 B1
 BS48 ....60 B1

Glastonbury Way BS22 ....89 A2
Glebe Ave BS20 ....45 E4
Glebe Cl BS41 ....62 C2
Glebe Field BS32 ....24 A5
Glebe Ho Bath BA2 ....102 B5
 Weston-Super-Mare BS22 ....88 F3
 Portishead BS20 ....45 E4
Glebe Inf Sch BS49 ....91 C4
Glebe Rd Bath BA2 ....101 B4
 Bristol BS5 ....64 E8
 Clevedon BS21 ....57 C2
 Long Ashton BS41 ....62 C2
 Portishead BS20 ....45 E4
 Weston-Super-Mare BS23 ....104 E8
Glebe The Freshford BA3 ....120 B4
 Hinton Charterhouse BA3 ....119 D2
 Pilning BS35 ....22 C7
 Timsbury BA3 ....116 B3
 Wrington BS40 ....92 D2
Glebe Wlk BS31 ....81 C4
Glebelands BA3 ....132 D1
Glebelands Rd BS34 ....36 A3
Gledemoor Dr BS36 ....38 D7
Glen Ave BS8 ....61 F8
Glen Brook BS9 ....48 D4
Glen Dr BS9 ....48 D5
Glen Hospl The BS6 ....49 A2
Glen La BS4 ....64 D2
Glen Park Gdns BS5 ....65 A8
Glen Pk Bristol, Eastville BS5 ....50 C2
 Bristol, St George BS5 ....65 A8
Glen The Bristol BS15 ....65 A8
 Bristol BS6 ....49 B3
 Saltford BS31 ....82 F1
 Weston-Super-Mare BS22 ....88 B2
 Yate BS37 ....27 E2
Glena Ave BS4 ....64 B2
Glenarm Rd BS4 ....64 E2
Glenarm Wlk BS4 ....64 E2
Glenavon Pk BS9 ....48 C4
Glenburn Rd BS15 ....51 B1
Glencairn Ct BA2 ....102 B6
Glencoe Bsns Pk BS23 ....105 A7
Glencoyne Sq BS10 ....35 C2
Glendale 16 Bristol BS8 ....62 F6
 Bristol, Downend BS16 ....51 E8
 Bristol, Hillfields BS16 ....51 C3
Glendare St BS5 ....64 C6
Glendevon Rd BS14 ....80 A3
Gleneagles BS37 ....27 E1
Gleneagles Cl Nailsea BS48 ....60 A1
 Weston-Super-Mare BS22 ....88 F3
Gleneagles Dr BS10 ....34 D3
Gleneagles Rd BS30 ....66 B6
Glenfall BS37 ....39 D7
Glenfrome Prim Sch BS5 ....50 B4
Glenfrome Rd BS2 ....50 B3
Glenluce BS15 ....51 N1
Glenside Cl BS16 ....51 C7
Glenside Pk 3 BS16 ....50 E5
Glentworth Rd Bristol BS6 ....49 C2
 Bristol BS8 ....140 B2
Glenview Rd BS4 ....64 D2
Glenview Ho BA2 ....133 D8
Glenview Rd BS4 ....64 D2
Glenwood BS16 ....51 C3
Glenwood Dr BS30 ....66 B4
Glenwood Mans BS23 ....87 D1
Glenwood Rd BS10 ....49 C3
Glenwood Rise BS20 ....44 F5
Gloster Ave BS5 ....50 D3
Gloucester Ct BS34 ....36 D5
Gloucester Ho 18 BS2 ....141 C3
Gloucester La 18 BS2 ....141 C3
Gloucester Rd
 Almondsbury BS32,BS35 ....24 C6
 Avonmouth BS11 ....33 A1
 Bath BA1 ....85 C3
 Bristol BS16 ....51 E3
 Bristol BS34 ....36 B7
 Bristol BS7 ....49 E4
 Knap BS35 ....8 C3
 Stone GL13 ....3 F3
 Upper Swainswick BA1 ....85 A7
Gloucester Row
 6 Bristol BS8 ....62 F7
 Kingswood GL12 ....11 F8
Gloucester St Bath BA1 ....142 B3
 5 Bristol BS2 ....141 B4
 Bristol BS5 ....64 B6
 Bristol BS8 ....62 F7
 Weston-Super-Mare BS23 ....104 D7
Glovers Field BS25 ....125 F7
Glyn Vale BS3 ....63 E1
Goddard Dr BS22 ....89 B3
Godfrey Ct 12 BS30 ....65 F4
Godwin Dr BS48 ....59 C3
Goffenton Dr BS16 ....51 B6
Goldcrest Rd BS37 ....39 F7
Golden Hill BS6 ....49 C5
Golden La GL12 ....11 F4
Golden Valley La BS30 ....66 F2
Golden Valley Sch BS9 ....59 F2
Goldfinch Way BS16 ....53 C4
Goldney Ave Bristol BS30 ....66 D7
 Bristol BS8 ....140 A2
Goldney Cl BS39 ....114 F1
Goldney Rd BS8 ....140 A2
Goldney Way BS8 ....140 A2
Goldsbury Wlk BS11 ....34 A1
Golf Club La BS31 ....82 E2
Golf Course La BS34 ....35 F3
Golf Course Rd BA2 ....102 D6
Gooch Cl BS30 ....66 C1
Gooch Way BS22 ....89 B3
Good Shepherd Cl 7 BS7 ....49 C4
Goodeve Pk BS9 ....48 D3

Goodeve Rd BS9 ....48 D3
Goodhind St BS5 ....64 A8
Goodneston Rd BS16 ....51 A3
Goodrich Cl BS37 ....27 B1
Goodring Hill BS11 ....34 A1
Goodwin Dr BS14 ....79 E5
Goodwood Gdns BS16 ....37 F1
Goold Cl BA2 ....100 A8
Goolden St BS4 ....64 A3
Goosard La BS39 ....131 E8
Goose Acre BS32 ....36 F4
Goose Gn Bristol BS30 ....52 C1
 Yate BS37 ....27 E3
Goose Green Way BS37 ....27 E4
Goosegreen BS36 ....38 C8
Gooseland Cl BS14 ....79 F3
Goosey La BS22 ....89 D2
Gordano Gdns BS20 ....47 B4
Gordano Rd BS20 ....46 D7
Gordano Sec Sch BS20 ....45 D3
Gordano Way BS20 ....46 F5
Gordon Ave BS5 ....50 E1
Gordon Bldgs BA3 ....133 A3
Gordon Cl BS5 ....50 E1
Gordon Rd Bath BA2 ....102 B5
 Bristol BS5 ....50 D1
 Bristol BS8 ....140 B3
 Peasedown St John BA2 ....133 D8
 Weston-Super-Mare BS23 ....104 F7
Gore Rd BS3 ....63 A3
Gore's Marsh Rd BS3 ....63 A2
Gores Pk BS39 ....115 B2
Gorham Cl BS11 ....34 C2
Gorlands Rd BS37 ....28 C1
Gorlanston Cl BS14 ....80 A7
Gorse Cover Rd BS35 ....22 A7
Gorse Hill BS16 ....51 C5
Gorse La Bristol BS8 ....140 B2
 Cold Ashton BS30,SN14 ....68 D7
Gosforth Cl BS10 ....35 B1
Gosforth Rd BS10 ....35 B1
Goslet Rd BS14 ....80 E5
Goss Barton BS48 ....59 D1
Goss Cl BS48 ....59 C1
Goss La BS48 ....59 C1
Goss View BS48 ....59 C1
Gotley Rd BS4 ....64 D2
Gott Dr BS4 ....64 D5
Goulston Rd BS13 ....79 A5
Goulston Wlk BS13 ....79 A5
Goulter St BS5 ....64 B6
Gournay Ct BS39 ....131 A1
Gourney Cl BS11 ....34 B2
Govenors Ho BA2 ....101 D6
Gover Rd BS15 ....65 C3
Govier Way BS35 ....22 C4
Grace Cl
 Chipping Sodbury BS37 ....28 C1
 Yatton BS49 ....91 B8
Grace Ct BS16 ....51 D6
Grace Dr Bristol BS15 ....66 A8
 Midsomer Norton BA3 ....132 A2
Grace Park Rd BS4 ....64 D1
Grace Rd Bristol BS16 ....51 C5
 Weston-Super-Mare BS22 ....89 B4
Gradwell Cl BS22 ....89 B3
Graeme Cl BS16 ....51 A4
Graham Rd Bristol BS5 ....51 A1
 4 Bristol BS23 ....63 C3
 21 Bristol BS5 ....50 B1
 Weston-Super-Mare BS23 ....104 E7
Grainger Cl BS11 ....47 E7
Graitney Cl BS49 ....92 A8
Grampian Cl BS30 ....66 C4
Granby Hill BS8 ....62 F6
Grand Par BA2 ....142 C2
Grand Pier BS23 ....104 D7
Grandmother's Rock La
 BS30 ....67 D2
Grange Ave Bristol BS15 ....65 D5
 Bristol BS34 ....36 C6
Grange Cl Bristol BS32 ....24 C2
Grange End BA3 ....138 B7
Grange Pk Bristol BS16 ....51 C8
 Bristol BS9 ....49 B6
Grange Rd Bristol BS13 ....79 A5
 Bristol BS8 ....140 A3
 Saltford BS31 ....82 C3
 Weston-Super-Mare BS23 ....104 E1
Grange The Bristol BS9 ....48 D7
 Flax Bourton BS48 ....76 F7
Grangeville Cl BS30 ....66 B3
Grangewood Cl BS16 ....51 C6
Granny's La BS15 ....65 E6
Grantham Ho BS15 ....51 C1
Grantham La BS15 ....65 C8
Grantham Rd BS15 ....51 C1
Grantson Cl BS4 ....64 E2
Granville Chapel 5 BS8 ....62 F5
Granville Cl BS15 ....65 C3
Granville Rd BA1 ....84 F1
Granville St BS5 ....64 C6
Grasmere Cl BS10 ....49 A8
Grasmere Dr BS23 ....104 F4
Grass Mead BS37 ....40 A8
Grassington Dr BS37 ....40 A8
Grassmere Gdns BS30 ....66 D6
Grassmere Rd BS49 ....91 B8

Gratitude Rd BS5 ....50 C1
Gravel Hill BS40 ....112 B7
Gravel Hill Rd BS37 ....28 A5
Gravel Wlk BA1 ....142 B3
Graveney Cl BS4 ....64 D1
Gray Cl BS10 ....34 E2
Gray Hollow BS40 ....128 F4
Grayle Rd BS10 ....35 A2
Grayling Ho BS9 ....48 F7
Grays Hill BA2 ....134 B5
Great Ann St BS2 ....141 C3
Great Bedford St BA1 ....142 B4
Great Brockeridge BS9 ....48 F6
Great Dowles BS30 ....66 A4
Great George St
 Bristol BS1 ....140 C2
 Bristol BS2 ....141 C3
Great Hayles Rd BS14 ....80 A6
Great Leaze BS30 ....66 A4
Great Park Rd BS32 ....24 B3
Great Pulteney St BA2 ....142 C3
Great Stanhope St BA1 ....142 A2
Great Stoke BS34 ....37 A5
Great Stoke Way
 Bristol, Harry Stoke BS34 ....37 A5
 Bristol, Harry Stoke BS34 ....36 D3
Great Western Cl BS34 ....36 F4
Great Western La BS5 ....64 C6
Great Western Rd BS21 ....57 D2
Great Weston Bsns Pk
 BS37 ....27 B3
Greatstone La BS40 ....94 F5
Green Cl BS7 ....50 A8
Green Cotts BA2 ....102 C2
Green Croft BS5 ....51 A1
Green Dell Cl BS10 ....34 D3
Green Ditch La BA3 ....137 B6
Green Dragon Rd BS36 ....37 D5
Green Hayes BS37 ....40 C8
Green Hill BS35 ....15 A4
Green La Avonmouth BS11 ....33 B1
 Blagdon BS40 ....111 A7
 Easter Compton BS35 ....22 C1
 Failand BS8 ....61 C4
 Farrington Gurney BS39 ....130 F6
 Felton BS40 ....94 C3
 Freshford BA3 ....120 B2
 Hinton Charterhouse BA3 ....119 E1
 Marshfield SN14 ....69 E8
 Priddy BS40 ....127 B7
 Rangeworthy BS37,GL12 ....17 B2
 Stratton On The Fosse BA3 ....137 E1
 Tytherington GL12 ....16 B8
 Winsley BA15 ....120 F6
 Winterbourne BS16 ....37 E2
Green Park Rd BA1 ....142 B2
Green Parlor Rd BA3 ....133 D1
Green Pastures Rd BS48 ....60 B2
Green Pk BA1 ....142 B2
Green Side BS16 ....51 D5
Green St Bath BA1 ....142 C2
 Bristol BS3 ....63 F4
 Peasedown St John BA2 ....133 E5
Green The Backwell BS48 ....76 A5
 Bath BA2 ....101 D1
 Bristol BS16 ....51 C2
 Bristol BS34 ....36 E4
 Cromhall GL12 ....17 B8
 Hinton Charterhouse BA3 ....119 F1
 Locking BS24 ....106 A4
 Olveston BS35 ....14 A2
 Pill BS20 ....47 D4
 Winscombe BS25 ....125 A7
Green Tree Rd BA3 ....132 B3
Greenacre BS22 ....88 E4
Greenacre Rd BS14 ....80 A3
Greenacres Bath BA1 ....84 B3
 Bristol BS9 ....48 E7
Greenacres Park Homes
 BS36 ....38 E5
Greenbank Ave BS5 ....50 C1
Greenbank Ave W BS5 ....50 C1
Greenbank Gdns BA1 ....84 B1
Greenbank Rd Bristol BS15 ....65 A4
 Bristol BS3 ....63 B3
 Bristol BS5 ....50 D2
Greenbank View BS5 ....50 D2
Greendale Rd Bristol BS3 ....63 E2
 Bristol BS6 ....49 B3
Greendown Ave BS13 ....79 C5
Greenditch Ave BS13 ....79 C5
Greenditch Ct BS13 ....79 C5
Greenditch St BS35 ....13 D1
Greendown BS5 ....65 A7
Greendown Pl BA2 ....102 A1
Greenfield Ave BS10 ....49 D8
Greenfield Cres BS48 ....59 F3
Greenfields Pk BS20 ....45 C3
Greenfield Pl BS23 ....104 D8
Greenfield Rd BS10 ....35 D1
Greenfields Ave BS29 ....107 A3
Greengage Cl BS22 ....105 E8
Greenhaven 5 BS5 ....50 C1
Greenhill BS35 ....15 A4
Greenhill Cl Nailsea BS48 ....59 D2
 Weston-Super-Mare BS22 ....105 C8
Greenhill Gdns BS35 ....15 A5
Greenhill Gr BS3 ....63 A2
Greenhill La Alveston BS35 ....14 F4
 Bristol BS11 ....34 B2
 Sandford BS25 ....108 B4
Greenhill Par 6 BS35 ....15 A5
Greenhill Pl BA3 ....132 A3

Greenhill Rd Alveston BS35 ....15 A5
 Midsomer Norton BA3 ....132 A3
 Sandford BS25 ....108 B4
Greenland Rd BS22 ....88 D1
Greenlands Rd BA2 ....133 C8
Greenlands Way BS10 ....34 F4
Greenleaze BS4 ....64 B1
Greenleaze Ave BS16 ....37 D1
Greenleaze Cl BS16 ....37 D1
Greenmore Rd BS4 ....64 B2
Greenore BS15 ....65 C7
Greenpark Rd BS10 ....35 E1
Greenridge BS39 ....114 F3
Greenridge Cl BS13 ....78 E4
Greenside Cl BS10 ....34 D3
Greenslade Gdns BS48 ....59 D3
Greenslade Inf Sch BS48 ....59 D3
Greensplott Rd BS11 ....33 E7
Greenvale Cl BA3 ....116 B1
Greenvale Dr BA3 ....116 B1
Greenvale Rd BS31 ....131 D5
Greenview BS30 ....66 A2
Greenway BA3 ....134 C1
Greenway Bush La BS3 ....63 A4
Greenway Ct BA2 ....101 F4
Greenway Dr BS10 ....49 D8
Greenway Ho 10 BS6 ....49 B2
Greenway La Bath BA2 ....102 A4
 Cold Ashton SN14 ....68 D5
Greenway Pk Bristol BS10 ....49 D8
 3 Clevedon BS21 ....57 F3
Greenway Rd BS6 ....49 B2
Greenway The BS16 ....51 C3
Greenways Bristol BS15 ....52 A1
 Chilcompton BA3 ....137 C2
Greenways Rd BS37 ....27 E3
Greenwell La BS40 ....109 C7
Greenwood Cl BS7 ....49 E7
Greenwood Dr BS35 ....14 F4
Greenwood Rd Bristol BS4 ....64 A1
 Weston-Super-Mare BS22 ....88 E2
Gregory Ct BS30 ....66 A6
Gregory Mead BS49 ....74 A1
Gregorys Gr BA2 ....118 D8
Gregorys Tyning BS39 ....131 F6
Greinton BS24 ....105 A2
Grenville Ave BS24 ....106 A4
Grenville Cl BS5 ....64 F8
Grenville Pl 7 BS1 ....62 F5
Grenville Rd BS6 ....49 E3
Greve Cl BS30 ....65 F4
Greville Rd BS3 ....63 B4
Greville St BS3 ....63 C4
Greyfield Comm BS39 ....115 C2
Greyfield Rd BS39 ....115 C2
Greyfield View BS39 ....114 F1
Greylands Rd BS13 ....78 F7
Greystoke Ave BS10 ....35 C1
Greystoke Gdns BS9 ....48 A8
Greystones BS16 ....37 F1
Grib La BS40 ....112 F2
Griffin Cl BS22 ....89 B2
Griffin Ct BA1 ....142 B2
Griffin Rd BS21 ....57 E3
Griggfield Wlk BS14 ....80 A7
Grimsbury Park Specl Sch
 BS30 ....66 B7
Grimsbury Rd BS15 ....66 A7
Grindell Rd BS5 ....64 D7
Grinfield Ave BS13 ....79 C4
Grinfield Cl BS13 ....79 C4
Grinfield Ct BS13 ....79 C4
Grittleton Rd BS7 ....49 E8
Grosvenor Bridge Rd BA1 ....85 C1
Grosvenor Ct 2 BS6 ....49 B1
Grosvenor High Sch BA1 ....85 B1
Grosvenor Pk BA1 ....85 C1
Grosvenor Pl BA1 ....85 C1
Grosvenor Rd BS2 ....49 F1
Grosvenor Terr BA1 ....85 C2
Grosvenor Villas 9 BA1 ....85 C2
Grove Ave Bristol BS1 ....141 A1
 3 Bristol BS16 ....50 F4
 Bristol BS9 ....48 C7
Grove Bank BS16 ....37 C1
Grove Ct BS9 ....48 C5
Grove Dr BS9 ....48 C5
Grove End BS34 ....36 B8
Grove Jun Sch BS48 ....75 D8
Grove La Faulkland BA3 ....134 D2
 Hinton SN14 ....54 C6
 Weston-Super-Mare BS23 ....104 D6
Grove Leaze BS11 ....47 D6
Grove Orch BS40 ....110 E2
Grove Park Ave BS4 ....64 D2
Grove Park Ct BS23 ....87 D1
Grove Pk Bristol BS6 ....49 B1
 Weston-Super-Mare BS23 ....87 D1
Grove Park Rd BS4 ....64 D2
Grove Park Terr BS16 ....50 F4
Grove Rd Bristol BS6 ....49 C2
 Bristol BS16 ....50 D6
 Bristol BS16 ....36 B7
 Bristol BS9 ....48 B6
 Paulton BS39 ....131 B7
 Rangeworthy BS37 ....27 A8
 Weston-Super-Mare BS25 ....107 F1

Grove The *continued*
Wraxall BS48 .... 60 C3
Grove View BS16 .... 50 E6
Grove Wood Rd BA3 .... 132 F1
Groves The BS13 .... 79 D4
Grovesend Rd
  Thornbury BS35 .... 15 D8
  Thornbury BS35 .... 8 B1
Guernsey Ave BS4 .... 64 F4
Guest Ave BS16 .... 52 B7
Gug The BS39 .... 115 C2
Guild Ct BS1 .... 141 B2
Guildford Rd BS4 .... 64 E6
Guinea La Bath BA1 .... 142 C3
  Bristol BS16 .... 51 A4
  Bristol BS16 .... 51 A5
Guinea St BS1 .... 141 A1
Gullen BA2 .... 134 A6
Gulliford's Bank BS21 .... 57 F2
Gullimores Gdns BS13 .... 79 B4
Gullivers Pl BS37 .... 40 A8
Gullock Tyning BA3 .... 132 B1
Gullon Wlk BS13 .... 78 F5
Gullons Cl BS13 .... 79 A6
Gully La BS35 .... 3 D2
Gully The BS36 .... 37 F7
Gullybrook La **3** BS5 ...... 64 B6
Gunning Cl BS15 .... 65 D6
Gunter's Hill BS5 .... 65 A6
Guthrie Rd BS8 .... 142 A4
Gwilliam St BS3 .... 63 D3
Gwyn St BS2 .... 49 E1
Gypsy La Keynsham BS31 ..... 99 B8
  Marshfield SN14 .... 69 F7

H

Haberfield Hill BS8 .... 47 E2
Haberfield Ho **6** BS8 .... 62 F6
Hacket Hill BS35 .... 15 F8
Hacket La BS35 .... 15 F8
Hadley Ct BS30 .... 66 B6
Hadley Rd BA2 .... 102 B2
Hadrian Cl BS9 .... 48 C4
Haig Cl BS9 .... 48 B7
Halbrow Cres BS16 .... 51 C5
Haldon Cl BS3 .... 63 D1
Hale Cl BS15 .... 65 D4
Hales Horn Cl BS32 .... 36 D6
Halfacre Cl BS14 .... 80 A3
Halfacre La BS14 .... 80 B4
Halfpenny Row BA3 .... 136 E1
Halifax Rd BS37 .... 27 D4
Hall End La Cold Ashton BA1 ... 68 B3
Hall La Cold Ashton BA1,SN14 ... 68 E2
  Horton BS37 .... 29 E5
Hall Sch The BS25 .... 125 B8
Hall St BS3 .... 63 C2
Hallam Cl BS21 .... 57 C4
Hallam Rd BS21 .... 57 C4
Hallards Cl BS11 .... 47 F8
Hallatrow Rd BS39 .... 131 C6
Hallen Cl BS10 .... 34 D2
Hallen Dr BS9 .... 48 C7
Hallen Ind Est BS10 .... 34 A7
Hallen Rd BS10 .... 34 D4
Halletts Way BS20 .... 45 D5
Halliwell Rd BS20 .... 44 D4
Halls Rd BS15 .... 65 D8
Halsbury Rd BS6 .... 49 B4
Halstock Ave BS16 .... 50 F3
Halston Dr BS2 .... 141 C4
Halswell Gdns BS13 .... 79 B4
Halswell Rd BS21 .... 57 D1
Halt End BS14 .... 80 C3
Halwyn Cl BS9 .... 48 D5
Ham Cl BS39 .... 114 F1
Ham Farm La BS16 .... 52 B6
Ham Gn BS20 .... 47 D3
Ham Gr BS39 .... 131 E5
Ham La Bishop Sutton BS39 .. 113 C5
  Bristol BS16 .... 50 E6
  Doynton BS30 .... 53 E1
  Dundry BS41 .... 78 A3
  Farrington Gurney BS39 ..... 130 F5
  Kingston Seymour BS21 ...... 73 B2
  North End BS49 .... 74 A3
  Paulton BS39 .... 131 E5
  Thornbury BS35 .... 7 C1
  Wraxall BS48 .... 60 B4
  Yatton BS49 .... 74 A3
Ham Link BS40 .... 109 F3
Ham Rd BS24,TA8 .... 121 B3
Ham Wood Cl BS24 .... 105 E2
Hamble Cl BS35 .... 15 C8
Hambledon Rd BS22 .... 89 C4
Hambrook La BS34 .... 37 A3
Hambrook Prim Sch BS16 .... 37 D3
Hamilton Rd Bath BA1 .... 84 E2
  Bristol BS3 .... 63 C3
  Bristol BS3 .... 64 B8
  Weston-Super-Mare BS23 .... 87 C1
Hamilton Terr BA2 .... 133 F5
Hamlet The BA2 .... 60 A3
Hammersley La BA1 .... 13 A3
Hammersmith Rd BS5 .... 64 D8
Hammond Cl BS4 .... 64 E1
Hammond Gdns BS9 .... 48 E7
Hampden Cl BS37 .... 27 D4
Hampden Rd Bristol BS4 ..... 64 B3
  Weston-Super-Mare BS22 .... 88 E2
Hampshire Way BS37 .... 27 F4

Hampstead Rd BS4 .... 64 C3
Hampton Cl BS30 .... 66 A5
Hampton Cnr BS11 .... 47 E6
Hampton Ct BS6 .... 49 B1
Hampton Ho **10** BA1 .... 85 C1
Hampton La **7** BS6 .... 49 B1
Hampton Pk BS6 .... 49 B1
Hampton Rd BS6 .... 49 B1
Hampton Row BA2 .... 102 B8
Hampton St BS15 .... 51 D1
Hampton View BA1 .... 85 B1
Hams La BS26 .... 123 C3
Hams Rd BS5 .... 81 F7
Hanbury Cl BS15 .... 65 D5
Hanbury Ct BS8 .... 140 A4
Hanbury Rd BS8 .... 140 A4
Handel Ave **2** BS5 .... 64 E7
Handel Rd BS31 .... 81 E5
Handford Way BS30 .... 66 B3
Hanford Ct BS14 .... 80 D7
Hang Hill BA2 .... 134 A6
Hanham Abbots Jun Sch
  BS15 .... 65 C4
Hanham Bsns Pk BS15 .... 65 B5
Hanham Hall Hospl BS15 ..... 65 C4
Hanham High Sch BS15 .... 65 C4
Hanham La BS39 .... 131 F7
Hanham Rd BS15 .... 65 C5
Hanham Way BS48 .... 59 B2
Hanna Cl BA2 .... 101 B6
Hannah More Cl BS40 .... 92 E2
Hannah More Inf Sch
  BS8 .... 75 D8
Hannah More Prim Sch
  BS1 .... 141 B2
Hannah More Rd BS48 .... 75 C8
Hanny's La BS40 .... 96 C3
Hanover Cl BS22 .... 89 A4
Hanover Ct Bath BA1 .... 85 B2
  Bristol BS1 .... 141 B3
  Bristol BS34 .... 36 A3
  Radstock BA3 .... 133 C2
Hanover Ho BS2 .... 64 A7
Hanover Pl Bath BA1 .... 102 B8
  Bristol BS1 .... 140 B1
Hanover St **2** Bath BA1 .... 85 B1
  2 Bristol BS1 .... 141 A2
  Bristol BS5 .... 64 A7
Hanover Terr **5** BA1 .... 85 B1
Hans Price Cl BS23 .... 104 E8
Hans Price Ho **18** BS23 ... 104 E8
Hansford Cl BA2 .... 101 E1
Hansford Sq BA2 .... 57 C2
Hanson's Way **3** BS21 ..... 57 C2
Hantone Hill BA2 .... 102 F8
Happerton La BS20 .... 47 D2
Hapsburg Cl BS22 .... 89 A4
Harbour Rd BS20 .... 45 E6
Harbour Road Trad Est
  BS20 .... 45 F6
Harbour Wall BS9 .... 48 B4
Harbour Way BS1 .... 140 C1
Harbury Rd BS9 .... 49 C7
Harbutts BA2 .... 85 F4
Harcombe Hill BS36 .... 37 E4
Harcombe Rd BS36 .... 37 D5
Harcourt Ave BS5 .... 65 A6
Harcourt Cl BS31 .... 82 E2
Harcourt Gdns BA1 .... 84 A3
Harcourt Hill BS6 .... 49 C3
Harcourt Rd BS6 .... 49 B3
Harden Rd BS14 .... 80 E5
Hardenhuish Rd BS4 .... 64 D5
Harding Pl BS31 .... 82 F3
Hardington Dr BS31 .... 82 A2
Hardwick Cl Bristol BS4 ...... 64 D5
  Bristol BS4 .... 64 E3
Hardwick Rd BS20 .... 47 C5
Hardwicke BS37 .... 39 C7
Hardy Ave BS3 .... 63 A3
Hardy Ct BS30 .... 65 F5
Hardy La BS32 .... 14 A1
Hardy Rd BS3 .... 63 B2
Hareclive Prim Sch BS13 ..... 79 C4
Hareclive Rd BS13 .... 79 C4
Harefield Cl BS15 .... 65 C2
Harescombe BS37 .... 39 E7
Harewood Cl BS6 .... 49 A3
Harewood Rd BS5 .... 51 A1
Harford Cl BS9 .... 48 C7
Harford Dr BS16 .... 37 C1
Harford Sq BS40 .... 96 B3
Harington Pl **2** BA1 .... 142 B2
Harlech Way BS30 .... 66 B2
Harleston St **4** BS5 .... 64 B7
Harley Ct **1** BS8 .... 62 F7
Harley La BS21 .... 58 C6
Harley Mews **2** BS8 .... 62 F7
Harley Pl **4** BS8 .... 62 F7
Harley St BA1 .... 142 B4
Harmony Dr BS20 .... 44 F4
Harnhill Cl BS13 .... 79 B4
Harolds Way BS15 .... 65 C6
Harptree BS24 .... 105 A2
Harptree Cl BS48 .... 75 D8
Harptree Ct **8** BS30 .... 66 A4
Harptree Gr BS3 .... 63 B2
Harptree Hill BS40 .... 128 B5
Harrington Ave BS14 .... 80 E6
Harrington Cl BS30 .... 82 D8
Harrington Gr BS14 .... 80 E6
Harrington Rd BS14 .... 80 E6
Harrington Wlk BS14 .... 80 E6
Harris Barton BS36 .... 38 B7
Harris Ct BS30 .... 65 F4
Harris La BS8 .... 61 F8
Harrison Cl BS16 .... 52 B6

Harrow Rd BS4 .... 64 D3
Harrowdene Rd BS4 .... 64 B3
Harry Stoke Rd BS34 .... 36 E2
Hart's La BS39 .... 131 B7
Hartcliffe Rd BS4 .... 79 E8
Hartcliffe Sch BS13 .... 79 E4
Hartcliffe Way
  BS3, BS4, BS13 .... 79 C7
Hartcliffe Wlk BS4 .... 79 F8
Hartfield Ave BS6 .... 140 C4
Hartgill Cl BS13 .... 79 B3
Hartington Pk BS6 .... 49 C2
Hartland **2** BS22 .... 89 A2
Hartland Ho BS5 .... 64 C6
Hartley Cl BS37 .... 28 C1
Harts Croft BS37 .... 27 F4
Harts Paddock BA3 .... 137 E7
Harvest Cl BS32 .... 24 D1
Harvest La BS24 .... 106 B8
Harvest Way BS22 .... 89 A5
Harvey Cl BS22 .... 89 A4
Harwood Gdns BS22 .... 88 E4
Harwood Ho **16** BS5 .... 64 B7
Haselbury Gr BS31 .... 82 E2
Haskins Ct **4** BS30 .... 66 A4
Haslands BS48 .... 75 D8
Haslemere Ind Est BS11 ..... 33 C2
Hassage Hill BA2 .... 134 E7
Hassell Dr BS2 .... 64 A7
Hastings Cl BS3 .... 63 C1
Hastings Rd BS3 .... 63 C1
Hatchet Hill BA3 .... 139 E4
Hatchet La BS34 .... 36 E5
Hatchet Rd BS34 .... 36 E5
Hatchmere BS35 .... 15 D8
Hatfield Bldgs BA2 .... 102 B5
Hatfield Rd Bath BA2 .... 101 F3
  Weston-Super-Mare BS23 .... 105 A8
Hatherley BS37 .... 39 E7
Hatherley Rd BS7 .... 49 E4
Hathway Wlk BS5 .... 64 A8
Hatters' La BS37 .... 28 C1
Havage Dro BS24 .... 107 D8
Haven The BS15 .... 51 E1
Haversham Cl BS22 .... 88 D1
Haverstock Rd BS4 .... 64 A3
Haviland Gr BA1 .... 84 B3
Haviland Ho **7** BS2 .... 141 C3
Haviland Pk BA1 .... 84 B2
Havory BA1 .... 85 C1
Haweya Rd BS40 .... 109 E8
Haw La BS35 .... 14 B3
Hawarden Terr BA1 .... 85 B1
Haweswater Cl BS30 .... 66 D6
Hawke Rd BS22 .... 88 E4
Hawkesbury Prim Sch
  GL9 .... 19 F3
Hawkesbury Rd
  Bristol BS16 .... 50 E3
  Hillesley GL12 .... 19 D6
Hawkesley Dr BS34 .... 36 C6
Hawkfield Bsns Pk BS14 ..... 79 D5
Hawkfield Cl BS14 .... 79 D5
Hawkfield Way BS14 .... 79 D5
Hawkins Cl BS30 .... 66 C5
Hawkins Cres BS32 .... 36 E8
Hawkins St BS2 .... 141 C3
Hawkley Dr BS32 .... 24 D3
Hawkmoor La BS16 .... 50 E8
Hawkridge Dr BS16 .... 53 C5
Hawksmoor Cl BS14 .... 80 A6
Hawksworth Dr
  Weston-Super-Mare BS22 .... 89 C4
Hawthorn Ave BS15 .... 65 B5
Hawthorn Cl Bristol BS34 ... 35 D7
  Charfield GL12 .... 11 A4
  Portishead BS20 .... 44 F5
Hawthorn Coombe BS22 ..... 88 E3
Hawthorn Cres
  Thornbury BS35 .... 8 C2
  .... 74 A2
Hawthorn Gdns BS22 .... 88 D2
Hawthorn Hill BS22 .... 88 E2
Hawthorn Hts BS22 .... 88 D3
Hawthorn Pk BS22 .... 88 E3
Hawthorn Rd BA3 .... 133 B2
Hawthorn Way Bristol BS34 . 36 E5
  Nailsea BS48 .... 60 A2
Hawthorne Cl BS16 .... 53 C5
Hawthorne Gdns BS16 .... 51 F4
Hawthorne St BS4 .... 64 A3
Hawthornes The BS16 .... 51 F4
Hawthorns La BS31 .... 81 E5
Hawthorns The BS21 .... 57 C3
Hay Ct BS20 .... 44 E4
Hay Hill BA1 .... 142 B3
Hay Leaze BS37 .... 27 D4
Hay St
  Farrington Gurney BS39 .... 137 A8
  .... 70 A8
Hayboro Way BS39 .... 131 E4
Haycombe BS14 .... 79 F6
Haycombe Dr BA2 .... 101 A4
Haycombe La BA2 .... 100 F3
Haycroft La GL13 .... 4 C6
Haycroft Rd BS34 .... 36 A3
Hayden Cl BA2 .... 142 A1
Haydock Cl BS16 .... 37 F1
Haydon Gate **12** BA3 ..... 49 A2
Haydon Gate BA3 .... 138 F8
Haydon Gdns BS7 .... 50 B5
Haydon Hill BA3 .... 139 A8

Haydon Ind Est BA3 .... 138 F8
Haye's La GL9 .... 30 F2
Hayeley Dr BS32 .... 36 E6
Hayes Cl BS2 .... 64 A7
Hayes Ct BS34 .... 36 A7
Hayes Park Rd BA3 .... 133 F1
Hayes Rd BA3 .... 131 F1
Hayesfield Pk BA2 .... 142 B1
Hayesfield Sch BA2 .... 101 D6
Hayesfield Sch Tech Coll
  BA2 .... 142 A1
Hayeswood Rd BA3 .... 115 E3
Hayfield SN14 .... 70 A8
Haygarth Ct BA1 .... 142 B4
Hayleigh Ho BS13 .... 79 C4
Haymarket The BS1 .... 141 A3
Hayne La BS24 .... 105 A2
Haynes La BS16 .... 51 D5
Hayter Ct BS10 .... 35 D3
Haythorn Ct **8** BS16 ...... 50 E3
Haytor Pk BS9 .... 48 D6
Hayward Cl BS21 .... 57 C1
Hayward Ind Est **1** BS16 ... 51 D3
Hayward Rd Bristol BS16 .... 51 D3
  Bristol BS5 .... 64 D7
Haywood Cl BS24 .... 105 A1
Haywood Gdns BS24 .... 105 B1
Hazel Ave BS6 .... 49 B2
Hazel Cote Rd BS14 .... 80 B4
Hazel Cres BS35 .... 8 D1
Hazel Gdns BS35 .... 15 A4
Hazel Gr Bath BA2 .... 101 D4
  Bristol BS7 .... 50 A8
Midsomer Norton BA3 ...... 138 B8
Hazel La Alveston BS35 ...... 14 F2
  Tockington BS32 .... 14 E3
Hazel Terr BA3 .... 138 C8
Hazel Way BA2 .... 118 D8
Hazelbury Dr BS30 .... 66 C6
Hazelbury Rd Bristol BS14 .. 80 C7
  Nailsea BS48 .... 59 D1
Hazeldene Rd Bristol BS34 .. 36 A7
  Weston-Super-Mare BS23 ... 105 A8
Hazelgrove BS36 .... 37 E5
Hazell Cl BS21 .... 57 E1
Hazelton Rd BS7 .... 49 C3
Hazelwood Ct BS9 .... 48 D3
Hazelwood Rd BS9 .... 48 D3
Hazleton Gdns BA2 .... 102 F3
Head Croft BS48 .... 77 B8
Headford Ave BS5 .... 65 B7
Headford Rd BS4 .... 63 D1
Headington Cl BS15 .... 65 D4
Headley Ct BS13 .... 79 B6
Headley La BS13 .... 79 B7
Headley Park Ave BS13 ...... 79 B7
Headley Park Prim Sch
  BS13 .... 79 B6
Headley Park Rd BS13 .... 79 A6
Headley Rd BS13 .... 79 A6
Headley Wlk BS13 .... 79 B6
Heart Meers BS14 .... 80 B5
Heath Cl BS16 .... 37 E6
Heath Ct BS16 .... 51 D7
Heath Gdns Bristol BS16 .... 51 D8
  Bristol BS16 .... 51 D8
Heath House La BS16,BS7 .... 50 C5
Heath Rd Bristol BS15 .... 65 B4
  Bristol BS16 .... 51 D8
  Bristol BS5 .... 50 B3
  Nailsea BS48 .... 59 F2
  Nailsea BS48 .... 59 F3
Heath Ridge BS41 .... 62 A2
Heath Rise BS30 .... 66 B5
Heath St BS5 .... 50 C3
Heath Wlk BS16 .... 51 D7
Heathcote Dr BS36 .... 38 D7
Heathcote La BS36 .... 38 D7
Heathcote Rd
  Bristol, Chester Park BS16 .. 51 B2
  Bristol, Staple Hill BS16 .... 51 E5
Heathcote Wlk BS16 .... 51 C2
Heather Ave BS36 .... 38 B6
Heather Cl BS15 .... 51 B1
Heather Dr BA2 .... 118 D8
Heatherdene BS14 .... 79 F7
Heathfield Cl Bath BA1 ...... 84 A3
  Keynsham BS31 .... 81 C5
Heathfield Cres BS14 .... 80 B4
Heathfield Rd BS48 .... 59 E2
Heathfield Way BS48 .... 59 E2
Heathfields BS16 .... 51 D8
Heathgate BS49 .... 91 B8
Heathgate BS23 .... 104 D4
Hebden Rd BA15 .... 120 E7
Heber St BS5 .... 64 C7
Hebron Rd **9** BS3 .... 63 C3
Hedge Cl BS24 .... 106 B8
Hedgemead Cl BS16 .... 50 E5
Hedgemead View BS16 ...... 50 E5
Hedges Cl **3** BS21 .... 57 B1
Hedges The BS22 .... 89 C3
Hedwick Ave BS5 .... 64 F7
Hedwick St BS5 .... 64 F7
Heggard Cl BS13 .... 79 A5
Helens Rd BS25 .... 108 B4
Hellier Wlk BS13 .... 79 C3
Helston Rd BS48 .... 60 A1
Helting Ct **7** BA1 .... 142 B2
Hemming Way BS24 .... 105 E3
Hemmings Par **3** BS5 ..... 64 B7
Hemplow Cl BS14 .... 80 D7

Hempton La BA2 ....
Hen La BS40 ....
Henacre Rd BS11 ....
Henbury Ct BS10 ....
Henbury Gdns BS10 ....
Henbury Hill BS9 ....
Henbury Manor Sch BS10 ... 3
Henbury Rd Bristol BS10 ....
  Bristol BS15 6
Henbury Road Henbury Hill
  BS9 ....
Henbury Sch BS10 3
Hencliffe Rd BS14 8
Hencliffe Way BS15 6
Henderson Ho **1** BS2 14
Henderson Rd BS15 6
Hendre Rd BS3 ....
Heneage La GL12 ....
Henfield Cres BS30 6
Henfield Rd BS36 3
Hengaston St BS3 6
Hengrove Ave BS14 8
Hengrove La BS14 8
Hengrove Rd BS4 6
Hengrove Sch BS14 8
Hengrove Way Bristol BS13 . 7
  Bristol BS14 7
Henleaze Ave BS9 4
Henleaze Gdns BS9 4
Henleaze Jun & Inf Schs
  BS9 4
Henleaze Park BS9 4
Henleaze Park Dr BS9 4
Henleaze Rd BS9 4
Henleaze Terr BS9 4
Henley Gr BS9 4
Henley La BS49 9
Henley Lodge Bath BA1 1
  Yatton BS49 9
Henley Pk BS49 9
Henley View BA2 11
Hennessy Cl BS14 8
Henrietta Ct BA2 14
Henrietta Gdns BA2 14
Henrietta Mews BA2 14
Henrietta Pl BA2 14
Henrietta Rd BA2 14
Henrietta St Bath BA2 14
  3 Bristol BS5 5
Henry Butt Ho **11** BS23 .. 10
Henry St Bath BA1 14
Henry Williamson Ct **1**
  BS30 6
Henshaw Cl BS15 5
Henshaw Rd BS15 5
Henshaw Wlk BS15 5
Hensley Gdns BA2 10
Hensley Rd BA2 10
Hensman's Hill BS8 14
Hepburn Rd BS2 ....
Herald Cl BS9 4
Herapath St BS5 6
Herbert Cres BS5 5
Herbert Rd Bath BA2 10
  Clevedon BS21 5
Herbert St Bristol BS3 6
  Bristol BS5 6
Hercules Cl BS34 ....
Hereford Rd BS2 5
Hereford St BS3 6
Heritage Cl BA2 11
Heritage The
  Peasedown St John BA3 11
  Peasedown St John BA3 13
Herkomer Cl BS7 5
Herluin Way BS22,BS23 4
Hermes Cl BS31 9
Hermitage Cl BS11 4
Hermitage Rd Bath BA1 8
Hern La BS48 7
Heron Cl BS22 10
Heron Ct BS21 5
Heron Gdns BS20 4
Heron Rd BS5 6
Heron Way BS37 4
Herridge Cl BS13 7
Herridge Rd BS13 7
Hersey Gdns BS13 7
Hesding Cl BS15 6
Hestercombe Rd BS13 7
Hewish Ct BS23 11
Hewland Ct BS11 3
Heyron Wlk BS13 7
Heywood Rd BS20 4
Heywood Terr BS20 4
Hibbs Cl SN14 7
Hickling Ct **8** BS15 5
Hicks Ct BS30 6
Hide Mkt BS2 6
High Acre BS39 13
High Bannerdown BA1 8
High Down Jun & Inf Schs
  BS20 4
High Elm BS15 6
High Gr BS9 4
High Mdws BA3 13
High Mead Gdns BS39 13
High Pk Bristol BS14 8
  Paulton BS39 13
High St Axbridge BS26 12
  Badminton GL9 ....

ontinued
3S29 ...107 A2
...142 C2
...101 B6
ston BA1 ...84 B1
ton BA2 ...85 F1
on BA1 ...85 F3
BA1 ...86 D2
30 ...82 E8
3S40 ...110 E3
1 ...141 A2
11 ...47 E6
16 ...51 D4
30 ...66 D4
5 ...50 B1
8 ...49 A2
9 ...49 A7
efferies Hill BS15 ...65 C5
ingswood BS15 ...65 E8
armley BS15 ...66 B8
gna BS40 ...96 A3
Sodbury BS37 ...28 B1
n BS49 ...74 F1
ury BS49 ...91 D4
BS30 ...53 F1
SN14 ...54 D4
otree BS40 ...128 F5
BA3 ...120 B5
ury Upton GL9 ...19 F3
eton BS39 ...115 D1
GL12 ...19 D8
arterhouse BA3 ...119 E1
n BS37 ...26 D4
n BS31 ...81 E6
d GL12 ...11 F4
d SN14 ...69 F8
r Norton BA3 ...132 B1
3S48 ...59 F3
Philip BA3 ...135 E4
S39 ...131 E5
Plummer's Hill
...131 E6
BS39 ...97 E4
BS20 ...46 E3
d BS20 ...45 D5
...136 F1
BS31 ...82 F3
ton BA3 ...130 E1
y BS35 ...15 B8
BA3 ...116 B2
A2 ...118 D1
Super-Mare BS22 ...88 E2
Super-Mare BS23 ...104 D8
0 ...67 D6
GL12 ...18 A5
3S40 ...95 A7
urne BS36 ...37 D6
BA1 ...84 F6
BS40 ...92 D2
49 ...91 C8
v BS20 ...45 A4
St 4 BS2 ...63 F4
Cotts 8 BA1 ...85 A1
Par BS23 ...87 C1
Pl BA1 ...85 A1
Rd Bristol BS3 ...63 C2
7 ...49 F7
S39 ...131 B7
Super-Mare BS23 ...87 C1
Terr 10 BA1 ...85 A1
Villas
BA1 ...85 A1
2 ...140 C4
t 4 Bristol BS30 ...66 C6
Super-Mare BS23 ...87 F1
t Jun Sch BS36 ...38 C8
Ave BS21 ...57 E3
Cl BS14 ...80 B4
Rd BS21 ...57 E3
Dr BS5 ...50 A1
Ave BS15 ...65 D5
Cl BA2 ...101 B5
Cres BA3 ...137 C4
Dr BS20 ...44 E3
Gdns BS30 ...66 C2
Gr BS7 ...49 D5
La
Martin BS40 ...128 B6
otree BS40 ...129 A3
37 ...29 E7
Rd
Sodbury BS37 ...28 A1
n BS31 ...81 F2
n St John BA2 ...133 C8
Super-Mare BS24 ...105 A1
s
ury Upton GL9 ...19 F2
Norton BA3 ...132 D2
BA3 ...132 E4
Drew BS39 ...96 F1
s Cl BS34 ...36 F3
e St BS4 ...64 A4
Cl BS22 ...88 B2
Cres 3 BS8 ...49 A2
Pl 13 BS8 ...49 A2
Rd BA2 ...101 B5
Sq 4 BS8 ...49 A2
Terr BA2 ...101 D6
s Dr GL11 ...5 E4
s La BS24 ...106 A8
s Rd
on BS41 ...62 A2
d BS20 ...45 B5
e Rd BS30 ...66 C4
d Gdns BS13 ...78 E4
e Ct BS7 ...50 B7
e Gdns BS7 ...50 C7
Cl BS34 ...24 B1

Highridge Cres BS13 ...78 F5
Highridge Gn BS13 ...78 E6
Highridge Inf Sch BS13 ...78 F6
Highridge Pk BS13 ...78 F6
Highridge Rd
Bristol BS13, BS41 ...78 E4
Bristol BS3 ...63 B2
Highridge Wlk BS13 ...78 E7
Highview Rd BS15 ...51 F2
Highwall La BS14, BS31 ...80 F1
Highway BS37 ...27 F2
Highwood La BS10, BS34 ...35 D7
Highwood Rd BS34 ...35 F7
Highworth Cres BS37 ...39 D8
Highworth Rd BS4 ...64 D6
Hildesheim Bridge BS23 ...104 F7
Hildesheim Cl BS23 ...104 F6
Hildeshiem Ct BS23 ...104 E7
Hilhouse BS9 ...48 C6
Hill Ave Bath BA2 ...101 F1
Bristol BS3 ...63 E3
Hill Burn BS9 ...49 C6
Hill Crest BS4 ...64 B1
Hill Ct BS39 ...131 E6
Hill Dr BS8 ...61 C3
Hill End Dr BS10 ...34 D3
Hill Gay Cl BS20 ...44 F4
Hill Gr BS9 ...49 C6
Hill House Rd BS16 ...51 F5
Hill La
Chipping Sodbury BS37 ...41 B7
Clevedon BS21 ...58 C4
Portishead BS20 ...44 F1
Rowberrow BS25 ...109 A1
Thornbury BS35 ...2 A2
Hill Lawn BS4 ...64 D3
Hill Moor BS21 ...57 E2
Hill Pk BS49 ...91 E5
Hill Rd Clevedon BS21 ...57 D4
Dundry BS41 ...78 D2
Sandford BS25 ...108 A3
Weston-Super-Mare BS22 ...88 E2
Weston-Super-Mare BS23 ...104 F8
Hill Rd E BS22 ...88 E2
Hill St Bristol BS1 ...140 C2
Bristol BS15 ...65 F8
Bristol BS3 ...63 F4
Bristol BS5 ...64 F8
Hill The Almondsbury BS32 ...24 B4
Freshford BA3 ...120 C5
Hill Top BS20 ...45 A4
Hill View Bristol BS16 ...51 D2
Bristol BS34 ...36 A3
Bristol BS8 ...140 B2
Bristol BS9 ...49 C6
Farrington Gurney BS39 ...131 B3
Marksbury BA2 ...99 B1
Priston BA2 ...117 A5
Hill View Cl BS30 ...66 C4
Hill View Ct BS22 ...105 D8
Hill View Rd Bath BA1 ...85 B2
Bristol BS13 ...79 A8
Pucklechurch BS16 ...53 C5
Weston-Super-Mare BS23 ...105 A7
Hill's Barton BS13 ...63 A1
Hillbrook Rd 5 BS35 ...15 D8
Hillburn Rd BS5 ...65 A8
Hillcote Est BS24 ...122 B8
Hillcrest
Peasedown St John BA2 ...133 C7
Pensford BS39 ...97 E3
Thornbury BS35 ...8 B1
Hillcrest Cl BS48 ...59 E1
Hillcrest Dr BA2 ...101 C4
Hillcrest Rd Nailsea BS48 ...59 E1
Portishead BS20 ...44 E4
Hillcroft Cl Bristol BS15 ...65 E4
Weston-Super-Mare BS22 ...88 A2
Hilldale Rd BS48 ...76 B5
Hillesley Prim Sch GL12 ...19 E8
Hillesley Rd GL12 ...11 F4
Hillfields Ave BS16 ...51 C3
Hillfields Prim Sch BS16 ...51 C2
Hillgrove St BS2 ...141 B4
Hillgrove St N BS2 ...141 A4
Hillgrove Terr BS23 ...104 D1
Hillier's La BS25 ...108 D4
Hillmead BS40 ...109 A5
Hillmer Rise BS29 ...106 F3
Hillpath BS29 ...107 B2
Hills Cl BS31 ...82 A5
Hillsborough BS8 ...140 A2
Hillsborough Ho BS23 ...105 A4
Hillsborough Rd BS4 ...64 C4
Hillsdon Rd BS9 ...48 F8
Hillside Bristol BS16 ...52 A5
Bristol BS6 ...140 C4
Burton SN14 ...43 A4
Portbury BS20 ...46 E3
Hillside Ave Bristol BS15 ...65 C8
Midsomer Norton BA3 ...137 F8
Hillside Cl
Frampton Cotterell BS36 ...38 C7
Paulton BS39 ...131 F6
Hillside Cres BA3 ...137 E8
Hillside Fst Sch BS22 ...88 E2
Hillside Gdns
Bishop Sutton BS39 ...113 C3
Weston-Super-Mare BS22 ...88 B1
Hillside Ho 5 BS6 ...49 D1
Hillside La BS36 ...38 C7
Hillside Rd Backwell BS48 ...76 A4
Bath BA2 ...101 D4
Bleadon BS24 ...122 B8
Bristol BS5 ...65 A7
Clevedon BS21 ...57 D3
Long Ashton BS41 ...62 B2
Midsomer Norton BA3 ...137 F8

Hillside Rd continued
Portishead BS20 ...44 D4
Hillside St BS4 ...64 A4
Hillside View
Midsomer Norton BA3 ...132 A3
Peasedown St John BA2 ...133 C8
Hillside W BS24 ...105 F2
Hilltop Gdns Bristol BS16 ...51 D2
Bristol BS5 ...65 A7
Hilltop Rd BS16 ...51 D2
Hilltop View BS5 ...65 A7
Hillview
Midsomer Norton BA3 ...137 E7
Timsbury BA3 ...116 B1
Hillview Ave BS21 ...57 D2
Hillview Gdns BS40 ...94 C8
Hillview Rd BS26 ...123 C4
Hillyfield Rd BS13 ...79 A6
Hillyfields BS25 ...125 B8
Hillyfields Way BS25 ...125 A8
Hilton Ct 5 BS5 ...64 B8
Hinckley Cl BS22 ...89 C4
Hind Pitts BS25 ...125 F7
Hinton BS24 ...105 A2
Hinton Cl Bath BA2 ...100 F6
Saltford BS31 ...82 E3
Hinton Dr BS30 ...66 C6
Hinton Hill BA2,BA3 ...119 A1
Hinton La 12 BS8 ...62 F6
Hinton Rd Bristol BS16 ...51 A4
Bristol BS5 ...50 C1
Hippisley Dr BS26 ...125 D2
Hiscocks Dr BA2 ...101 E4
Hitchen Cl SN14 ...69 F8
Hither Gn BS21 ...57 F2
Hither Green Ind Est BS21 ...57 F2
Hither Mead BS36 ...38 B6
Hoare's La BA3 ...139 B3
Hobart Rd BS23 ...104 F3
Hobb's La BS1 ...140 C2
Hobbiton Rd BS22 ...89 A4
Hobbs Ct BS48 ...59 F2
Hobbs La
Barrow Gurney BS48 ...77 E3
Bristol BS30 ...52 B1
Hobhouse Cl BS9 ...49 C7
Hobwell La BS41 ...62 C2
Hockeys La BS16 ...51 A4
Hockley Ct BA1 ...84 D1
Hoddon La BS16 ...53 D5
Hodshill BA2 ...118 F6
Hoecroft Gdns BA3 ...137 D3
Hogarth Mews BS22 ...89 A3
Hogarth Wlk Bristol BS7 ...50 C7
Weston-Super-Mare BS22 ...89 A3
Hogues Wlk BS13 ...79 B4
Holbeach Way BS14 ...80 A2
Holbrook Cres BS13 ...79 D4
Holbrook La BS30 ...67 B7
Holburne Mus
& Crafts Study Ctr BA2 ...102 B7
Holcombe BS14 ...80 A5
Holcombe Cl BA2 ...85 F1
Holcombe Gn BA1 ...84 B2
Holcombe Gr BS31 ...81 D5
Holcombe La BA2 ...85 F1
Holcombe Vale BA2 ...85 F1
Holdenhurst Rd BS15 ...51 C1
Holders Wlk BS41 ...77 F8
Holford Cl BS48 ...59 E1
Holford Ct BS14 ...80 B5
Holland Rd Bath BA1 ...85 B1
Clevedon BS21 ...57 B1
Holland St BS23 ...105 A8
Hollidge Gdns 3 BS3 ...63 D4
Hollies La BA1 ...86 A6
Hollies The Bristol BS15 ...65 E6
Midsomer Norton BA3 ...132 A1
Hollis Ave BS20 ...45 C3
Hollis Cl BS41 ...78 A8
Hollis Cres BS20 ...45 C3
Hollis Gdns SN14 ...31 E4
Hollister's Dr BS13 ...79 D4
Hollow La BS22 ...88 F3
Hollow Marsh La
BA3, BS39 ...130 B4
Hollow Rd
Almondsbury BS32 ...24 A4
Bristol BS15 ...65 E8
Shipham BS25 ...125 F8
Hollow The Bath BA2 ...101 B4
Peasedown St John BA2 ...117 D4
Holloway BA2 ...142 B1
Holloway Hill SN14 ...56 F7
Holloway Rd BS35 ...22 C4
Hollowbrook La
BS39,BS40 ...113 D6
Hollowmead BS49 ...91 E8
Hollowmead Cl BS49 ...91 F8
Hollows The BS36 ...38 D2
Hollway Cl BS14 ...80 E5
Hollway Rd BS14 ...80 E5
Holly Cl Alveston BS35 ...14 F4
Bristol BS5 ...51 A2
Nailsea BS48 ...60 A3
Pucklechurch BS16 ...53 C5
Weston-Super-Mare BS22 ...89 A1
Holly Cres BS15 ...51 E1
Holly Ct BS2 ...140 C4
Holly Dr Bath BA2 ...118 D8
Colerne SN14 ...70 F6
Holly Gn BS15 ...52 A1
Holly Gr BS16 ...51 C3
Holly Hill BS37 ...26 E3
Holly Hill Rd BS15 ...51 F1
Holly Ho BS11 ...34 C2
Holly La BS21 ...57 F6
Holly Lodge Cl BS5 ...51 A2

Holly Lodge Rd BS5 ...50 F2
Holly Ridge BS20 ...45 A5
Holly Wlk Keynsham BS31 ...81 D4
Radstock BA3 ...132 E1
Hollybush Cl
Acton Turville GL9 ...43 A6
Winsley BA15 ...120 E7
Hollybush La Bristol BS9 ...48 E5
Bristol BS9 ...48 F4
Hollyguest Rd BS15 ...65 E6
Hollyleigh Ave BS34 ...35 F2
Hollyman Wlk 5 BS21 ...57 F3
Hollymead La BS9 ...48 E4
Hollyridge BS14 ...80 C6
Hollywood La BS10, BS35 ...35 A7
Hollywood Rd BS4 ...64 D2
Holm La BS35 ...13 B2
Holm Rd BS24 ...105 E2
Holmdale Rd BS34 ...36 C3
Holmes Ct BS9 ...49 B5
Holmes Gr BS9 ...49 B5
Holmes Hill Rd BS5 ...64 F8
Holmes St BS5 ...64 B6
Holmesdale Rd BS3 ...63 E3
Holmlea BS20 ...45 F5
Holmoak Rd BS31 ...81 C4
Holms Rd BS23 ...105 A5
Holmwood BS15 ...65 C5
Holmwood Cl BS36 ...37 D6
Holmwood Gdns BS9 ...49 B8
Holroyd Ho BS3 ...63 D3
Holsom Cl BS14 ...80 F6
Holsom Rd BS14 ...80 F6
Holst Gdns BS4 ...79 D7
Holton Rd BS7 ...50 A6
Holtsdown La BA1 ...85 F7
Holwell Cl BS39 ...131 E4
Holy Cross
Catholic Prim Sch BS3 ...63 C4
Holy Family Prim Sch
BS34 ...36 B8
Holy Trinity Prim Sch
BS32 ...24 C2
Holy Well Cl BS4 ...64 E6
Holymead Inf Sch BS4 ...64 D2
Holymead Jun Sch BS4 ...64 D3
Holyrood Cl BS34 ...36 D4
Home Cl Bristol BS10 ...35 E2
Wrington BS40 ...92 E3
Home Farm Cl BA2 ...133 B7
Home Farm Rd BS8 ...62 B8
Home Farm Way BS35 ...23 A1
Home Field Cl BS16 ...52 B6
Home Ground Bristol BS11 ...47 D7
Bristol BS9 ...49 B7
Home Mead Bristol BS30 ...66 A4
Bristol BS4 ...79 E7
Home Orch
Chew Stoke BS40 ...112 D8
Yate BS37 ...27 D2
Homeapple Hill BS30 ...66 F6
Homeavon Ho BS31 ...81 F5
Homefield
Congresbury BS49 ...91 E3
Locking BS24 ...106 A5
Thornbury BS35 ...15 D8
Timsbury BA3 ...116 C2
Yate BS37 ...27 E3
Homefield Cl
Locking BS24 ...106 A5
Saltford BS31 ...82 E3
Winscombe BS25 ...107 F1
Homefield Dr BS16 ...51 A5
Homefield Ind Est BS24 ...106 A5
Homefield Rd
Pucklechurch BS16 ...53 B5
Saltford BS31 ...82 F3
Homeground Bristol BS16 ...52 B6
Clevedon BS21 ...57 F2
Homelea Pk E BA1 ...101 A7
Homelea Pk W BA1 ...101 A7
Homeleaze Rd BS10 ...35 D3
Homemead Dr BS4 ...64 D1
Homestead BS20 ...44 E3
Homestead Gdns BS16 ...51 B8
Homestead Rd BS34 ...36 A3
Homestead The
Clevedon BS21 ...57 C3
Keynsham BS31 ...81 F2
Homestead Way BS25 ...125 A8
Honey Garston Cl BS13 ...79 B4
Honey Garston Rd BS13 ...79 B4
Honey Hill Rd BS15 ...65 F8
Honey Suckle La BS16 ...50 E5
Honeyborne Way GL12 ...18 B5
Honeyhall La BS49 ...108 D7
Honeylands BS20 ...45 C3
Honeymead BS14 ...80 C6
Honeysuckle Cl BS32 ...24 E2
Honeysuckle Pl 4 BS24 ...106 A8
Honister Ho BS34 ...36 A8
Honiton 9 BS22 ...89 A2
Honiton Rd Bristol BS16 ...51 A3
Clevedon BS21 ...57 E1
Hook Hill BA3 ...116 D2
Hook La BA3, BS39 ...129 E4
Hooks Batch BS40 ...110 C4
Hooper Rd BS14 ...80 D5
Hope Ct BS1 ...140 B1
Hope Rd Bristol BS3 ...63 C2
Yate BS37 ...27 A2
Hope Sq BS8 ...62 F6
Hope Terr BA3 ...132 B1
Hopechapel Hill 10 BS8 ...62 F6
Hopetoun Rd BS2 ...49 F3
Hopewell Gdns BS11 ...47 F7
Hopkin Cl BS35 ...15 D7
Hopkins Ct 13 BS6 ...49 B1

Hopkins St BS23 ...104 E8
Hopland Cl BS30 ...66 B3
Hopp's Rd BS15 ...65 D7
Horesham Gr BS13 ...79 C5
Horfield CE Prim Sch
BS10 ...49 D7
Horfield Ct BS7 ...49 E4
Horfield Rd BS2 ...141 A4
Horley Rd BS2 ...50 A2
Horn's La BS26 ...125 B2
Hornbeam Wlk BS31 ...81 C3
Hornbeams The BS16 ...37 B1
Horne Cl BA3 ...137 F1
Horse La BS35 ...8 D5
Horse Race La BS8 ...61 A6
Horse St BS37 ...28 C1
Horsecastle Cl BS49 ...74 A1
Horsecastle Farm Rd
BS49 ...74 A1
Horsecombe Brow BA2 ...102 A1
Horsecombe Gr BA2 ...102 A1
Horsecombe Vale BA2 ...102 A1
Horsecroft Gdns BS30 ...66 A6
Horsefair The BS1 ...141 B3
Horseleaze La BS25 ...108 D1
Horsepool La BS30 ...67 F8
Horsepool Rd BS13 ...78 E3
Horseshoe Dr BS9 ...48 C4
Horseshoe La BS37 ...28 B1
Horseshoe Wlk BA2 ...102 B5
Horsford Rd GL12 ...11 B5
Hortham La BS32 ...24 E5
Horton Ct BS37 ...29 D7
Horton Hill BS37 ...29 C5
Horton Ho BA2 ...142 C4
Horton Prim Sch BS37 ...29 C5
Horton Rd
Chipping Sodbury BS37 ...28 C2
Chipping Sodbury,
Little Sodbury End BS37 ...28 D4
Horton St BS2 ...141 C3
Horwood Ct 3 BS30 ...66 A4
Horwood La GL12 ...18 B4
Horwood Rd BS48 ...59 F1
Hosey Wlk BS13 ...79 A5
Host St BS1 ...141 A3
Hot Bath St 6 BA1 ...142 B2
Hot Water La BS15 ...52 A3
Hottom Gdns BS7 ...50 A7
Hotwell Rd BS8 ...140 B1
Hotwells Prim Sch BS8 ...62 F6
Houlgate Way BS26 ...125 B1
Houlton St BS2 ...141 C4
Hounds Cl BS37 ...28 B1
Hounds Rd BS37 ...28 B1
How Hill BA2 ...101 A6
Howard Ave BS5 ...64 E8
Howard Cl BS31 ...82 D3
Howard Rd Bristol BS16 ...51 D4
Bristol BS3 ...63 C4
Bristol BS6 ...49 B4
Thornbury BS35 ...8 C2
Howard St BS5 ...50 E1
Howecroft Ct BS9 ...48 E4
Howecroft Gdns BS9 ...48 E4
Howells Mead BS16 ...52 B7
Howes Cl BS30 ...66 A6
Howett Rd 16 BS5 ...64 C7
Howsmoor La Bristol BS16 ...52 B8
Bristol BS16 ...52 C8
Hoylake BS37 ...39 E8
Hoylake Dr BS30 ...66 B6
Huckford La BS36 ...38 A4
Huckford Rd BS36 ...37 E5
Huckley Way BS32 ...36 F6
Hudd's Hill Gdns 2 BS5 ...64 F8
Hudd's Hill Rd BS5 ...64 F8
Hudd's Vale Rd BS5 ...64 E8
Hudson Cl BS37 ...39 F8
Hugh Littleton Prim Sch
BS39 ...115 C1
Hughenden Rd Bristol BS7 ...49 E5
Bristol BS8 ...49 A2
Weston-Super-Mare BS23 ...105 A8
Huish Ct BA3 ...133 B2
Hulbert Cl BS4 ...65 A2
Hulse Rd BS4 ...64 D1
Humber Way BS11 ...33 D5
Humberstan Wlk BS11 ...47 E8
Humphry Davy Way 6
BS8 ...62 F5
Humphrys Barton BS4 ...64 F5
Hung Rd BS11 ...47 E5
Hungerford Cl BS4 ...80 E8
Hungerford Cres BS4 ...64 E1
Hungerford Gdns BS4 ...80 E8
Hungerford Rd Bath BA1 ...101 C7
Bristol BS4 ...80 E8
Hungerford Terr BA2 ...118 D1
Hungerford Wlk BS4 ...64 E1
Hunstrete Rd BA3 ...115 F7
Hunt's La BS49 ...91 E8
Hunter's Way BS34 ...36 B3
Hunters Cl BS15 ...65 C5
Hunters Dr BS15 ...51 F1
Hunters Mead GL9 ...20 A2
Hunters Rd BS15 ...65 C5
Hunters Rd E BS15 ...65 C4
Huntingham Rd BS13 ...78 F4
Huntley Gr BS48 ...60 A1
Hunts Ground Rd BS34 ...36 F4
Hunts La BS7 ...49 E6
Hurle Cres BS8 ...49 B1
Hurle Rd BS8 ...49 B1
Hurlingham Rd BS7 ...49 F2

Hurn La BS31 . . . . .82 A3
Hurn Rd BS21 . . . . .57 F2
Hursley Hill BS14 . . . . .97 D8
Hursley La BS14 . . . . .80 E1
Hurst Rd Bristol BS4 . . . . .79 F8
　Weston-Super-Mare BS23 . .105 B6
Hurst Wlk BS4 . . . . .79 F8
Hurston Rd BS4 . . . . .79 D7
Hurstwood Rd BS16 . . . . .51 D5
Hutton CE Prim Sch
　BS24 .105 E2
Hutton Cl Bristol BS9 . . . . .48 E7
　Keynsham BS31 . . . . .82 A2
Hutton Hill BS24 . . . . .105 F2
Hutton Moor La
　BS22,BS24 . . . . .105 C6
Hutton Moor Rd BS22 . . . . .105 C7
Huyton Rd BS5 . . . . .50 C3
Hyatts Wood Rd BS48 . . . . .76 E1
Hyde Ave BS35 . . . . .8 B3
Hyde The BS21 . . . . .73 C8
Hyde's La SN14 . . . . .69 A6
Hyland Gr BS9 . . . . .48 F8

I

Ida Rd **2** BS5 . . . . .64 C8
Iddesleigh Rd BS6 . . . . .49 B3
Idstone Rd BS16 . . . . .51 B4
Idwal Cl BA2 . . . . .133 C8
Iford Cl BS31 . . . . .82 E3
Iford Hill BA15 . . . . .120 E2
Iford La BA3,BA15 . . . . .120 C3
Ilchester Cres BS13 . . . . .63 B1
Ilchester Rd BS13 . . . . .79 B8
Iles Cl BS15 . . . . .65 D4
Ilex Ave BS21 . . . . .57 E2
Ilex Cl BS13 . . . . .78 F6
Ilex La BS25 . . . . .107 F1
Ilminster BS24 . . . . .105 A2
Ilminster Ave BS4 . . . . .79 F8
Ilminster Avenue Prim Sch
　BS4 . . . . .80 A8
Ilminster Cl Clevedon BS21 . . . .57 E2
　Nailsea BS48 . . . . .75 D8
Ilsyn Gr BS14 . . . . .80 D7
Imber Court Cl BS14 . . . . .80 B8
Imperial Arc BS3 . . . . .63 D4
Imperial Rd Bristol BS14 . . . . . . .80 C8
　Bristol BS6 . . . . .49 B3
Imperial Wlk BS14 . . . . .64 B1
Ingleside Rd BS15 . . . . .51 C1
Inglestone Rd GL12 . . . . .18 B5
Ingleton Dr BS22 . . . . .89 A4
Ingmire Rd BS5 . . . . .50 B3
Ingst Hill BS35 . . . . .13 B3
Ingst Rd BS35 . . . . .13 D4
Inkerman Cl BS7 . . . . .49 E7
Inman Ho BA1 . . . . .142 C4
Inn Cotts BS11 . . . . .48 A7
Inner Down The BS12 . . . . .14 D3
Inner Elm Terr BA3 . . . . .132 C1
Innicks Cl BS40 . . . . .111 D1
Innocks Est GL11 . . . . .5 D4
Innox Gdns BS13 . . . . .79 A5
Innox Gr BA2 . . . . .100 F2
Innox La BA1 . . . . .85 B5
Innox Rd BA2 . . . . .101 B5
Inns Court Ave BS4 . . . . .79 D7
Inns Court Dr BS4 . . . . .79 D6
Instow **1** BS22 . . . . .89 A2
Instow Rd BS4 . . . . .79 E8
Instow Wlk BS4 . . . . .79 E8
International Helicopter
　Mus BS24 . . . . .105 E5
International Sch
　of Choueifat SN14 . . . . .70 C4
International Trad Est
　BS11 . . . . .33 B2
Interplex 16 BS32 . . . . .24 C3
Inverness Rd BA2 . . . . .101 C6
Ipswich Dr BS4 . . . . .64 C6
Irby Rd BS3 . . . . .63 A3
Irena Rd BS16 . . . . .50 F3
Ireton Rd BS3 . . . . .63 B3
Iron Acton CE Prim Sch
　BS37 . . . . .26 E4
Iron Acton Way BS37 . . . . .27 B3
Iron Hogg La GL12 . . . . .9 C3
Ironchurch Rd BS11 . . . . .33 C5
Ironmould La BS4 . . . . .51 E4
Irving Cl Bristol BS16 . . . . .51 E4
　Clevedon BS21 . . . . .57 F3
Irving Ho BS1 . . . . .140 C3
ISF Rd BS11 . . . . .33 C3
Island Gdns BS16 . . . . .50 C4
Island The BA3 . . . . .132 A1
Isleys Ct BS30 . . . . .65 F3
Islington Rd BS3 . . . . .63 C4
Ison Hill Rd BS10 . . . . .34 E3
Itchington Rd
　Alveston BS35 . . . . .15 F4
　Tytherington GL12 . . . . .16 B4
Ivo Peters Rd BA2 . . . . .142 A2
Ivor Rd BS5 . . . . .64 C8
Ivy Ave BA2 . . . . .101 C4
Ivy Bank Pk BA2 . . . . .101 F2
Ivy Cl BS48 . . . . .59 D1
Ivy Ct BS20 . . . . .44 F5
Ivy Gr BA2 . . . . .101 C4
Ivy House Cotts BS29 . . . . .106 D7
Ivy La Bristol BS16 . . . . .51 A3
　Weston-Super-Mare BS24 . . .106 A8
Ivy Pl BA2 . . . . .101 C4

Ivy Terr BS37 . . . . .39 B4
Ivy Wlk Banwell BS29 . . . . .106 E4
　Midsomer Norton BA3 . . . . .138 B8
Ivybridge **8** BS22 . . . . .89 A2
Ivywell Rd BS9 . . . . .48 E3
Iwood La BS40 . . . . .92 A2

J

Jack Knight Ho BS7 . . . . .49 F5
Jackson Cl BS35 . . . . .22 D7
Jacob St Bristol BS2 . . . . .141 B3
Jacob's Cl BA1 . . . . .141 C3
Jacob's Ct BS1 . . . . .140 C2
Jacob's Wells Rd BS8 . . . . .140 B2
Jacobs Mdw BS20 . . . . .45 F4
Jamaica St BS2 . . . . .141 B4
James Cl BS16 . . . . .51 E4
James Rd Bristol BS16 . . . . .51 E4
James St Bristol BS2 . . . . .50 A2
　Bristol BS5 . . . . .141 C4
James St W BA1 . . . . .142 B2
Jane St BS5 . . . . .64 B7
Jarvis St BS5 . . . . .64 B6
Jasmine Cl **8** BS23 . . . . .104 E8
Jasmine Gr BS11 . . . . .34 C2
Jasmine La BS49 . . . . .74 F2
Jasmine Way BS24 . . . . .89 A1
Jasper St BS3 . . . . .63 B3
Jays The GL12 . . . . .16 B6
Jean Rd BS4 . . . . .64 E2
Jefferies Hill Bottom
　BS15 . . . . .65 B5
Jeffery Ct BS30 . . . . .66 B6
Jeffreys Ct **9** BS16 . . . . .50 E3
Jellicoe Ave BS16 . . . . .50 E8
Jellicoe Ct BS22 . . . . .88 E4
Jena Ct BS31 . . . . .82 D3
Jenner Cl BS37 . . . . .40 D8
Jersey Ave BS4 . . . . .64 F4
Jesmond Rd Clevedon BS21 . . . .57 C3
　Weston-Super-Mare BS22 . . . .89 C4
Jesse Hughes Ct BA1 . . . . .85 C2
Jessop Ct BS1 . . . . .141 B2
Jessop Underpass BS3 . . . . .62 F4
Jews La Bath BA2 . . . . .101 C6
　Churchill BS25 . . . . .108 F4
Jim O'Neil Ho BS11 . . . . .47 D7
Jocelin Dr BS22 . . . . .88 F4
Jocelyn Rd BS7 . . . . .49 F7
Jockey La BS5 . . . . .65 A7
John Cabot Ct BS1 . . . . .140 A1
John Cabot Cty Tech Coll
　BS15 . . . . .65 C7
John Carr's Terr BS8 . . . . .140 B2
John Cozens Ho **6** BS2 . . . . . .141 C3
John James Ct BS7 . . . . .50 B7
John Slessor Ct BA1 . . . . .142 B4
John St Bath BA1 . . . . .142 B3
　Bristol BS1 . . . . .141 A3
　Bristol BS15 . . . . .65 C8
　Bristol BS2 . . . . .50 A2
John Wesley Rd BS5 . . . . .65 B6
John Wesleys Chapel
　BS1 . . . . .141 B3
Johnson Dr BS30 . . . . .65 F5
Johnson Rd BS16 . . . . .52 C6
Johnsons La BS5 . . . . .50 D1
Johnsons Rd BS5 . . . . .50 C1
Johnstone St BA2 . . . . .142 C2
Jones Cl BS49 . . . . .74 A1
Jordan Wlk BS32 . . . . .36 D8
Jorrocks Ind Est BS37 . . . . .39 C4
Joy Hill BS8 . . . . .62 F6
Jubilee Cres BS16 . . . . .52 A6
Jubilee Dr Failand BS8 . . . . .61 B4
　Thornbury BS35 . . . . .8 D1
Jubilee Gdns BS37 . . . . .28 A2
Jubilee Ho BS34 . . . . .36 C8
Jubilee La Cromhall GL12 . . . . . .17 B7
　Langford BS40 . . . . .109 A6
Jubilee Pl Bristol BS1 . . . . .141 A1
　Clevedon BS21 . . . . .57 D1
Jubilee Rd Axbridge BS26 . . . . .125 C2
　Bristol BS15 . . . . .51 E3
　Bristol BS2 . . . . .50 A1
　Bristol BS5 . . . . .64 F7
　Radstock BA3 . . . . .132 D1
Jubilee St BS2 . . . . .141 C2
Jubilee Terr BS39 . . . . .131 E6
Jubilee Way BS11 . . . . .33 B2
Julian Cl BS9 . . . . .48 E3
Julian Ct BS9 . . . . .48 E3
Julian Rd Bath BA1 . . . . .142 B3
　Bristol BS9 . . . . .48 E3
Julier Ho BA1 . . . . .142 C4
Julius Rd BS7 . . . . .49 D3
Junction Ave BA2 . . . . .142 A1
Junction Rd Bath BA2 . . . . .142 A1
　Bristol BS4 . . . . .64 D4
Juniper Ct **2** BS5 . . . . .50 C2
Juniper Pl BS22 . . . . .88 F4
Juniper Way BS34 . . . . .37 A7
Jupiter Rd BS34 . . . . .35 E7
Justice Ave BS31 . . . . .82 E3
Justice Rd BS16 . . . . .51 A3
Jutland Rd BS11 . . . . .33 B1

K

Karelean Ct BS10 . . . . .35 D3
Karen Cl BS48 . . . . .76 A4
Karen Dr BS48 . . . . .76 A5

Kathdene Gdns BS7 . . . . .49 F3
Katherine Dr BS12 . . . . .11 A5
Katherine Lady Berkeley's
　Sch GL12 . . . . .11 A4
Kaynton Mead BA1 . . . . .101 B7
Keats Ho **4** BS23 . . . . .104 F4
Keats Rd BA3 . . . . .138 C8
Keble Ave BS13 . . . . .78 F5
Keeds La BS41 . . . . .61 F1
Keedwell Hill BS41 . . . . .61 F1
Keel Cl BS5 . . . . .64 F6
Keel's Hill BA2 . . . . .133 C8
Keen's Gr BS35 . . . . .22 C7
Keene's Way BS21 . . . . .57 C2
Keep The Bristol BS30 . . . . .66 D5
　Weston-Super-Mare BS22 . . . .89 A3
Keinton Wlk BS10 . . . . .35 A2
Kelbra Cres BS36 . . . . .38 B6
Kellaway Ave BS7 . . . . .49 D5
Kellaway Cres BS9 . . . . .49 D6
Kellaway Ct BS6 . . . . .49 D6
Kellways BS48 . . . . .76 A4
Kelso Pl BA1 . . . . .101 D7
Kelso Villas BA1 . . . . .101 D7
Kelston CE Prim Sch BS10 . . .49 D8
　Weston-Super-Mare BS22 . . . .89 B5
Kelston Gr BS15 . . . . .65 E6
Kelston Rd Bath BA1 . . . . .83 E1
　Bristol BS10 . . . . .49 D8
　Keynsham BS31 . . . . .81 D5
　Weston-Super-Mare BS22 . . . .89 B5
Kelston View BA2 . . . . .101 A5
Kelston Wlk BS16 . . . . .51 C4
Kelting Gr BS21 . . . . .57 F2
Kemble Cl Bristol BS15 . . . . .65 E6
　Nailsea BS48 . . . . .60 A1
Kemble Gdns BS11 . . . . .47 F5
Kemble Ho BS34 . . . . .23 F1
Kempe's Cl BS41 . . . . .62 A2
Kemperleye Way BS32 . . . . .36 D7
Kempton Cl Bristol BS16 . . . . . . .37 F1
　Thornbury BS35 . . . . .8 B3
Kencot Wlk BS13 . . . . .79 B3
Kendal Rd BS7 . . . . .50 A7
Kendall Gdns BS16 . . . . .51 D4
Kendall Rd BS16 . . . . .51 D4
Kendon Dr BS10 . . . . .49 D7
Kendon Way BS10 . . . . .49 D8
Kenilworth BS37 . . . . .39 F8
Kenilworth Cl BS31 . . . . .81 D4
Kenilworth Rd BS6 . . . . .49 C1
Kenmare Rd BS4 . . . . .63 E1
Kenmeade Cl BS25 . . . . .125 E8
Kenmore Cres BS7 . . . . .35 E1
Kenmore Dr BS7 . . . . .35 E1
Kenn Cl BS23 . . . . .105 A5
Kenn Court Bsns Pk BS4 . . . . . .79 E7
Kenn Moor Dr BS21 . . . . .57 E1
Kenn Moor Rd BS49 . . . . .74 F1
Kenn Rd Bristol BS5 . . . . .65 A7
　Clevedon BS21 . . . . .73 F6
Kenn St BS21 . . . . .73 F7
Kennard Cl BS15 . . . . .65 C7
Kennard Rd BS15 . . . . .65 C8
Kennard Rise BS15 . . . . .65 C8
Kennaway Rd BS21 . . . . .57 E2
Kennedy Way BS37 . . . . .27 F1
Kennel Dr Gl 9 . . . . .30 E2
Kennel La BS26 . . . . .123 E3
Kennel Lodge Rd BS3 . . . . .62 E4
Kennet Pk BA2 . . . . .85 E1
Kennet Rd BS31 . . . . .82 A4
Kennet Way **4** BS35 . . . . .15 D8
Kenneth Rd BS4 . . . . .64 D2
Kennford **8** BS22 . . . . .89 A2
Kennington Ave
　3 Bristol BS15 . . . . .51 D1
　Bristol BS7 . . . . .49 F4
Kennington Rd BA1 . . . . .101 B7
Kennion Rd BS5 . . . . .65 A7
Kennmoor Cl BS30 . . . . .66 A6
Kennmoor Rd BS21 . . . . .74 A6
Kensal Ave BS3 . . . . .63 E3
Kensal Rd BS3 . . . . .63 E3
Kensington Cl BS35 . . . . .8 B2
Kensington Ct Bath BA1 . . . . . . .85 B2
　Bristol BS8 . . . . .140 A3
Kensington Gdns BA1 . . . . .85 B1
Kensington Park Rd BS4 . . . . . . .64 C2
Kensington Pk **12** BS5 . . . . .50 A1
Kensington Pl Bath BA1 . . . . .85 B1
　Bristol BS8 . . . . .140 A3
Kensington Rd
　6 Bristol BS15 . . . . .51 D1
　Bristol BS6 . . . . .49 B3
　Bristol BS6 . . . . .49 C1
　Weston-Super-Mare BS23 . . .104 F5
Kent Ave BS37 . . . . .27 F3
Kent Cl BS34 . . . . .36 D4
Kent La BS30 . . . . .53 D7
Kent Rd Bristol BS7 . . . . .49 D3
Kent St BS3 . . . . .63 C3
Kent Way BS22 . . . . .89 B4
Kenton Ho BS34 . . . . .23 F1
Kenton Mews BS9 . . . . .49 C5
Kents Gn BS15 . . . . .51 E2
Kentshare La BS40 . . . . .95 B6
Keppel Cl BS31 . . . . .82 D2
Kerry Rd BS4 . . . . .63 E1
Kersteman Rd BS6 . . . . .49 B3
Kestrel Cl Bristol BS34 . . . . .35 E8
　Chipping Sodbury BS37 . . . . . .39 F8

Kestrel Cl continued
　Thornbury BS35 . . . . .8 D2
Kestrel Dr
　Puxton/Churchill BS16 . . . . . .53 C4
　Weston-Super-Mare BS22 . . . .88 E1
Keswick Wlk BS10 . . . . .35 C2
Ketch Rd BS3 . . . . .63 F3
Kew Rd BS23 . . . . .87 E1
Kew Wlk BS4 . . . . .80 C8
Kewside BS22 . . . . .88 B4
Kewstoke Prim Sch BS22 . . . . . .88 B3
Kewstoke Rd Bath BA2 . . . . . . .102 A2
　Bristol BS9 . . . . .48 E4
　Weston-Super-Mare BS22 . . . .88 C3
Keyes Path BS22 . . . . .88 F4
Keyhaven Bglws BS21 . . . . .88 B4
Keynes Bsy-Pass BS31 . . . . .81 E7
Keynsham Hospl BS31 . . . . .81 F4
Keynsham Prim Sch BS31 . . . . .81 D5
Keynsham Rd BS30,BS31 . . . . . .82 A8
Keynsham Sta BS31 . . . . .81 F6
Keys Ave BS7 . . . . .49 F7
Kidney Hill BS37 . . . . .39 A3
Kielder Dr BS22 . . . . .88 F3
Kilbirnie Rd BS14 . . . . .80 A3
Kilburn St **11** BS5 . . . . .64 B8
Kilburn St **11** BS5 . . . . .64 B8
Kildare Rd BS3 . . . . .102 B7
Kildare Rd BS4 . . . . .63 D1
Kilkenny La BA2 . . . . .118 B8
Kilkenny St **2** BS2 . . . . .141 C2
Killcott Rd GL12 . . . . .19 D6
Kilmersdon CE Prim Sch
　BA3 . . . . .139 A6
Kilmersdon Hill BA3 . . . . .139 A5
Kilmersdon Rd Bristol BS13 . . . .79 B4
　Radstock BA3 . . . . .138 E8
Kilminster Rd BS11 . . . . .47 C8
Kiln Cl BS15 . . . . .51 B2
Kiln Cl BS15 . . . . .51 B2
Kiln Pk BS23 . . . . .105 A6
Kilnhurst Cl BS30 . . . . .65 F2
Kilve BS24 . . . . .105 A2
Kilvert Cl BS4 . . . . .64 D5
Kimberley Ave BS16 . . . . .51 C5
Kimberley Cl BS16 . . . . .51 F7
Kimberley Cres BS16 . . . . .51 C5
Kimberley Rd Bristol BS15 . . . . .51 D1
　Bristol BS16 . . . . .51 C5
Kimsbury Cl BS16 . . . . .52 D6
Kinber Cl BA1 . . . . .84 A3
King Alfred Way BA15 . . . . . . .120 D7
King Dick's La **6** BS5 . . . . .64 B7
King Edmund Com Sch
　BS37 . . . . .27 E1
King Edward Cl BS14 . . . . .80 A6
King Edward Rd BA2 . . . . .101 D5
King Edward's Jun Sch
　BA2 . . . . .102 C7
King Edward's Senior Sch
　BA2 . . . . .102 C7
King George V Pl **6** BS1 . . . . .141 A2
King George's Rd
　Bath BA2 . . . . .101 C6
　Bristol BS13 . . . . .78 F5
King John's Rd BS15 . . . . .51 B2
King La Clutton BS39 . . . . .114 F4
　Litton BA3 . . . . .129 A1
King Rd Bristol BS4 . . . . .64 C1
　Churchill Green BS49 . . . . . . .108 E6
King Road Ave BS11 . . . . .33 B2
King Sq BS2 . . . . .141 A4
King Square Ave BS2 . . . . .141 A4
King St Avonmouth BS11 . . . . . .33 A1
　Bristol BS1 . . . . .141 A2
　Bristol BS15 . . . . .65 B8
　Bristol BS15 . . . . .50 C1
King William Ave BS1 . . . . .141 A2
King William St BS3 . . . . .63 B4
King's Ave BS6,BS7 . . . . .49 C4
King's Dr BS7 . . . . .49 C4
King's Head La BS13 . . . . .78 F7
King's La Clevedon BS21 . . . . . . .57 D5
King's Parade Ave **1** BS8 . . . . .49 B1
King's Parade Mews BS8 . . . . . .49 A1
King's Rd Bristol BS4 . . . . .140 A3
　Bristol BS8 . . . . .140 A3
　Clevedon BS21 . . . . .57 D5
　Portishead BS20 . . . . .44 F6
　Westerleigh BS37 . . . . .38 E8
Kingcott Mdw BS39 . . . . .114 E2
Kings Park Ave BS2 . . . . .64 C6
Kings Rd BS40 . . . . .94 B3
Kings Sq BS30 . . . . .82 D8
Kings Sq BS30 . . . . .82 D8
Kings Weston Ave BS11 . . . . . . .47 E8
Kings Weston La
　Avonmouth BS11 . . . . .33 E3

Kings Weston La continue
　Bristol BS11 . . . . .47 F8
Kings Weston Rd
　BS11, BS10 . . . . .34 B2
Kings Wlk BS13 . . . . .78 E5
Kingscote BS37 . . . . .39 D7
Kingscote Pk BS5 . . . . .65 B6
Kingscourt Cl BS14 . . . . .80 A4
Kingsdown Gr SN13 . . . .
Kingsdown Par BS6 . . . .
Kingsdown View **10** BA1 . . . . . .
Kingsfield BA2 . . . .
Kingsfield La Bristol BS15 . . . . . .
　Bristol BS30 . . . .
Kingshill Sch BS15 . . . .
Kingshill BS48 . . . .
Kingshill Gdns BS48 . . . .
Kingshill Ho BS4 . . . .
Kingshill La BS40 . . . .
Kingshill Rd BS4 . . . .
Kingsholm Ct BS23 . . . .
Kingsholme Rd BS15 . . . .
Kingsholme Rd BS15 . . . .
Kingsland Cl **11** BS2 . . . .
Kingsland Rd BS2 . . . .
Kingsland Road Bridge
　BS2 . . . .
Kingsland Trad Est BS2 . . . .
Kingsleigh Ct BS15 . . . .
Kingsleigh Gdns BS15 . . . .
Kingsleigh Pk BS15 . . . .
Kingsley Ho Bristol BS2 . . . .
　Bristol BS9 . . . .
Kingsley Pl **1** BS3 . . . .
Kingsley Rd Bristol BS5 . . . .
　Bristol BS6 . . . .
　Clevedon BS21 . . . .
　Radstock BA3 . . . .
　Weston-Super-Mare BS23 . . .
Kingsmarsh Ho **3** BS5 . . . .
Kingsmead BA1 . . . .
Kingsmead BS48 . . . .
Kingsmead Ct **8** BA1 . . . .
Kingsmead N BA1 . . . .
Kingsmead Sq BA1 . . . .
Kingsmead St BA1 . . . .
Kingsmead Wlk BS5 . . . .
Kingsmill BS9 . . . .
Kingston Ave
　Clevedon BS21 . . . .
　Saltford BS31 . . . .
Kingston Cl BS16 . . . .
Kingston Dr Bristol BS16 . . . .
　Nailsea BS48 . . . .
Kingston La BS40 . . . .
Kingston Mead BS40 . . . .
Kingston Rd Bath BA1 . . . .
　Bristol BS1 . . . .
　Nailsea BS48 . . . .
Kingston Way BS48 . . . .
Kingstree St BS4 . . . .
Kingsway Bath BA2 . . . .
　Bristol BS3 . . . .
　Bristol BS5 . . . .
Kingsway Ave BS15 . . . .
Kingsway Cres BS15 . . . .
Kingsway Sh Prec BS5 . . . .
Kingsway BS15 . . . .
Kingswear Rd BS3 . . . .
Kingsweston Down
　Nature Res BS9, BS11 . . . .
Kingswood Abbey
　Gatehouse GL12 . . . .
Kingswood Cty Prim Sch
　GL12 . . . .
Kingswood Day Prep Sch
　BA1 . . . .
Kingswood Rd GL12 . . . .
Kingswood Sch BA1 . . . .
Kingswood Trad Est **6**
　BS15 . . . .
Kington La BS35 . . . .
Kington Rd BS35 . . . .
Kingwell View BS39 . . . .
Kinsale Rd BS14 . . . .
Kinsale Wlk BS4 . . . .
Kinvara Rd BS4 . . . .
Kipling Rd Bristol BS7 . . . .
　Radstock BA3 . . . .
　Weston-Super-Mare BS23 . . .
Kirkby Rd BS11 . . . .
Kirkstone Gdns BS10 . . . .
Kirtlington Rd BS5 . . . .
Kite Hay Cl BS16 . . . .
Kites Cl BS32 . . . .
Kitley Hill BA3 . . . .
Knap La Gl 12 . . . .
Knapp Rd Thornbury BS35 . . . . .
　Thornbury,Crossways BS35 . . .
Knapp The BS37 . . . .
Knapps Cl BS25 . . . .
Knapps Dr BS25 . . . .
Knapps La BS5 . . . .
Knightcott BS29 . . . .
Knightcott Gdns BS29 . . . .
Knightcott Ind Est BS29 . . . .
Knightcott Pk BS29 . . . .
Knightcott Rd
　Abbots Leigh BS8 . . . .
　Banwell BS29 . . . .
Knighton Rd BS10 . . . .
Knights Cl Bristol BS9 . . . .

Long Mdw BS16 50 D6
Long Mead BS37 27 E5
Long Rd BS16 52 A5
Long Row BS1 141 B2
Long Thorn La BS40 111 E7
Long Valley Rd BA2 100 F5
Longacre BS21 73 B8
Longacre Rd BS14 80 A3
Longbottom BS25 125 F6
Longcross GL12 10 B1
Longden Rd BS16 51 F6
Longdown Dr BS22 89 B4
Longfellow Ave BA2 101 F4
Longfellow Rd BA3 138 C8
Longfield Rd BS7 49 E3
Longford BS37 39 C8
Longford Ave BS10 49 D8
Longlands Ho 13 BS5 64 C7
Longleat Cl BS9 49 C5
Longleaze Gdns BS24 105 F3
Longmead Ave BS7 49 D5
Longmead Cl BA3 135 F5
Longmead Croft BS13 78 F4
Longmead Rd BS16 38 B1
Longmeadow Rd BS31 81 C4
Longmoor Ct BS3 63 A2
Longmoor Rd BS3 63 A2
Longney Pl BS34 23 F1
Longreach Gr BS14 80 D6
Longridge Way BS24 106 A8
Longs Dr BS37 27 C2
Longs View GL12 11 A5
Longton Grove Rd 3 BS23 104 E8
Longton Ind Est BS23 104 F6
Longvernal BA3 131 F1
Longvernal Prim Sch BA3 131 F1
Longway Ave BS13, BS14 79 F4
Longwell Green Prim Sch
BS30 65 F3
Longwell Ho BS30 65 F3
Longwood BS4 65 A2
Longwood Ho BS8 61 D4
Longwood La BS41 61 F4
Lons The BS30 66 C1
Lonsdale Ave BS23 104 F4
Lonsdale Bsns Ctr BS15 51 C2
Lorain Wlk BS10 34 F2
Lorne Rd BA2 101 D6
Lorton Cl BS10 35 B1
Lorton Rd BS10 35 B1
Lotts' Ave BS48 76 B5
Lotus Ct BS22 88 C1
Loughman Cl BS15 65 E8
Louisa St BS2 141 C2
Louise Ave BS16 52 A5
Love La
Chipping Sodbury BS37 40 A8
Yate BS37 28 A4
Love's La BA3 115 F6
Lovelinch Gdns BS41 61 F1
Lovell Ave BS30 66 D4
Lovell's Hill BS15 65 B5
Lovells Mill BS39 113 D4
Loveringe Cl BS10 34 F4
Lovers La BA3, BS39 132 A5
Lovers' Wlk BS23 104 D8
Loves Hill BA3 116 A1
Lowbourne BS14 79 F6
Lower Ashley Rd
13 Bristol BS2 49 F1
Bristol BS2,BS5 50 A1
Lower Batch BS40 96 B3
Lower Borough
Walls BA1 142 C2
Lower Bristol Rd
Bath BA2 101 B6
Bath BA2 142 A2
Clutton BS39 114 F4
Lower Camden Pl BA1 142 C4
Lower Castle St BS1 141 B3
Lower Chapel La BS36 38 C7
Lower Chapel Rd BS15 65 C5
Lower Cheltenham Pl
BS6 49 F1
Lower Church La BS2 141 A3
Lower Church Rd BS23 104 D8
Lower Claverham BS49 74 F3
Lower Clifton Hill BS8 140 B2
Lower Cock Rd BS15 65 F7
Lower College St BS1 140 C2
Lower Court Rd BS32 24 A5
Lower Down Rd BS20 45 B5
Lower East Hayes BA1 102 B8
Lower Fallow Cl BS14 79 F3
Lower Gay St BS2 141 A4
Lower Grove Rd BS16 50 F4
Lower Guinea St BS1 141 A1
Lower Hanham Rd BS15 65 C6
Lower Hedgemead Rd
BA1 142 C4
Lower High St BS11 47 D7
Lower House Cres BS34 36 B4
Lower Kingsdown Rd
SN13 86 F3
Lower Knole La BS10 35 A3
Lower Knowles Rd BS21 57 C2
Lower Lamb St BS1 140 C2
Lower Linden Rd BS21 57 D3
Lower Maudlin St BS1 141 A3
Lower Moor Rd BS37 27 E4
Lower Northend BA1 85 F5
Lower Norton La
Weston-Super-Mare BS22 88 E4
Weston-Super-Mare, Norton
BS22 88 C4
Lower Oldfield Pk BA2 142 A1
Lower Parade Ground Rd
BS24 106 C5
Lower Park Row BS1 141 A3
Lower Queen's BS21 57 D3
Lower Rd BS39 129 E6
Lower RedlandMews 2
BS6 49 B2
Lower Redland Rd BS6 49 B2
Lower Sidney St BS3 63 A4
Lower St BA3 136 E1
Lower Station Rd
4 Bristol, Ridgeway BS16 51 A4
Bristol, Staplehill BS16 51 C4
Lower Stoke BA2,BA3 120 A8
Lower Stone Cl BS36 38 C7
Lower Strode BS40 112 A7
Lower Strode Rd BS21 73 A7
Lower Thirlmere Rd BS34 36 A8
Lower Tockington Rd
BS32 14 B1
Lower Whitelands BA3 133 B3
Lowlis Cl BS10 34 F3
Lowther Rd BS10 35 C2
Loxley Gdns BA2 101 C4
Loxton Dr BA2 101 B6
Loxton Rd BS23 104 F2
Loxton Sq BS14 80 A6
Lucas Cl BS4 64 D1
Luccombe Hill BS6 49 B2
Luckington Court Gdns
SN14 31 F5
Luckington Cross
BA11 139 B2
Luckington Cty Prim Sch
SN14 31 E5
Luckington Rd BS7 49 E8
Lucklands Rd BA1 84 C1
Luckley Ave BS13 79 C5
Luckwell Prim Sch BS3 63 A3
Luckwell Rd BS3 63 B3
Lucky La BS3 63 D4
Ludlow Cl Bristol BS2 49 F1
Bristol BS30 66 B2
Keynsham BS31 81 D5
Ludlow Ct BS30 66 B1
Ludlow Rd BS7 50 A7
Ludwell Cl BS36 37 D5
Ludwells Orch BS39 131 E5
Lullington Rd BS4 64 B2
Lulsgate Rd BS13 79 A8
Lulworth Cres BS16 51 F8
Lulworth Rd BS31 81 E4
Lurgan Wlk BS4 63 D1
Luvers La BS40 110 D1
Lux Furlong BS9 48 B7
Luxton St BS5 64 B8
Lychgate Pk BS24 106 A4
Lydbrook Cl BS37 39 D8
Lyddington Rd BS7 49 F8
Lyddon Rd BS22 89 B3
Lyddyieth Ct BA15 120 E7
Lyde Green Rdbt BS16 52 B8
Lydford Wlk BS3 63 C2
Lydiard Croft BS15 65 C4
Lydney Rd Bristol BS10 35 D1
Bristol BS16 51 E4
Lydstep Terr BS3 63 C4
Lye Cross Rd BS40 93 C1
Lye Hole La BS40 93 D2
Lye Mead BS40 95 A6
Lyefield Rd BS22 88 E4
Lyes The BS49 91 D3
Lyme Gdns BA1 101 B7
Lyme Rd BA1 101 B7
Lymore Ave BA2 101 C5
Lymore Gdns BA2 101 C5
Lymore Terr BA2 101 C4
Lympsham Gn BA2 118 D8
Lympsham Prim Sch
BS24 122 B1
Lympsham Rd BS24 122 B1
Lynbrook BS41 61 F1
Lynbrook La BA2 101 F3
Lynch Cl BS22 88 F3
Lynch Cres BS25 124 F7
Lynch Ct BS30 65 F4
Lynch Hill BA3 137 A3
Lynch The BS25 124 F7
Lynchmead BS25 125 A7
Lyncombe Hill BA2 142 C1
Lyncombe Vale BA2 102 B4
Lyncombe Vale Rd BA2 102 A4
Lyncombe Wlk BS16 51 B2
Lyndale Ave BS9 48 D5
Lyndale Rd Bristol BS5 64 D8
Yate BS37 27 D1
Lynde Cl BS13 79 B4
Lyndhurst Rd
Bath BA2 101 C6
Bristol BS9 48 F7
Keynsham BS31 81 F3
Midsomer Norton BA3 138 B8
Weston-Super-Mare BS23 104 E4
Lyndhurst Terr BA1 142 C4
Lynfield Pk BA1 84 C1
Lynmouth Cl BS22 89 A2
Lynmouth Rd 3 BS2 50 A2
Lynn Rd BS16 50 D5
Lynton 3 BS15 66 A8
Lynton Cl BS20 45 E4
Lynton Pl 9 BS5 64 C8
Lynton Rd Bristol BS3 63 D2
Midsomer Norton BA3 138 B8
Lynton Way BS16 37 B1
Lynwood Cl BA3 138 A8
Lynwood Rd BS3 63 B2
Lynx Cres BS24 105 B2
Lyons Court Rd BS14 80 D7
Lyons Ct BS23 104 F7
Lyppiatt Rd BS5 64 D8
Lyppincourt Rd BS10 35 A3
Lysander Rd BS10, BS34 35 C6
Lysander Wlk BS34 36 E5
Lytchet Dr BS16 51 F8
Lytes Cary Rd BS31 82 A3
Lytton Gdns BA2 101 B4
Lytton Gr Bristol BS7 50 A8
Keynsham BS31 82 A5
Lyveden Gdns BS13 79 B5
Lyvedon Way BS41 62 B1

M

Macaulay Bldgs BA2 102 C4
Macauley Rd BS7 50 A8
Macdonald Wlk 3 BS15 65 D8
Macey's Rd BS13 79 D3
Machin Cl BS10 34 F3
Machin Gdns BS10 35 A3
Machin Rd BS10 35 A3
Macies The BA1 84 B3
Mackie Ave BS34 36 B2
Mackie Gr BS34 36 B2
Mackie Rd BS34 36 B2
Mackley La BA3 135 E3
Macleod Cl BS21 57 A2
Macquarie Farm Cl BS49 74 A1
Macrae Ct BS15 65 E8
Macrae Rd BS20 47 E4
Madam La
Weston-Super-Mare BS22 88 F2
Weston-Super-Mare BS22 89 A3
Weston-Super-Mare BS22 89 A4
Madam's Paddock BS40 96 B3
Madeira Ct BS23 104 C8
Madeira Rd Clevedon BS21 57 D3
Weston-Super-Mare BS23 87 C1
Madeline Rd BS16 50 F2
Madison Cl BS37 27 D2
Maesbury BS15 65 E6
Maesbury Rd BS31 82 A2
Maesknoll La BS14,BS39 97 B8
Maesknoll Rd BS4 64 A2
Magdalen Ave BA2 142 B1
Magdalen Rd BA2 142 B1
Magdalen Way BS22 89 A3
Magdalene Pl BS2 49 F1
Magdalene Rd BA3 133 C2
Magellan Cl BS22 88 F4
Maggs Cl BS10 35 C3
Maggs Hill BA3 116 B2
Maggs La Bristol BS5 50 E2
Whitchurch BS14 80 C4
Magnolia Ave BS22 89 A1
Magnolia Cl BS22 105 E7
Magnolia Rd BA3 132 E1
Magpie Bottom La
Bristol BS15 65 C6
Bristol BS5 65 B6
Magpie Cl BS22 105 E8
Maiden Way BS11 47 C8
Maidenhead Rd BS13 79 D3
Maidstone Gr BS24 105 A1
Maidstone St BS3 63 F3
Main Rd Bristol BS16 52 D5
Brockley BS49 75 D2
Flax Bourton BS48 76 F7
Hutton BS24 105 E2
Main St BS39 131 A4
Main View BS36 38 D7
Maisemore BS37 39 E6
Maisemore Ave BS34 24 B1
Makin Cl BS30 66 C5
Malago Rd BS3 63 D3
Malago Vale Est BS3 63 D3
Malago Wlk BS13 78 E4
Maldowers La 2 BS5 65 A8
Mall The Bath BA1 142 C2
Bristol BS34 35 D6
Bristol BS8 62 F7
Mallard Cl Bristol BS32 24 D2
Bristol BS5 50 F1
Chipping Sodbury BS37 40 A8
Mallow Cl Clevedon BS21 57 E2
Thornbury BS35 8 D2
Malmains Dr BS16 37 B1
Malmesbury Cl Bristol BS30 65 F5
Bristol BS6 49 C4
Maltings Ind Est The BA1 101 B6
Maltings The BS22 88 F2
Maltlands BS22 105 D8
Malvern Bldgs BA1 85 A2
Malvern Ct BS5 64 F7
Malvern Dr Bristol BS30 66 C5
Thornbury BS35 15 D8
Malvern Rd Bristol BS4 64 D3
Bristol BS5 64 F7
Weston-Super-Mare BS23 104 E5
Malvern Terr 4 BA1 85 A1
Malvern Villas 3 BA1 85 A1
Mancroft Ave BS11 47 F7
Mandy Mdws BA3 131 F1
Mangotsfield CE Sch BS16 52 B6
Mangotsfield Rd BS16 52 A5
Mangotsfield Sch BS16 52 B4
Manilla Cres BS23 87 C1
Manilla Pl BS23 87 C1
Manilla Rd BS8 140 A3
Manmoor La BS21 58 A1
Manor Cl
Coalpit Heath BS36 38 C6
Easton-In-Gordano BS20 47 A4
Farrington Gurney BS39 131 A3
Portishead BS20 45 A5
Manor Cl *continued*
Tockington BS32 14 C1
Wellow BA2 118 D1
Manor Cl The BS8 62 A8
Manor Copse Rd BA3 133 C2
Manor Cotts GL11 5 F5
Manor Court Dr BS7 49 E7
Manor Ct Backwell BS48 76 A5
Bristol BS16 50 E4
9 Bristol BS5 50 B1
Locking BS24 106 B4
Weston-Super-Mare BS23 105 A8
Manor Dr BA1 86 C2
Manor Farm BS32 36 D8
Manor Farm Cl BS24 105 B2
Manor Farm Cres
Bristol BS32 24 D1
Weston-Super-Mare BS24 105 B2
Manor Gardens Ho BS16 51 A5
Manor Gdns
Farmborough BA3 115 F6
Farrington Gurney BS39 131 A3
Locking BS24 106 A4
Weston-Super-Mare BS22 88 B4
Manor Gr Bristol BS16 52 A4
Bristol BS34 24 B2
Manor Grange BS24 122 B7
Manor Ho 6 BS5 50 B1
Manor House
Sacred Heart Sch BS40 96 A3
Manor La Abbots Leigh BS8 61 F8
Charfield GL12 11 A4
Winterbourne BS36 37 F7
Manor Pk Bath BA1 101 B8
Bristol BS6 49 B3
Radstock BA3 133 C2
Tockington BS32 14 C1
Manor Pl BS16 37 C1
Manor Prim Sch The
BS36 38 D6
Manor Rd Abbots Leigh BS8 61 F7
Bath BA1 84 C1
Bristol BS13 79 A6
Bristol BS7 49 E4
Bristol, Fishponds BS16 51 A5
Bristol, Mangotsfield BS16 52 A4
Radstock BA3 133 C2
Rangeworthy BS37 27 A7
Saltford BS31 82 C2
Weston-Super-Mare BS23 105 A8
Wick BS30 67 C5
Manor Terr BA3 133 C2
Manor Valley BS23 88 A1
Manor Villas BA1 84 C1
Manor Way
Chipping Sodbury BS37 28 C2
Failand BS8 61 C4
Manor Wlk BS35 8 B3
Mansel Cl BS31 82 C3
Mansfield Ave BS23 105 B8
Mansfield St BS3 63 C2
Manston Cl BS14 80 C7
Manvers St BA1 142 C1
Manworthy Rd BS4 64 D3
Manx Rd BS7 49 F8
Maple Ave Bristol BS16 51 C3
Thornbury BS35 8 C1
Maple Cl Bristol BS14 80 D5
Bristol BS30 66 B4
Bristol BS34 36 C7
Weston-Super-Mare BS23 105 A8
Maple Ct Bristol BS9 48 F8
5 Bristol BS15 51 D1
Maple Dr BA3 132 E1
Maple Gdns BA2 101 E4
Maple Gr BA2 101 E4
Maple Leaf Ct BS8 140 A3
Maple Rd Bristol BS4 64 D5
Bristol BS7 49 E5
Maple Rise BA3 133 B2
Maple Wlk Keynsham BS31 81 D4
Pucklechurch BS16 53 C5
Mapleleaze BS4 64 D3
Maplemeade BS7 49 C4
Mapleridge La BS37 28 D7
Maples The BS48 59 C1
Maplestone Rd BS14 80 A3
Mapstone Cl BS16 37 B3
Marbeck Rd BS10 35 B1
Marchants Pass BA1 142 C1
Marchfields Way BS23 105 A5
Marconi Rd BS20 44 F5
Mardale Cl BS10 35 C2
Marden Rd BS31 82 A4
Mardon Rd BS4 64 D6
Mardyke Ferry Rd BS1 140 B1
Margaret Rd BS13 78 F4
Margaret's Bldgs BA1 142 B3
Margaret's Hill BA1 142 C4
Margate St BS3 63 F3
Marguerite Rd BS13 78 F7
Marigold Wlk BS3 63 A2
Marina Gdns BS16 50 E3
Marindrin Dr BS22 89 B4
Marine Hill BS21 57 C5
Marine Par Clevedon BS21 57 C4
Pill BS20 47 C5
Weston-Super-Mare BS23 104 D6
Weston-Super-Mare BS23 87 B1
Mariner's Cl BS22 88 D1
Mariner's Way BS20 47 C5
Mariners Cl BS48 76 A6
Mariners Dr Backwell BS48 76 A6
Bristol BS9 48 D4
Mariners' Path BS9 48 E3
Marion Rd BS15 65 B3
Marion Wlk BS5 65 A7
Marissal Cl BS10 34 E3
Marissal Rd BS10
Mariston Way BS30
Marjoram Pl BS32
Mark La BS1
Market Ind Est BS49
Market La BS23
Market Pl Marshfield SN14
Winford BS40
Market Sq BS16
Marketside BS2
Markham Cl BS11
Marklands BS9
Marksbury BA2
Marksbury CE Prim Sch
BA2
Marksbury Rd BS3
Marlborough Ave 13 BS16
Marlborough Bldgs BA1
Marlborough Dr
Bristol BS16
Weston-Super-Mare BS22
Marlborough Flats 8
BS2
Marlborough Hill BS2
Marlborough Hill Pl BS2
Marlborough La BA1
Marlborough St Bath BA1
Bristol BS2
Bristol BS5
Marlbrook Prim Sch BS35
Marlepit Gr BS13
Marlfield Wlk BS13
Marling Rd BS5
Marlowe Ho 3 BS23
Marlwood Dr BS10
Marlwood Sch BS32
Marmaduke St BS3
Marmion Cres BS10
Marne Cl BS14
Marron Cl BS26
Marsden Rd BA2
Marsh Cl BS36
Marsh Comm BS35
Marsh La Bristol BS3
Bristol BS5
Burton SN14,GL9
Farrington Gurney BS39
Portbury BS20
Temple Cloud BS39
Marsh Rd Bristol BS3
Rode BA3
Yatton BS49
Marsh St Avonmouth BS11
4 Bristol BS1
Marshacre La BS35
Marshall Ho 1 BS16
Marshall Wlk BS4
Marsham Way BS30
Marshfield CE Prim Sch
SN14
Marshfield La BS30
Marshfield Rd
Bristol, Frenchay BS16
Bristol, Hillfields BS16
Tormarton GL9
Marshfield Way BA1
Marshwall La BS32
Marson Rd BS21
Marston Rd BS4
Mart The BS23
Martcombe Rd BS20
Martin Cl BS34
Martin Ct 12 BS16
Martin St 2 BS3
Martin's Rd BS15
Martindale Ct BS22
Martindale Rd BS22
Martingale Rd BS4
Martins Cl BS15
Martins Gr BS22
Martlock Cres BS3
Martock BS24
Martock Rd Bristol BS3
Keynsham BS31
Martor Ind Est SN14
Marwood Rd BS4
Mary Carpenter Pl 15 BS2
Mary Ct 1 BS5
Mary Elton Prim Sch BS21
Mary St BS5
Marybush La 7 BS2
Marygold Leaze BS30
Mascot Rd BS3
Masefield Ho BS23
Masefield Way BS7
Maskelyne Ave BS10
Masons View BS36
Matchells Cl BS4
Materman Rd BS14
Matford Cl Bristol BS10
Winterbourne BS36
Matford La GL13
Matthew's Rd 17 BS5
Matthews Cl BS14
Maules La BS16
Maunsell Rd BS11
Maurice Rd BS6
Mautravers Cl BS32
Mawdeley Ho 11 BS3
Max Mill La BS25
Maxse Rd BS4
May Gr GL12
May Park Prim Sch BS5
May St BS15
May Tree Cl BS48
May Tree Rd BA3
May Tree Wlk BS31
May's La BS24

ank Rd BS37 .... 27 D1
ec Gdns BS5 .... 65 A6
bourne BS4 .... 65 A2
rick Rd BA2 .... 101 D5
iffe Pk BS6 .... 49 F2
air BS48 .... 59 E5
low Ave Bristol BS16 .. 51 A2
on-Super-Mare BS22 ... 88 E1
eld Ct BS16 .... 51 A3
eld Pk BS16 .... 51 A2
eld Pk N BS16 .... 51 A2
eld Pk S BS16 .... 51 A2
eld Rd BA2 .... 101 D5
elds BS31 .... 81 E5
ellands BS48 .... 60 A2
ard Cl Bristol BS13 .. 79 C5
everdon BS21 .... 57 F3
ard Rd BS13 .... 79 C5
ars Bldgs BS16 ...... 51 B5
ole Cl BS39 .... 114 E3
nield Cl BS20 .... 45 D3
green La BS24 .... 90 B3
ee Ave BS40 .... 109 C6
ee Ave BS13 .... 79 B7
ee Cl BS13 .... 79 B7
lle Ave BS34 .... 36 A3
ood Ave B4 BS16 ..... 51 B4
ood Cres BS16 .... 51 B4
ood Rd BS16 .... 51 C4
St BS5 .... 64 B6
iam Way BS1 .... 62 F5
ae Rd BS24 .... 106 B5
Cl Bath BA2 .... 101 E3
ol BS11 .... 47 E6
l Ct Bsns Pk BS15 .. 15 B8
La Blagdon BS40 .... 110 E3
ford BS3 .... 82 F4
ford BS25 .... 107 E4
ngton BS35 .... 13 D2
Lands BA2 .... 100 B7
Rd Bristol BS34 ..... 36 F5
ping Sodbury BS37 ... 28 C1
shead BS20 .... 45 C2
Rise BS3 .... 63 F4
St BS3 .... 141 C1
Terr BS40 .... 110 E2
The Alveston BS35 ... 15 A5
on BS34 .... 36 B4
on BS39 .... 114 E3
rry BS41 .... 78 D2
borough BA3 .... 116 A6
nam BS25 .... 125 E8
ton On The Fosse BA3 . 137 F2
bury BA3 .... 116 C3
ley BA15 .... 120 E7
Vale BS22 .... 105 E8
Vale Prim Sch BS22 .. 88 E1
f Way BS35 .... 15 B7
sgate 51 C7
low Cl Backwell BS48 . 76 B6
ol BS16 .... 51 F7
La BS48 .... 59 E2
shead BS20 .... 44 F5
low Court Dr BS30 ... 66 C3
low Croft BS34 ...... 105 B2
low Dr Bath BA2 ..... 118 D8
ping BS24 .... 106 B4
shead BS20 .... 44 F1
low Gdns BA1 .... 84 A1
low Gr BS11 .... 47 D7
low La BA2 .... 85 D1
low Mead
apton Cotterell BS36 . 38 B8
Bristol BS21 .... 57 E3
nhall Gl12 .... 10 B4
on BS39 .... 131 F4
low St
nmouth BS11 .... 33 A1
dge BS26 .... 125 C2
ol BS2 .... 141 C4
ton-Super-Mare BS23 .. 104 E7
low Vale BS5 .... 51 A1
low View
apton Cotterell BS36 . 38 D7
dock BA3 .... 133 A1
low View Cl BA1 .... 101 A8
low Villas 14 BS23 .. 104 E8
low Way BS37 ...... 36 E7
owbank BS22 .... 88 A6
owcroft BS35 ...... 52 A8
owland BS49 ...... 74 A1
owland Rd BS10 .... 34 E4
owlands BS22 ..... 89 C2
ows End BS25 ..... 108 D4
ows Prim Sch The
.... 82 D8
low Tts BS5 ...... 65 D4
lowside 2 BS35 .... 15 D8
lowside Dr BS4 .... 80 A8
losweet Ave BS34 ... 36 B3
ys The Bristol BS16 .. 51 F7
on BS14 .... 43 B3
dway Bristol BS9 .... 48 C6
combe La BS24 ..... 122 F6
rdon Rd BS14 ...... 80 E6
ene BS14 .... 79 C4
ere Rd BA2 .... 102 A2
ace Cl BS1 .... 141 B1
ical Ave BS2, BS8 ... 140 C3
ford BS35 .... 15 C7

Medway Cl BS31 ...... 82 A3
Medway Ct BS35 ...... 15 D8
Medway Dr
Frampton Cotterell BS36 . 38 B7
Keynsham BS31 .... 82 A3
Meere Bank BS11 ..... 34 B1
Meetinghouse La BS49 . 75 A1
Meg Thatcher's Gdns BS5 65 B7
Meg Thatchers Cl BS5 . 65 B7
Melbourne Dr BS37 ... 28 C1
Melbourne Rd BS7 ... 49 D4
Melbourne Terr 2 BS21 57 D2
Melbury Rd BS4 ...... 64 A2
Melcombe Ct BS21 ... 101 D4
Melcombe Rd BA2 ... 101 D4
Melita Rd BS6 .... 49 E3
Mellent Ave BS13 .... 79 C3
Mells Cl BS31 .... 82 A2
Mells La BA3 .... 133 B1
Melrose Ave Bristol BS8 140 B4
Yate BS37 .... 28 A2
Melrose Gr BA2 ..... 101 B3
Melrose Pl BS8 ..... 140 B4
Melrose Terr BA1 ... 85 A2
Melton Cres BS7 .... 50 A7
Melville Rd BS6 .... 49 B1
Melville Terr BS3 .. 63 C3
Melvin Sq BS4 ...... 63 E1
Memorial Cl BS15 ... 65 B4
Memorial Rd Bristol BS15 65 B4
Wrington BS40 ...... 92 E2
Mendip Ave BS22 ... 88 F2
Mendip Centre (Coll) The
.... 110 D2
Mendip Cl Axbridge BS26 125 D2
Keynsham BS31 ..... 81 D5
2 Nailsea BS48 .... 59 E1
Paulton BS39 ...... 131 E4
Yatton BS49 .... 91 B7
Mendip Cres BS16 ... 52 A8
Mendip Edge BS24 .. 121 F8
Mendip Fields BA3 .. 137 C2
Mendip Gdns Bath BA2 118 D8
Yatton BS49 .... 91 B7
Mendip Green Fst Sch
.... 88 E1
Mendip Lodge BS25 . 125 A8
Mendip Rd Bristol BS3 . 63 D3
Locking BS24 ...... 106 D4
Portishead BS20 ... 45 B5
Weston-Super-Mare BS23 105 A7
Yatton BS49 .... 91 B7
Mendip Rise BS24 .. 106 B4
Mendip View BS30 .. 67 C7
Mendip View Ave BS16 51 A3
Mendip Villas BS40 . 110 E2
Mendip Way BA3 ... 132 F3
Menlea BS40 .... 110 D3
Mercer Ct BS14 .... 80 B8
Merchant St BS1 ... 141 B3
Merchants Ct BS8 .. 140 A1
Merchants Quay BS1 141 A1
Merchants Rd Bristol BS8 140 A3
Bristol BS8 .... 140 A3
Merchants The SN14 . 31 E4
Merchants Trad Pk BS2 64 C6
Mercia Dr BS2 ...... 50 A2
Mercier Cl BS37 .... 27 F2
Meredith Ct BS1 ... 140 A1
Merfield Rd BS4 ... 64 B2
Meriden BA1 .... 101 D8
Meridian Pl BS8 ... 140 B3
Meridian Rd BS6 ... 49 C1
Meridian Vale BS8 . 140 B3
Meriet Ave BS13 ... 79 B4
Merioneth St BS3 .. 63 F3
Meriton St BS2 .... 64 B5
Merlin Cl Bristol BS9 . 48 F8
Weston-Super-Mare BS22 105 E8
Merlin Rd BS10 ... 49 B7
Merlin Pk BS20 ... 45 A4
Merlin Rd BS34 ... 35 C6
Merlin Ridge BS16 53 C4
Merlin Way BS37 . 39 F8
Merrett Ct BS7 ... 50 B6
Merrick Ct BS1 .. 141 A1
Merrimans Rd BS11 47 D8
Merrivale Rd BS22 106 B6
Merryweather Cl BS32 36 D8
Merryweathers BA4 64 F2
Merrywood Cl 8 BS5 63 C4
Merrywood Rd BS4 . 63 F1
Mersham BA1 12 BS2 50 A2
Merton Dr BS24 ... 106 A8
Merton Rd BS7 .... 49 E5
Mervyn Rd BS7 .... 49 E4
Meryl Cl BS4 ...... 49 B1
Metford Gr BS6 ... 49 B3
Metford Pl BS6 ... 49 B3
Metford Rd BS6 ... 49 B3
Methwyn Cl BS22 .. 105 C7
Mews The BA1 .... 101 A8
Michaels Mead BA1 84 B2
Middle Ave BS1 ... 141 A2
Middle La Bath BA1 . 85 B1
Kingston Seymour BS21 72 F4
Middle Rd BS15 ... 51 F3
Middle St BS40 ... 128 F4
Middle Yeo Gn BS48 59 D3
Middledown Rd SN14 55 C1
Middleford Ho BS13 79 D4
Middlemead BA3 .. 137 F3
Middlepiece La BA2,BS31 99 B7
Middleton Rd BS11 47 F8
Midford BS24 ..... 104 F2

Midford Hill BA2,BA3 ... 119 C5
Midford La BA2,BA3 .... 119 E7
Midford Rd BA2 ...... 119 B7
Midhaven Rise BS22 ... 88 E4
Midland Bridge Rd
BA1,BA2 .... 142 A2
Midland Rd Bath BA1 . 101 D7
Bristol BS16 .... 51 C4
Bristol BS2 .... 141 C3
Midland St BS2 ..... 141 C2
Midland Terr BS16 .. 50 F3
Midland Way BS35 .. 15 C7
Midsomer Ent Pk BA3 132 C2
Midsomer Norton
Prim Sch BA3 ..... 132 B1
Midsomer Norton
Railway Ctr BA3 ... 138 A8
Midsummer Bldgs BA1 85 B2
Milbourne Cl BA15 .. 120 D7
Milburn Rd BS23 ... 104 F7
Milbury Gdns BS22 . 88 C2
Mildred St BS5 ..... 64 C7
Mile Wlk BS14 ..... 80 A6
Miles Ct BS30 ..... 65 F4
Miles Rd BS8 ...... 49 A1
Miles St BA2 ...... 142 C1
Miles's Bldgs BA1 . 142 B3
Milestone Ct BS22 . 89 D2
Milford Ave BS30 .. 67 B7
Milford St BS3 ..... 63 C4
Milk St BA1 .... 142 B2
Mill Ave BS1 ...... 141 A2
Mill Cl
Frampton Cotterell BS36 . 38 C7
Portbury BS20 ..... 46 D2
Mill Cres BS37 .... 39 B4
Mill Hill BA2 ..... 118 E1
Mill Ho 10 BS5 .... 50 A1
Mill La Bath BA2 .. 101 B6
Bathampton BA2 ... 85 F2
Bitton BS30 ...... 82 E8
Bristol BS3 ...... 63 D4
Bristol BS30 ...... 66 C5
Chew Stoke BS40 . 112 D8
Chipping Sodbury BS37 . 40 E6
Compton Martin BS40 . 129 A7
Congresbury BS49 . 91 D4
Doynton BS30 .... 53 F1
Falfield GL12 .... 9 F7
Frampton Cotterell BS36 . 26 B1
Monkton Combe BA2 . 119 E8
Portbury BS20 .... 46 E3
Priston BA2 ...... 117 A7
Redhill BS40 ..... 111 A8
Timsbury BA3 ..... 116 B1
Tockington BS32 .. 14 B1
Upton Cheyney BS30 . 66 F1
Wrington BS40 .... 109 F8
Winterbourne BS36 . 37 D4
Mill Rd Radstock BA3 . 133 B2
Winterbourne BS36 . 37 D4
Mill Road Ind Est BA3 . 133 B3
Mill Slps BS36 .... 37 E4
Mill Stream Cl BS26 125 C1
Millard Cl BS10 ... 35 D2
Millard's Hill BA3 . 132 C3
Millards Hill BA3 . 132 B3
Millbank Cl BS4 ... 64 E3
Millbook Ct 1 BS6 . 49 E1
Millbrook Ave BS4 . 64 F3
Millbrook Cl BS30 . 66 C6
Millbrook Ct BA2 . 142 C1
Millbrook Pl BA2 . 142 C1
Millcross BS21 .... 73 C8
Miller Cl BS23 .... 104 F8
Miller Ho BS8 .... 140 A2
Miller Wlk BA2 ... 85 F1
Millers Cl BS20 ... 47 C4
Millers Dr BS30 .. 66 D5
Millers Rise BS22 . 89 A4
Millfield
Midsomer Norton BA3 . 137 F8
Thornbury BS35 .... 8 C2
Millfield Dr BS30 . 66 C6
Millground Rd BS13 78 F5
Millier Rd BS49 ... 92 B8
Millman Cl BS13 .. 79 C5
Millmead Ho BS13 . 79 C4
Millmead Rd BA2 .. 101 C5
Millpond Prim Sch BS5 50 A1
Millpond St 8 BS5 . 50 A1
Millpool Ct BS10 .. 35 B1
Millpool Ct EPD BS9 49 B8
Millward Gr BS16 . 51 C4
Millward Terr BS39 131 E6
Milner Gn BS30 ... 66 A4
Milner Rd BS7 .... 49 F6
Milsom St Bath BA1 142 B3
Bristol BS5 ...... 64 B8
Milton Ave Bath BA2 . 101 F4
Weston-Super-Mare BS23 104 E4
Milton Brow BS22 . 88 B2
Milton Cl Nailsea BS48 59 E3
Yate BS37 .... 27 D2
Milton Gn BS22 ... 88 C1
Milton Hill BS22 .. 88 B2
Milton Inf & Jun Schs
BS22 .... 88 C1
Milton Park Rd BS22 88 C1
Milton Pk 1 BS5 .. 64 C7
Milton Rd Bristol BS7 49 E6
Radstock BA3 ..... 132 C1
Weston-Super-Mare
BS22,BS23 .... 105 B8
Yate BS37 .... 27 D2
Milton Rise BS22 .. 88 C1

Miltons Cl BS13 ..... 79 D4
Milverton BS24 ..... 104 F2
Milverton Gdns BS6 . 49 F2
Milward Rd BS31 ... 81 E6
Mina Rd BS2 .... 50 A2
Minehead Rd BS4 .. 63 F1
Minerva Gdns BA2 . 101 C4
Minor's La BS10 ... 34 A8
Minsmere Rd BS31 . 82 A4
Minster Cl 1 BS37 . 39 D7
Minster Way BA2 .. 102 C8
Minto Rd BS2 ...... 50 A2
Minto Road Ind Ctr 8
BS2 .... 50 A2
Minton Cl BS14 .... 80 B5
Mission Rd BS37 ... 27 B4
Mitchell La BS1 ... 141 B2
Mitchell Wlk BS30 . 66 D7
Mitford-Slade Ct BS49 91 C7
Mivart St BS5 ..... 50 B2
Mizzymead Cl 1 BS48 59 D1
Mizzymead Rd BS48 59 E1
Mizzymead Rise BS48 59 E1
Modecombe Gr BS10 34 F3
Mogg St BS2 ...... 50 A2
Molesworth Cl BS13 79 A4
Molesworth Dr BS13 79 A4
Molly Cl BS39 ..... 130 E8
Monger Cotts BS39 . 131 F4
Monger La
Midsomer Norton BA3 . 132 A3
Paulton BS39 ...... 132 A4
Monk Rd BS7 ...... 49 D4
Monk's Park Ave BS7 49 E8
Monks Ave BS15 ... 65 B8
Monks Hill BS22 .. 88 B3
Monks Ho 8 BS37 . 39 D7
Monks Park Sch BS7 49 F8
Monks Park Way BS7 49 E8
Monksdale Rd BA2 . 101 D4
Monkton Ave BS24 . 105 A2
Monkton Combe Jun Sch
BA2 .... 102 C1
Monkton Combe Jun Sch
(Pre-Prep) BA2 ... 102 C1
Monkton Combe
Senior Sch BA2 ... 102 E1
Monkton Farleigh
Prim Sch BA15 ... 103 E7
Monkton Rd BS15 .. 65 B5
Monmouth Cl BS20 44 F4
Monmouth Ct BA1 . 142 A2
Monmouth Hill BS32 23 E4
Monmouth Paddock BA2 135 E4
Monmouth Pl BA1 . 142 B2
Monmouth Rd Bristol BS7 49 D4
Bristol BS15 ...... 51 F1
Pill BS20 .... 47 C5
Monmouth St Bath BA1 142 B2
Bristol BS3 ...... 63 F3
Monsdale Cl BS10 . 35 A3
Monsdale Dr BS10 . 35 A2
Montacute Cl BS34 36 E5
Montague Ct 4 BS2 141 A4
Montague Flats 6 BS2 141 A4
Montague Ho 8 BA1 85 C1
Montague Pl BS6 . 141 A4
Montague St
Peasedown St John BA2 133 E5
Saltford BS31 .... 82 D2
Monteplier BS23 . 141 A4
Montgomery St BS3 63 F3
Montpelier E BS23 87 F1
Montpelier Sta BS6 49 F2
Montpelier 2 BS23 87 F1
Montreaux Ho 2 BS16 51 D4
Montrose Ave BS6 . 49 C1
Montrose Dr BS30 . 66 B6
Montrose Pk BS4 .. 64 B1
Montserrat 5 BA1 . 85 C1
Monument The 1 BS1 141 B2
Moon St BS2 ..... 141 B4
Moor Croft Dr BS30 65 F3
Moor Croft Rd BS24 105 E3
Moor End Spout BS48 59 D2
Moor La Backwell BS48 75 F6
Clapton In Gordano BS20 45 E1
Clevedon BS21 ... 57 E2
Clevedon BS21 ... 58 A2
Hutton BS24 ..... 105 D3
Tickenham BS21 .. 58 F4
Tockington BS32 .. 24 A8
Weston-Super-Mare BS24 105 C7
Weston-Super-Mare BS23 104 E4
Moor Pk BS21 .... 57 E2
Moor Rd Banwell BS29 107 B5
Yatton BS49 ...... 74 B2
Moordell Cl BS37 . 27 D1
Moorend Gdns BS11 47 E7
Moorend Rd BS16 . 37 D3
Moorfield Rd BS48 76 A6
Moorfields Cl BA2 . 101 D3
Moorfields Ho 1 BS5 50 E1
Moorfields Rd Bath BA2 101 D3
Clevedon BS21 ... 57 E2
Moorfields Rd Bristol BS5 64 C7
Moorgrove Ho BS9 . 48 C7
Moorham Rd BS25 . 108 A1
Moorhill St 4 BS5 . 50 B1
Moorhouse La BS10 34 B4
Moorings The BS20 47 C4
Moorland Rd Bath BA2 101 D5
Weston-Super-Mare BS23 104 E4

Moorland Rd continued
Yate BS37 .... 27 D1
Moorland St BS26 . 125 C1
Moorlands Cl BS48 59 D2
Moorlands Dr BA3 . 120 B6
Moorlands Inf Sch BA2 101 D4
Moorlands Jun Sch BA2 101 D3
Moorlands Rd
Bristol, Mayfield Park BS16 51 A2
Bristol, Ridgeway BS16 51 F7
Moorledge La BS39,BS40 113 F7
Moorledge Rd BS40 96 B1
Moorpark Ave BS37 27 D1
Moorside BS49 .... 74 B1
Moorside Ct BS21 . 57 E2
Moorside Villas BS21 57 E2
Moorslade La GL12 . 3 D1
Moravian Ct 4 BS15 65 D8
Moravian Rd BS15 . 65 D8
Morden Wlk BS14 . 80 D7
Moreton Cl BS14 .. 80 A4
Moreton La BS40 . 112 E2
Morford St BA1 .. 142 B4
Morgan Cl BS31 .. 82 D2
Morgan Way BA2 . 133 E2
Morgan's La BS40 128 F2
Morgans Bldgs BS20 59 F8
Morgans Hill Cl BS48 75 D8
Morley Ave BS16 . 52 A4
Morley Cl Bristol BS16 51 D4
Bristol BS34 ..... 36 C7
Morley Rd Bristol BS16 51 D4
Bristol BS3 ...... 63 C4
Morley Sq BS7 ... 49 E4
Morley St Bristol BS5 49 F1
Bristol BS2 ...... 64 B7
Morley Terr Bath BA2 101 D6
1 Bristol BS15 .. 51 D1
Radstock BA3 .... 133 A3
Mornington Rd 14 BS8 49 A2
Morpeth Rd BS4 . 79 D8
Morris La BA1 .... 86 B3
Morris Rd BS7 ... 50 A5
Morse Rd BS5 .... 64 C7
Mortimer Cl BA1 . 84 B2
Mortimer Rd Bristol BS34 36 B2
Bristol BS8 ...... 140 A3
Morton St BS5 .. 64 B7
Morton St Bristol BS5 64 B7
Thornbury BS35 .. 8 C4
Morton Way BS35 . 8 D1
Moseley Gr BS23 . 104 E2
Motorway Distribution Ctr
BS11 .... 33 C2
Mount Beacon Row 1
BA1 .... 85 A1
Mount Cl BS36 ... 37 F8
Mount Cres BS36 . 37 D7
Mount Gdns BS15 65 D6
Mount Gr BA2 ... 101 B3
Mount Hill Rd BS15 65 D6
Mount Pleasant Bath BA2 102 D1
Hallen BS10 ..... 34 C2
Pill BS20 .... 47 D4
Radstock BA3 ... 133 B2
Mount Pleasant Terr BS3 63 C4
Mount Rd BA1 ... 142 B4
Mount The BS49 .. 91 E8
Mount View Bath BA1 85 A1
Bath BA2 .... 101 B3
Mountain Ash BA1 84 D1
Mountain Wood BA1 86 C2
Mountain's La BA3 115 E6
Mountbatten Cl
Weston-Super-Mare BS22 88 E4
Yate BS37 .... 27 D3
Mounteney's La GL12 18 D7
Mow Barton Bristol BS13 78 F6
Yate BS37 .... 27 D2
Mowbray Rd BS14 . 80 C7
Mowcroft Rd BS13 . 79 D4
Moxham Dr BS13 .. 79 C4
Mud La BS49 ..... 74 D2
Muddy La BS22 ... 89 A8
Muirfield Bristol BS30 66 A6
Yate BS37 .... 39 E8
Mulberry Ave BS20 45 E5
Mulberry Cl Backwell BS48 76 A6
Bristol BS15 ..... 65 C5
Portishead BS20 . 45 F5
Weston-Super-Mare BS22 89 A1
Mulberry Dr BS15 . 51 F1
Mulberry La BS24 122 C6
Mulberry Rd BS49 91 E3
Mulberry Wlk BS9 48 C8
Mule St GL13 ... 4 B3
Muller Ave BS7 ... 49 F4
Muller Rd BS5,BS7 50 B3
Mulready Cl BS7 . 50 C6
Mumbleys Hill BS35 14 E7
Mumbleys La Thornbury,
Alveston Down BS35 14 E6
Thornbury, Kington BS35 14 E8
Munford Ave BS13 79 B4
Mundy Wlk BS13 . 79 B4
Murhill BA3 ...... 120 C6
Murray St 9 BS3 . 63 C4
Mus Of Costume BA1 142 B3
Mus of East Asian Art
BA1 .... 142 B3
Musgrove Cl BS11 33 C2
Myrtle Dr BS11 ... 47 E5
Myrtle Gdns BS49 91 B8
Myrtle Hill BS20 . 47 C5

Myrtle Ave BS2 ... 140 C4
Myrtle St BS3 ... 63 B3
Myrtleberry Mead BS22 ... 89 A5
Myrtles The BS24 ... 105 D2

N

Nags Head Hill BS5 ... 65 A7
Nailsea & Backwell Sta BS48 ... 75 F7
Nailsea Christ Church Jun Sch BS48 ... 59 D3
Nailsea Cl BS13 ... 79 A7
Nailsea Moor La BS48 ... 74 F7
Nailsea Park Cl BS48 ... 59 F2
Nailsea Pk BS48 ... 59 F2
Nailsea Sec Sch BS48 ... 59 E1
Nailsea Wall BS21 ... 74 C8
Nailsea Wall La BS48 ... 74 E7
Nailsworth Ave BS37 ... 27 E1
Naish Hill BS20 ... 45 F1
Naish Ho BA2 ... 101 A6
Naish La BS48 ... 77 D3
Naish's Cross BA3 ... 137 D3
Naishcombe Hill BS30 ... 67 C7
Nanny Hurn's La BS39 ... 114 A1
Napier Ct BS1 ... 140 B1
Napier Miles Rd BS11 ... 48 A8
Napier Rd Avonmouth BS11 ... 33 B1
  Bath BA1 ... 84 B1
  Bristol BS5 ... 50 B2
  Bristol BS6 ... 49 B2
Napier Sq BS11 ... 33 A1
Napier St BS5 ... 64 B6
Narrow La BS16 ... 51 E4
Narrow Plain BS2 ... 141 B2
Narrow Quay BS1 ... 141 A2
Narroways Rd BS2 ... 50 A3
Naseby Wlk BS5 ... 50 F1
Nash Cl BS31 ... 82 A5
Nash Dr BS7 ... 50 C7
Nates La BS40 ... 92 F1
Naunton Way BS22 ... 88 B2
Neads Dr BS30 ... 66 C5
Neale Way BS11 ... 33 C1
Neate Ct BS4 ... 36 C8
Neath Rd BS5 ... 64 D8
Nelson Bldgs BA1 ... 142 C4
Nelson Ct BS22 ... 88 E4
Nelson Ho Bath BA1 ... 142 C4
  Bristol BS16 ... 51 D5
Nelson Par BS3 ... 63 D4
Nelson Pl BA1 ... 142 C4
Nelson Pl W BA1 ... 142 A2
Nelson St Bristol BS16 ... 51 D5
  Bristol BS1 ... 141 A3
  Bristol BS3 ... 63 A2
Nelson Terr BA1 ... 142 C4
Nelson Villas BA1 ... 142 B2
Nempnett St BS40 ... 111 D5
Neston Wlk BS4 ... 79 F8
Netham Park Ind Est BS5 ... 64 D6
Netham Rd BS5 ... 64 C6
Netham View Ind Pk BS5 ... 64 D7
Netherton Wood La BS48 ... 75 A6
Netherways BS21 ... 57 B1
Nettlestone Cl BS10 ... 34 E4
Nettleton & Burton CE Prim Sch SN14 ... 43 B2
Nettleton Rd SN14 ... 43 B2
Neva Rd BS23 ... 104 E6
Nevalan Dr BS5 ... 65 A6
Nevil Rd BS7 ... 49 E4
Neville Rd BS15 ... 51 E2
New Bldgs BS16 ... 50 C6
New Bond St BA1 ... 142 C2
New Bond Street Pl BA1 ... 142 C2
New Bristol Rd BS22 ... 88 E1
New Brunswick Ave BS5 ... 65 B7
New Charlotte St BS3 ... 63 E4
New Cheltenham Rd BS15 ... 51 E1
New Church Rd BS23 ... 104 D2
New Cut Bow BS21 ... 73 A6
New Fosseway Rd BS14 ... 80 B6
New Fosseway Sch BS14 ... 80 B6
New John St BS3 ... 63 C3
New King St BA1 ... 142 B2
New Kingsley Rd BS2 ... 141 C2
New La BS35 ... 15 C5
New Leaze BS32 ... 24 C3
New Mills La GL12 ... 19 E8
New Orchard St BA1 ... 142 C2
New Park Ho BS21 ... 57 D5
New Pit Cotts BA3 ... 116 F1
New Queen St Bristol BS15 ... 65 B8
  Bristol BS3 ... 63 D4
New Rd Banwell BS29 ... 106 E4
  Bathford BA1 ... 86 D2
  Bristol, Filton BS34 ... 35 F3
  Bristol, Harry Stoke BS34 ... 36 D3
  Churchill BS25 ... 108 E4
  Clevedon BS21 ... 57 D2
  Freshford BA3 ... 120 B5
  High Littleton BS39 ... 115 C3
  Kilmersdon BA3 ... 139 E4
  Kingswood GL12 ... 11 E6
  North Nibley GL11 ... 5 E4
  Olveston BS35 ... 14 A2
  Pensford BS39 ... 97 D3
  Pill BS20 ... 47 C4
  Rangeworthy BS37 ... 17 C1

New Rd continued
  Rangeworthy BS37 ... 27 A8
  Redhill BS40 ... 94 A4
  Shipham BS25 ... 108 E1
  Tytherington GL12 ... 16 C6
New Rock Ind Est BA3 ... 137 D2
New Siblands Sch BS35 ... 8 D1
New St Bath BA1 ... 142 B2
  Bristol BS2 ... 141 C3
  Charfield GL12 ... 11 A6
New Stadium Rd BS5 ... 50 B2
New Station Rd BS16 ... 51 A4
New Station Way BS16 ... 51 A4
New Street Flats BS2 ... 141 C3
New Thomas St BS2 ... 141 C2
New Tyning La BS39 ... 29 C4
New Walls BS4 ... 63 F4
New Wlk BS15 ... 65 B5
Newark St BA1 ... 142 C1
Newbolt Cl BS22 ... 89 A2
Newbourne Rd BS22 ... 105 C8
Newbrick Rd BS34 ... 37 A5
Newbridge Cl BS4 ... 64 D5
Newbridge Ct BA1 ... 101 B7
Newbridge Gdns BA1 ... 101 A8
Newbridge Hill BA1 ... 101 B7
Newbridge Ho BS9 ... 48 C4
Newbridge Jun Sch BA1 ... 101 B7
Newbridge Rd Bath BA1,BA2 ... 101 B7
  Bristol BS4 ... 64 E6
Newbridge St John's Inf Sch BA1 ... 101 B7
Newbridge Trad Est BS4 ... 64 D5
Newbury Rd BS7 ... 50 A7
Newclose La BS40 ... 112 D1
Newcombe Dr BS9 ... 48 C4
Newcombe Rd BS9 ... 48 F7
Newditch La BS40 ... 77 C1
Newent Ave BS15 ... 65 C7
Newfields BS40 ... 126 C8
Newfoundland Rd
  Bristol BS2 ... 50 A1
Newfoundland St BS2 ... 141 C4
Newfoundland Way BS2 ... 141 C4
Newgate BS1 ... 141 B3
Newhaven Pl BS20 ... 44 E4
Newhaven Rd BS20 ... 44 D4
Newland Dr BS13 ... 79 A4
Newland Rd Bristol BS13 ... 79 A3
  Weston-Super-Mare BS23 ... 104 F6
Newland Wlk BS13 ... 79 A3
Newlands Ave BS36 ... 38 C7
Newlands Cl BS20 ... 45 C5
Newlands Gn BS21 ... 57 G1
Newlands Hill BS20 ... 45 C4
Newlands Rd BS31 ... 81 D4
Newlands The BS16 ... 51 B7
Newleaze BS34 ... 36 A2
Newlyn Ave BS9 ... 48 D5
Newlyn Way BS37 ... 27 F2
Newlyn Wlk BS4 ... 64 B1
Newman Cl BS37 ... 39 B4
Newmans La ... 116 B2
Newmarket Ave BS1 ... 141 A3
Newnham Cl BS14 ... 80 D7
Newnham Pl BS34 ... 23 F1
Newpit La BS30 ... 66 F2
Newport Cl Clevedon BS21 ... 57 C2
  Portishead BS20 ... 44 F4
Newport Rd BS20 ... 47 C5
Newport St BS3 ... 63 E3
Newquay Rd BS4 ... 63 F1
Newry Wlk BS4 ... 63 E1
Newsome Ave BS20 ... 47 C4
Newton Cl Bristol BS15 ... 51 F1
  West Harptree BS40 ... 128 E6
Newton Dr BS30 ... 66 A5
Newton Gn BS48 ... 75 C8
Newton Rd Bath BA2 ... 100 F6
  Bristol BS30 ... 66 A5
  Weston-Super-Mare BS23 ... 104 E6
Newton St BS5 ... 64 A8
Newton's Rd
  Weston-Super-Mare BS23 ... 88 E3
  Weston-Super-Mare BS23 ... 88 E4
Newtown GL12 ... 11 A5
Niblett Cl BS15 ... 65 F6
Nibley La BS37 ... 28 A8
Nibley Rd BS11 ... 47 F5
Nichol's Rd BS20 ... 44 F5
Nicholas La BS5 ... 65 A6
Nicholas Rd BS5 ... 50 B1
Nicholas St BS3 ... 63 E4
Nicholettes BS30 ... 66 D5
Nicholls La BS36 ... 37 E6
Nigel Pk BS11 ... 47 E7
Nightingale Cl Bristol BS4 ... 64 E6
  Frampton Cotterell BS36 ... 38 A6
  Thornbury BS35 ... 8 D2
Nightingale Ct BA1 ... 101 A8
Nightingale Gdns BS48 ... 59 D3
Nightingale La BS36 ... 38 A8
Nightingale Rise BS20 ... 44 F3
Nightingale Valley BA3 ... 138 B8
Nile St BA1 ... 142 A2
Nine Tree Hill BS1 ... 49 E1
Ninth Ave BS7 ... 36 B1
Nippors Way BS25 ... 124 F8
Nithsdale Rd BS23 ... 104 E4
Nixon Trad Units BS24 ... 105 A3
No 1 Royal Cres Mus BA1 ... 142 B3
Noble Ave BS30 ... 66 C4

Nomis Pk BS49 ... 91 E2
Nore Gdns BS20 ... 45 C6
Nore Park Dr BS20 ... 44 F5
Nore Rd BS20 ... 44 F5
Norfolk Ave Bristol BS2 ... 141 B4
  Bristol BS6 ... 49 E2
Norfolk Bldgs BA1 ... 142 A2
Norfolk Cres BA1 ... 142 A2
Norfolk Gr BS31 ... 81 C4
Norfolk Pl BS3 ... 63 C3
Norfolk Rd Portishead BS20 ... 45 E4
  Weston-Super-Mare BS23 ... 104 F5
Norland Rd BS8 ... 62 F8
Norley Rd BS7 ... 49 F7
Norman Gr BS15 ... 51 C2
Norman Rd Bristol BS2 ... 50 A2
  Saltford BS31 ... 82 E3
Normanby Rd BS5 ... 50 B1
Normans The BA2 ... 85 F2
Normanton Rd BS8 ... 49 A2
Norrisville Rd BS6 ... 49 E1
North Chew Terr BS40 ... 96 B3
North Croft BS30 ... 66 D4
North Ct BS32 ... 24 D3
North Devon Rd BS16 ... 51 A5
North Down Cl BS25 ... 125 F8
North Down La BS25 ... 125 F8
North Dro BS48 ... 59 A2
North East Rd BS35 ... 8 C2
North End BS49 ... 74 A2
North End Rd BS49 ... 73 F3
North Gr BS20 ... 47 C4
North Green St BS8 ... 62 F6
North Hills Cl BS24 ... 105 B2
North La Bath BA2 ... 102 D5
  Nailsea BS48 ... 59 B1
  Weston-Super-Mare BS23 ... 104 E7
North Leaze BS41 ... 62 B2
North Mdws BA2 ... 133 E8
North Par Bath BA2 ... 102 C6
  Yate BS37 ... 27 E2
North Parade Bldgs BA1 ... 142 C2
North Parade Pas BA1 ... 142 C2
North Parade Rd BA2 ... 102 B6
North Pk BS15 ... 51 E1
North Rd Banwell BS29 ... 107 A3
  Bath BA2 ... 102 B2
  Bathampton BA2 ... 102 C6
  Bristol BS3 ... 63 A4
  Bristol BS6 ... 49 E2
  Bristol BS8 ... 49 B2
  Leigh Woods BS8 ... 62 D7
  Lympsham BS24 ... 122 D2
  Midsomer Norton BA3 ... 132 A1
  Thornbury BS35 ... 8 B3
  Timsbury BA3 ... 116 C2
  Winterbourne BS36 ... 37 F7
  Yate BS37 ... 27 B3
  Yate, Engine Common BS37 ... 27 B5
North Side Rd BS48 ... 93 F8
North St Bristol BS1 ... 141 B4
  Bristol BS16 ... 51 E5
  Bristol BS3 ... 63 B3
  Bristol BS30 ... 66 C4
  Nailsea BS48 ... 59 B1
  Norton St Philip BA3 ... 135 E4
  Weston-Super-Mare BS23 ... 104 E8
  Wickwar GL12 ... 18 A6
North Stoke La BS30 ... 83 B8
North Terr Bristol BS6 ... 49 A4
  Bristol, Mangotsfield BS16 ... 51 E5
  Bristol, Upper Soundwell BS15 ... 51 D4
  Radstock BA3 ... 133 B2
North View Cl BA2 ... 101 B5
North View Dr BS29 ... 107 A2
North Way Bath BA2 ... 101 A5
  Bristol BS34 ... 36 B4
  Midsomer Norton BA3 ... 132 A1
North Wlk BS37 ... 27 E1
Northampton Bldgs BA1 ... 142 B4
Northampton Ho BS48 ... 60 D3
Northampton St BA1 ... 142 B4
Northanger Ct BA2 ... 27 C3
Northavon Bsns Ctr BS37 ... 27 C3
Northcote Rd Clevedon BS21 ... 51 F6
  Bristol BS5 ... 64 F7
  Bristol BS8 ... 48 F1
Northdown Rd BA3 ... 132 E5
Northend Ave BS15 ... 51 D2
Northend Gdns BS15 ... 51 D2
Northend Rd BS15 ... 51 E1
Northern Path BS21 ... 57 F3
Northern Way BS21 ... 57 F3
Northfield Radstock BA3 ... 133 A3
  Timsbury BA3 ... 116 C3
  Winsley BA15 ... 120 F7
  Yate BS37 ... 39 D8
Northfield Ave BS15 ... 65 D5
Northfield Ho Bath BA1 ... 63 C4
  Bristol BS3 ... 63 C4
Northfield La SN14 ... 55 F1
Northfield Rd Bristol BS5 ... 65 B7
  Portishead BS20 ... 44 E3
Northfields BA1 ... 84 F1
Northgate St BA1 ... 142 C2
Northleach Wlk BS11 ... 47 F5
Northleaze Prim Sch BS41 ... 62 B2
Northleigh Ave BS22 ... 88 C1
Northmead Ave BA3 ... 131 F2
Northmead Cl BA3 ... 131 F2
Northmead La BS37 ... 26 D6
Northmead Rd BA3 ... 131 F2
Northover Ct BS16 ... 22 E6

Northover Rd BS9 ... 35 A1
Northumberland Bldgs BA1 ... 142 B2
Northumberland Pl BA1 ... 142 C2
Northumberland Rd BS6 ... 49 C2
Northumbria Dr BS9 ... 49 B4
Northville Rd BS7 ... 36 A1
Northwick Gdns BS39 ... 113 D4
Northwick Rd Bristol BS7 ... 49 F8
  Chew Magna BS39,BS40 ... 96 B3
  Pilning BS35 ... 12 E1
Northwoods Wlk BS10 ... 35 D3
Norton Cl Bristol BS15 ... 65 F7
  Chew Magna BS40 ... 96 B3
Norton Down La BA3 ... 137 F5
Norton Hall La BA3 ... 138 B8
Norton Ho Bristol BS1 ... 141 B1
Norton La
  Chew Magna BS39,BS40 ... 96 D5
  Wellow BA2,BA3 ... 135 B7
  Weston-Super-Mare BS22 ... 88 C4
  Whitchurch BS14 ... 80 C2
Norton Radstock Coll BA3 ... 132 F2
Norton Rd BS4 ... 64 A3
Norton St Philip CE Prim Sch BA3 ... 135 E4
Nortons Wood La BS21 ... 58 A5
Norwich Dr BS4 ... 64 F6
Norwood Ave BA2 ... 102 E5
Norwood Farm BA3 ... 135 F7
Norwood Gr BS20 ... 44 F5
Notgrove Cl BS22 ... 88 B2
Nottingham Rd BS7 ... 49 E3
Nottingham St BS3 ... 63 E3
Nova Scotia Pl BS1 ... 140 A1
Nova Way BS11 ... 33 B1
Nover's Lane Inf Sch BS4 ... 79 C7
Nover's Lane Jun Sch BS4 ... 79 C7
Novers Cres BS4 ... 79 C8
Novers Hill BS4 ... 79 D8
Novers Hill Trad Est BS3 ... 63 C1
Novers La BS4 ... 79 D7
Novers Park Dr BS4 ... 79 C8
Novers Park Rd BS4 ... 79 C8
Novers Rd BS4 ... 79 C8
Nowhere La BS48 ... 60 A1
Nugent Hill BS6 ... 49 D1
Nunney Cl BS31 ... 82 A2
Nupdown Rd BS35 ... 1 E5
Nursery Gdns BS10 ... 35 A3
Nursery The GL12 ... 16 B5
Nursery Rise BS23 ... 63 B3
Nursery Thy BS3 ... 63 B3
Nutfield Gr BS34 ... 36 B2
Nutgrove Ave BS3 ... 63 E3
Nutgrove La BS40 ... 96 A4
Nuthatch Dr BS16 ... 50 F6
Nuthatch Gdns BS16 ... 51 A6
Nutwell Rd BS22 ... 88 E2
Nutwell Sq BS22 ... 88 E2
Nye Dro BS24 ... 107 E8
Nympsfield BS15 ... 51 E2

O

Oak Ave BA2 ... 101 C3
Oak Cl Bristol BS34 ... 36 D7
  Yate BS37 ... 27 D3
Oak Ct BS14 ... 80 A5
Oak Dr BS20 ... 45 B4
Oak Gr BS20 ... 47 C5
Oak Ho BS13 ... 79 D4
Oak La BS5 ... 50 F2
Oak Lodge BS37 ... 39 D8
Oak Rd Bristol BS7 ... 49 E5
  Colerne SN14 ... 70 F7
Oak Tree Ave BS16 ... 53 B4
Oak Tree Cl BS15 ... 65 C3
Oak Tree Wlk BS31 ... 81 D3
Oakdale Ave BS16 ... 51 D8
Oakdale Cl BS16 ... 51 D8
Oakdale Ct BS16 ... 51 D7
Oakdale Gdns BS22 ... 88 F2
Oakdale Rd Bristol BS14 ... 80 A8
  Bristol BS16 ... 51 D8
Oakdene Ave BS5 ... 50 D3
Oakenhill Rd BS4 ... 64 E2
Oakenhill Wlk BS4 ... 64 E2
Oakes La GL9 ... 42 B5
Oakfield Bsns Pk BS15 ... 65 D7
Oakfield Cl BA1 ... 101 D8
Oakfield Gr BS8 ... 140 B4
Oakfield Pl BS8 ... 140 B4
Oakfield Rd Bristol BS15 ... 65 D7
  Bristol BS8 ... 140 B4
  Keynsham BS31 ... 81 E4
Oakford Ave BS23 ... 104 F8
Oakford La SN14 ... 70 B2
Oakhanger Dr BS11 ... 34 B1
Oakhill BS24 ... 105 A2
Oakhill Ave BS30 ... 66 C2
Oakhill Cl BS48 ... 60 B1
Oakhill La BS10 ... 34 C4
Oakhill Rd BA2 ... 101 F2
Oakhurst Rd BS9 ... 48 F5
Oakland Bsn Pk BS37 ... 27 B3
Oakland Rd Bristol BS6 ... 49 C3
  Bristol BS5 ... 64 E8
  Bristol BS6 ... 49 B1
Oaklands Clevedon BS21 ... 57 C4
  Paulton BS39 ... 131 E4

Oaklands continued
  Temple Cloud BS39 ... 114 E1
Oaklands Cl BS16 ... 51 F5
Oaklands Dr
  Almondsbury BS32 ... 23 F3
  Bristol BS16 ... 51 F5
  Bristol BS30 ... 66 C2
Oaklands Rd BS16 ... 51 E5
Oakleaze BS35 ... 8 D3
Oakleaze Rd BS35 ... 8 C2
Oakleigh Ave BS5 ... 64 C8
Oakleigh Cl BS48 ... 76 A6
Oakleigh Gdns BS30 ... 66 C2
Oakley Bath BA2 ... 101 A6
  Clevedon BS21 ... 57 E1
Oakley Rd BS7 ... 49 F6
Oakmeade Pk BS4 ... 64 C3
Oakridge Cl Bristol BS15 ... 65 F8
  Winscombe BS25 ... 125 A8
Oaks The Nailsea BS48 ... 60 A2
  Winford BS40 ... 95 A5
Oaksey Gr BS48 ... 60 A1
Oaktree Cres BS32 ... 24 C3
Oaktree Ct BS11 ... 47 E6
Oaktree Gdns BS13 ... 78 E5
Oakwood Ave BS9 ... 49 C6
Oakwood Gdns BS36 ... 37 E5
Oakwood Pk BS16 ... 51 C6
Oakwood Rd BS9 ... 49 C5
Oatfield BS48 ... 76 A7
Oatlands Ave BS14 ... 80 A5
Oberon Ave BS5 ... 50 E1
Odins Rd BA2 ... 101 F1
Okebourne Cl BS10 ... 35 B3
Okebourne Rd BS10 ... 35 B3
Old Ashley Hill BS6 ... 49 F2
Old Aust Rd BS32 ... 24 C3
Old Banwell Rd BS24 ... 106 B4
Old Barn La BS40 ... 93 F4
Old Barrow Hill BS11 ... 47 D7
Old Bond St BA1 ... 142 B2
Old Bread St BS2 ... 141 C2
Old Brewhouse The BA1 ... 84 F1
Old Bristol Rd
  Priddy BA5 ... 126...
  Weston-Super-Mare BS22 ... 88 F3
Old Chapel BA1 ... 142 C4
Old Chelsea La BS8 ... 61 C4
Old Church Rd
  Axbridge BS26 ... 125 B2
  Clevedon BS21 ... 57 F3
  Nailsea BS48 ... 59 D1
  Weston-Super-Mare BS23 ... 104 E7
Old Coach Rd BS26 ... 123 F1
Old Down Hill BS32 ... 13 F2
Old Down Rd GL9 ... 30 F...
Old England Way BA2 ... 135 E1
Old Farm La BS5 ... 65 B6
Old Ferry Rd BA2 ... 102 D5
Old Forge Way BA2 ... 135 E1
Old Fosse Rd BA2 ... 101 E1
Old Frome Rd BA2 ... 119 E8
Old Gloucester Rd
  Alveston BS35 ... 15 A4
  Bristol BS16 ... 37 B3
  Bristol BS36 ... 37 B3
  Frampton Cotterell BS36 ... 26 C1
  Thornbury BS35 ... 15 A4
Old Hill Winford BS40 ... 95 A4
  Wrington BS40 ... 92 F2
Old King St BA1 ... 142 B3
Old King Street Ct BS1 ... 141 B3
Old La BS16 ... 51 F8
Old Manor Cl GL12 ... 11 F5
Old Market St GL12 ... 141 C3
Old Midford Rd BA2 ... 119 C6
Old Mill Cl BS37 ... 27 F1
Old Mill Rd BS20 ... 45 E4
Old Mill Way BS24 ... 106 A4
Old Millard's Hill BA3 ... 133 A3
Old Mills Ind Est BS39 ... 131 F7
Old Mills La BS39 ... 131 F7
Old Mixon Rd BS24 ... 105 C3
Old Newbridge Hill BA1 ... 100 E7
Old Orch BA1 ... 142 C2
Old Orchard St BA1 ... 142 C2
Old Park Hill BS2 ... 140 C3
Old Park Rd Bristol BS11 ... 47 E7
  Clevedon BS21 ... 57 D4
Old Pit Rd BA3 ... 138 D3
Old Pit Terr BA3 ... 133 E4
Old Police Sta The BS4 ... 64 F4
Old Post Office La BS23 ... 104 D8
Old Priory Rd BS20 ... 47 C4
Old Quarry BA2 ... 101 E3
Old Quarry Rd BS11 ... 47 F7
Old Quarry Rise BS11 ... 47 F6
Old Rd BA3 ... 134 C3
Old Rectory Rd GL12 ... 16 B6
Old School Ho The BA1 ... 142 C4
Old School La BS24 ... 122 B1
Old Sneed Ave BS9 ... 48 D4
Old Sneed Cotts BS9 ... 48 E4
Old Sneed Pk BS9 ... 48 D4
Old Sneed Rd BS9 ... 48 D4
Old Sodbury CE Prim Sch BS37 ... 40 D5
Old St BS21 ... 57 F3
Old Station Cl BS40 ... 109 C8
Old Tarnwell BS39 ... 97 A2
Old Tk BA3 ... 139 C1
Old Vicarage Ct BS14 ... 80 C5
Old Vicarage Gn BS31 ... 81 E5

ge Pl BS8 ....49 A1
ie The
.................49 E1
...35 ....14 A3
...24 ....121 D5
Gdns The
.................110 E2
Rd BA2 ....101 F3
n Rd
y BS49 ....91 B5
se BS48 ....77 B8
e BS14 ....80 A3
nase BS30 ....44 C2
Rd BS14 ....80 C3
nase BS30 ....66 A2
urt Prim Sch
.................51 B6
urt Rd BS16 .....51 A5
— Thornbury BS35 ...7 B4
.................67 D5
rim Sch BS35 .....7 B5
n-Severn
.....................7 B4
...21 ....57 E1
ris Sch BA1 .....83 F1
...BA2 ....101 E4
...ark Halt BA2 ...101 D6
...BS8 ....62 F5
d Bath BA2 .....142 A1
.....................140 A1
...a BS35 ....25 D7
...ve BS36 ....38 C6
...Wlk BS37 .....78 E7
...Cres BS24 ....105 A3
...Prim Sch BS24 ...105 A2
...son BS24 ......105 B1
...y Pk BS32 .....14 C4
...e BS21 ....57 D2
...n BS37 ....27 B8
...— BS35 ....14 F4
...oks Rd BA3 ....137 E7
...rim Sch BS35 ...14 A3
...ld BS7 ....49 E5
...l BS34 ....36 D6
...d BS34 ....35 D7
...BA1 ....142 A3
...BA2 ....142 A3
...BA2 ....101 D1
...BA2 ....101 D1
...s30 ....65 F4
...BA1 ....142 C2
...BS2 ....141 C4
...ive Bristol BS11 ...140 C2
...Norton BA3 ....131 F1
...BS21 ....58 E4
.....................8 D1
...nd BS30 ....66 B4
...Banwell BS29 ...107 B3
...BS39 ....113 C3
...s 65 E8
....................48 F5
...LL2 ....11 A5
...ry BS49 ....91 D4
...o 94 C8
...n BS48 ....77 A8
...BS31 ....81 D6
...BS30 ....45 D5
...per-Mare,
...BS22 ....88 B3
...per-Mare,
.......................88 F2
...BA15 ....120 F3
...ne BS36 ....37 E5
...BS40 ....92 E2
.......................27 F2
...l The BS24 ....105 F4
...otts BA1 ....116 F1
...res BS11 ....36 A2
...t Bristol BS34 ...36 A2
...BS5 ....64 D7
...BS4 ....74 F1
...BS23 ....88 B3
...r Aust BS35 ....13 A7
...BS25 ....108 A4
...nd BS40 ....128 F4
...dns Bristol BS15 ...65 F8
...e BS39 ....131 E6
...range BS35 ......8 B2
...s BA1 ....140 C2
...ea
...l BS35 ....15 A5
...BS23 ....47 D4
...d Axbridge BS26 ...125 C1
...BS48 ....76 A6
.......................65 E8
.......................64 F6
.......................49 E4
...s32 ....57 D2
...ath BS36 ....38 D7
...24 ....105 E2
...on BS41 ....61 F1
...-48 ....59 D1
...39 ....131 E6
...36 ....53 B5
...Rise BS35 ....14 A3
...g BS5 ....64 D7
...e BS3 ....140 C2
...uper-Mare BS23 ...104 E8
...uper BA2 ....101 B6
...The
...s29 ....107 A3
...I Bristol BS16 ...36 D4
...BA3 ....120 C5
...s24 ....106 A5

P

Pack Horse La BA2 ......118 F7
Paddock Cl Bristol BS16 ...52 C6
...........................24 E2
Paddock Gdn BS14 ....79 F4
Paddock Gdns BS35 ......15 A5
Paddock The
Banwell BS29 ....107 A3
Clevedon BS21 ....57 D2
Corston BA2 ....100 B7
Portishead BS20 ....45 D4
Paddock Woods BA2 ......102 D2
Paddocks The Bath BA2 ...102 B1
Sandford BS25 ....108 C4
Thornbury BS35 ....8 B2
Weston-Super-Mare BS23 ...104 D2
Padfield Cl BA2 ....101 B5
Padleigh Hill BA2 ....101 B2
Padmore Ct **7** BS5 ....64 D7
Padstow Rd BS4 ....79 F8
Pagans Hill BS40 ....95 D2
Page Ct BS16 ....51 D4
Page Rd BS16 ....51 D4
Page's Ct BS49 ....91 C8

Orchard The continued
Pensford BS39 ....97 E4
Pill BS20 ....47 C4
Stanton Drew BS39 ....97 A2
Tytherington GL12 ....16 B5
Orchard Vale Bristol BS15 ...65 F7
Midsomer Norton BA3 ...131 F1
Orchard View
Ham Green Hospl BS20 ...47 E4
Orchard Way BA2 ......133 D7
Orchard Wlk
Churchill BS25 ....108 E4
Kingswood GL12 ....11 F4
Orchards The Bristol BS11 ...47 E6
Bristol BS15 ....65 C8
Oriel Gdns BA1 ....85 C2
Oriel Gr BA2 ....101 B4
Orion Dr BS21 ....36 D6
Orland Way BS30 ....66 A3
Orlebar Gdns BS11 .....34 B2
Orme Dr BS21 ....57 D5
Ormerod Rd BS9 ....48 E5
Ormonds Cl BS32 ....24 E1
Ormsley Cl BS34 ....36 C8
Orpen Gdns BS7 ....50 B5
Orpen Pk BS32 ....24 B3
Orpheus Ave BS34 ......36 D6
Orwell Dr BS31 ....82 A4
Orwell St BS3 ....63 E3
Osborne Ave BS7 ....49 F3
Weston-Super-Mare BS23 ...104 F7
Osborne Cl BS34 ....36 D4
Osborne Rd Bath BA1 ...101 B7
Bristol BS3 ....63 C4
Bristol BS8 ....49 A1
Severn Beach BS35 ....22 A2
Weston-Super-Mare BS23 ...104 F7
Osborne Terr BS3 ....63 D3
Osborne Villas BS2 ....140 C4
Osborne Wallis Ho BS8 ...140 A1
Oslings La BA1 ....86 B2
Osprey Cl BS34 ....36 A8
Osprey Gdns BS22 ......88 F1
Osprey Pk BS35 ....8 D3
Osprey Rd **13** BS5 ......64 C7
Ottawa Rd BS23 ....104 F3
Otter Rd **8** BS21 ....57 E1
Otterford Cl BS14 ......80 B5
Ottery Cl BS11 ....34 A1
Ottrells Mead BS32 .....24 C3
Our Lady of Lourdes
Prim RC Sch BS15 ....65 E7
Our Lady of the Rosary
Cath Prim Sch BS11 ....48 A8
Our Lady of the Rosary
Prim Sch BS11 ....34 A1
Oval The BA2 ....101 C4
Over La BS35 ....23 D2
Overdale
Peasedown St John BA3 ...116 F3
Radstock BA3 ....132 E5
Overhill BS20 ....47 D4
Overndale Rd BS16 ....51 C6
Overndale Rd BS37 ......41 A7
Overnhill Cl BS16 ....51 D5
Overnhill Rd BS16 ......51 D5
Overnhurst Ct **2** BS16 ...51 D5
Overton **3** BS6 ....64 D1
Overton Rd BS6 ....49 E2
Owen Dr BS8 ....61 B4
Owen Gr BS9 ....49 B5
Owen St **10** BS5 ....64 B8
Owls Head Rd BS15 .....65 E6
Oxbarton BS34 ....36 F5
Oxen Leaze BS32 ....24 E2
Oxford Pl **14** Bristol BS1 ...50 B1
10 Bristol BS8 ....62 F6
Weston-Super-Mare BS23 ...104 D7
Oxford Row BA1 ....142 B3
Oxford Sq BS24 ....106 B6
Oxford St Bristol BS2 ...140 C4
Bristol BS3 ....64 A6
Bristol BS3 ....63 F4
7 Bristol BS5 ....64 C7
Weston-Super-Mare BS23 ...104 D7
Oxhouse La Failand BS8 ...61 B6
Winford BS40 ....94 D6
Oxleaze BS13 ....79 D4
Oxleaze La BS41 ....78 E3
Ozenhay BS39 ....129 E6
Ozleworth BS15 ....66 A8

Pages Mead BS11 ....47 C8
Painswick Ave BS34 .....36 B8
Painswick Dr BS37 ......27 E1
Palace Yard Mews BA1 ...142 B2
Palmdale Cl BS30 ....66 A3
Palmer Row **7** BS23 ...104 E8
Palmer St BS23 ....104 E7
Palmer's Way BS24 .....105 D2
Palmers Cl BS30 ....66 A6
Palmers Leaze BS34 ....37 A6
Palmerston Rd BS6 ......49 C4
Palmerston St **6** BS3 ...63 C3
Palmyra Rd BS3 ....63 B2
Paquet Ho BS20 ....47 C5
Parade The Bath BA2 ....101 B6
Bristol BS11 ....47 E6
Bristol BS13 ....79 A6
Chipping Sodbury BS37 ...28 A1
Paradise Row BS39 ......98 A6
Paragon Ct BS21 ....87 C1
Paragon Rd BS23 ....87 C1
Paragon Sch The BA2 ...102 A3
Paragon The Bath BA1 ...142 C3
Bristol BS8 ....62 F6
Parbrook Cl BS14 ....80 B5
Parfitt's Hill **5** BS5 ....64 F6
Parish Brook Rd BS48 ...59 B2
Parish Wharf Est BS20 ...45 D6
Park Ave Bath BA2 ......101 B6
Bristol BS3 ....63 E3
Bristol BS32 ....24 A2
Bristol BS5 ....50 D3
Bristol BS8 ....64 E8
Frampton Cotterell BS36 ...38 B6
Winterbourne BS36 ......37 E7
Yatton BS49 ....74 B1
Park Batch BS40 ....110 F3
Park Cl Bristol BS15 ....65 E7
Bristol BS30 ....66 A6
Keynsham BS31 ....81 D5
Paulton BS39 ....131 D5
Park Cres Bristol BS16 ...37 C1
Bristol BS30 ....66 B5
Park Ct **6** BS23 ....104 E5
Park End BS29 ....106 E4
Park Farm Ct **13** BS30 ...65 F4
Park Farm Village Gn
BS36 ....38 B6
Park Gdns BA1 ....101 D8
Park Gr BS9 ....49 C5
Park Hill BS11 ....47 F6
Park La Bath BA1 ....101 D7
Blagdon BS40 ....110 F2
Bristol BS2 ....140 C3
Faulkland BA3 ....134 B1
North Nibley GL11 ....5 E7
Winterbourne BS36 ......38 B6
Park Pl Bath BA1 ....142 A4
Bristol BS2 ....140 B3
Bristol BS8 ....50 E3
Bristol BS8 ....140 B3
Weston-Super-Mare BS23 ...104 E5
Park Prep Sch for Boys
BA1 ....101 C8
Park Prim Sch The BS15 ...65 E8
Park Rd Bath BA1 ....101 B7
Bristol BS11 ....47 F6
Bristol BS15 ....65 D8
Bristol BS16 ....51 E5
Bristol BS3 ....140 B1
Bristol BS30 ....66 B5
Bristol BS7 ....36 A1
Clevedon BS21 ....57 D3
Congresbury BS49 ....91 E3
Cromhall GL12 ....10 B4
Keynsham BS31 ....81 E4
Paulton BS39 ....131 D5
Thornbury BS35 ....8 B2
Park Row Bristol BS1 ....140 C3
Frampton Cotterell BS36 ...38 A8
Park St Bath BA1 ....142 A4
Bristol BS1 ....140 C3
Bristol BS5 ....64 A3
Bristol BS5 ....64 B8
Hawkesbury Upton GL9 ...20 A2
Iron Acton BS37 ....26 D4
Park Street Ave BS1 ....140 C3
Park Street Mews BA1 ...142 A4
Park The Bristol BS15 ...65 D8
Bristol BS30 ....66 B1
Bristol BS32 ....24 C3
Keynsham BS31 ....81 E6
Portishead BS20 ....45 D4
Yatton BS49 ....74 B1
Park View Bath BA2 .....101 D6
Bristol BS15 ....65 E7
Yate BS37 ....39 E8
Park View Ave BS35 .....8 C2
Park View Terr BS5 .....64 E8
Park Villas BS23 ....104 D8
Park Way Bristol BS30 ...66 B5
Midsomer Norton BA3 ...138 A8
Park Wood Cl BS14 ......79 F4
Parker St **5** BS3 ....63 B3
Parkers Ave BS30 ....67 C7
Parkers Barton BS5 .....64 B6
Parkers Cl BS10 ....35 E4
Parkers Rd BS24 ....106 C5
Parkfield Ave **4** BS5 ...64 D7
Parkfield Gdns BS39 ....113 D3
Parkfield Rd
Axbridge BS26 ....125 D1
Pucklechurch BS16 ....53 A6

Parkhouse La BS31 ......81 C2
Parkhurst Ave **4** BS16 ...51 B4
Parkhurst Rd BS23 .....105 A7
Parkland Way BS35 ....8 C3
Parklands Bristol BS15 ...65 C8
High Littleton BS39 ....115 D2
Parklands Ave BS22 .....89 A4
Parklands Rd BS3 ....62 E4
Parkside Ave BS36 ......37 E6
Parkside Gdns BS5 ......50 B4
Parkside Inf Sch BA1 ...142 B3
Parkstone Ave BS7 ......49 F6
Parkwall Cres BS30 ......65 F4
Parkwall Rd BS30 ....66 A4
Parkway BS34 ....37 A4
Parkway La BA3 ....116 D3
Parkway N BS34 ....37 A4
Parkway Trad Est **5** ...37 A4
Parkwell Cty Prim Sch
BS30 ....66 A4
Parliament St BS4 ....64 A4
Parnall Cres BS37 ....27 C2
Parnall Rd BS16 ....51 A3
Parnall Road Ind Est BS16 ...51 A3
Parnell Rd Bristol BS16 ...50 D7
Clevedon BS21 ....57 D3
Parry Cl BA2 ....101 B4
Parry's Cl BS9 ....48 E5
Parry's La BS9 ....48 F5
Parrys Gr BS9 ....48 E5
Parslow Barton **4** BS5 ...64 D7
Parson St BS3 ....63 B2
Parson Street Prim Sch
BS3 ....63 C2
Parson Street Sta BS3 ...63 B2
Parsonage Cl BS40 ......94 F6
Parsonage La
Axbridge BS26 ....125 E2
Bath BA1 ....142 B2
Chilcompton BA3 ....137 C4
Pensford BS39 ....97 E4
Winford BS40 ....94 F6
Parsonage Rd BS41 ......62 C2
Parsons Ave BS34 ....36 F5
Parsons Gn Clevedon BS21 ...73 C8
Weston-Super-Mare BS22 ...89 A3
Parsons Mead BS48 ......79 F2
Parsons Paddock BS14 ...80 A7
Parsons Way BS25 ......124 E6
Parsons Wlk BS30 ....66 D7
Partis Coll BA1 ....101 A8
Partis Way BA1 ....101 A8
Partition St BS1 ....140 C2
Partridge Cl BS22 ....88 F1
Partridge Rd BS16 ......53 C4
Passage Leaze BS11 .....47 D6
Passage Rd Bristol BS10 ...34 F3
Bristol BS9 ....49 A8
Passage Road Brentry Hill
BS9, BS10 ....35 A2
Passage St BS2 ....143 B2
Pastures The BA15 .....120 E3
Patch Croft BS21 ....73 C8
Patch Elm La BS37 ......28 F7
Patch La BS37 ....27 A8
Patcham High Sch BS22 ...89 A2
Patchway BS34 ....36 B8
Patchway Brook BS32 ...24 C2
Patchway CE Prim Sch
BS34 ....24 C1
Patchway Sta BS34 ......24 F4
Patchway Trad Est BS34 ...35 E7
Patterson Ho **8** BS1 ...143 B1
Paul St BS2 ....140 C4
Paul's Cswy BS49 ....91 D4
Paulman Gdns BS41 ......77 F8
Paulmont Rise BS39 .....114 E1
Paulto' Hill BA3, BS39 ...132 B6
Paulton Dr BS7 ....49 C4
Paulton Inf Sch BS39 ...131 E5
Paulton Jun Sch BS39 ...131 E5
Paulton La BA3 ....132 D7
Paulton Meml Hospl
BS39 ....131 F4
Paulton Rd
Farrington Gurney BS39 ...131 B4
Midsomer Norton BA3 ...131 F1
Paulton BS39 ....131 B7
Paultow Ave BS3 ....63 E3
Paultow Rd BS3 ....63 E3
Paulwood Rd BS39 ......114 E1
Pavey Cl BS13 ....79 C4
Pavey Rd BS13 ....79 C4
Pawlett BS24 ....105 A2
Pawlett Rd BS13 ....79 C3
Pawlett Wlk BS13 ....79 C3
Paxton BS16 ....50 E8
Paybridge Rd BS13 ......79 A4
Payne Dr BS5 ....64 B7
Payne Rd BS24 ....105 D2
Peache Ct BS16 ....51 E6
Peache Rd BS16 ....51 F6
Peacocks La BS15 ....65 C8
Pear Tree Ave BS24 ....122 C6
Pear Tree Hey BS37 .....27 E5
Pear Tree Rd BS32 ......24 C2
Pearces Hill BS16 ....51 C3
Pearl St BS3 ....63 B3
Pearsall Rd BS30 ....65 F3
Pearse Cl BS22 ....89 B5
Peart Cl BS13 ....78 E5
Peart Dr BS13 ....78 E4
Peartree Field BS20 .....45 F4
Peartree La Bristol BS15 ...51 F2
Bristol BS5 ....65 B6
Peasedown St John
Prim Sch BA2 ....133 C7

Pedder Rd BS21 ....57 D1
Peel St BS5 ....141 C4
Peg Hill BS37 ....27 F4
Pegasus Rd BS34 ....35 D7
Pelican Cl BS22 ....105 F8
Pemberton Ct BS16 .....51 C5
Pembery Rd BS3 ....63 C3
Pembroke Ave BS11 .....47 E6
Pembroke Ct BS21 ......57 E4
Pembroke Gate BS8 .....49 A1
Pembroke Gr BS8 ....140 A3
Pembroke Mans BS8 ....140 A4
Pembroke Pl BS8 ....140 A1
Pembroke Rd Bristol BS11 ...47 E6
Bristol BS15 ....51 E2
Bristol BS3 ....63 C4
Bristol BS8 ....140 A3
Portishead BS20 ....44 E4
Weston-Super-Mare BS23 ...104 F4
Pembroke St BS2 ....141 B4
Pembroke Vale BS8 ......140 A4
Pen Park Rd BS10 ....35 D2
Pen Park Sch BS10 ......35 D2
Penard Way BS15 ....65 F7
Penarth Dr BS22 ....105 A1
Pendennis Ave BS16 .....51 D4
Pendennis Ho **8** BS16 ...51 D4
Pendennis Pk BS4 ....64 D2
Pendennis Rd BS16 ......51 D5
Pendlesham Gdns BS23 ...88 A1
Pendock Cl BS30 ....66 C1
Pendock Ct BS16 ....52 B7
Pendock Rd Bristol BS16 ...51 C2
Winterbourne BS36 ......37 E5
Penfield Rd BS2 ....50 A2
Penlea Ct BS11 ....47 D7
Penn Dr BS16 ....37 C1
Penn Gdns BA1 ....101 A8
Penn Hill Rd BA1 ....84 A1
Penn Lea Ct BA1 ....101 B8
Penn Lea Rd BA1 ....101 B8
Penn St BS1 ....141 B3
Penn Way BS26 ....125 D5
Pennard BS24 ....105 A2
Pennard Ct BS14 ....80 B5
Pennard Gn BA2 ....101 A6
Penngrove BS30 ....66 A3
Pennine Gdns BS23 ......88 A1
Pennine Rd BS30 ....66 C4
Pennlea BS13 ....79 C7
Penns The BS21 ....57 E2
Pennycress BS22 ....105 D7
Pennyquick BA2 ....100 D6
Pennyquick View BA2 ...100 F6
Pennyroyal Gr BS16 .....50 E4
Pennywell Ct **3** BS5 ...64 A8
Pennywell Est **2** BS21 ...57 D2
Pennywell Rd BS5 ....64 A8
Penpole Ave BS11 ....47 E6
Penpole Cl BS11 ....47 D7
Penpole La BS11 ....47 E7
Penpole Pk BS11 ....47 E7
Penrice Cl BS22 ....88 C2
Penrith Gdns BS10 ......49 D8
Penrose BS14 ....79 F7
Penrose Dr BS32 ....36 D2
Pensfield Pk BS10 ....35 D4
Pensford Ct BS14 ....80 D5
Pensford Cty Prim Sch
BS39 ....97 D3
Pensford Hill BS39 ......97 D5
Pensford La BS39 ....97 A3
Pensford Old Rd BS39 ...97 E3
Pentagon The BS9 ....48 B5
Pentire Ave BS13 ....79 A6
Pentland Ave BS35 ......15 C8
Peppershells La BS39 ...98 C6
Pepys Cl BS31 ....82 D2
Pera Pl BA1 ....142 C4
Pera Rd BA1 ....142 C4
Percival Rd BS8 ....62 F8
Percy Pl **13** BA1 ....85 B1
Percy St **8** BS3 ....63 D4
Percy Walker Ct BS16 ...51 C6
Peregrine Cl BS22 ....88 F1
Perfect View BA1 ....85 A1
Perretts Ct BS1 ....140 C1
Perrinpit Rd BS36 ....25 E8
Perrings The BS48 ......75 E8
Perrinpit Rd BS36 ....23 E2
Perrott Rd BS15 ....52 A1
Perry Cl BS36 ....37 D4
Perry Court Inf Sch BS14 ...80 A6
Perry Court Jun Sch BS14 ...80 A6
Perry Rd BS1 ....143 A3
Perry St BS5 ....64 A8
Perrycroft Ave BS13 ....79 A6
Perrycroft Rd BS13 .....79 A6
Perrymans Ct BS16 ......51 A4
Perrymead Bath BA2 ....102 B3
Weston-Super-Mare BS22 ...89 B5
Perrys Lea BS32 ....24 D2
Pesley Cl BS13 ....79 A4
Peter's Terr BS5 ....64 B7
Petercole Dr BS13 ......79 A6
Peterside BS39 ....130 E8
Peterson Sq BS13 ....79 C3
Petersway Gdns BS5 .....65 E7
Petherbridge Way BS7 ...50 B5
Petherton Cl BS15 ......65 E7
Petherton Gdns BS14 ...80 B7
Petherton Rd BS14 ......80 B7
Petherton Road Inf Sch
BS14 ....80 B7

Pethick Ho BS4 .... 79 F8
Peto Garden at
  Iford Manor The BA15 .. 120 E3
Pettigrove Gdns BS15 ... 65 E7
Pettigrove Rd BS15 ...... 65 E6
Pevensey Wlk BS4 .... 79 D7
Peverell Cl BS10 .... 34 F3
Peverell Dr BS10 .... 34 F3
Philadelphia Ct **6** BS1 . 141 B3
Philip St Bristol BS2 .... 64 B5
  Bristol BS3 .... 63 D4
Philippa Cl BS14 .... 80 A7
Philips Ho **8** BS1 ...... 141 B4
Phillips Rd BS23 .... 105 A6
Phillis Hill BS39 .... 131 F4
Phippen St **1** BS1 ..... 141 B1
Phipps St BS3 .... 63 B4
Phoenix Gr BS6 .... 49 C5
Phoenix Ho Bath BA1 .... 142 B4
  Bristol BS5 .... 64 B6
Pickedmoor La BS35 ...... 7 E5
Pickwick Rd BA1 .... 85 A2
Picton La BS6 .... 49 E1
Picton St BS6 .... 49 E1
Pier Rd BS20 .... 45 E7
Pierrepont Pl BA1 .... 142 C2
Pierrepont St BA1 .... 142 C2
Pigeon House Dr BS13 ... 79 C4
Pigeon La BS40 .... 93 E1
Pigott Ave BS13 .... 79 A4
Pile Marsh BS5 .... 64 D7
Pilgrims Way
  Bristol BS16 .... 51 D8
  Chew Stoke BS40 .... 112 D8
  Shirehampton BS11 ..... 47 C7
  Weston-Super-Mare BS22 . 88 E3
Pilgrims Wharf BS4 ...... 64 E7
Pilkington Cl BS34 ...... 36 C2
Pill Rd Abbots Leigh BS8 . 47 F1
  Pill BS20 .... 47 E2
Pill St BS20 .... 47 D4
Pill Way BS21 .... 57 B2
Pillingers Rd BS15 ...... 65 C7
Pilning St BS35 .... 23 C8
Pilning Sta BS35 .... 22 F5
Pimm's La BS22 .... 88 B2
Pimms La BS22 .... 88 B3
Pimpernel Mead BS32 .... 36 E7
Pinchay La BS40 .... 95 A4
Pincots La GL12 .... 18 B3
Pine Cl Thornbury BS35 .. 8 C1
  Weston-Super-Mare BS22 . 88 D2
Pine Ct Chew Magna BS40 . 96 B3
  Keynsham BS31 .... 81 C4
  Radstock BA3 .... 133 A2
Pine Gr BS7 .... 36 A1
Pine Grove Pl BS7 .... 49 D3
Pine Hill BS22 .... 88 D2
Pine Lea BS24 .... 122 B6
Pine Rd BS10 .... 35 B3
Pine Ridge Cl BS9 ...... 48 C4
Pine Wlk BA3 .... 132 E1
Pinecroft Bristol BS14 .. 79 F7
  Portishead BS20 .... 44 F6
Pines Cl BA3 .... 137 D3
Pines La BS35 .... 14 D3
Pines Rd BS30 .... 66 C1
Pines Way Bath BA2 ..... 142 A2
  Radstock BA3 .... 133 A2
Pines Way Ind Est BA2 .. 142 A2
Pinetree Rd BS24 .... 106 D4
Pinewood BS15 .... 51 F1
Pinewood Ave BA3 ...... 131 F1
Pinewood Cl BS9 .... 49 B7
Pinewood Gr BA3 .... 131 F1
Pinewood Rd BA3 .... 131 F1
Pinewood Way SN14 .... 70 F7
Pinhay Rd BS13 .... 79 B6
Pinkers Mead BS16 ..... 52 C6
Pinkhams Twist BS14 ... 80 A5
Pinnell Gr BS16 .... 52 C7
Pioneer Ave BA2 ...... 101 F1
Pioneer Pk BS4 .... 64 C5
Pipe La BS1 .... 140 C2
Pipehouse La BA3 ..... 119 F4
Piper Rd BS37 .... 27 E3
Pippin Cl BA2 .... 133 D7
Pippin Ct **4** BS30 .... 65 F4
Pit La BS40 .... 111 F5
Pit Rd BA3 .... 138 F2
Pitch & Pay La BS9 ... 48 E3
Pitch & Pay Pk BS9 .. 48 E3
Pitch La BS6 .... 49 D1
Pitchcombe BS37 ..... 39 C7
Pitchcombe Gdns BS9 . 48 D7
Pitching The BA3 ..... 137 D5
Pitfour Terr BA3 ..... 116 B2
Pithay Cl BS1 .... 141 A3
Pithay The Bristol BS1 . 141 A3
  Paulton BS39 .... 116 A6
Pitlochry Cl BS7 ..... 35 F1
Pitman Ct BA1 .... 85 C2
Pitman Ho BA2 .... 101 D4
Pitman Rd BS23 ...... 104 E6
Pitt Rd BS7 .... 49 E5
Pitt's La BS40 .... 96 B1
Pittville Cl BS35 ..... 8 C3
Pitville Pl **10** BS6 .... 49 B1
Pitway Cl BS39 ...... 130 F4
Pitway La BS39 ...... 130 F4
Pixash Bsns Ctr BS31 . 82 B5
Pixash La BS31 ...... 82 C5
Pizey Ave BS21 ...... 57 B2
Pizey Ave Ind Est **2** BS21 . 57 C2
Pizey Cl BS21 .... 57 B2

Plain The
  Norton St Philip BA3 ... 135 E4
  Thornbury BS35 .... 8 B1
Players Ct BS16 .... 37 B3
Playford Gdns BS11 .... 47 E8
Pleasant Ho **4** BA16 .... 51 D5
Pleasant Pl BA1 ...... 86 D2
Pleasant Rd BS16 ..... 51 D5
Pleshey Cl BS22 ...... 88 D2
Plimsoll Ho **3** BS1 ... 141 A1
  5 Bristol BS5 .... 64 B6
Ploughed Paddock BS48 . 59 D1
Plover Cl
  Weston-Super-Mare BS22 . 88 F1
  Yate BS37 .... 27 C2
Plovers Rise BA3 ..... 133 A3
Plowright Ho **7** BS16 .. 65 B5
Plumers Cl BA21 ...... 57 E1
Plumley Cres BS24 .... 106 A4
Plumley Ct BS23 ...... 104 D4
Plummer's Hill BS5 ... 64 E8
Plumpton Ct BS16 .... 37 F1
Plumptre Cl BS39 .... 131 E5
Plumptre Rd BS39 .... 131 E5
Plumtree Cl BS25 .... 108 A1
Plumtree Rd BS22 .... 105 E8
Plunder St BS49 ..... 92 B7
Podgers Dr BA1 ...... 84 B2
Podium The BA1 ...... 142 C2
Poets' Cl BS5 .... 64 D8
Polar Gdns SN14 .... 31 E4
Polden Cl BS48 ..... 59 E1
Polden Ho BS3 ...... 63 D3
Polden Rd Portishead BS20 . 45 B5
Polestar Way BS24 ... 106 A8
Pollard Way BS22 .... 105 F8
Polly Barnes Cl **4** BS15 . 65 B5
Polly Barnes Hill BS15 . 65 B5
Polygon Rd BS8 ..... 140 A2
Polygon The
  Avonmouth BS11 .... 33 D1
  15 Bristol BS8 .... 62 F6
Pomfrett Gdns BS14 .. 80 E5
Pomphrey Hill BS16 .. 52 C4
Ponsford Rd BS4 .... 80 B1
Ponting Cl BS5 ..... 51 A1
Pool Cnr BS32 ...... 14 B2
Pool Ho BS34 ...... 36 A8
Pool La BS40 .... 95 A2
Pool Rd BS15 ...... 51 E3
Poole Court Dr BS37 . 27 E2
Poole Ho BA2 ...... 100 F5
Poole St BS11 ..... 47 B8
Pooles Wharf BS8 .. 140 A1
Pooles Wharf Ct BS8 . 140 A1
Poorhouse Rd BA2 .. 100 F5
Poor Hill BA3 ..... 115 F6
Pope's Wlk BA2 .... 102 B3
Poplar Ave BS9 .... 48 D6
Poplar Cl Bath BA2 .. 101 D4
  Bristol BS30 ...... 66 D6
Poplar Dr BS16 .... 53 B5
Poplar La GL12 .... 18 B4
Poplar Pl Bristol BS16 . 51 A3
  18 Weston-Super-Mare
  BS23 .... 104 E8
Poplar Rd Bath BA2 . 118 D8
  Bristol BS13 ..... 78 F7
  Bristol BS15 ..... 65 A5
  Bristol BS30 ..... 66 D6
  Bristol BS5 ...... 50 F1
Poplar Terr BS15 ... 65 F8
Poplar Wlk BS24 ... 70 F5
Poplar Wlk BS24 ... 105 E5
Poplars
  Easton-In-Gordano BS20 . 47 B4
  Weston-Super-Mare BS22 . 89 A1
Pople's La BA3 .... 139 F1
Poppy Cl BS22 .... 89 A5
Poppy Mead BS32 .. 36 E7
Porlock Cl
  3 Clevedon BS21 .... 57 E1
  Weston-Super-Mare BS23 . 104 F2
Porlock Gdns BS48 . 59 E1
Porlock Rd Bath BA2 . 102 A1
  Bristol BS3 ..... 63 D3
Port Elizabeth Ho BS10 . 35 B1
Port Side Cl **5** BS5 . 64 F6
Port View BS20 .... 47 C5
Portal Rd BS24 .... 106 D4
Portbury Comm BS20 . 45 F4
Portbury Gr BS11 ... 47 D6
Portbury Hundred The
  BS20 .... 46 C4
Portbury La BS20 ... 60 E7
Portbury Way BS20 . 46 E5
Portbury Wlk BS11 . 47 D6
Portishead Bsns Pk BS20 . 45 E5
Portishead La BS20 . 45 D6
Portishead Prim Sch BS20 . 45 C5
Portishead Way BS3 . 62 F3
Portishead Wlk BS4 . 80 B1
Portland Cl BS48 ... 59 D1
Portland Ct BS1 ... 140 B1
Portland Dr BS20 .. 45 E4
Portland Pl Bath BA1 . 142 B4
  Bristol BS16 ..... 51 D3
Portland Rd BA1 ... 142 B4
Portland Sq BS2 ... 141 B4
Portland St Bristol BS16 . 51 D3
  Bristol BS8 ...... 62 F7
Portland Terr BA1 .. 142 B4
Portmeade Dro BS26 . 125 C1
Portmeirion Cl BS14 . 80 B5
Portview Rd BS11 .. 47 B8
Portwall La BS1 ... 141 B1
Portwall La E **10** BS1 . 141 B1

Portway Bristol BS11 ... 47 C6
  Bristol BS8 .... 48 C3
Portway Com Sch BS11 . 47 E7
Portway La BS37 ...... 28 E2
Portway Rdbt BS11 .... 47 C8
Post Office La
  Blagdon BS40 .... 110 D3
  Flax Bourton BS48 .... 76 F7
Post Office Rd BS24 ... 106 C5
Postlebury Cl BS48 ... 120 C7
Pottery Cl BS23 ...... 105 A6
Potts Cl BA1 .... 85 F3
Pound Dr BS16 ...... 50 F5
Pound La Bristol BS16 . 50 F4
  Nailsea BS48 .... 59 D3
Pound Mead BS40 .... 94 C8
Pound Rd BS15 ...... 51 F2
Pound The
  Almondsbury BS32 .... 24 A5
  Redhill BS40 .... 93 D3
  Thornbury BS35 ..... 7 B6
Pountney Dr BS5 ... 64 B8
Pow's Hill BA3 .... 132 C1
Pow's Orch BA3 .... 132 A1
Powis Cl BS22 ..... 88 C2
Powis Cl BS22 ..... 88 C2
Powlett Ct BA2 .... 102 B7
Powlett Rd BA2 .... 102 B8
Poyntz Ct BS30 .... 65 F3
Poyntz Rd BS4 .... 79 F8
Pratten's La BS16 .. 51 D4
Preacher Cl BS5 ... 65 B6
Preanes Gn BS22 .. 89 A2
Precinct The BS20 . 45 D5
Preddy's La BS5 .. 65 A6
Prescot Cl BS22 .. 88 B2
Prescott BS37 .... 39 D8
Press Moor Dr BS30 . 65 F4
Prestbury BS37 ... 39 D8
Preston Wlk BS4 . 64 A1
Prestwick Cl BS4 . 64 D1
Pretoria Rd BS34 . 35 F8
Prewett St BS1 ... 141 B1
Priddy Cl BA2 .... 101 B5
Priddy Ct BS14 ... 80 B5
Priddy Dr BS14 ... 80 B5
Priests Way BS22 . 88 D2
Priestwood Cl BS10 . 35 A3
Primrose Cl Bristol BS15 . 65 C8
  Bristol BS32 .... 24 D2
Primrose Dr BS35 .. 8 D2
Primrose Hill BA1 .. 84 D1
Primrose La Bristol BS15 . 51 C1
  Midsomer Norton BA3 . 132 B1
Primrose Terr BS15 . 51 C1
Prince St BS1 .... 141 A1
Prince Street Rdbt BS1 . 141 A2
Prince's Bldgs BS8 . 62 F6
Prince's Bldgs **17** BS8 . 62 F6
Prince's Rd BS21 ... 57 D3
Prince's St Bristol BS2 . 141 C4
  Radstock BA3 ..... 132 E5
Princes Bldgs BA1 . 142 B3
Princes Ct BS30 .. 65 F4
Princes St BA1 ... 142 B2
Princes' La BS8 .. 62 F6
Princes' Pl BS7 .. 49 E3
Princess Cl BS31 . 81 D4
Princess Gdns BS16 . 50 D6
Princess Row BS2 . 141 A4
Princess St Bristol BS2 . 64 A7
  Bristol BS3 ...... 63 E4
Princess Victoria St BS8 . 62 F6
Prinknash Cl **4** BS37 . 39 D7
Prior Park Bldgs BA2 . 102 B5
Prior Park Coll BA2 . 102 C2
Prior Park Cotts BA2 . 142 C1
Prior Park Gdns BA2 . 102 B5
Prior Park Landscape Gdn
  BA2 .... 102 C3
Prior Park Rd BA2 . 102 B4
Prior's Hill **11** BS6 . 49 D1
Priors Lea BS37 .. 116 A2
Priors Rd BS37 ... 27 D1
Priory Ave BS9 ... 49 A7
Priory Cl Bath BA2 . 102 B2
  Midsomer Norton BA3 . 132 A1
Priory Comm Sch BS22 . 89 B3
Priory Court Rd BS9 . 49 A7
Priory Ct Bristol BS15 . 65 C3
  Bristol BS5 ...... 64 B2
Priory Dene BS9 .. 49 A7
Priory Farm Trad Est
  BS20 .... 46 D3
Priory Gdns Bristol BS11 . 47 D7
  Bristol BS7 ...... 49 F8
  Easton-In-Gordano BS20 . 47 B4
  Priory Mews BS23 . 105 B7
Priory Rd Bristol BS4 . 64 B3
  Bristol BS8 ...... 140 C4
  Bristol, Shirehampton BS8 . 47 D6
  Easton-In-Gordano BS20 . 47 B4
  Keynsham BS31 .... 81 E7
  Portbury BS20 ..... 46 D3
  Weston-Super-Mare BS23 . 105 A7
Priory Wlk BS20 ... 46 D3
Priston Cl BS22 ... 89 B5
Priston La BA2,BA3 . 117 A5
Priston Mill BA2 .. 117 B8
Priston Rd BA2 ... 117 C8
Pritchard St BS2 . 141 B4
Probyn Cl BS16 ... 51 A7
Proctor Cl BS4 ... 64 D1
Proctor Ho BS1 .. 141 B1
Prospect Ave BS15 . 65 B8
Prospect Ave BS15 . 65 D2
Prospect Cl
  Easter Compton BS35 . 23 A2
  Frampton Cotterell BS36 . 37 F8

Prospect Cl continued
  Winterbourne BS36 ... 37 E4
Prospect Cres BS15 .. 51 F2
Prospect Gdns BA1 .. 85 F5
Prospect La BS36 ... 37 F8
Prospect Pl
  Bath, Beacon Hill BA1 . 85 A1
  Bath, Weston BA1 .. 84 C2
  Bathford BA1 ..... 86 D2
  Bristol BS3 ...... 63 C3
  Bristol BS5 ...... 64 C8
  Bristol BS6 ...... 49 D2
  9 Weston-Super-Mare
  BS23 .... 104 E8
Prospect Rd Bath BA2 . 102 C4
  Severn Beach BS35 .. 22 A5
Proud Cross BS40 .. 128 E4
Providence La BS41 . 61 F2
Providence Pl BS2 . 141 C2
Providence View BS41 . 62 A1
Prowse's La BS26 .. 125 C1
Prudham St **7** BS5 . 50 C1
Publow La BS39 ... 97 E5
Pucklechurch CE Prim Sch
  BS16 .... 53 B4
Pucklechurch Trad Est
  BS16 .... 53 B4
Pudding Pie Cl BS40 . 109 A5
Pudding Pie La BS40 . 109 A6
Puffin Cl BS22 ... 105 F8
Pullin Gr BS10 ... 66 D4
Pullins Gn BS35 .. 8 B1
Pulteney Ave BA2 . 102 B6
Pulteney Gdns BA2 . 102 B6
Pulteney Gr BA2 .. 102 B6
Pulteney Mews BA2 . 102 B7
Pulteney Rd BA2 .. 102 B6
Pulteney Terr BA2 . 102 B6
Pump La Bathford BA1 . 86 B2
  Bristol BS1 ...... 141 B1
  Redhill BS40 ..... 93 D2
Purcell Wlk BS7 .. 79 D7
Purdown Rd BS7 .. 49 F5
Purdue Cl BS22 .. 89 B3
Purlewent Dr BA1 . 84 C1
Purn La BS24 .... 122 A8
Purn Rd BS24 ... 121 F8
Purn Way BS24 .. 122 B7
Pursey Dr BS32 .. 36 F6
Purton Cl BS15 .. 65 C6
Purton Rd BS7 .. 49 D2
Purving Row BS24 . 122 C1
Purving Row La BS24 . 122 C1
Puttingthorpe Dr BS22 . 105 C7
Puxley Cl BS14 .. 80 E6
Puxton La BS24 . 90 D3
Puxton Moor La BS24 . 90 E2
Pye Cnr BS25 ... 108 D4
Pye Croft BS32 . 24 E3
Pyecroft Ave BS9 . 49 C7
Pylewell La BS25 . 108 D1
Pylle Hill Cres BS3 . 63 F4
Pyne Point BS21 . 57 C3
Pynne Cl BS14 .. 80 F5
Pynne Rd BS14 .. 80 F5
Pyracantha Wlk BS14 . 80 A6

Q

Quadrangle The BS37 . 39 C4
Quadrant BS32 .... 24 B3
Quadrant E BS16 ... 51 C3
Quadrant The Bristol BS32 . 24 A3
  Bristol BS6 ...... 49 B3
Quadrant W BS16 .. 51 C3
Quaker La BS35 ... 8 B1
Quaker's Cl BS16 . 51 D8
Quaker's Rd BS16 . 51 E8
Quakers' Friars BS1 . 141 B3
Quantock Cl BS30 . 66 C5
Quantock Rd Bristol BS3 . 63 D3
  Portishead BS20 .. 45 B5
  Weston-Super-Mare BS23 . 104 E4
Quantocks BA2 ... 102 A1
Quarries The BS16 . 24 C6
Quarrington Rd BS7 . 49 E5
Quarry Barton BS16 . 37 C4
Quarry Cl Bath BA2 . 101 F1
  Limpley Stoke BA3 . 120 D6
Quarry Hay BS40 . 112 D8
Quarry La Bristol BS11 . 34 C1
  Winterbourne BS36 . 37 E4
Quarry Mead BS35 . 14 F5
Quarry Rd Alveston BS35 . 14 F5
  Bath BA2 .... 102 D6
  Bristol BS15 .... 65 D6
  Bristol BS16 .... 51 C7
  Chipping Sodbury BS37 . 28 A1
  Sandford BS25 ... 108 A2
Quarry Rock Gdns Cvn Pk
  BA2 .... 102 D4
Quarry Stps BS8 . 49 A2
Quarry Vale Cotts BA2 . 102 B1
Quarry Way Bristol BS16 . 38 A1
  Bristol BS16 .... 52 A6
Quarryman's Ct BA2 . 102 B1
Quay St BS1 .... 141 A3
Quays The BS1 .. 140 C1
Quayside **4** BS5 . 64 F6
Quedgeley BS37 .. 39 C8
Queen Ann Rd BS5 . 64 B6

Queen Charlotte St BS1
Queen Charlton La BS1
Queen Elizabeth's
  Hospital Sch BS8
Queen Quay BS1
Queen Sq Bath BA1
  Bristol BS1
Saltford BS31
Queen Square Ave **7**
  BS1
Queen Sq Pl BA1
Queen St Avonmouth BS11
  Bath BA1
  Bristol BS15
  Bristol BS2
  Bristol BS5
Queen Victoria Rd BS6
Queen Victoria St BS2
Queen's Ave Bristol BS8
  Portishead BS20
Queen's Ct BS8
Queen's Dr Bath BA2
Queen's Par
  Bristol BS1
Queen's Par BA1
Queen's Parade Pl BA1
Queen's Rd
  Bristol BS13, BS41
  Bristol BS30
  Bristol BS4
  Bristol BS5
  Clevedon BS21
  Pucklechurch BS16
  Radstock BA3
  Weston-Super-Mare BS23
Queen's Way BS22
Queens Down BS34
Queens Down Gdns BS4
Queens Dr BS9
Queens Gate BS9
Queens Par BS1
Queens Rd Banwell BS29
  Bristol BS4
  Keynsham BS31
  Nailsea BS48
  Portishead BS20
Queens Way BS20
Queens Wlk BS35
Queenscote BS20
Queensdale Cres BS4
Queensdown Gdns BS4
Queenshill Rd BS4
Queensholm Ave BS16
Queensholm Cl BS16
Queensholm Cres BS16
Queensholm Dr BS16
Queensway BS34
Queenswood Ave BA1
Quickthorn Cl BS14
Quiet St BA1
Quilter Gr BS4

R

Raby Mews BA2
Raby Pl BA2
Rackfield Pl BA2
Rackham Cl BS7
Rackhay BS1
Rackley La BS26
Rackvernal Ct BA3
Rackvernal Rd BA3
Radford Hill BA3
Radley Rd BS16
Radnor Bsns Ctr BS7
Radnor Rd Bristol BS7
  Bristol BS9
Radstock & District Mus
  BA3
Radstock Inf Sch BA3
Radstock Rd BA3
Raeburn Rd BS5
Rag Hill BA3
Rag La GL12
Raglan Cl BA3
Raglan La Bristol BS5
  Winford BS40
Raglan Pl Bristol BS7
  Thornbury BS35
  Weston-Super-Mare BS23
Raglan Rd BS7
Raglan Terr BA1
Raglan Wlk BS31
Ragland La BA1
Ragland St BA1
Railton Jones Cl BS34
Railway Cotts BS37
Railway St BA1
Railway Terr BS16
Railway View Pl BA3
Rainbow Ct BS37
Rainbow Wood Farm
  BA2
Rains Batch BS40
Rainham Ct BS23
Raleigh Cl BS31
Raleigh Ct **8** BS23
Raleigh Rd BS3
Raleigh Rise BS20
Ralph Allen Dr BA2
Ralph Allen Sch BA2
Ralph Rd BS7
Ram Hill BS36
Ram Hill Bsns Pk BS36
Ramsay Cl BS22

scombe La BA1 .....85 F6
sey Rd BS7 .....49 F7
chways BS20 .....44 F4
dall CI BS15 .....51 F2
dall Rd BS38 .....140 B2
dolph Ave Bristol BS13 .....79 B5
  n BS37 .....27 C4
dolph CI BS13 .....79 B5
gers Wlk BS15 .....65 C4
ieworthy CE Prim Sch 16 F1
gs Ave BS19 .....98 C5
noch Rd BS7 .....35 F1
scombe Ave BS22 .....88 D2
sford BS21 .....57 B1
nael Ct BS1 .....141 B1
fe Dr BS34 .....36 E5
bone CI BS36 .....38 C5
en CI BS22 .....88 E1
en CI BS7 .....48 F8
endale Dr BS30 .....66 D2
nglass Cres BS10 .....35 D2
enhead Dr BS14 .....80 B8
enhill Ave BS13 .....63 F2
enhill Rd BS13 .....63 F3
enscourt Rd BS34 .....36 A2
enswood BS30 .....66 B3
enswood Rd BS9 .....49 C1
enswood Special Sch
lins Ave BS22 .....59 D3
nsley Ho 15 BS5 .....50 A1
ens CI BS41 .....61 F1
ens Cross Rd BS13 .....61 F1
eigh Rd BS9 .....48 E7
mend Rd BS3 .....63 E3
mer's Wlk BS13 .....63 E2
mill BS4 .....65 A2
enon Ho BS16 .....51 F4
enore Rise BS41 .....61 F1
enre Rd BS13 .....63 A3
neswood BS23 .....104 F8
field Inf Sch BS37 .....39 F8
field Jun Sch BS37 .....39 F8
ol's Row GL12 .....19 D7
or's Way BS23 .....104 F6
ory CI
  nborough BA3 .....116 A6
  dall BS48 .....60 A2
  on BS37 .....27 F3
ory Dr BS49 .....91 C7
ory La g Bleadon BS24 .....122 C6
  tol BS54 .....36 A3
  pton Martin BS40 .....128 B6
  emhall GL12 .....17 A8
  nbury BA3 .....116 B2
ory Way
  ton-in-Gordano BS20 .....47 B3
  pton Cotterell BS36 .....38 A8
tory Way
  enham BS24 .....121 F2
  on BS49 .....91 C7
nium Lodge BS26 .....125 B2
Hill
  esedown St John BA3 .....116 E1
  dall BS40 .....93 D2
House La
  ndbury BS32 .....24 B4
  tol BS9 .....48 E6
Maids La BS59 .....49 A6
Maids Sch BS9 .....49 A6
Post Ct BA2 .....133 B7
Rd TA8 .....121 A2
cre BS40 .....93 D3
beer CI BS16 .....37 F1
catch Rd BS4 .....63 F2
liff Backs BS1 .....141 B2
liff Cres BS3 .....63 D4
liff Hill BS1 .....141 B1
liff Mead La BS1 .....141 B1
liff Ct BS20 .....44 E3
liffe Par BS1 .....141 A1
liffe Par W BS1 .....141 A1
liffe Rd BS1 .....141 B1
croft BS40 .....93 D3
cross Mews 14 BS2 .....141 C3
cross St BS2 .....141 C3
ding Pk La BS40 .....94 E4
dings The Bristol BS1 .....51 F2
  pton Martin BS40 .....128 B7
ield Edge Prim Sch 66 D4
Bar Rd BA3 .....138 A8
Hill BS40 .....66 E3
ield Rd Bristol BS34 .....36 B7
  somer Norton BA3 .....138 A8
ford Cres BS13 .....78 F3
ford La BS16 .....53 D4
ham La BS13 .....78 F3
ham La BS35 .....22 F8
nill CI BS16 .....50 E3
nill Dr BS16 .....50 E3
nill La BS35 .....13 E6
and Court
  arls High Sch) BS49 .....49 C2
and Court Rd BS49 .....49 C2
and Green BS49 .....49 C2
and High Jun Sch 49 C2
and High Sch BS49 .....49 C2
and Hill BS49 .....49 B2
and Hill Rd BA2 .....100 F6
  tol BS5 .....49 B2
and Rd Bristol BS16 .....49 C2
  tbury BS20 .....46 F6
and Sta BS6 .....49 C2

Redland Terr 8 BS6 .....49 B2
Redlands Terr BA3 .....137 F8
Redlynch La BS31 .....81 D2
Redshard La BS40 .....109 B7
Redshell Wlk BS10 .....35 C3
Redwick & Northwick
  CE Sch BS35 .....12 D2
Redwick CI BS11 .....34 C2
Redwick Gdns BS11 .....22 C7
Redwick Rd BS35 .....22 C8
Redwing Dr BS22 .....88 F1
Redwing Gdns BS16 .....50 E6
Redwood CI Bristol BS30 .....66 A3
  Nailsea BS48 .....60 A2
  Radstock BA3 .....138 C8
Redwood Ho BS13 .....79 D3
Redwood La BS48 .....77 C7
Reed CI BS10 .....49 D6
Reed Ct BS30 .....65 F3
Reed's Row GL12 .....19 D7
Reedley Rd BS9 .....48 F5
Reedling CI BS16 .....50 E6
Regency Dr BS4 .....65 A2
Regent Rd BS3 .....63 D4
Regent St Bristol BS15 .....65 D8
  Bristol BS8 .....140 A2
  Weston-Super-Mare BS23 .....104 E7
Regents CI BS31 .....81 F6
Regents CI BS8 .....8 B2
Regil La BS40 .....95 A6
Regil Rd BS40 .....94 F1
Regine The BA1 .....142 B3
Remenham Dr BS9 .....49 B5
Remenham Pk BS9 .....49 B5
Rendcomb CI BS22 .....88 B2
Rendle Ho BS16 .....51 C4
Rene Rd 18 BS5 .....50 B1
Rennison CI BS23 .....104 E4
Repton Rd BS4 .....64 D3
Retford Ho BA2 .....102 E4
Reto Gr BA15 .....120 F1
Retort Rd BS11 .....33 C3
Retreat The BA3 .....133 E3
Reubens CI BS22 .....88 F3
Reynold's Wlk BS7 .....50 A7
Reynolds CI BS31 .....82 A3
Rhode CI BS31 .....82 A3
Rhodyate BS40 .....110 D2
Rhodyate Hill BS49 .....91 F6
Rhodyate La BS49 .....92 A7
Rhodyate The BS29 .....107 C1
Rhyne Terr BS23 .....104 D2
Rhyne View BS48 .....59 B1
Ribblesdale BS35 .....15 D8
Richards CI BS22 .....89 B4
Richeson CI BS10 .....34 F2
Richeson Ho BS10 .....34 F2
Richmond Ave Bristol BS34 .....36 E5
  Bristol BS6 .....49 F2
Richmond CI Bath BA1 .....84 F1
  Keynsham BS31 .....81 D4
  Portishead BS20 .....45 E5
Richmond Ct 2 Bristol BS3 .....63 B1
  7 Bristol BS8 .....49 A2
Richmond Dale 6 BS8 .....49 A2
Richmond Gn BS48 .....59 F1
Richmond Hill Bath BA1 .....84 F1
  Bristol BS8 .....140 B3
Richmond Hill Ave BS8 .....140 B3
Richmond Hts Bath BA1 .....84 F2
  Bristol BS8 .....140 B3
Richmond La Bath BA1 .....84 F2
  Bristol BS8 .....140 B3
Richmond Mews BS8 .....140 A3
Richmond Park Rd BS8 .....140 A3
Richmond Rd Bath BA1 .....84 F1
  Bristol BS16 .....52 A6
  Bristol BS5 .....64 F7
  Bristol BS6 .....49 E1
Richmond St BS3 .....63 F4
  Weston-Super-Mare BS23 .....104 D7
Richmond Terr
  Avonmouth BS11 .....33 B1
  Bristol BS8 .....140 A3
Ricketts La BS22 .....89 A2
Rickford La BS40 .....110 A3
Rickford Rd BS48 .....59 F1
Rickford Rise BS40 .....110 A3
Rickyard Rd BS32 .....24 C2
Ride The BS15 .....52 A2
Ridge CI BS20 .....45 A4
Ridge Cres BS40 .....112 E8
Ridge Green CI BA2 .....118 D8
Ridge Jun Sch The BS37 .....27 F2
Ridge La BS40 .....128 D5
Ridge The Bristol BS11 .....47 E7
  Coalpit Heath BS36 .....38 D7
Ridgehill BS9 .....49 C6
Ridgemeade BS14 .....80 B4
Ridgeview BS41 .....61 B2
Ridgeway
  Coalpit Heath BS36 .....38 D7
  Nailsea BS48 .....59 C1
  Yate BS37 .....28 A2
Ridgeway Ave BS23 .....104 E6
Ridgeway CI BS40 .....128 E6
Ridgeway Ct BS10 .....35 A1
Ridgeway Gdns BS14 .....80 C5
Ridgeway Ind Ctr BS5 .....50 E2
Ridgeway La BS14 .....80 B5
Ridgeway Par BS5 .....50 E3
Ridgeway Rd Bristol BS16 .....50 E3
  Long Ashton BS41 .....62 A2
Ridgeway The Bristol BS10 .....35 A1
  Weston-Super-Mare BS22 .....88 A2
Ridgewood BS9 .....48 D3

Riding Barn Hill BS30 .....67 A6
Ridingleaze BS11 .....34 A1
Ridings CI BS37 .....28 D1
Ridings High Sch The
  BS36 .....37 D6
Ridings Rd BS36 .....38 C6
Ridings The Bristol BS14 .....78 E4
  Coalpit Heath BS36 .....38 C6
Ringspit La BS14,BS39 .....97 E8
Ringswell Gdns BA1 .....85 B1
Ringwell BA1 .....135 E4
Ringwell La BA1 .....135 E4
Ringwood Cres BS10 .....35 D1
Ringwood Gr BS23 .....88 A1
Ringwood Rd BA2 .....101 C5
Ripley Rd BS5 .....51 A1
Ripon Ct BS16 .....37 F2
Ripon Rd BS4 .....64 E6
Ripple The BS21 .....59 D4
Rippleside BS20 .....45 C5
Rippleside Rd BS21 .....57 E5
Risdale Rd BS3 .....62 F1
Risedale BS15 .....65 D5
Risedale Rd BS25 .....125 A8
River Mead BS21 .....73 D8
River Rd
  Chipping Sodbury BS37 .....28 A1
  Portbury BS20 .....46 F8
River St BS2 .....141 C3
River Street PI BA1 .....142 B3
River Terr BS31 .....81 F5
River View BS16 .....50 E5
Riverland Dr BS13 .....78 F5
Riverleaze Bristol BS9 .....48 C5
  Portishead BS20 .....44 F6
Rivers St BA1 .....142 B3
Rivers Street Mews BA1 .....142 B3
Riverside Bsns Pk BS4 .....64 D6
  Cleeve BS21 .....57 B1
Riverside Cotts
  Bristol BS15 .....65 B1
  Radstock BA3 .....133 A2
Riverside Ct Bath BA2 .....142 B1
  2 Bristol BS4 .....64 F6
Riverside Gdns Bath BA1 .....142 B2
  Midsomer Norton BA3 .....137 F7
Riverside Mews BS4 .....64 F6
Riverside Pk BS35 .....21 F6
Riverside Rd Bath BA2 .....142 B2
  Midsomer Norton BA3 .....137 F7
Riverside Stps BS1 .....64 E7
Riverside Wlk BS15 .....65 C3
Riverside Wlk
  6 Bristol BS5 .....64 F6
  Midsomer Norton BA3 .....137 F7
Riverway BS48 .....59 F3
Riverwood Rd BS16 .....37 C1
Riviera Cres BS16 .....51 E4
Roach's La GL9 .....30 D2
Road Hill SN13 .....86 E8
Road Two BS30 .....22 A3
Roath Rd BS20 .....45 D5
Rob-Lynne Ct BS25 .....124 F8
Robbins CI Bristol BS32 .....36 F6
  Marshfield SN14 .....
Robbins Ct BS16 .....52 B6
Robel Ave BS36 .....38 A8
Robert Ct BS16 .....52 B7
  Leigh Woods BS8 .....62 D7
Robert St
  Bristol, Baptist Mills BS5 .....50 B2
  18 Bristol, Russell Town BS5 .....64 B7
Robertson Dr BS4 .....64 F6
Robertson Rd BS5 .....50 C2
Robin CI Bristol BS10 .....35 B2
  Bristol BS14 .....80 D6
  Midsomer Norton BA3 .....138 B8
  Weston-Super-Mare BS22 .....105 E8
Robin Dr BS24 .....105 E2
Robin La BS21 .....57 D5
Robin Way BS37 .....40 A7
Robinia Wlk BS14 .....80 A7
Robinson CI BS48 .....76 A5
Robinson Dr BS5 .....64 A8
Robinson Way BS48 .....76 A5
Rochester CI BS24 .....105 A1
Rochester Rd BS4 .....64 F5
Rochfort Ct BA1 .....102 B8
Rock Ave BS48 .....59 C2
Rock CI BS4 .....64 E2
Rock Cotts BS20 .....47 E4
Rock Hall Ho BA2 .....102 B1
Rock Hall La BA2 .....102 B1
Rock Ho BS10 .....35 C3
Rock La Bristol BS34 .....36 B4
  Bristol BS34 .....36 E4
Rock Rd Chilcompton BA3 .....137 D3
  Keynsham BS31 .....81 E5
  Midsomer Norton BA3 .....138 A3
Rock St BS35 .....15 B8
Rock The BS35 .....64 E3
Rock Villas BS20 .....45 E4
Rockeries The BS25 .....124 F8
Rockhill Est BS31 .....81 F4
Rockingham Gdns BS11 .....48 A8
Rockingham Gr BS23 .....88 A1
Rockland Gr BS16 .....50 D5
Rockland Rd BS16 .....51 D7
Rocklease BS35 .....8 B2
Rockleaze BS9 .....48 E2
Rockleaze Ave BS9 .....48 E3
Rockleaze Ct BS9 .....48 E3

Rockleaze Mans BS23 .....87 C1
Rockleaze Rd BS9 .....48 E3
Rockliffe Ave BA2 .....102 B8
Rockliffe Rd BA2 .....102 B8
Rocks La BS40 .....77 F1
Rockside Ave BS16 .....51 F8
Rockside Dr BS9 .....49 C6
Rockside Gdns Bristol BS16 .....51 F8
  Frampton Cotterell BS36 .....38 C8
Rockstowes Way BS10 .....35 D3
Rockwell Ave BS11 .....34 B1
Rockwood Ho BS37 .....28 A4
Rodborough BS37 .....39 C7
Rodborough Way BS15 .....66 A7
Rodbourne Rd BS10 .....49 E6
Rode Bird Gdns BA3 .....136 D2
Rode Hill BA1 .....136 E1
Rodford Prim Sch BS37 .....39 D7
Rodford Way BS37 .....39 D7
Rodfords Mead BS14 .....80 A7
Rodmead Wlk BS13 .....79 A4
Rodmoor Rd BS20 .....45 D6
Rodney Ave BS30 .....105 A2
Rodney Ave BS15 .....65 A8
Rodney Cres BS34 .....36 A4
Rodney Ho BA2 .....101 A6
Rodney PI BS8 .....140 A3
Rodney Rd Backwell BS48 .....76 A6
  Bristol BS15 .....65 A8
  Saltford BS31 .....82 E2
Rodney Wlk BS15 .....52 B3
Rodway Ho BS16 .....52 A4
Rodway Rd Bristol BS16 .....52 A5
  Bristol BS34 .....35 F7
Rodway View BS15 .....51 F2
Roebuck CI BS22 .....89 B4
Roegate Dr BS4 .....64 E6
Roegate Ho BS5 .....51 A1
Rogers CI Bristol BS30 .....66 B5
  Clutton BS39 .....114 E3
Rokeby Ave BS6 .....49 C1
Roman Baths
  & Pump Room BA1 .....142 C2
Roman Farm Ct BS11 .....34 C2
Roman Farm Rd BS4 .....79 F7
Roman Ho BA1 .....142 C4
Roman Rd Bath BA1 .....142 C3
  Bleadon BS24 .....122 C8
  Bristol BS5 .....50 B1
  Sandford BS25 .....
Roman Way Bristol BS9 .....48 C4
  Paulton BS39 .....131 C6
Roman Wlk Bristol BS14 .....36 E5
  Midsomer Norton BA3 .....
Romney Ave BS7 .....50 B6
Romney Avenue Inf Sch
  BS7 .....50 B6
Romney Avenue Jun Sch
  BS7 .....50 B6
Ron Jones Ho 8 BS1 .....141 C4
Ronald Rd BS16 .....50 E6
Ronayne Wlk BS16 .....51 C6
Rookery CI BS22 .....88 E3
Rookery La Pilning BS35 .....23 A6
  Pucklechurch BS30,SN14 .....53 F4
Rookery Rd BS4 .....64 A2
Rookery Way BS14 .....79 F4
Rooksbridge Wlk BA2 .....101 B5
Rope Wlk BS48 .....76 A5
Roper's La BS40 .....92 E3
Rosary The BS16 .....52 F7
Rose Acre BS10 .....35 A3
Rose CI BS36 .....37 E4
Rose Cotts BS22 .....89 C2
Rose Gdns BS22 .....89 B4
Rose Green CI BS5 .....50 E2
Rose Green Rd BS5 .....50 D2
Rose Hill BA1 .....85 C3
Rose La BS36 .....38 D6
Rose Mead BS7 .....50 A7
Rose Meare Gdns BS13 .....78 E7
Rose Oak Dr BS36 .....38 D7
Rose Oak Gdns BS36 .....38 D7
Rose Oak La BS36 .....38 D7
Rose Rd BS5 .....64 E7
Rose Terr Bath BA2 .....102 C2
  Bristol BS8 .....140 B2
Rose Tree Ho BS16 .....51 F4
Rose Wlk BS16 .....51 C3
Rosebay Mead BS16 .....50 E5
Roseberry Pk BS5 .....64 D8
Roseberry PI BA2 .....101 C6
Roseberry Rd Bath BA2 .....101 C6
  Bristol BS5 .....64 C7
Rosebery Ave BS2 .....50 A1
Rosebery Terr BS8 .....140 B2
Rosedale Ave BS23 .....105 A6
Rosedale Rd BS16 .....51 C3
Roselarge Gdns BS10 .....35 A2
Rosemary CI BS32 .....36 F7
Rosemary La Bristol BS5 .....50 C2
  Freshford BA3 .....
Rosemont Terr BS8 .....140 A2
Rosemount Ct BS15 .....65 B8
Rosemount La BA2 .....102 B4
Rosemount Rd BS48 .....77 B8
Rosery CI BS9 .....49 A8
Rosery The BS16 .....51 E3
Rosevear BS2 .....64 A7
Roseville Ave BS30 .....66 A2
Rosewarn CI BA2 .....101 A4
Rosewell Ct BA1 .....142 B2
Rosewood Ave BS35 .....15 D7
Roshni Gar 5 BS5 .....50 B1
Roshni Gar W 18 BS5 .....50 B1
Rosling Rd BS7 .....49 E6
Roslyn La BS22 .....88 C1

Roslyn Rd BS6 .....49 C1
Ross CI BS37 .....28 B1
Rossall Ave BS34 .....36 C6
Rossall Rd BS4 .....64 D3
Rossendale CI BS22 .....88 F3
Rossiter Rd BA2 .....142 C1
Rossiter Wood Ct BS11 .....34 B2
Rossiter's La BS5 .....65 A6
Rosslyn Rd BA1 .....101 B7
Rosslyn Way BS35 .....8 C3
Rotcombe La BS39 .....115 D2
Rotcombe Vale BS39 .....115 D2
Rounceval St BS37 .....28 A1
Roundhill Gr BA2 .....101 B3
Roundhill Pk BA2 .....101 A4
Roundmoor CI BS31 .....82 D3
Roundmoor Gdns BS14 .....80 D7
Roundways BS36 .....38 D6
Rousham Rd BS5 .....50 A3
Row La BA3 .....135 C1
Row Of Ashes La BS40 .....93 F4
Row The BS35 .....13 A7
Rowacres Bath BA2 .....101 B3
  Bristol BS14 .....79 F6
Rowan CI Bristol BS16 .....51 A2
  Nailsea BS48 .....60 A2
Rowan Ct 9 Bristol BS5 .....64 B7
  Radstock BA3 .....132 E1
  Yate BS37 .....27 C3
Rowan Ho BS13 .....79 D4
Rowan PI BS24 .....89 B1
Rowan Tree Ho BS16 .....51 F4
Rowan Way Bristol BS15 .....65 B3
  Langford BS40 .....109 A5
Rowan Wlk BS31 .....81 C4
Rowans The Bristol BS16 .....37 B1
  Portishead BS20 .....45 C4
Rowberrow BS14 .....79 F7
Rowberrow La
  Rowberrow BS25 .....108 F2
  Shipham BS25 .....125 F8
Rowberrow Way BS48 .....59 E1
Rowland Ave BS16 .....50 D4
Rowlands CI BA1 .....86 B2
Rowlandson Gdns BS7 .....50 B6
Rowley St BS3 .....63 C3
Rownham CI BS3 .....62 E4
Rownham Ct BS8 .....140 A1
Rownham Hill BS8 .....62 E6
Rownham Mead BS8 .....140 A1
Rows The BS22 .....88 E2
Roy King Gdns BS30 .....66 C6
Royal Albert Rd BS6 .....49 A4
Royal Ave BA1 .....142 B3
Royal CI BS10 .....34 D3
Royal Cres Bath BA1 .....142 A3
  Weston-Super-Mare BS23 .....104 D8
Royal Ct BS23 .....104 D4
Royal Fort Rd BS2,BS8 .....140 C2
Royal High Sch The BA1 .....142 B4
Royal Hospl
  for Sick Children BS2 .....140 C3
Royal National Hospl
  for Rheumatic Diseases
  BA1 .....142 B2
Royal Par BS23 .....104 D8
Royal Pk BS8 .....140 B3
Royal Photographic
  Society BA1 .....142 B3
Royal Portbury Dock Rd
  BS20 .....46 E5
Royal Prom BS8 .....140 B3
Royal Rd BS16 .....52 A6
Royal Sands BS23 .....104 D4
Royal Sch The BA1 .....84 F2
Royal United Hospl BA1 .....101 B8
Royal West of England
  Acad BS8 .....140 B3
Royal York Cres BS8 .....62 F6
Royal York Ho BS8 .....140 A2
Royal York Mews BS8 .....140 A2
Royal York Villas BS8 .....140 A2
Royate Hill BS5 .....50 D2
Roycroft Rd BS34 .....36 B2
Royston Lodge BS23 .....104 D6
Royston Wlk BS10 .....35 D2
Rozel Rd BS7 .....49 E5
Rubens CI BS31 .....82 A5
Ruby St BS3 .....63 B3
Ruddymead BS21 .....57 D2
Rudford CI BS34 .....24 B1
Rudge CI BS15 .....51 F2
Rudgeway Pk BS35 .....14 F1
Rudgeway Rd BS39 .....131 E4
Rudgewood CI BS13 .....79 D4
Rudgleigh Ave BS20 .....47 C4
Rudgleigh Rd BS20 .....47 C4
Rudhall Gn BS22 .....89 B3
Rudhall Gr BS10 .....49 E7
Rudmore Pk BA1 .....101 A7
Rudthorpe Rd BS7 .....49 E5
Ruett La BS39 .....131 B4
Ruffet Rd BS36 .....38 B4
Rugby Rd BS4 .....64 D3
Runnymead Ave BS4 .....64 D2
Runnymede BS15 .....51 E1
Runswick Rd BS4 .....64 C3
Rupert St Bristol BS1 .....141 A3
  Bristol BS5 .....64 B7
Rush CI BS32 .....24 D2
Rush Hill Bath BA2 .....101 C2
  Farrington Gurney BS39 .....130 F3
Rusham BS13 .....78 F4
Rushgrove Gdns BS39 .....113 C4
Rushmead La SN14 .....55 F2

Rushmoor BS21 . . . . .57 A1
Rushmoor Gr BS48 . . . . .76 A5
Rushmoor La BS48 . . . . .76 A5
Rushton Dr BS36 . . . . .38 D7
Rushway BS40 . . . . .109 F4
Rushy BS30 . . . . .66 A4
Rushy Way BS16 . . . . .38 A1
Ruskin Gr BS7 . . . . .50 A8
Ruskin Ho BS34 . . . . .36 A8
Ruskin Rd BA3 . . . . .132 C1
Russ La BS21 . . . . .73 E4
Russ St BS2 . . . . .141 C2
Russell Ave BS15 . . . . .65 E7
Russell Cl BS40 . . . . .95 A6
Russell Gr BS6 . . . . .49 C5
Russell Rd Bristol BS16 . . . .51 B2
  Bristol BS6 . . . . .49 B4
  Clevedon BS21 . . . . .57 C3
  Locking BS24 . . . . .106 C6
Russell St BA1 . . . . .142 B3
Russell Town Ave BS5 . . . . . .64 B8
Russell Town Ind Pk **18**
  BS5 . . . . .64 C7
Russet Cl BS35 . . . . .14 A3
Russet Ct GL12 . . . . .11 F4
Russet Way BA2 . . . . .133 D7
Russett Cl BS48 . . . . .76 B6
Russett Gr BS48 . . . . .75 C8
Russetts Cotts BS48 . . . . . . .76 B8
Rutherford Cl BS30 . . . . .66 A3
Ruthven Rd BS4 . . . . .79 E8
Rutland Ave BS30 . . . . .66 A2
Rutland Cl BS22 . . . . .105 C8
Rutland Rd BS7 . . . . .49 E3
Rydal Ave BS24 . . . . .106 A4
Rydal Ho BS34 . . . . .36 A8
Rydal Rd BS23 . . . . .104 F4
Ryde Rd BS4 . . . . .64 B2
Rye Cl BS13 . . . . .78 E6
Ryecroft Ave BS22 . . . . .88 E2
Ryecroft Rd BS36 . . . . .38 C8
Ryecroft Rise BS41 . . . . .62 B1
Ryedown La BS30 . . . . .66 D2
Ryland Pl **1** BS2 . . . . .50 A2
Rylestone Cl BS36 . . . . .37 F8
Rylestone Gr BS9 . . . . .48 F5
Rysdale Rd BS9 . . . . .48 F6

S

Sabrina Way BS9 . . . . .48 C4
Sadbury Cl BS22 . . . . .89 B4
Sadlier Cl BS11 . . . . .48 A8
Saffron Ct BA1 . . . . .142 C4
Saffron Ho **10** BS23 . . . . . .104 E8
Saffrons The **7** BS22 . . . . .89 B4
Sage Cl BS20 . . . . .44 E4
Sages Mead BS32 . . . . .36 E8
St Agnes Ave BS4 . . . . .63 F2
St Agnes Cl Bristol BS4 . . . .63 F2
  Nailsea BS48 . . . . .60 A1
St Agnes Wlk BS4 . . . . .63 F2
St Aidan's Cl BS5 . . . . .65 B6
St Aidan's Rd BS5 . . . . .65 B6
St Alban's Rd BS6 . . . . .49 B4
St Aldams Dr BS16 . . . . .53 B5
St Aldwyns Cl BS7 . . . . .49 F8
St Andrew's CE Prim Sch
  BA1 .142 B4
St Andrew's CE Prim Sch
  GL12 .10 A1
St Andrew's Dr BS21 . . . . . . .57 A2
St Andrew's Jun Sch
  BS49 . . . . .91 C4
St Andrew's Par **1** BS23 . .104 F4
St Andrew's Rd
  Avonmouth BS11 . . . . .33 B1
  Avonmouth BS11 . . . . .33 B4
  Bristol BS6 . . . . .49 E2
St Andrews Bristol BS30 . . . .66 B6
  Yate BS37 . . . . .27 F1
St Andrews Cl
  Nailsea BS48 . . . . .60 A1
  Weston-Super-Mare BS22 . . .88 F3
St Andrews Gate Rdbt
  BS11 .33 C2
St Andrews Rd BS48 . . . . . . .76 B5
St Andrews Road Sta
  BS11 .33 B4
St Andrews Trad Est BS11 . .33 C2
St Ann's Pl BA1 . . . . .142 B2
St Ann's Way BA2 . . . . .102 C6
St Anne's Ave BS31 . . . . .81 D6
St Anne's CE Prim Sch
  BS30 .66 C3
St Anne's Dr
  BS24 .90 B5
St Anne's Cl BS30 . . . . .66 B4
St Anne's Ct BS31 . . . . .81 D6
St Anne's Dr
  Coalpit Heath BS36 . . . . .38 C5
  Wick BS30 . . . . .67 B7
St Anne's Inf Sch BS4 . . . . . .64 E5
St Anne's Park Prim Sch
  BS4 . . . . .64 E5
St Anne's Park Rd BS4 . . . . .64 E5
St Anne's Rd Bristol BS4 . . . .64 D6
  Bristol BS5 . . . . .65 B6
St Anne's Terr BS4 . . . . .64 E5
St Annes Ct **7** BS4 . . . . . . .64 F6
St Annes Dr BS4 . . . . .64 D5

St Annes Dr BS30 . . . . .66 C2
St Anthony's Cl BA3 . . . . . .132 A2
St Anthony's Dr BS30 . . . . . .67 B7
St Aubin's Ave BS4 . . . . .64 F3
St Aubyn's Ave BS23 . . . . . .104 D2
St Augustine of
  Canterbury RC Sch BS16 . .51 F7
St Augustine's Par BS1 . . . .141 A2
St Augustine's Pl **1** BS1 . .141 A2
St Austell Cl BS48 . . . . .76 A8
St Austell Rd BS22 . . . . .105 B8
St Barnabas CE Prim Sch
  Bristol BS6 . . . . .49 F1
  Portishead BS20 . . . . .45 B5
St Barnabas Cl Bristol BS6 . .49 F2
  Bristol BS4 . . . . .63 F1
  Midsomer Norton BA3 . . . . .132 B3
St Bartholomew's Rd BS7 . . .49 F3
St Bede's Rd BS15 . . . . .34 B2
St Bede's Rd BS15 . . . . .51 D2
St Benedict's RC Prim Sch
  BA3 .138 C7
St Bernadette RC Prim Sch
  BS14 .80 B6
St Bernadette RC Sch
  BS14 .80 B6
St Bernard's RC Sch BS11 . .47 E6
St Bernard's Rd BS11 . . . . . .47 E6
St Bonaventure's
  RC Prim Sch BS7 . . . . .49 D4
St Brandon's Sch BS21 . . . . .57 B3
St Brelades Gr BS4 . . . . .64 F5
St Brendan's
  Sixth Form Coll BS4 . . . . . .65 A1
St Brendan's Way BS11 . . . . .33 B1
St Brendans Rdbt BS11 . . . . .33 C1
St Briavels Dr BS37 . . . . .39 D8
St Bridges Cl BS22 . . . . .88 A6
St Cadoc Ho BS31 . . . . .81 F5
St Catherine's Cl BA2 . . . . .102 C6
St Catherine's Ind Est
  BS3 . . . . .63 D3
St Catherine's Mead BS20 . .47 D3
St Catherine's Terr BS3 . . . . .63 D3
St Catherines Pl **7** BS3 . . .63 D4
St Chad's Ave BS34 . . . . . . .132 A1
St Chad's Gn BA3 . . . . .138 A8
St Charles Cl BA3 . . . . .132 A2
St Christopher's Ct BS1 . . . .57 C5
St Christopher's Specl Sch
  BS6 . . . . .49 B4
St Christophers Cl BA2 . . . .102 C8
St Clements Ct Bath BA1 . . .84 C1
  Bristol BS16 . . . . .51 D3
  Clevedon BS21 . . . . .57 C4
  Keynsham BS31 . . . . .81 E4
  Weston-Super-Mare BS22 . . .89 A2
St Clements Rd BS31 . . . . . . .81 E4
St David's Ave BS30 . . . . .66 B5
St David's Cl BS22 . . . . .88 B2
St David's Rd BS5 . . . . .64 F6
St Dunstan's Rd BS3 . . . . . . .63 C2
St Edward's Rd BS8 . . . . . . .140 B2
St Edyth's Rd BS9 . . . . .48 C6
St Fagans Ct BS30 . . . . .66 B2
St Frances RC Sch BS48 . . . .59 F1
St Francis Dr Wick BS30 . . . .67 B7
  Winterbourne BS36 . . . . .37 F6
St Francis Rd
  5 Bristol BS3 . . . . .63 A4
  Keynsham BS31 . . . . .81 D6
St Gabriel's Rd BS5 . . . . .64 B8
St George CE Prim Sch
  BS1 .140 B2
St George Com Sch BS5 . . . .64 C8
St George's Hill Bath BA2 . .102 D8
  Easton-In-Gordano BS20 . . .47 A3
St George's Ho BS48 . . . . . . .59 D2
St George's Rd
  Keynsham BS31 . . . . .81 D6
  Portbury BS20 . . . . .46 E7
St Georges Ave **10** BS5 . . .64 F6
St Georges Ho BS5 . . . . .64 E8
St Georges Ind Est BS11 . . . .33 B3
St Georges Rd BA1 . . . . .140 C2
St Giles Barton GL12 . . . . . . .19 D8
St Gregory's Rd BS7 . . . . .49 F8
St Gregory's Wlk BS7 . . . . . .49 F8
St Helen's Wlk BS5 . . . . .51 A1
St Helena Rd BS6 . . . . .49 B4
St Helens CE Prim Sch
  BS35 .15 A4
St Helens Dr Bristol BS30 . . .66 C2
  Wick BS30 . . . . .67 C7
St Helier Ave BS4 . . . . .64 F3
St Hilary Cl BS9 . . . . .48 C5
St Ivel Way BS30 . . . . .66 C6
St Ives Cl BS48 . . . . .60 A1
St Ives Rd BS23 . . . . .105 A5
St James Cl BS35 . . . . .8 C3
St James Ct BS32 . . . . .24 C3
St James' Barton BS1 . . . . .141 B4
St James's Par BA1 . . . . .142 B2
St James's Pk BA1 . . . . .142 B4
St James's Sq BA1 . . . . .142 A3
St James's St Bath BA1 . . . .142 B4
  Bristol BS16 . . . . .52 A5
St John St
  Hawkesbury Upton GL9 . . . .20 A3
  Thornbury BS35 . . . . .8 B1
St John the Evangelist
  CE Prim Sch BS21 . . . . .57 C1
St John's Ave BS21 . . . . .57 D3
St John's Bridge **2** BS1 . .141 A3

St John's CE Prim Sch
  BS8 . . . . .49 A2
St John's CE Sch BA3 . . . . .132 A1
St John's Cl
  Peasedown St John BA2 . . .133 B7
  Weston-Super-Mare BS23 . . .87 D1
St John's Cres Bristol BS3 . .63 E2
  Midsomer Norton BA3 . . . . .132 A2
St John's Ho **6** BS5 . . . . . .64 D8
St John's La BS3 . . . . .63 E2
St John's Mead
  CE Prim Sch BS37 . . . . .28 B1
St John's Pl BA1 . . . . .142 B2
St John's Prim Sch BS1 . . . .81 E5
St John's RC Prim Sch
  BA2 .102 B6
St John's St
  (Annexe) BA2 . . . . .101 D4
St John's Rd Backwell BS48 . .76 B5
  Bath BA1 . . . . .101 C7
  Bath BA2 . . . . .142 C3
  Bristol BS8 . . . . .49 A1
  Bristol, Bedminster BS3 . . . . .63 C3
  Bristol, Southville BS3 . . . . . .63 D4
  Clevedon BS21 . . . . .57 D3
St John's St BS3 . . . . .63 E3
St Johns Cl Axbridge BS26 .125 B2
  Bristol BS16 . . . . .51 A3
  Keynsham BS31 . . . . .81 E6
St Johns Rd BA3 . . . . .116 B1
St Johns Way BS37 . . . . .28 C2
St Joseph's RC Prim Sch
  Bristol BS16 . . . . .51 B3
  Portishead BS20 . . . . .45 C6
St Joseph's Rd Bristol BS10 .35 B3
  Weston-Super-Mare BS23 . . .87 E1
St Jude's Terr BS22 . . . . .88 C1
St Julian's CE Prim Sch
  BA2 .118 E1
St Julian's Rd BA2 . . . . .133 F5
St Julians Ct BS39 . . . . .131 E4
St Katherine's Sch BS20 . . . .47 E3
St Kenya Ct BS31 . . . . .81 F5
St Keyna Rd BS31 . . . . .81 E5
St Kilda's Rd BA2 . . . . .101 D5
St Ladoc Rd BS31 . . . . .81 D6
St Laud Cl BS9 . . . . .48 D5
St Leonard's Rd
  Bristol BS5 . . . . .50 C2
  Bristol BS7 . . . . .49 E5
St Lucia Cl BS7 . . . . .49 E7
St Lucia Cres BS7 . . . . .49 E7
St Luke St **6** BS5 . . . . .64 B7
St Luke's Cres BS3 . . . . .63 F4
St Luke's Ct BS3 . . . . .63 E4
St Luke's Gdns BS4 . . . . .64 E2
St Luke's Rd BS3 . . . . .63 E3
  Bristol BS3 . . . . .63 E4
  Midsomer Norton BA3 . . . . .131 F2
St Margaret's Cl BS31 . . . . . .81 D6
St Margaret's Dr BS9 . . . . . . .49 C5
St Margaret's Terr BS23 . . .104 D8
St Margarets Cl BS48 . . . . . . .76 A5
St Mark's Ave **1** BS5 . . . . .50 B1
St Mark's CE Sch BA1 . . . . . .85 B2
St Mark's CE/Methodist
  Ecumenical Prim Sch
  BS22 .88 F4
St Mark's Gr **8** BS5 . . . . . .50 B1
St Mark's Rd Bath BA2 . . . .142 C1
  Bristol BS5 . . . . .50 B1
  Midsomer Norton BA3 . . . . .132 A2
  Weston-Super-Mare BS22 . . .89 A3
St Mark's Terr **2** BS5 . . . . .50 B1
St Marks Church Ho **4**
  BS5 . . . . .50 B1
St Marks Cl BS31 . . . . .81 E6
St Marks Gdns BA1 . . . . . . .142 C1
St Marks Ho **13** BS5 . . . . . .50 B1
St Martin's Ct BA2 . . . . .101 E1
St Martin's Gdns BS4 . . . . . .64 B1
St Martin's La SN14 . . . . .69 F8
St Martin's Wlk BS4 . . . . . . .64 B1
St Martins BS22 . . . . .57 C5
St Martins CE Jun Sch
  BS22 .88 D2
St Martins Cl BS4 . . . . .64 B1
St Martins Ct BS22 . . . . .88 E3
St Martins Hospl BA2 . . . . .101 E1
St Mary Prim Sch Bath BA2 .102 C8
St Mary Redcliffe &
  Temple CE Sch BS1 . . . . .141 B1
St Mary Redcliffe
  Prim Sch BS3 . . . . .63 E4
St Mary St BS35 . . . . .15 B8
St Mary's Bldgs BA2 . . . . . .142 B1
St Mary's CE Prim Sch
  BS20 .46 E3
St Mary's CE Prim Sch
  BA3 .133 C1
St Mary's CE Prim Sch
  Timsbury BA3 . . . . .116 C3
  Yate BS37 . . . . .27 E2
St Mary's Cl Bath BA2 . . . .102 B6
St Mary's Ct BS24 . . . . .105 A1
St Mary's Gdns BS40 . . . . . .109 B5
St Mary's Gr BS48 . . . . .75 C8
St Mary's Hospl BS8 . . . . . .140 B3
St Mary's Park Rd BS20 . . . .45 C4
St Mary's Pk BS48 . . . . .75 C8
St Mary's RC Inf Sch BA1 . .84 B1
St Mary's RC Prim Sch BS11 .47 D7
  Hutton BS24 . . . . .105 D2
  Leigh Woods BS8 . . . . .62 D6

St Mary's Rd continued
  Portishead BS20 . . . . .45 C4
St Mary's Sch BS26 . . . . . . .125 C2
St Mary's Way BS37 . . . . . . .27 F2
St Mary's Wlk BS11 . . . . .47 D6
St Marys Cl BS24 . . . . .105 D2
St Marys RC Prim Sch
  BS34 .37 A7
St Marys Rise BA3 . . . . .133 C2
St Marys Way BS35 . . . . .8 B1
St Mathew's Pl BA2 . . . . . . .102 B5
St Mathias Ho BS2 . . . . .141 C3
St Matthew's Ave **10** BS6 . .49 D1
St Matthew's Cl BS23 . . . . . .87 D1
St Matthew's Rd BS6 . . . . . .141 A4
St Matthias & Dr Bell's
  CE Prim Sch BS16 . . . . .51 A4
St Matthias Pk BS2 . . . . . . .141 C3
St Michael's Ave
  Clevedon BS21 . . . . .57 D1
  Weston-Super-Mare BS22 . . .89 A3
St Michael's CE Jun Sch
  BA2 .101 A6
St Michael's CE Prim Sch
  BS36 .36 E5
St Michael's Cl BS36 . . . . . . .37 E7
St Michael's Ct BA2 . . . . . . .119 E8
St Michael's Hill BS2 . . . . . .140 C4
St Michael's Hospl BS2 . . . .140 C4
St Michael's Pk BS2 . . . . . . .140 C4
St Michael's Pl BA1 . . . . . . .142 B2
St Michael's Rd BA1 . . . . . .101 D7
St Michaels CE Prim Sch
  BS36 .37 E6
St Michaels Cl BS37 . . . . .49 E4
St Michaels Ct BS15 . . . . . . .65 B8
St Michaels Rd BA2 . . . . . . .101 A5
St Nicholas Chantry
  Prim Sch BS21 . . . . .57 E3
St Nicholas Cl BA15 . . . . . . .120 D7
St Nicholas Cres BS42 . . . . . .85 F1
St Nicholas of Tolentine
  RC Prim Sch BS5 . . . . .64 A8
St Nicholas Pk **10** BS5 . . .50 B1
St Nicholas Rd
  Weston-Super-Mare BS23 . .104 D2
  Whitchurch BS14 . . . . .80 C4
St Nicholas Way BS48 . . . . . .75 D2
St Nicholas' Inf Sch BS23 . .132 F2
St Nicholas' Rd BS2 . . . . . . .49 F3
St Nicholas's Church Mus
  BS1 .141 A2
St Oswald's Ct BS13 . . . . . . .79 A8
St Oswald's Ct BS6 . . . . .49 B3
St Oswald's Rd BS6 . . . . .49 B3
St Patrick's Ct BA2 . . . . .102 B6
St Patrick's RC Prim Sch
  BS5 . . . . .64 D7
St Patricks Ct BS31 . . . . .81 E5
St Paul St BS2 . . . . .141 B4
St Paul's RC Prim Sch
  BS37 .39 E8
St Paul's Rd **2** Bristol BS3 .63 D4
  Weston-Super-Mare BS22 . .104 B5
St Paul's St BS2 . . . . .141 B2
St Peter's Ave BS23 . . . . .87 D1
St Peter's Cres BS36 . . . . . . .38 B8
St Peter's Ho BS8 . . . . .140 B2
St Peter's Rd BA3 . . . . .133 C8
St Peter's Rise BS13 . . . . .79 B7
St Peter's Terr BA2 . . . . .101 D6
St Peter's Wlk **3** BS9 . . . . .49 B6
St Peters CE Prim Sch
  BS20 .45 D4
St Peters Rd BS20 . . . . .45 D4
St Philip's CE Prim Sch
  BA2 .101 D2
St Philips Central BS2 . . . . . .64 A5
St Philips Cswy BS2 . . . . . . .64 A5
St Philips Rd BS2 . . . . .64 A7
St Pius X RC Prim Sch
  BS13 .79 A5
St Pierre Dr BS30 . . . . .66 B6
St Ronan's Ave BS6 . . . . .49 C1
St Saviour's Inf Sch BA1 . . .85 B2
St Saviour's Jun Sch BA1 . . .85 B2
St Saviour's Rd BA1 . . . . .85 C2
St Saviour's Rise BS36 . . . . .38 B6
St Saviour's Terr **10** BA1 . .85 B2
St Saviours Way BA1 . . . . . . .85 C1
St Silas St BS2 . . . . .64 A5
St Stephen's Ave **3** BS1 . .141 A2
St Stephen's CE Jun Sch
  BS16 .51 D2
St Stephen's Cl Bristol BS10 .35 C4
  BA1 . . . . .84 F1
St Stephen's Ct BA1 . . . . . . .84 F1
St Stephen's Pl BA1 . . . . . . .142 B4
St Stephen's Rd Bath BA1 . .142 B4
  Bristol BS16 . . . . .51 D2
St Stephen's St BS1 . . . . . . .141 A2
St Stephens Bsns Ctr
  BS30 .66 C5
St Stephens Cl BS16 . . . . . . .51 E3
St Swithin's Pl BA1 . . . . .85 B1
St Teresa's RC Prim Sch
  BS7 . . . . .35 E1
St Thomas More RC Sch
  BS7 . . . . .50 A3
St Thomas Rd BA3 . . . . .132 B2
St Thomas St BS1 . . . . .141 B2
St Thomas St E BS1 . . . . . . .141 B2
St Ursula's High Sch BS9 . . .49 A6

St Vigour & St John
  Prim Sch BA3 . . . . .132 —
St Vincent's Hill **1** BS6 . . .49 —
St Vincent's Rd BS8 . . . . . . .140 —
St Vincents Trad Est BS2 . . .64 —
St Werburgh's Pk BS2 . . . . . .50 —
St Werburgh's Rd BS2 . . . . . .49 —
St Werburgh's Sch BS5 . . . . .50 —
St Whytes Rd BS4 . . . . .79 —
St Winifred's Dr BA2 . . . . . .102 —
SS Gt Britain BS1 . . . . .141 —
SS Peter & Paul
  Catholic Sch BS8 . . . . .140 —
SS Peter & Paul RC Cath
  BS8 .140 —
Salcombe Gdns BS22 . . . . . . .89 —
Salcombe Rd BS4 . . . . .64 —
Salem Rd BS34 . . . . .3 —
Salisbury Ave BS15 . . . . .6 —
Salisbury Gdns BS16 . . . . . . .5 —
Salisbury Pk BS16 . . . . .5 —
Salisbury Rd Bath BA1 . . . . . .8 —
  Bristol BS16 . . . . .5 —
  Bristol BS6 . . . . .6 —
  Bristol BS4 . . . . .6 —
  Paulton BS39 . . . . .13 —
  Weston-Super-Mare BS22 . . .88 —
Salisbury St
  Bristol, Pile Marsh BS5 . . . . . .6 —
  Bristol, Russell Town BS5 . . . .6 —
Salisbury Terr BS23 . . . . .6 —
Sally In The Wood
  BA1,BA15 . . . . .103 —
Sally Lunn's Kitchen Mus
  BA1 .142 —
Sallybarn Cl BS30 . . . . .6 —
Sallys Way BS36 . . . . .3 —
Sallysmead Cl BS13 . . . . .7 —
Salmons Way BS16 . . . . .5 —
Saltford CE Prim Sch
  BS31 .8 —
Saltford Ct BS31 . . . . .8 —
Salthouse Ct BS21 . . . . .5 —
Salthouse Rd BS21 . . . . .5 —
Salthrop Rd BS7 . . . . .4 —
Saltings Cl BS21 . . . . .5 —
Saltmarsh Dr BS11 . . . . .3 —
Saltwell Ave BS14 . . . . .8 —
Sambourne La BS20 . . . . .4 —
Samian Way BS34 . . . . .3 —
Sampson House Bsns Pk
  BS10 .3 —
Sampsons Rd BS13 . . . . .7 —
Samuel St **3** BS5 . . . . .6 —
Samuel White Rd BS15 . . . . .6 —
Samuel Whites Inf Sch
  BS15 .6 —
Samuel Wright Cl BS30 . . . . .6 —
San Andreas BS34 . . . . .3 —
Sanctuary Gdns BS9 . . . . .4 —
Sand Farm La BS22 . . . . .8 —
Sand Hill BS4 . . . . .6 —
Sand Rd BS22 . . . . .8 —
Sandbach Rd BS4 . . . . .6 —
Sandbed Rd BS2 . . . . .5 —
Sandburrows Rd BS13 . . . . . .7 —
Sandburrows Wlk BS13 . . . . .7 —
Sandcroft BS14 . . . . .7 —
Sandcroft Ave BS23 . . . . . . .104 —
Sandford Cl **2** BS21 . . . . . . .5 —
Sandford Prim Sch BS25 . . .108 —
Sandford Rd Bristol BS8 . . .140 —
  Weston-Super-Mare BS23 . .105 —
Winscombe BS25 . . . . .10 —
Sandgate Rd BS4 . . . . .6 —
Sandholme Cl BS16 . . . . .5 —
Sandholme Rd BS4 . . . . .6 —
Sandhurst BS37 . . . . .3 —
Sandhurst Cl BS34 . . . . .2 —
Sandhurst Rd BS4 . . . . .6 —
Sandling Ave BS7 . . . . .5 —
Sandmead Rd BS25 . . . . . . .108 —
Sandown Cl BS16 . . . . .3 —
Sandown Rd Bristol BS34 . . .3 —
  Bristol BS4 . . . . .6 —
Sandpiper Dr BS22 . . . . .8 —
Sandpits La GL9 . . . . .2 —
Sandringham Ave BS16 . . . . .5 —
Sandringham Ct BS23 . . . . .104 —
Sandringham Pk BS16 . . . . . .5 —
Sandringham Rd
  Bristol BS30 . . . . .6 —
  Bristol BS34 . . . . .3 —
  Weston-Super-Mare BS23 . .104 —
Sandringham Road Rd
  BS23 . . . . .104 —
Sands Hill SN14 . . . . .6 —
Sands La BS36 . . . . .2 —
Sandstone Rise BS36 . . . . . . .3 —
Sandwich Rd BS4 . . . . .6 —
Sandy Cl BS32 . . . . .3 —
Sandy Lady La Aust BS35 . . . .3 —
  Aust BS35 . . . . .3 —
Sandy Lodge BS37 . . . . .3 —
Sandy Park Rd BS4 . . . . .6 —
Sandyleaze BS9 . . . . .4 —
Sarabeth Dr BA3 . . . . .117 —
Saracen St BA1 . . . . .142 —
Sarah St BS5 . . . . .6 —
Sargent St BS3 . . . . .6 —
Sarum Cres BS10 . . . . .3 —
Sassoon Ct BS30 . . . . .6 —
Satchfield Cl BS10 . . . . .3 —

Cres BS10 .... 34 F2
sns Pk BS5 .... 64 D6
Rd BS16 .... 51 E4
lk BS4 .... 79 F8
ood BS12 .... 36 E8
ood Rd BS32 .... 36 D8
Rd BS22 .... 88 F3
s BS22 .... 105 C8
e Cl BS9 .... 48 F6
ews BS6 .... 141 A4
S8 .... 140 A2
e BS9 .... 48 F3
er-Mare BS22 .... 105 C8
w BA1 .... 142 B3
S4 .... 64 D8
.... 142 B2
S 8 B1
dns BA3 .... 137 D3
st BS20 .... 46 E7

BA3 .... 137 D3
8 .... 60 A2
BS21 .... 57 E3
levedon BS21 .... 57 B1
er-Mare BS22 .... 89 B4
evedon BS22 .... 50 A2
er-Mare BS22 .... 105 C8
S40 .... 109 D6
st Bristol BS22 .... 24 C1
St John BA2 .... 133 E8
.... 120 F7
30 .... 66 D7
40 .... 109 B4
5 .... 65 B5
S23 .... 88 A2
Cl BS10 .... 34 E2
ry Cl BS16 .... 51 D8
S22 .... 88 F2
Banwell BS29 .... 107 B3
.... 79 F4
.... 36 C8
Badminton GL9 .... 30 E2
ney BS48 .... 77 D5
BA1 .... 85 F4
Cl BS40 .... 112 D8
Gurney BS39 .... 131 A4
r BS25 .... 109 A1
Christ the King
Sch BS4 .... 79 E8
Bristol BS15 .... 65 C8
hom Hill BS4 .... 64 E3
sbury Heath BS30 .... 66 A4
illand
n BS30 .... 66 C3
Beacon BS4 .... 64 A3
otterell BS36 .... 38 A8
S40 .... 92 E2
ay BS35 .... 22 A6
ke BS35 .... 50 D1
.... 27 E2
e BS39 .... 115 C2
S32 .... 24 B5
S40 .... 110 E2
S40 .... 110 D7
La BS40 .... 112 D7
r BS24 .... 89 D1
40 .... 95 D1
rn Cl BS48 .... 59 F2
rn Way BS48 .... 59 F2
e Ave BS48 .... 59 F2
S30 .... 65 F5
rence Cl BS16 .... 51 A7
S23 .... 105 A4
S37 .... 39 F8
BS30 .... 66 D7
n La BS39 .... 115 C2
BS20 .... 32 E1
Inf Sch BS7 .... 48 C7
Jun Sch BS9 .... 48 B5
La BS9 .... 48 C5
Sta BS9 .... 48 B4
Rd BS22 .... 88 D1
BS10 .... 35 E1
urt Ave BS4 .... 64 E4
s BS23 .... 105 B6
BS21 .... 57 E2
.... 63 D1
BS5 .... 50 C1
lews BS21 .... 57 C4
d BS21 .... 57 C4
d Homeschool,
ay BS20 .... 44 F4
l, West Hill BS20 .... 44 F6
S19 .... 48 D2
Rd BS9 .... 48 D2
te Bath BA2 .... 101 D5
e La 80 B7
BA3 .... 138 C7
ay BS11 .... 33 D1
J BS2 .... 50 A2
Gdns BS16 .... 37 F1
er Cl BS48 .... 75 E8
er Rd Bath BA2 .... 101 F2
per-Mare BS23 .... 87 F1
Ho BS11 .... 47 E7
rk Jun & Inf Schs
.... 49 F3
rk BA2 .... 94 D4
Ave BA2 .... 106 A8
Rd BS7 .... 49 F5
r Cl BA1 .... 101 A8
r Rd BS23 .... 123 E1
Cres BS16 .... 51 C6
S5 .... 50 F1
BS14 .... 80 E5

Selkirk Rd BS15 .... 51 C1
Selley Wlk BS13 .... 79 A5
Selway Ct BA2 .... 102 B2
Selwood Cl BS22 .... 105 C7
Selworthy BS15 .... 65 C7
Selworthy Cl BS31 .... 81 D5
Selworthy Gdns ▲ BS48 .... 59 E1
Selworthy Ho BA2 .... 101 F2
Selworthy Rd Bristol BS4 .... 64 B2
Weston-Super-Mare BS23 .... 105 A4
Semington Rd BA2 .... 101 F2
Seneca Pl ◆ BS5 .... 64 D7
Seneca St BS5 .... 64 D7
Septimus Bldgs BS14 .... 79 D5
Serbert Cl BS20 .... 45 E5
Serbert Rd BS20 .... 45 E5
Serbert Way BS20 .... 45 E5
Serbrook Pk BS21 .... 57 E1
Serlo Ct BS22 .... 89 A4
Serridge La BS36 .... 38 D4
Seven Acres La BA1 .... 83 F5
Seven Acres The BS24 .... 105 F7
Seven Dials BA1 .... 142 B2
Seventh Ave Bristol BS14 .... 80 A7
BS7 .... 36 B1
Severn Ave BS23 .... 104 E5
Severn Beach Prim Sch
BS35 .... 22 A6
Severn Beach Sta BS35 .... 22 A6
Severn Cl BS12 .... 11 A4
Severn Dr BS35 .... 8 B2
Severn Grange BS10 .... 34 D3
Severn La GL13 .... 2 F8
Severn Rd Avonmouth BS11 .... 33 C4
Bristol BS11 .... 47 D6
Hallen BS10 .... 34 A2
Pill BS20 .... 47 C5
Portishead BS20 .... 45 C5
Severn Beach BS35 .... 21 F3
Weston-Super-Mare BS23 .... 104 E5
Severn View Rd BS35 .... 8 C2
Severn Way Bristol BS34 .... 23 F1
Keynsham BS31 .... 82 A5
Severnleigh Gdns BS9 .... 48 F3
Severnmeade BS20 .... 44 F5
Severnside Trad Est BS35 .... 13 C5
Severnwood Gdns BS35 .... 22 A5
Sevier Rd BS26 .... 123 C3
Sevier St BS2 .... 49 F2
Seville Rd BS20 .... 45 E7
Seward Terr BA2 .... 133 C2
Sewell Ho BS25 .... 125 A8
Seymour Ave BS7 .... 49 E4
Seymour Cl Clevedon BS21 .... 57 E3
Weston-Super-Mare BS22 .... 88 F4
Seymour Rd Bath BA1 .... 142 C4
Bristol BS15 .... 51 C1
Bristol BS16 .... 51 E4
Bristol BS5 .... 50 A1
Bristol BS7 .... 49 E4
Seyton Wlk BS34 .... 36 E5
Shackel Hendy
Mews BS16 .... 52 B5
Shackleton Ave BS37 .... 39 F8
Shadow Wlk BS34 .... 106 C3
Shadwell Rd BS7 .... 49 D3
Shaft Rd BA2 .... 102 E1
Severn Beach BS35 .... 22 A8
Shaftesbury Ave
Bath BA1 .... 101 C7
Bristol BS6 .... 49 E1
Shaftesbury Cl BS48 .... 75 D8
Shaftesbury Rd Bath BA2 .... 101 D5
Weston-Super-Mare BS23 .... 105 B8
Shaftesbury Terr
▣ Bristol BS5 .... 64 D7
Radstock BA3 .... 133 A3
Shakespeare Ave
Bath BA2 .... 101 F4
Bristol BS7 .... 50 A8
Shakespeare Rd BA3 .... 132 C1
Shaldon Rd BS7 .... 50 A8
Shallowbrooks La SN14 .... 31 F8
Shallows The BS31 .... 82 F3
Sham Castle La BA2 .... 102 C2
Shamrock Rd BS5 .... 50 D3
Shanklin Dr BS34 .... 36 B3
Shannon Ct BS35 .... 15 F8
Shapcott Cl BS4 .... 64 B1
Shaplands BS9 .... 48 F4
Sharland Cl BS9 .... 48 E3
Sharland Gr BS13 .... 79 C4
Shaw Cl ▣ BS5 .... 50 B1
Shaws Way BA2 .... 100 F5
Shaymoor La BS35 .... 23 A4
Shearmore Cl BS7 .... 50 A7
Sheene La ▣ BS3 .... 63 C3
Sheene La BS3 .... 63 C3
Sheene Way BS3 .... 63 C3
Sheep Fair La SN14 .... 69 F8
Sheephouse Caravan Pk
BS20 .... 46 E7
Sheeps Croft BS13 .... 79 A5
Sheepway BS20 .... 46 A5
Sheepway La BS20 .... 46 C5
Sheepwood Cl BS10 .... 35 A2
Sheepwood Rd BS10 .... 35 A2
Sheiling Sch The BS35 .... 8 B2
Sheldare Barton BS5 .... 65 B7
Sheldon Cl BS21 .... 57 F2
Sheldrake Dr BS16 .... 50 E6
Shellard Rd BS34 .... 36 A2
Shellards La BS35 .... 15 E2
Shellards Rd BS30 .... 65 F3
Shelley Ave BS21 .... 57 D2
Shelley Cl BS5 .... 64 F8
Shelley Ho BS34 .... 24 A1
Shelley Rd Bath BA2 .... 101 F4

Shelley Rd continued
Radstock BA3 .... 132 C1
Weston-Super-Mare BS23 .... 105 A4
Shelley Way BS7 .... 50 A8
Shellmor Ave BS34 .... 24 B1
Shellmor Cl BS32 .... 24 D1
Shepherds Cl BS16 .... 51 E5
Sheppard Rd BS16 .... 51 C6
Sheppards Gdns BA1 .... 84 B1
Shepperdine Rd BS35 .... 1 D2
Sheppy's Mill BS49 .... 91 D5
Shepton BS24 .... 105 A2
Shepton Wlk BS3 .... 63 C2
Sherbourne Ave BS32 .... 36 E7
Sherbourne Cl BS15 .... 51 F2
Sherbourne St BS5 .... 64 E7
Sherbourne's Brake BS32 .... 36 E6
Sheridan Rd Bath BA2 .... 100 F5
Bristol BS7 .... 50 A8
Sheridan Way BS30 .... 66 A2
Sherrin Way BS13 .... 78 E3
Sherrings The BS34 .... 36 B8
Sherston Cl Bristol BS16 .... 51 B5
Nailsea BS48 .... 60 A1
Sherston Rd Bristol BS7 .... 49 F8
Luckington SN14 .... 31 F5
Sherwell Rd BS4 .... 64 E3
Sherwood Cl BS31 .... 81 E5
Sherwood Cres BS22 .... 88 F3
Sherwood Rd Bristol BS15 .... 51 E5
Keynsham BS31 .... 81 E5
Shetland Rd BS10 .... 35 D1
Shetland Way BS48 .... 60 A1
Shickle Gr BA2 .... 101 D1
Shield Ret Ctr BS34 .... 36 A3
Shield Road Prim Sch
BS7 .... 36 A1
Shields Ave BS7 .... 36 A1
Shiels Dr BS32 .... 36 D7
Shilton Cl BS15 .... 65 F7
Shimsey Cl BS16 .... 51 C6
Shiners Elms BS49 .... 91 B8
Ship La BS1 .... 141 B1
Shipham Cl Bristol BS14 .... 80 B5
Nailsea BS48 .... 75 F8
Shipham Fst Sch BS25 .... 125 E8
Shipham La BS25 .... 108 B1
Shipham Rd Cheddar BS27 .... 125 F7
Shipham BS25,BS27 .... 125 F5
Shipley Mow BS16 .... 52 B6
Shipley Rd BS9 .... 49 A8
Shipman Ct BS16 .... 51 E4
Shire Gdns BS11 .... 47 D8
Shire Hill SN14 .... 56 A7
Shire Way BS37 .... 39 D6
Shirehampton Inf Sch
BS11 .... 47 D6
Shirehampton Rd BS9 .... 48 C6
Shirehampton Sta BS11 .... 47 D5
Shires Yd BA1 .... 142 B3
Shockerwick La BA1 .... 86 D4
Shop La GL9 .... 30 E2
Shophouse Rd BA2 .... 101 B5
Shopland Ho ◤ BS21 .... 57 C2
Shoredick Cl BS40 .... 112 C7
Shorland Ho BS8 .... 49 A1
Short La Litton BA3 .... 129 F2
Long Ashton BS41 .... 62 A2
Short St BS2 .... 64 A5
Short Way Failand BS8 .... 61 B4
Thornbury BS35 .... 8 D1
Shorthill Rd BS37 .... 39 C4
Shortlands Rd BS11 .... 34 A1
Shortwood Hill BS16 .... 52 E4
Shortwood Rd Bristol BS13 .... 79 E3
Pucklechurch BS16 .... 53 C2
Shortwood View BS15 .... 65 F8
Shortwood Wlk BS13 .... 79 E3
Shoscombe CE Prim Sch
BA2 .... 133 F5
Showering Cl BS14 .... 80 D5
Showering Rd BS14 .... 80 D5
Shrewsbury Bow BS24 .... 106 A8
Shrubbery Ave BS23 .... 87 D1
Shrubbery Cotts ◤ BS6 .... 49 B2
Shrubbery Ct ◤ BS16 .... 51 D5
Shrubbery Rd Bristol BS16 .... 51 D5
Weston-Super-Mare BS23 .... 87 D1
Shrubbery Terr BS23 .... 87 C1
Shrubbery Wlk W BS23 .... 87 D1
Shuter Rd BS13 .... 78 E5
Sibland ▣ BS35 .... 15 D8
Sibland Cl ▣ BS35 .... 15 D8
Sibland Rd BS35 .... 15 D8
Sibland Way BS35 .... 15 D8
Sidcot BS24 .... 105 A2
Sidcot La BS25 .... 125 A7
Sidcot Sch BS25 .... 125 B7
Sideland Cl BS14 .... 80 E6
Sidelands Rd BS16 .... 51 C6
Sidelings The BS40 .... 127 D8
Sidings The GL12 .... 11 B5
Sidmouth Ct BS3 .... 63 D1
Sidmouth Gdns BS3 .... 63 D2
Sidmouth Rd BS3 .... 63 E2
Sidney Hill Cottage Homes
BS25 .... 108 E4
Signal Rd BS16 .... 51 F4
Silbury Rd BS3 .... 62 E2
Silbury Rise BS31 .... 82 A2
Silcox Rd BS13 .... 79 C4
Silklands Gr BS9 .... 48 C6
Silver Ct BS48 .... 59 C2
Silver Mead BS49 .... 91 D2
Silver Moor La BS29 .... 106 F7

Silver St Bristol BS1 .... 141 A3
Chew Magna BS40 .... 96 B3
Congresbury BS49 .... 91 D2
Holcombe BA3 .... 138 C1
Kilmersdon BA3 .... 139 B5
Midsomer Norton BA3 .... 138 A7
Nailsea BS48 .... 59 D2
Portishead BS20 .... 44 F1
Thornbury BS35 .... 8 B1
Wrington BS40 .... 92 E2
Silverberry Rd BS22 .... 89 A1
Silverbirch Cl BS34 .... 36 D7
Silvercombe ▣ BS23 .... 104 E5
Silverhill Brake BS35 .... 14 E1
Silverhill Rd BS10 .... 34 E3
Silverhill Sch BS37 .... 28 A4
Silverhill Sch (Jun) BS36 .... 37 E7
Silverlow Rd BS48 .... 59 D2
Silverstone Way BS49 .... 91 D3
Silverthorne La BS2 .... 64 A6
Silverthorne Wharf BS2 .... 64 B6
Silverton Ct BS4 .... 63 F1
Simmonds View BS34 .... 36 F5
Simon's Cl BS39 .... 131 F5
Simons Cl BS22 .... 89 A2
Simplex Ind Est The BS30 .... 66 D4
Sinclair Ho Bristol BS8 .... 36 A2
Bristol BS8 .... 140 A2
Singapore Rd BS23 .... 104 E3
Sion Hill Bath BA1 .... 84 E1
Bristol BS8 .... 62 F7
Sion Hill Pl BA1 .... 84 E1
Sion La BS8 .... 62 F7
Sion Pl Bath BA2 .... 102 B6
Bristol BS8 .... 62 F7
Sion Rd Bath BA1 .... 84 E1
▣ Bristol BS3 .... 63 C3
Sir Bernard Lovell Sch
BS30 .... 66 C4
Sir Bernard Lovell Sch
(annexe) BS30 .... 66 D5
Sir Bevil Grenville's Mon
BA1 .... 68 A1
Sir John's La Bristol BS5 .... 50 B4
Bristol BS7 .... 50 B5
Siston Cl BS15 .... 52 A2
Siston Comm Bristol BS15 .... 52 A2
Bristol BS30 .... 52 B1
Siston Hill BS30 .... 52 B2
Siston La BS30 .... 52 F2
Siston Pk BS15 .... 52 A2
Six Streams BA1 .... 84 B2
Six Ways BS21 .... 57 C4
Sixpence BS39 .... 115 D2
Sixth Ave Bristol BS14 .... 80 A7
Bristol BS7 .... 36 B1
Sixty Acres Cl BS8 .... 61 B4
Skinner's Hill BA2 .... 132 F7
Skinners La BS25 .... 108 F4
Skippon Ct BS15 .... 65 E5
Sladacre La BS40 .... 110 E2
Slade La
Barrow Gurney BS48 .... 77 C4
Lympsham BS24 .... 122 B1
Slade Rd BS20 .... 45 D5
Sladebrook Ave BA2 .... 101 C3
Sladebrook Ct BA2 .... 101 C3
Sladebrook Rd BA2 .... 101 B4
Slate La BS14,BS31 .... 98 B7
Sleep La BS14 .... 80 D3
Slimbridge Cl BS37 .... 39 F7
Sloan St BS5 .... 64 D8
Slough La SN14 .... 68 F5
Slymbridge Ave BS10 .... 35 A3
Small Down End BS25 .... 107 F2
Small La BS16 .... 50 E5
Small St Bristol BS1 .... 141 A3
Bristol BS2 .... 64 A6
Smallbrook La BS39 .... 98 B6
Smallcombe Cl BA3 .... 132 E5
Smallcombe Rd BA3 .... 132 E4
Smallway BS49 .... 91 D5
Smarts BS40 .... 40 C8
Smeaton Rd BS1 .... 62 F5
Smith's Forge Ind Est
BS49 .... 73 F3
Smithcourt Dr BS34 .... 36 D6
Smithmead BS13 .... 79 B5
Smoke La BS11 .... 33 D6
Smyth Rd BS3 .... 63 A3
Smyth Terr ▣ BS3 .... 63 C4
Smythe Croft BS14 .... 80 A3
Smyths Cl BS11 .... 33 A1
Snow Hill Bath BA1 .... 85 A1
Snow Hill Ho BA1 .... 142 C4
Snowberry Cl BS22 .... 89 A1
Snowberry Wlk BS5 .... 50 E1
Snowdon Cl BS16 .... 50 F4
Snowdon Rd BS16 .... 50 F4
Snowdon Vale BS23 .... 88 A1
Soapers La BS35 .... 15 B8
Soaphouse Ind Est BS5 .... 64 E8
Sodbury Rd GL12 .... 18 A4
Solent Way BS35 .... 15 C7
Solon Ct BS13 .... 78 F5
Solsbury Ct BA1 .... 85 F3
Solsbury La BA1 .... 85 F4
Solsbury View ▣ BA1 .... 85 A1
Solsbury Way BA1 .... 85 A2
Somer Ave BA3 .... 131 F2
Somer Ho BA3 .... 132 A1
Somer Lea BA3 .... 137 D5
Somer Rd BA3 .... 131 F2
Somerby Cl BS32 .... 36 D7
Somerdale Ave Bath BA2 .... 101 D2
Bristol BS4 .... 64 A1
Weston-Super-Mare BS22 .... 105 C8
Somerdale Cl BS22 .... 105 C8

Somerdale Rd BS31 .... 81 F7
Somerdale Rd N
BS30, BS31 .... 81 F8
Somerdale View BS4 .... 101 C2
Somerford Ct BS10 .... 34 F1
Somermead BS3 .... 63 C1
Somerset Ave
Weston-Super-Mare
BS2,BS24 .... 106 F7
Yate BS37 .... 27 F3
Somerset Cl GL12 .... 11 F4
Somerset Cres BS34 .... 36 F5
Somerset Folly BA2 .... 116 B2
Somerset Ho Bath BA2 .... 101 D3
▣ Bristol BS2 .... 141 C3
Somerset La BA1 .... 84 E1
Somerset Mews BS23 .... 104 F6
Somerset Pl BA1 .... 84 E1
Somerset Rd Bristol BS4 .... 64 B3
Clevedon BS21 .... 57 E3
Portishead BS20 .... 44 F5
Somerset Sq Bristol BS1 .... 141 B1
▣ Nailsea BS48 .... 59 E2
Somerset St Bath BA1 .... 142 C1
Bristol BS1 .... 141 B1
Bristol BS2 .... 141 A4
Somerset Terr 63 D3
Somerset Way BS39 .... 133 C6
Somerton Cl BS15 .... 65 C7
Somerton Rd Bristol BS7 .... 49 E6
Clevedon BS21 .... 57 I
Somervale Rd BA3 .... 133 E2
Somervale Sch BA3 .... 132 A1
Somerville Cl BS31 .... 82 E2
Somerville Rd BS25 .... 108 A4
Sommerville Rd BS7 .... 49 F4
Sommerville Rd S ▣ BS6 .... 49 F3
Sophia Gdns BS22 .... 89 B4
Sopworth Rd SN14 .... 31 E5
Sorrel Cl BS35 .... 8 D2
Soundwell Coll
Bristol BS16 .... 51 E2
Bristol BS16 .... 36 D3
Soundwell Rd BS15,BS16 .... 51 D2
Soundwell Tech Coll
(Downend division)
BS16 .... 52 A8
South Ave Bath BA2 .... 101 D5
Portishead BS20 .... 45 D6
Yate BS37 .... 27 B1
South Bristol Trad Pk BS3 .... 62 F3
South Combe BS24 .... 122 B6
South Croft Bristol BS9 .... 49 C7
Winscombe BS25 .... 107 F2
South Ct BS32 .... 24 D3
South Dene BS9 .... 48 E6
South Gloucestershire
Central Teaching Unit
BS16 .... 52 A5
South Green St ▣ BS8 .... 62 F6
South Hayes BS5 .... 50 B4
South Hill BS25 .... 107 F2
South Lawn BS24 .... 105 F4
South Lawn Cl BS24 .... 105 F4
South Lea Rd BA1 .... 101 A8
South Liberty La BS3 .... 135 A1
South Mdws BS40 .... 92 E2
South Par Bath BA2 .... 142 C2
Chew Magna BS40 .... 96 B3
Weston-Super-Mare BS23 .... 104 D8
Yate BS37 .... 27 C1
South Parade Cotts BA2 .... 102 C1
South Rd Almondsbury BS32 .... 24 E6
Bristol BS15 .... 65 C8
▣ Bristol BS3 .... 63 C3
Bristol BS6 .... 49 C2
Lympsham BS24 .... 132 B1
Midsomer Norton BA3 .... 132 B1
Portishead BS20 .... 45 D7
Timsbury BA3 .... 116 B2
Weston-Super-Mare BS23 .... 87 C1
South Rock Ind Est BA3 .... 137 A1
South Side BS49 .... 91 E5
South St Bristol BS3 .... 63 B3
Stratton On The Fosse BA3 .... 137 F2
South Street Prim Sch
BS3 .... 63 B3
South Terr ▣ Bristol BS6 .... 49 B2
Weston-Super-Mare BS23 .... 104 D8
South Twerton Jun Sch
BA2 .... 101 C4
South View Bath BA2 .... 102 E1
Bristol BS16 .... 51 E5
Frampton Cotterell BS36 .... 38 B7
Paulton BS39 .... 131 E6
Portishead BS20 .... 45 D7
Radstock BA3 .... 116 B2
South View Bsns Pk BS16 .... 51 F5
South View Cres BS36 .... 38 D6
South View Pl BA3 .... 132 B2
South View Rd BA2 .... 101 D6
South View Rise BS36 .... 38 D6
South View Terr BS49 .... 74 B1
South Wlk BS37 .... 27 E1
Southbourne Gdns BA1 .... 85 B1
Southbourne Mans BA2 .... 142 C2
Southbow Ho ▣ BS3 .... 63 A3
Southcot Pl BA2 .... 142 C1
Southdown BS22 .... 88 F4

Southdown Ave BA2 . . . . . . 101 B3
Southdown Jun Sch BA2 . . 101 B3
Southdown Jun Sch BA2 . . 101 B3
Southdown Rd Bath BA2 . . 101 B4
Bristol BS9 . . . . 48 F8
Southend Ho GL12 . . . . 18 A5
Southend Rd BS23 . . . . . . 104 E4
Southern Ring Path 4
BS21 . . . . 57 B1
Southern Way BS21 . . . . . . 57 C1
Southernhay Bristol BS16 . . 51 D4
Bristol BS8 . . . . 140 B2
Southernhay Ave BS8 . . . . 140 B2
Southernhay Cres BS8 . . . 140 B2
Southey Ave BS15 . . . . 51 E1
Southey Ct BS15 . . . . 51 D1
Southey Rd BS21 . . . . 57 D2
Southey St BS2 . . . . 49 F2
Southfield
Norton St Philip BA3 . . . . . . 135 F4
Radstock BA3 . . . . 133 A2
Southfield Ave BS15 . . . . . . 51 E1
Southfield Cl
Nailsea BS48 . . . . 59 E3
Weston-Super-Mare BS23 . 104 D2
Southfield Ct BS9 . . . . 49 A7
Southfield Rd Bristol BS6 . . 49 D1
Nailsea BS19 . . . . 59 E3
Southfield Rd Trad Est
BS48 . . . . 59 F3
Southgate BA1 . . . . 142 C2
Southlands Bath BA1 . . . . . 84 B1
Bristol BS4 . . . . 64 B1
Southlands Dr BA3 . . . . . . 116 B2
Southlands Way BS49 . . . . 91 E5
Southleaze BS25 . . . . 125 A6
Southleigh BS25 . . . . 124 F8
Southleigh Rd BS8 . . . . . . 140 B4
Southmead BS25 . . . . 125 A8
Southmead Hospl BS10 . . . 49 E8
Southmead Rd
Bristol BS10, BS34 . . . . 35 E1
Weston-Super-Mare BS22 . 105 B7
Southmead Way BS10 . . . . . 49 D8
Southover Cl BS9 . . . . 49 A8
Southover Rd BS39 . . . . . . 115 D1
Southridge Hts BS24 . . . . . 122 A8
Southside BS23 . . . . 104 E8
Southside Cl BS9 . . . . 48 B8
Southside Cres BS22 . . . . . . 88 A4
Southstoke La BA2 . . . . . . 118 F8
Southstoke Rd BA2 . . . . . . 101 F1
Southview Cl BS24 . . . . . . 105 E2
Southville Pl BS3 . . . . 63 D4
Southville Prim Sch BS3 . . 63 C4
Southville Rd Bristol BS3 . . 63 C4
Weston-Super-Mare BS23 . 104 F7
Southville Terr BA2 . . . . . . 102 B4
Southway Ct BS21 . . . . 57 D1
Southway Dr BS15 . . . . 66 D5
Southwell St BS2 . . . . 140 C4
Southwood Ave BS9 . . . . . . 48 C8
Southwood Dr BS9 . . . . 48 B8
Southwood Dr E BS9 . . . . . . 48 C8
Sovereign Sh Ctr BS23 . . . 104 D7
Spalding Cl BS7 . . . . 50 A3
Spaniorum View BS35 . . . . . 22 F2
Spar Rd Avonmouth BS11 . . 33 D4
Yate BS37 . . . . 27 D2
Spartley Dr BS13 . . . . 78 F6
Spartley Wlk BS13 . . . . 78 F6
Specklemead BS39 . . . . . . 131 D5
Speedwell Ave BS5 . . . . 64 D7
Speedwell Cl BS35 . . . . 8 D2
Speedwell Est BS21 . . . . . . 57 C2
Speedwell Rd BS5,BS15 . . . 51 A1
Speedwell Sch BS15 . . . . . . 51 A1
Spencer Dr
Midsomer Norton BA3 . . . . 132 A2
Weston-Super-Mare BS22 . . 89 B3
Spencer Ho 6 BS1 . . . . . . 141 B1
Spencer's Ct BS35 . . . . 15 B5
Spencers Belle Vue BA1 . . 142 B4
Sperring Cl BA3 . . . . 137 F8
Spey Cl BS35 . . . . 15 C8
Spindleberry Gr BS48 . . . . . 60 A2
Spinners End BS22 . . . . 89 B4
Spinney Croft BS13 . . . . 78 F5
Spinney Rd BS24 . . . . 106 D4
Spinney The Bristol BS32 . . 36 E7
Frampton Cotterell BS36 . . . 38 B7
Portishead BS20 . . . . 45 C4
Weston-Super-Mare BS24 . . 105 E7
Spires View 4 BS16 . . . . . . 50 E5
Spratts Bridge BS40 . . . . . . 96 A3
Spring Cres BA2 . . . . 142 C2
Spring Gardens Rd BA2 . . 142 C2
Spring Gdns BS4 . . . . 64 A1
Spring Ground Rd BS39 . . 131 E5
Spring Hill Bristol BS15 . . . . 51 E2
Bristol BS2 . . . . 141 A4
Weston-Super-Mare BS22 . . 88 D2
Spring Hill Dr BS22 . . . . 88 E1
Spring Hill Prim Sch BS5 . . 51 C2
Spring La Bath BA1 . . . . 85 B2
Dundry BS41 . . . . 79 A1
Spring Rise BS20 . . . . 45 C3
Spring St BS3 . . . . 63 E4
Spring Street Pl BS3 . . . . . . 63 E4
Spring Terr BS22 . . . . 88 C2
Spring Vale BA1 . . . . 85 B2
Spring Valley BS22 . . . . 88 C2
Spring Wood Gdns BS24 . 105 E3

Springfield
Norton St Philip BA3 . . . . . . 135 E4
Peasedown St John BA2 . . . 133 C7
1 Thornbury BS35 . . . . 15 D8
Springfield Ave
Bristol BS11 . . . . 47 D6
Bristol BS7 . . . . 52 A7
Bristol BS7 . . . . 49 F5
Weston-Super-Mare BS22 . . 88 D1
Springfield Bldgs
Midsomer Norton BS39 . . . 131 D2
Radstock BA3 . . . . 133 A3
Springfield Cl Bath BA2 . . 101 B5
Bristol BS16 . . . . 52 A7
Springfield Cotts BS30 . . . 83 A8
Springfield Cres BA3 . . . . 133 A3
Springfield Gdns BS29 . . . 107 A3
Springfield Gr BS6 . . . . 49 C5
Springfield Ho
Bristol BS6 . . . . 140 C4
Portishead BS20 . . . . 45 C4
Springfield Hts BA3 . . . . . . 132 E4
Springfield Lawn BS11 . . . . 47 D6
Springfield Pl BA3 . . . . 132 E4
Springfield Rd Bristol BS16 . 52 A7
Bristol BS6 . . . . 49 D1
Pill BS20 . . . . 47 C4
Portishead BS20 . . . . 45 B5
Springfields BS34 . . . . 36 A2
Springhill Cl BS39 . . . . 131 C6
Springleaze Bristol BS16 . . 52 A7
Bristol BS4 . . . . 64 A1
Springville Cl BS30 . . . . 66 A3
Springwater Pk Trad Est
BS5 . . . . 64 E7
Springwood Dr BS10 . . . . . . 34 E3
Spruce Way Bath BA2 . . . . 118 E8
Bristol BS34 . . . . 35 F7
Weston-Super-Mare BS22 . 105 E8
Square The
Axbridge BS26 . . . . 125 C2
Bath BA2 . . . . 142 B1
Bristol BS4 . . . . 64 A1
Shipham BS25 . . . . 125 E7
Temple Cloud BS39 . . . . 114 E1
Wellow BA2 . . . . 118 D1
Winscombe BS25 . . . . 124 E6
Squire La BS40 . . . . 111 C1
Squires Ct BS30 . . . . 65 F4
Squires Leaze BS35 . . . . 8 D2
Stabbins Cl BS22 . . . . 89 B5
Stable Yd BA2 . . . . 101 D6
Stackpool Rd BS3 . . . . 63 C4
Staddlestones BA3 . . . . . . 137 F7
Stadium Rd BS6 . . . . 49 C5
Stafford Cres BS35 . . . . 8 B1
Stafford Pl BS23 . . . . 104 E8
Stafford Rd Bristol BS2 . . . . 50 A2
Portishead BS20 . . . . 45 E4
Stafford St BS3 . . . . 63 D4
Stainer Cl BS4 . . . . 79 D7
Stalcombe La BA2 . . . . 99 B4
Stall St BA1 . . . . 142 C2
Stambrook Pk BA1 . . . . 86 A5
Stanbridge Cl BS16 . . . . 51 F6
Stanbridge Cty Prim Sch
BS16 . . . . 51 F6
Stanbridge Rd BS16 . . . . . . 51 F6
Stanbury Ave BS16 . . . . 51 C5
Stanbury Rd BS3 . . . . 63 E3
Stancombe La BS48 . . . . 76 E7
Standfast Rd BS10 . . . . 34 F3
Standish Ave BS34 . . . . 24 C1
Standish Cl BS10 . . . . 34 F1
Standon Way BS10 . . . . 35 C2
Stane Way BS11 . . . . 47 C7
Stanfield Cl BS7 . . . . 50 C6
Stanford Cl BS36 . . . . 37 F8
Stanford Pl BS4 . . . . 79 D7
Stanhope Pl BA1 . . . . 142 A2
Stanhope Rd Bristol BS30 . . 65 F2
Weston-Super-Mare BS23 . 104 E3
Stanhope St BS2 . . . . 64 A5
Stanier Rd BA2 . . . . 142 A2
Stanley Ave Bristol BS34 . . . 36 B2
Bristol BS7 . . . . 49 E3
Stanley Chase BS5 . . . . 50 E2
Stanley Cres BS34 . . . . 36 B2
Stanley Ct BA3 . . . . 132 B2
Stanley Gdns BS30 . . . . 66 B4
Stanley Gr BS23 . . . . 104 F5
Stanley Hill BS4 . . . . 64 A4
Stanley Mead BS32 . . . . 24 E2
Stanley Park Rd BS16 . . . . . 51 E3
Stanley Pk BS5 . . . . 50 C1
Stanley Rd Bristol BS15 . . . . 66 B8
Bristol BS6 . . . . 49 C1
Weston-Super-Mare BS23 . 104 F7
Stanley St 5 BS3 . . . . 63 C3
Stanley St N 8 BS3 . . . . 63 C3
Stanley St S BS3 . . . . 63 C2
Stanley Terr Bristol BS3 . . . 63 C2
Radstock BA3 . . . . 133 A3
Stanley Villas 12 BA1 . . . . . 85 A1
Stanshalls Cl BS40 . . . . 94 C8
Stanshalls Dr BS40 . . . . 94 C8
Stanshalls La BS40 . . . . 94 C8
Stanshaw Cl BS16 . . . . 51 A7
Stanshaw Rd BS16 . . . . 51 A7
Stanshawe Cres BS37 . . . . . 27 E1
Stanshawes Court Dr
BS37 . . . . 39 E8
Stanshawes Dr BS37 . . . . . . 27 D1
Stanshaws Cl BS32 . . . . 24 C2
Stanton Cl BS15 . . . . 51 F1

Stanton Drew Prim Sch
BS39 . . . . 97 A2
Stanton La BS39 . . . . 97 D4
Stanton Rd Bristol BS10 . . . . 35 E2
Chew Magna BS40 . . . . 96 B3
Stanton Wick La BS39 . . . . . 97 B1
Stanway BS30 . . . . 66 C1
Stanway Cl BA2 . . . . 101 D1
Staple Gr BS31 . . . . 81 D5
Staple Grove Cres BS5 . . . . 65 B7
Staple Hill Cty Prim Sch
BS16 . . . . 51 D4
Staplehill Rd BS16 . . . . 51 B4
Staples Cl BS21 . . . . 57 E1
Staples Gn BS22 . . . . 89 B3
Staples Hill BA3 . . . . 120 C4
Stapleton Cl BS16 . . . . 50 D5
Stapleton Rd Bristol BS5 . . . 50 B1
Bristol, Eastville BS5 . . . . 50 C3
Stapleton Road Junc BS5 . . 50 B1
Star Barn Rd BS36 . . . . 37 E7
Star La Bristol BS16 . . . . 50 F3
Pill BS20 . . . . 47 D4
Starcross Rd BS22 . . . . 89 A2
Starling Cl BS22 . . . . 105 E8
Starrs Cl BS26 . . . . 125 B2
Station App Pensford BS39 . 97 D5
Weston-Super-Mare BS23 . 104 E7
Station Avenue S 3 BS16 . . 51 A4
Station Cl Backwell BS48 . . . 75 F7
Bristol BS15 . . . . 66 C8
Chipping Sodbury BS37 . . . . 40 D8
Congresbury BS49 . . . . 91 C4
Station Ct BS5 . . . . 64 E8
Station La BS7 . . . . 50 A4
Station Lodge BS23 . . . . . . 104 E7
Station Mead BA3 . . . . 137 D3
Station Rd
Acton Turville GL9 . . . . 42 F8
Axbridge BS26 . . . . 125 B2
Backwell BS48 . . . . 76 A6
Bath BA1 . . . . 101 C7
Blagdon BS40 . . . . 110 E3
Bristol BS10 . . . . 34 F4
Bristol BS3 . . . . 51 C3
Bristol BS15 . . . . 51 A4
Bristol BS30 . . . . 66 C7
Bristol BS4 . . . . 64 D2
Bristol BS36 . . . . 49 E2
Bristol BS7 . . . . 49 F4
Bristol, Filton BS34 . . . . 36 A3
Bristol, Newleaze BS34 . . . . . 36 B2
Bristol, Patchway BS34 . . . . . 36 C7
Bristol, Shirehampton BS11 . . 47 D5
Bristol, Shirehampton BS11 . . 47 E6
Charfield GL12 . . . . 11 A5
Clevedon BS21 . . . . 57 D3
Clutton BS39 . . . . 114 E3
Coalpit Heath BS36 . . . . 38 C5
Congresbury BS49 . . . . 91 C4
Flax Bourton BS48 . . . . 77 A8
Freshford BA3 . . . . 120 C5
Iron Acton BS37 . . . . 26 D3
Keynsham BS31 . . . . 81 E6
Midsomer Norton BA3 . . . . . 132 B2
Nailsea BS48 . . . . 59 F1
Pill BS20 . . . . 47 C4
Pilning BS35 . . . . 22 F4
Portbury BS20 . . . . 46 D3
Portishead BS20 . . . . 45 D6
Sandford BS25 . . . . 107 F4
Severn Beach BS35 . . . . 22 A6
Wellow BA2 . . . . 118 D1
Weston-Super-Mare BS23 . 104 E7
Weston-Super-Mare, Worle
BS22 . . . . 88 F2
Wickwar GL12 . . . . 18 B7
Winterbourne BS36 . . . . 37 E4
Wrington BS40 . . . . 92 D2
Yate BS37 . . . . 27 C2
Yatton BS49 . . . . 74 B1
Station Road Bsns Ctr
BS15 . . . . 52 A3
Station Road Workshops
BS15 . . . . 52 A3
Staunton Fields BS14 . . . . . 80 C4
Staunton La BS14 . . . . 80 D3
Staunton Way BS14 . . . . 80 D4
Staveley Cres BS10 . . . . 35 C2
Staverton Cl BS32 . . . . 24 C1
Staverton Way BS15 . . . . . . 66 A7
Stavordale Gr BS14 . . . . 80 B6
Staynes Cres BS15 . . . . 65 E8
Steam Mills BA3 . . . . 137 F8
Stean Bridge Rd BS32 . . . . . 36 E6
Steanbridge BS32 . . . . 36 D6
Steel Cl BS30 . . . . 65 F3
Steel Mills BS31 . . . . 81 F4
Steevens Ho
(Almshouses) 12 BS2 . . . . 141 C3
Stephen Dr BS10 . . . . 34 D3
Stephen St BS5 . . . . 64 C8
Stephens Dr BS30 . . . . 65 F5
Stepney Rd BS5 . . . . 50 C1
Stepney Wlk BS5 . . . . 64 C1
Stepping Stones The BS4 . . 64 E6
Sterncourt Rd BS16 . . . . 51 A7
Stevens Cres BS3 . . . . 63 F4
Stevens La BS24 . . . . 122 C3
Stevens Wlk BS32 . . . . 36 D8
Steway La BA1 . . . . 86 F6
Stibbs Ct BS30 . . . . 65 F4
Stibbs Hill BS5 . . . . 65 A7
Stickland BS21 . . . . 57 C1
Stidcot La GL12 . . . . 16 D5

Stidcote La GL12 . . . . 16 E5
Stile Acres BS11 . . . . 34 A1
Stilemead La BS40 . . . . 111 D1
Stillhouse La BS3 . . . . 63 D4
Stillingfleet Rd BS13 . . . . . . 79 C5
Stillman Cl BS13 . . . . 78 E4
Stinchcombe BS37 . . . . 27 E1
Stirling Cl BS37 . . . . 27 D4
Stirling Rd BS4 . . . . 64 C3
Stirling Way BS31 . . . . 81 E4
Stirtingale Ave BA2 . . . . . . 101 C3
Stirtingale Rd BA2 . . . . 101 C3
Stitchings La BA2 . . . . 117 D7
Stitchings Shord La
BS39 . . . . 114 D2
Stock Hill BS35 . . . . 7 C1
Stock La BS40 . . . . 109 A7
Stock Way N BS48 . . . . 59 F2
Stock Way S BS48 . . . . 59 E2
Stockhill Cl BA3 . . . . 137 C3
Stockhill Rd BA3 . . . . 137 C2
Stockmead BS40 . . . . 109 B5
Stockton Cl Bristol BS14 . . . 79 F4
Bristol BS30 . . . . 66 B3
Stockwell Ave BS16 . . . . 52 A6
Stockwell Cl BS16 . . . . 51 F6
Stockwell Dr BS16 . . . . 52 A6
Stockwell Gdns BS16 . . . . . . 51 F6
Stockwood Hill BS31 . . . . . . 81 C7
Stockwood La BS14 . . . . 80 E5
Stockwood Mews BS4 . . . . . 64 F5
Stockwood Rd BS4, BS14 . . . 81 A7
Stodelegh Cl BS22 . . . . 89 B3
Stoke Bishop CE Prim Sch
BS9 . . . . 48 D5
Stoke Bridge Ave BS34 . . . . 36 D6
Stoke Cotts BS9 . . . . 48 E4
Stoke Gr BS9 . . . . 48 E6
Stoke Hamlet BS9 . . . . 48 F6
Stoke Hill Bristol BS9 . . . . . . 48 E3
Chew Stoke BS40 . . . . 112 D7
Stoke La Bristol BS16 . . . . . . 50 E7
Bristol BS34 . . . . 36 C3
Bristol BS9 . . . . 48 F6
Stoke Lodge Jun & Inf Sch
BS34 . . . . 36 C8
Stoke Mdws BS32 . . . . 24 D1
Stoke Mead BA3 . . . . 119 F7
Stoke Paddock Rd BS9 . . . . 48 D6
Stoke Park Rd BS9 . . . . 48 F4
Stoke Park Rd S BS9 . . . . . . 48 E3
Stoke Rd Bristol BS8,BS9 . . . 49 A2
Portishead BS20 . . . . 45 D5
Stoke View BS34 . . . . 36 A3
Stoke View Pk 8 BS16 . . . . 50 F4
Stoke View Rd BS16 . . . . 50 F3
Stokefield Cl BS35 . . . . 8 B1
Stokeleigh Wlk BS9 . . . . 48 C5
Stokemead BS34 . . . . 36 C8
Stokes Croft BS1 . . . . 141 B4
Stokes Ct 8 BS30 . . . . 66 A4
Stone House Mews BS37 . . 28 B1
Stone La BS36 . . . . 37 F3
Stone Monolith BS34 . . . . . . 35 E6
Stone with Woodford
CE Sch GL12 . . . . 3 E4
Stone's Cotts BS10 . . . . 34 C4
Stoneable Rd BA3 . . . . 133 A3
Stoneage La BA2 . . . . 117 B1
Stoneberry Rd BS14 . . . . . . 80 B3
Stonebridge BS21 . . . . 57 D1
Stonebridge Rd BS23 . . . . . 104 F4
Stonechat Gdns BS16 . . . . . 50 E6
Stonehenge La BS48 . . . . . . 59 E4
Stonehill BS15 . . . . 65 E4
Stonehill Ctr BS30 . . . . 65 E4
Stonehouse Cl BA2 . . . . . . 102 B2
Stonehouse La BA2 . . . . . . 102 B2
Stoneleigh BS40 . . . . 96 B3
Stoneleigh Cres BS4 . . . . . . 64 A2
Stoneleigh Ct BA1 . . . . 84 E3
Stoneleigh Dr BS30 . . . . 65 F5
Stoneleigh Rd BS4 . . . . 64 A2
Stoneleigh Wlk BS4 . . . . 64 A2
Stones Cross BA3 . . . . 132 B2
Stonewell Dr BS49 . . . . 91 D3
Stonewell Gr BS49 . . . . 91 D3
Stonewell La BS49 . . . . 91 D3
Stonewell Park Rd BS49 . . . 91 D3
Stoney Steep BS48 . . . . 60 A5
Stoney Stile Rd BS35 . . . . . . 15 A5
Stoneyard La BA3 . . . . 129 D2
Stoneyfield Cl BS20 . . . . 47 B5
Stoneyfields BS20 . . . . 47 B4
Storms Rd BS31 . . . . 33 C4
Stormont Cl BS23 . . . . 104 F3
Stothard Rd BS7 . . . . 50 B7
Stottbury Rd BS7 . . . . 50 A3
Stoulton Gr BS10 . . . . 35 A3
Stourden Cl BS16 . . . . 51 A7
Stourton Dr BS30 . . . . 65 F4
Stourton Rd BS4 . . . . 64 E2
Stover Rd BS37 . . . . 27 B2
Stover Trad Est BS37 . . . . . . 27 B2
Stow Hill Rd GL12 . . . . 16 B6
Stowborough Cotts BA2 . . 133 C7
Stowell Hill Rd GL12 . . . . . . 16 B6
Stowey Bottom BS39 . . . . . 113 E5
Stowey Pk BS49 . . . . 91 D7
Stowey Rd BS49 . . . . 91 C8
Stowick Cres BS11 . . . . 34 C1
Stradbrook Ave BS5 . . . . 65 B7
Stradling Ave BS23 . . . . . . 104 F5
Stradling Rd BS11 . . . . 34 C2
Straight St BS2 . . . . 141 C2
Straightmead BA3 . . . . 129 F1

Straits Par BS16 . . . .
Stratford Cl BS14 . . . .
Stratford Ct BS9 . . . .
Stratford La BS40 . . . .
Stratheden BS8 . . . .
Strathmore Rd BS7 . . . .
Stratton Cl BS34 . . . .
Stratton Rd Saltford BS3 . . . .
Stratton On The Fosse BA3 . .
Stratton St BS2 . . . .
Strawberry Cl BS48 . . . .
Strawberry Field BS26 . . . .
Strawberry Gdns 3 BS48 . .
Strawberry Hill BS21 . . . . . .
Strawberry La BS13, BS41 . .
Strawbridge Rd 10 BS5 . . . .
Stream Cl BS10 . . . .
Stream Side BS16 . . . .
Stream The BS16 . . . .
Streamcross BS49 . . . .
Streamleaze BS35 . . . .
Streamleaze . . . .
Chew Magna BS40 . . . .
Thornbury BS35 . . . .
Streamside . . . .
Chew Magna BS40 . . . .
1 Clevedon BS21 . . . .
Streamside Rd BS37 . . . .
Streamside Wlk BS4 . . . .
Stredlings Yd BS2 . . . .
Street End BS40 . . . .
Street End La BS40 . . . .
Street The Alveston BS35 . . .
Bishop Sutton BS39 . . . .
Bishop Sutton, Stowey BS39 .
Burton SN14 . . . .
Chew Stoke BS40 . . . .
Chilcompton BA3 . . . .
Compton Martin BS40 . . . . . .
Farmborough BA3 . . . .
Luckington SN14 . . . .
North Nibley GL11 . . . .
Olveston BS35 . . . .
Radstock BA3 . . . .
Ubley BS40 . . . .
Winford BS40 . . . .
Stretford Ave BS5 . . . .
Stretford Rd BS5 . . . .
Stride Cl BS20 . . . .
Strode Comm BS35 . . . .
Strode Gdns BS35 . . . .
Strode Rd BS21 . . . .
Strode Way BS21 . . . .
Stroud Rd . . . .
Bristol, Patchway BS34 . . . . .
Bristol, Shirehampton BS11 . .
Stuart Pl BA2 . . . .
Stuart Rd BS23 . . . .
Stuart St BS5 . . . .
Studland Ct BS9 . . . .
Stumpwell La GL12 . . . .
Sturden La BS16 . . . .
Sturdon Rd BS3 . . . .
Sturmer Cl BS37 . . . .
Sturmey Way BS20 . . . .
Sturminster Cl BS14 . . . .
Sturminster Rd BS14 . . . . . .
Sulis Manor Rd BA2 . . . .
Sullivan Cl BS4 . . . .
Sumerlin Dr BS21 . . . .
Summer Hill BS4 . . . .
Summer La Banwell BS29 . . .
Burton SN14 . . . .
Monkton Combe BA2 . . . .
Weston-Super-Mare
BS22, BS24 . . . .
Weston-Super-Mare BS29 . . .
Summer La N BS22 . . . .
Summer St 9 BS3 . . . .
Summerfield BS22 . . . .
Summerfield Rd BA1 . . . . . .
Summerfield Sch BA1 . . . . .
Summerfield Terr BA1 . . . . .
Summerhayes BS30 . . . .
Summerhill Jun & Inf Sch
BS5 . . . .
Summerhill Rd Bath BA1 . . .
Bristol BS5 . . . .
Summerhill Terr BS5 . . . . . .
Summerhouse BS21 . . . .
Summerlands Rd BS23 . . . . .
Summerlands BS48 . . . .
Summerleaze BA2 . . . .
Summerleaze Bristol BS16 . .
Keynsham BS31 . . . .
Summers Dr BS30 . . . .
Summers Mead BS37 . . . . . .
Summers Rd 4 BS2 . . . .
Summers Terr 3 BS2 . . . . . .
Sundays Hill BS32 . . . .
Sundayshill La GL12 . . . .
Sunderland Pl BS8 . . . .
Sunderland St BA2 . . . .
Sundridge Pk BS37 . . . .
Sunfield Rd BS24 . . . .
Sunningdale Bristol BS8 . . . .
Yate BS37 . . . .
Sunningdale Cl BS48 . . . . . .
Sunningdale Dr BS30 . . . . . .
Sunningdale Rd BS22 . . . . . .
Sunny Bank Bristol BS15 . . .
Wick BS30 . . . .
Sunny Hill BS9 . . . .
Sunny Wlk BS15 . . . .
Sunnybank Bath BA2 . . . . . .
Bristol BS16 . . . .
Westerleigh BS37 . . . .

Tyning Rd continued
Bristol BS3 ....63 F3
Peasedown St John BA2 .133 D7
Saltford BS31 ....82 E2
Wrinsley BA15 ....120 E7
Tyning The Bath BA2 .....102 B5
Freshford BA3 ....133 B8
Tynings BS39 ....114 D3
Tynings Cty Prim Sch
BS16 ....51 E4
Tynings Mews BS23 ......104 E4
Tynings The Clevedon BS21 .57 A1
Portishead BS20 ....44 F1
Tynings Way Churton BS39 .114 E3
Westwood BA15 ....120 F3
Tynning Terr 15 BA1 ....85 A1
Tynte Ave BS13 ....79 E3
Tyntesfield Rd BS13 ....79 A8
Tyrone Wlk BS4 ....79 E8
Tyrrel Way BS34 ....36 E5
Tythe Ct SN14 ....70 A8
Tytherington Rd BS35 .....16 A6

U

Ubley Dro BS40 ....127 B7
Ubley Prim Sch BS40 .....111 D1
Ullswater Cl Bristol BS30 ...66 D6
Weston-Super-Mare BS23 .105 A4
Yate BS37 ....27 E3
Ullswater Dr BA1 ....85 A2
Ullswater Rd BS10 ....35 C1
Uncombe Cl BS48 ....76 D7
Under Knoll BA2 ....133 E8
Under La BS40 ....93 D1
Underbanks BS20 ....47 D4
Underdown Ho BS1 ......141 A1
Underhill Ave BA3 ....131 F2
Underhill Dr BS23 ....104 D4
Underhill La BA3 ....131 F2
Underhill Rd GL12 ....11 A5
Underleaf Way BA2 ......133 D7
Undertown BS40 ....128 A7
Undertown La BS40 ......128 A7
Underwood Ave BS22 .....88 B1
Underwood Cl BS35 ....15 A4
Underwood End BS25 ....108 A4
Underwood Rd BS20 ......45 C3
Unicorn Bsns Pk BS4 .....64 D5
Union Pas BA1 ....142 C2
Union Pl BS23 ....104 D7
Union Rd 2 BS2 ....64 A6
Union St Bath BA1 ....142 C2
Bristol BS1 ....143 A2
Nailsea BS48 ....59 C1
Weston-Super-Mare BS23 .104 D7
Unity Ct BS31 ....82 A5
Unity Rd BS31 ....82 A6
Unity St Bristol BS1 .....140 C2
Bristol BS1 ....143 A2
Bristol BS2 ....141 C3
Univ of Bath BA2 ....102 E5
Univ of Bristol BS8 ......142 C4
Univ of Bristol
Dept of Economics BS8 .140 C3
BS8 ....140 C4
Univ of Bristol Sch
of Vetinary Science BS2 .140 C4
Univ of the West
of England Bristol BS3 ...62 E4
Bristol BS16 ....49 B2
Univ of the West
of England Faculty of
Health & Social Care
BS16 ....50 E5
Univ of the West
of England
Frenchay Campus BS16 ..36 E1
Univ of the West
of England,
Frenchay Campus BS16 ..50 E8
Univ of the West
of England, St Matthias
BS16 ....51 A5
University Cl BS9 ....48 F4
University Rd BS8 ....140 C3
University Wlk BS8 ......140 C3
Uphill Ct BS23 ....104 D2
Uphill Dr BA1 ....85 B2
Uphill Prim Sch BS23 ...104 D2
Uphill Rd BS7 ....49 F5
Uphill Rd N BS23 ....104 D4
Uphill Rd S BS23 ....104 D2
Uphill Way BS23 ....104 D1
Upjohn Cres BS13 ....79 D3
Uplands Cl BA1 ....119 F7
Uplands Dr BS31 ....82 F2
Uplands Rd Bristol BS16 ..51 D3
Saltford BS31 ....82 F2
Uplands The BS48 ....75 D8
Upper Bath Rd BS35 ......15 B8
Upper Belgrave Rd BS8 ...49 A2
Upper Belmont Rd BS7 ...49 E3
Upper Berkeley Pl BS8 ...140 B3
Upper Bloomfield Rd
BA2 ....101 D1
Upper Borough Walls
BA1 ....142 C2
Upper Bristol Rd
Bath BA1 ....101 D7
Clutton BS39 ....114 D3
Weston-Super-Mare BS22 .88 B1
Upper Byron Pl BS8 .....140 B3

Upper Camden Pl BA1 ...142 C4
Upper Chapel La BS36 .....38 C7
Upper Cheltenham Pl BS6 .49 E1
Upper Church La
Bristol BS2 ....142 C3
Hutton BS24 ....105 E2
Upper Church Rd BS23 ...87 D1
Upper Church St BA1 ....142 B3
Upper Cranbrook Rd BS6 .49 B4
Upper East Hayes BA1 ....85 B1
Upper Farm Cl BA3 .....135 F4
Upper Furlong BA2 ......116 B3
Upper Green La BS40 ....111 B7
Upper Hedgemead Rd
BA1 ....142 C4
Upper Horfield Prim Sch
BS7 ....50 A8
Upper Kewstoke Rd BS23 .87 B1
Upper Lambridge St BA1 ..85 C2
Upper Lansdown Mews
BA1 ....84 F1
Upper Maudlin St BS2 ...141 A3
Upper Mount Pleasant
BA3 ....120 A4
Upper Myrtle Hill BS20 ...47 C4
Upper New Rd BS27 ....125 F1
Upper Oldfield Pk BA2 ...142 A1
Upper Perry Hill BS3 ......63 C4
Upper Pitching BA3 .....137 D5
Upper Rd BS39 ....129 E6
Upper Sandhurst Rd BS4 ..64 D4
Upper St Bristol BS4 ......64 A4
Dyrham SN14 ....54 D4
Upper Stanton BS39 ......97 A2
Upper Station Rd BS16 ...51 D4
Upper Stone Cl BS36 ......38 C7
Upper Strode BS40 ......111 F7
Upper Sydney St BS3 .....63 B3
Upper Terr BS11 ....34 B1
Upper Tockington Rd
BS32 ....14 A2
Upper Town La BS40 .....94 C8
Upper Wells St BS1 .....140 C2
Upper York St BS2 ....141 B4
Upton BS24 ....105 A2
Upton La BS41 ....96 A8
Upton Rd BS3 ....63 B4
Urchinwood La BS49 .....91 F4
Urfords Dr BS16 ....51 C6
Usk Ct 5 BS35 ....15 C8

V

Valda Rd BS22 ....88 C2
Vale Cres BS22 ....89 C2
Vale Ct BS8 ....140 A4
Vale End BS48 ....59 D1
Vale La BS3 ....79 C8
Vale Mill Way BS24 .....105 F8
Vale St BS4 ....64 A4
Vale The BS16 ....52 F6
Vale View BA3 ....133 A2
Vale View Terr BA1 ....85 F3
Valentine Cl BS14 ....80 B5
Valerian Cl BS11 ....47 F6
Valetta Cl BS23 ....104 F3
Valley Cl 6 BS48 ....59 E2
Valley Gdns Bristol BS16 ..51 F8
Nailsea BS48 ....59 E2
Valley Rd Bristol BS13 ...79 A8
Bristol BS30 ....66 D6
Clevedon BS21 ....57 B1
Leigh Woods BS8 ....62 C7
Portishead BS20 ....45 A2
Valley View Cl BA1 ......85 B3
Valley View Rd Bath BA1 ..85 C3
Paulton BS39 ....131 E6
Valley Way Rd BS48 ......59 E3
Valley Wlk BA3 ....132 B2
Valls The BS32 ....36 F6
Valma Rocks BS5 ....65 A6
Van Diemen's La BA1 .....84 F2
Vandyck Ave BS31 ....81 F6
Vane St 3 BA2 ....102 B7
Varsity Way BS24 ....106 B6
Vassall Ct BS16 ....51 B5
Vassall Rd BS16 ....51 B5
Vattingstone La BS35 .....14 F5
Vaughan Cl BS10 ....34 F3
Vauxhall Terr 2 BS3 .....63 A4
Vayre Cl BS37 ....28 C1
Veale The BS24 ....122 C2
Vee La BS40 ....94 D8
Vellore La BA2 ....102 C7
Ventnor Ave 1 BS5 ......64 F8
Ventnor Rd Bristol BS34 ..36 B3
Bristol BS5 ....50 E1
Venton Ct 5 BS15 ....65 B5
Venus La BS39 ....114 E3
Venus St BS49 ....91 E2
Vera Rd BS16 ....50 F2
Verbena Way BS22 ....89 A1
Vereland Rd BS24 ....105 E3
Verlands BS49 ....91 E5
Vernals La GL12 ....11 B1
Vernham Gr BA2 ....101 C1
Vernon Cl BS31 ....82 D3
Vernon La BS26 ....124 B3
Vernon Pk BA2 ....101 C6
Vernon St 6 BS2 ....63 F4
Vernon Terr BA2 ....101 C6
Vernslade BA1 ....84 A2
Verrier Rd BS5 ....64 C7
Verwood Dr BS30 ....66 A3
Vian End BS22 ....88 F4

Vicarage Cl BS22 ....89 A3
Vicarage Cotts BS16 ......51 D5
Vicarage Ct 8 BS15 ......65 B5
Vicarage Gdns BA2 .....133 B7
Vicarage La
Barrow Gurney BS48 ......77 C6
Compton Bishop BS26 ...124 B3
Compton Dando BS39 .....98 D6
Hillesley GL12 ....19 D8
Norton St Philip BA3 ....135 E4
Olveston BS35 ....14 B3
Vicarage Rd Bristol BS13 ..79 A6
Bristol BS3 ....63 B5
Bristol BS3 ....63 B4
Bristol BS5 ....64 C8
Coalpit Heath BS36 ....38 C6
Leigh Woods BS8 ....62 B6
Pilning BS35 ....22 C7
Vicars Cl BS16 ....51 B4
Victor Ho BS34 ....36 C7
Victor Rd BS3 ....63 C3
Victor St Bristol BS2 ......64 A4
4 Bristol BS5 ....64 B6
Victoria Ave BS5 ....64 C7
Victoria Bldgs BA2 .....101 D6
Victoria Bridge Rd
BA1,BA2 ....142 A2
Victoria Cl Bath BA2 ....101 C5
Portishead BS20 ....45 D5
Thornbury BS35 ....8 B3
Victoria Cotts BA2 ......118 F7
Victoria Cres BS35 ....22 A6
Victoria Ct Bristol BS6 ...49 A3
6 Bristol BS6 ....49 D1
Portishead BS20 ....45 D5
Victoria Gdns
Batheaston BA1 ....85 F3
7 Bristol BS6 ....49 D1
Victoria Gr BS3 ....63 E4
Victoria Ho Bath BA1 ...101 D8
Keynsham BS31 ....81 F4
Victoria Jubilee Homes
BS40 ....109 C6
Victoria Lodge BS22 ......88 E2
Victoria Par BS5 ....64 B8
Victoria Park Bsns Ctr
BA1 ....101 D7
Victoria Park Com Jun
& Inf Schs BS23 ....63 E3
Bristol BS3 ....51 A5
Weston-Super-Mare BS23 .87 D1
Victoria Pl Bath BA2 ......85 C1
Bath BA2 ....102 C1
Bristol BS3 ....63 C3
Paulton BS39 ....131 D5
Weston-Super-Mare BS23 .104 D8
Victoria Quadrant BS23 .104 E8
Victoria Rd
Avonmouth BS11 ....47 B7
Bath BA2 ....101 D6
Bristol BS5 ....65 C5
Bristol BS2 ....64 A5
Bristol BS30 ....66 D5
Clevedon BS21 ....57 C3
Saltford BS31 ....82 D3
Victoria Sq Bristol BS8 ..140 A3
Weston-Super-Mare BS23 .104 D7
Victoria St Bristol BS1 ...141 B2
Bristol BS16 ....51 D5
Victoria Terr Bath BA2 ...101 D6
Bristol BS2 ....64 B5
8 Bristol BS8 ....62 F6
Paulton BS39 ....131 E6
Victoria Wlk BS6 ....49 D1
View Ct BS30 ....67 C6
Vigor Rd BS13 ....79 B5
Villa Rosa BS23 ....87 C1
Village Cl BS37 ....27 D1
Villice La BS40 ....128 A7
Villiers Rd BS5 ....50 B1
Vilner La BS35 ....15 B7
Vimpany Cl BS10 ....34 F3
Vimpennys La BS35 ....22 E1
Vincent Cl BS11 ....34 C2
Vincent Ct 2 BS16 ......51 D3
Vine Gdns BS22 ....89 A2
Viner's La BS9 ....40 F4
Vinery The BS25 ....125 A7
Vineyard La GL12 ....11 F5
Vining Wlk 4 BS5 ....64 B8
Vinney La BS37 ....28 F8
Vinny Ave BS16 ....52 A7
Vintery Leys BS9 ....49 A7
Virginia Cl BS37 ....28 A1
Vivian St BS3 ....63 D3
Vivien Ave BA3 ....132 A2
Vowell Cl BS13 ....79 B4
Vowles Cl BS48 ....60 A2
Vulcan Ho BA2 ....142 C3
Vynes Cl BS48 ....60 A1
Vynes Ind Est BS48 ......60 A3
Vynes Way BS48 ....60 A1
Vyvyan Rd BS8 ....140 A3
Vyvyan Terr BS8 ....140 A3

W

Wade Rd BS37 ....27 A3
Wade St BS2 ....141 C3
Wadehurst Ind Pk BS2 ...64 A7
Wades Rd BS34 ....36 B3
Wadham Dr BS16 ....37 B1
Wadham Gr BS16 ....52 A6
Wadham St BS23 ....104 D8
Wagtail Gdns BS22 ......105 E8

Wainbridge Cres BS35 ...22 D7
Wainbrook Dr BS5 ....50 D2
Wains Cl 5 BS21 ....57 C2
Wainwright Cl 6 BS22 ...89 B4
Waits Cl BS39 ....106 F3
Wakedean Gdns BS49 ....74 A1
Wakeford Rd 1 BS16 .....52 A7
Walcot Bldgs BA1 ......142 C4
Walcot Ct BA1 ....142 C4
Walcot Gate BA1 ....142 C4
Walcot Ho BA1 ....142 C4
Walcot Inf Sch BA1 ....142 C4
Walcot Par BA1 ....142 C4
Walcot St BA1 ....142 C3
Walcot Terr BA1 ....142 C4
Waldegrave Rd BA1 ......84 E1
Waldegrave Terr BA3 ...133 A3
Walden Rd BS31 ....82 A4
Walford Ave BS22 ....89 C4
Walk Mill La GL12 ....11 F4
Walk The GL12 ....11 F5
Walker Cl Bristol BS16 ...52 A7
Bristol BS5 ....64 B8
Walker Ct BS16 ....51 F5
Walker St BS2 ....140 C4
Walker Way BS35 ....15 B7
Wall Gn BS26 ....125 C2
Wallace La BS40 ....128 E3
Wallace Rd BA1 ....85 B1
Wallcroft Ho BS6 ....49 A3
Wallenge Cl BS39 ......131 F6
Wallenge Dr BS39 ......131 F6
Walley La BS40 ....113 B7
Wallingford Rd BS4 ......79 D7
Walliscote Ave BS9 ......49 C6
Walliscote Grove Rd
BS23 ....104 E7
Walliscote Prim Sch
BS23 ....104 E7
Walliscote Rd Bristol BS9 .49 C6
Weston-Super-Mare BS23 .104 D6
Walliscote Rd S BS23 ...104 D4
Wallscourt Rd BS34 ......36 B2
Wallscourt Rd S BS34 ....36 B1
Wallsend La SN14 ....55 C5
Wallycourt Rd BS40 ....112 E8
Walmsley Terr 4 BA1 .....85 B1
Walnut Ave BS37 ....28 A2
Walnut Bldgs BA3 ......133 A3
Walnut Cl Axbridge BS26 .125 B1
Bristol BS31 ....51 F1
Easton-In-Gordano BS20 ..47 A3
Frampton Cotterell BS36 ..26 A1
Keynsham BS31 ....81 C4
Nailsea BS48 ....75 E8
Thornbury BS35 ....8 D1
Weston-Super-Mare BS24 .105 B2
Walnut Cres BS15 ....65 B8
Walnut Dr Bath BA2 ....101 E4
Coleme SN14 ....70 F6
Walnut La BS15 ....66 A8
Walnut Tree Cl BS32 .....24 A5
Walnut Wlk Bristol BS13 ..79 A6
Keynsham BS31 ....81 C4
Walsh Ave BS14 ....80 A7
Walsh Cl BS24 ....105 B2
Walshe Ave BS37 ....28 C1
Walsingham Rd BS6 .....49 E2
Walter St BS3 ....63 A4
Waltham End 2 BS24 ...106 A8
Walton BS24 ....105 A2
Walton Ave BS4 ....64 D5
Walton Bay House
Park Homes BS21 ....44 B1
Walton Cl Bristol BS30 ...66 C1
Keynsham BS31 ....81 D4
Walton Dro BS21 ....58 C6
Walton Heath BS37 ......27 F1
Walton Rd Bristol BS11 ...47 D6
Clevedon BS21 ....57 F4
Walton Rise BS9 ....49 A7
Walton St BS5 ....50 B1
Walwyn Cl BA2 ....101 A6
Wanscombe Prim Sch
BS14 ....79 F4
Wansbeck Rd BS31 ....82 A4
Wansbrough Rd BS22 ....89 B4
Wanscow Wlk BS9 ....49 B6
Wansdyke Bsns Ctr BA2 .101 D4
Wansdyke Ct BS14 ....80 B5
Wansdyke Rd BA2 ......101 D1
Wansdyke Sch BA2 ......118 E8
Wansdyke Workshops
BS31 ....82 A6
Wapley Hill BS37 ....39 E4
Wapley Rd BS37 ....40 B3
Wapping Rd BS1 ....141 A1
Warden Rd BS3 ....63 C4
Wardour Rd BS4 ....79 D8
Ware Ct BS36 ....37 D5
Wareham Cl BS48 ....59 D1
Warend Hill GL11 ....5 F6
Waring Ho BS1 ....141 A1
Warleigh Dr BA1 ....86 A3
Warleigh La BA1 ....103 C5
Warleigh Manor Sch
BA1 ....103 C6
Warleys La BS24 ....89 C1
Warman Cl BS14 ....80 F6
Warman Rd BS14 ....80 F6
Warmington Rd BS14 ....80 C8
Warminster Rd
Bath BA2,BA3 ....103 B5
Bristol BS2 ....64 B7
Warmley CE Prim Sch
BS30 ....66 C6

Warne Pk BS23 10
Warne Rd BS23 1
Warner Cl Bristol BS15 ....
Cleeve BS49 ....
Warns The BS30 ....
Warren Cl Bristol BS32 ....
Hutton BS24 1
Warren Croft GL11 ....
Warren Gdns BS14 ....
Warren La BS41 ....
Warren Rd BS34 ....
Warren Way BS37 ....
Warrilow Cl BS22 ....
Warrington Rd BS4 ......
Warry Cl BS48 ....
Warth La Pilning BS35 ....
Weston-Super-Mare BS22 .
Warwick Ave BS5 ....
Warwick Cl Bristol BS30 ..
Thornbury BS35 ....
Weston-Super-Mare BS22 ..1
Warwick Rd Bath BA1 1
Bristol BS5 ....
Bristol BS6 ....
Keynsham BS31 ....
Washing Pound La
Bristol BS14 ....
Nailsea BS48 ....
Washingpool Hill BS35 ....
Washingpool Hill Rd BS32 .
Washingpool La BS11 ....
Washington Ave BS5 .....
Washpool La BA2 ....
Watch Elm Cl BS32 ....
Watchhouse Rd BS20 ....
Watchill Ave BS13 ....
Watchill Cl BS13 ....
Water La Bristol BS1 1
Bristol BS3 ....
Bristol BS3 ....
Bristol BS4 ....
Paulton BA3,BS39 1
Pill BS20 ....
Water St BS40 ....
Water's La BS9 ....
Waterbridge Rd BS13 ....
Watercress Cl BS48 ......
Watercress Rd BS2 ....
Waterdale Cl BS9 ....
Waterdale Gdns BS9 .....
Waterford Cl BS35 ....
Waterford Pk BA3 1
Waterford Rd BS9 ....
Waterhouse La BA2 1
Waterloo Bldgs BA2 ......
Waterloo Ho BS20 ....
Waterloo Pl 10 BS2 .....
Radstock BA3 1
Waterloo Rd Bristol BS2 ..1
8 Bristol BS2 ....
Weston-Super-Mare BS23 ..1
Watermead Ct 2 BA1 ....
Watermill Cl GL12 ....
Watermore CI BS36 ....
Waters Rd BS15 ....
Waterside Cres BA3 1
Waterside Dr BS32 ......
Waterside La BA3 1
Waterside Pk BS20 ......
Waterside Rd BA3 1
Waterside Way BA3 1
Watery La Bath BA2 1
Doynton BS30 ....
Nailsea BS48 ....
Stratton On The Fosse BA3 .1
Winford BS40 ....
Watkins Ho BS16 ....
Watkins Yd BS9 ....
Watley's End Rd BS36 ....
Watling Way BS11 ....
Watson Ave BS4 ....
Watson's Rd BS30 ....
Watters Cl BS36 ....
Wavell Cl BS37 ....
Waveney Rd BS31 ....
Waverley Ct BS49 ....
Waverley Rd Backwell BS48 .
Bristol BS6 ....
Bristol BS6 ....
Weston-Super-Mare BS23 ..1
Yate BS37 ....
Waverley St BS5 ....
Wayacre Dro BS24 1
Waycroft Prim Sch BS14 ..
Wayfield Gdns BA1 ......
Wayford Cl BS31 ....
Wayland Rd BS22 ....
Wayleaze
Coalpit Heath BS36 ......
Westerleigh BS37 ....
Wayside BS22 ....
Wayside Cl BS36 ....
Wayside Dr BS21 ....
Weal Terr BA1 ....
Weal The BA1 ....
Weare Ct BS1 1
Weatherley Dr BS20 .....
Weatherly Ave BA2 1
Weathers The BS35 ......
Weavers Cl GL12 ....
Webb St BS5 ....
Webbington Rd BS26 1
Webbs Heath BS30 ....
Webbs Mead BS40 1
Webbs Wood Rd BS32 ...

Weal The BA1 ....66 B7
Wedgewood Cl BS14 .....80 B7

iewood Rd BS16 .... 37 D1
.wood Cl BS14 .... 80 B5
.ore Rd BA2 .... 101 A5
.ore Cl Bristol BS15 ...... 65 F7
.on-Super-Mare BS21 .... 124 F2
.ore Pk BA2 .... 101 A3
.ore Rd
.oon BS21 .... 57 B1
.a BS48 .... 75 E8
.shi BS31 .... 82 D4
.ore Vale BS3 .... 63 E2
.on Cl 2 BA2 .... 50 A2
.esley La BA3 .... 116 D1
.wood Rd BS49 .... 91 E5
.nt Rd 2 BS5 .... 64 C7
.d The BS22 .... 88 D2
.La Abbots Leigh BS8 ..... 61 F5
.nfield SN14 .... 69 F8
.Rd BS49 .... 91 E3
.Cl Long Ashton BS41 ..... 62 B1
.on-Super-Mare BS24 ...... 105 B2
.come BS5 .... 125 A8
.House Cl BS9 .... 48 E3
.La Badminton GL9 .... 30 E5
.ell BS29 .... 106 E3
.in BS49 .... 91 C8
.Rd BS49 .... 91 E4
.nd Rd BS31 .... 81 F4
.Ho Cl 1 BS22 .... 89 B4
.isley Prim Sch BS47 ...... 39 D6
.arth Rd BA2 .... 64 A2
.arth Wlk BS4 .... 64 A2
.ington Ave BS6 .... 49 E1
.ington Bldgs BA1 .... 84 B2
.ington Cres BS7 .... 49 E6
.ington Ct BS21 .... 57 C5
.ington Dr Bristol BS9 .... 49 D6
.BS37 .... 27 E3
.ington Hill BS7 .... 49 E6
.ington Wlk BS7 .... 49 D7
.ington La BS6 .... 49 E1
.ington Mews BS11 .... 47 D5
.ington Pk BS6 .... 49 E1
.ington Pl Bristol BS16 .... 37 B1
.on-Super-Mare BS23 ...... 104 D7
.ington Rd Bristol BS15 ... 51 D2
.ol BS2 .... 141 C4
.BS37 .... 27 E3
.ington Terr
.istol BS8 .... 62 F6
.edon BS21 .... 57 D5
.ington Wlk BS10 .... 49 C7
.w Brook Mdw BA3 .... 132 B2
.w La
.n Charterhouse BA3 ...... 119 D1
.on St Philip BA1 .... 135 D5
.edown St John BA2 .... 133 C6
.edown St John BA2 .... 133 B4
.ar Mead BA2 .... 133 B7
.wn Rd BA2 .... 134 B8
.wn Tyning BA2 .... 133 D7
.Cl Bristol BS14 .... 80 C5
.a BS48 .... 60 B1
.Rd Bath BA2 .... 142 B1
.ol BS4 .... 64 B2
.ompton BA3 .... 137 F4
.on BS21 .... 57 D1
.ry BS40,BS41 .... 94 A1
.on St Philip BA3 .... 135 C3
.on BS20 .... 131 B7
.stock BA3 .... 132 E2
.Sq BA3 .... 132 D1
.St BS3 .... 63 A4
.ea Gr BS23 .... 105 B7
.stead Ave BS37 .... 27 D1
.sway Bath BA2 .... 101 F3
.BS31 .... 81 F3
.sway Pk BA2 .... 118 D8
.way Sec Sch BS11 ...... 82 A5
.ford Ave BS16 .... 50 D4
.ford Rd BS34 .... 36 C4
.n Back BS1 .... 141 A2
.or BA3 .... 132 B3
.on Prim Sch BA3 .... 132 B2
.on Rd BA1 .... 132 E2
.on Vale BA3 .... 132 B2
.wn Wlk BS15 .... 51 C2
.yn Gdns BS13 .... 79 C3
.berham Cres BS49 ...... 74 A1
.berham La BS49 .... 90 E8
.ury Rd Bristol BS16 ...... 37 D1
.forth Dr 2 BS25 .... 51 C2
.wood Dr BS24 .... 105 A1
.worth Bristol BS30 .... 66 A6
.BS37 .... 27 C1
.worth Cl BS22 .... 89 A3
.worth Rd BS7 .... 49 D3
.ott Gr BS11 .... 34 C2
.sway Cl Bristol BS16 .... 51 D3
.tock BA3 .... 132 D1
.sy St BS3 .... 63 C3
.ey Theological Coll

.ex Ave BS7 .... 49 F7
.ex Ho 10 BS2 .... 141 C3
.ex Rd BS24 .... 105 B2
.Ave BA2 .... 101 C5
.Broadway BS9 .... 49 D6
.Cl BA2 .... 101 A5
.Coombe BS9 .... 48 D6

West Country Water Pk
BS36 .... 24 F2
West Croft Blagdon BS40 . 110 E2
.ington BS9 .... 49 C7
Clevedon BS21 .... 57 B2
West Dene BS9 .... 48 E6
West Dundry La BS41 ..... 78 E2
West End Bristol BS2 ..... 141 A4
.Bristol BS3 .... 140 C1
.Thornbury BS35 .... 7 C6
West End La BS48 .... 75 A8
West End Trad Est BS48 .. 59 B1
West Garston BS29 .... 107 A3
West Gdns BS20 .... 45 C5
West Gr BS6 .... 49 F1
West Harptree Rd BS40 .. 128 F5
West Hay Rd BS40 .... 92 C3
West Hill Nailsea BS48 ... 60 A5
.Portishead BS20 .... 45 B5

West Hill Gdns
.Radstock BA3 .... 132 C5
.Radstock BA3 .... 132 E1
West Hill Rd BA3 .... 132 D1
West La BS40 .... 94 C8
West Lea Rd BA1 .... 84 A1
West Leaze Pl BS32 ...... 36 E6
West Leigh City Inf Sch
BS48 .... 76 A6
West Links BS23 .... 104 D2
West Links Cl BS22 ...... 88 B3
West Littleton Rd SN14 .. 55 E2
West Mall BS8 .... 62 F7
West Par BS9 .... 48 C7
West Park Rd BS16 ...... 51 E5
West Pk BS8 .... 140 B4
West Point Row BS32 .... 24 C3
West Priory Cl BS9 ...... 48 F7
West Rd Lympsham BS24 . 122 B1
.Midsomer Norton BA3 .... 132 A3
.Yatton BS49 .... 91 B7
West Ridge BS36 .... 38 C7
West Rocke Ave BS9 .... 48 D6
West Rolstone Rd BS24 .. 90 A1
West Shrubbery 6 BS6 .. 49 B2
West St Axbridge BS26 ... 125 B2
.Banwell BS29 .... 107 B3
.2 Bedminster BS3 .... 63 C3
.Bristol BS2 .... 141 C3
.Bristol BS3 .... 63 C3
.Bristol BS30 .... 66 C4
.Tytherington GL12 ...... 16 B5
.Weston-Super-Mare BS23 104 D8
West Town Ave BS4 ...... 64 D1
West Town Dr 2 BS4 ..... 64 D1
West Town Gr BS4 ...... 80 D8
West Town La BS4 .... 64 D1
West Town Lane
Jun & Inf Schs BS4 ..... 64 C1
West Town Pk BS4 ...... 64 D1
West Town Rd
.Backwell BS48 .... 76 A5
.Bristol BS11 .... 47 C7
West Tyning BA2 .... 99 B1
West View 2 BS4 .... 14 F4
West View Rd
.Batheaston BA1 .... 86 A3
.Bristol BS3 .... 63 B3
.Keynsham BS31 .... 81 E5
West Way
.Bristol BS10, BS34 ..... 35 E4
.Clevedon BS21 .... 57 C3
West Wick BS24 .... 89 C1
West Wick Rdbt BS24 ... 106 B8
Westacre Cl BS10 .... 35 A2
Westaway Cl BS49 ...... 91 C7
Westaway Pk BS49 ...... 91 D7
Westbourne Ave
.Clevedon BS21 .... 57 B2
.Keynsham BS31 .... 81 E5
Westbourne Cl 2 BS16 .. 52 A7
Westbourne Cres BS21 .. 57 B2
Westbourne Gr 8 BS3 .. 63 C3
Westbourne Pl BS8 ..... 140 B3
Westbourne Rd
.Bristol BS16 .... 51 F8
.8 Bristol BS5 .... 64 B8
Westbourne Terr BS16 .. 51 B7
Westbrook Pk BA1 ...... 84 A2
Westbrook Rd
.Bristol BS4 .... 80 D8
.Weston-Super-Mare BS22 88 D1
Westbrooke Ct BS1 ..... 140 A1
Westbury Court Rd BS9 . 49 A7
Westbury Cres BS23 .... 104 F2
Westbury Ct BS9 .... 49 A7
Westbury Hill BS9 ...... 49 A7
Westbury La BS9 .... 48 C7
Westbury Park Prim Sch
BS6 .... 49 B3
Westbury Pk BS6 .... 49 A4
Westbury Rd BS6 ...... 49 A4
Westbury View BA2 .... 133 D8
Westbury-on-Trym
.CE Prim Sch BS9 ...... 49 A8
Westcliff Coll F Ed BS23 . 87 B1
Westcourt Dr BS30 ..... 66 B4
Westend La BS35 .... 7 B6
Westend Rd GL12 ...... 17 E5
Westering Cl BS16 ..... 52 A5
Westerleigh Cl BS16 ... 51 F7
Westerleigh Rd Bath BA2 102 B1
.Bristol BS16 .... 51 F6
.Clevedon BS21 .... 57 B2
.Henfield BS36 .... 38 C2
.Pucklechurch BS16 ..... 53 C7
.Westerleigh BS36,BS37 . 39 B5
.Yate BS37 .... 39 C8

Western Approach
Distribution Pk BS35 ... 22 C4
Western Ave BS36 ...... 26 A1
Western Ct BS21 .... 57 D3
Western Dr BS14 .... 79 E6
Western Grange BS34 ... 36 A3
Western La BS40 .... 128 C3
Western Rd BS7 .... 49 E6
Westex Ho BS23 .... 105 B5
Westfield BS31 .... 73 D8
Westfield Cl Backwell BS48 76 A6
.Bath BA2 .... 101 E3
.Bristol BS15 .... 65 D5
.Keynsham BS31 .... 81 C5
.Weston-Super-Mare BS23 104 D2
Westfield Cres BS29 .... 107 A3
Westfield Cty Prim Sch
BA2 .... 138 C8
Westfield Dr BS40 ...... 78 A6
Westfield Ho BA2 ...... 142 B1
Westfield Ind & Trad Est
BA3 .... 138 C7
Westfield La BS34 ..... 36 E3
Westfield Pk BA1 ...... 101 A7
.Bristol BS6 .... 49 B1
Westfield Pk S BA1 .... 101 A7
Westfield Rd BS48 ..... 62 F7
Westfield Rd Backwell BS48 76 A6
.Banwell BS29 .... 107 A3
.Bristol BS9 .... 49 A8
.Weston-Super-Mare BS23 104 D2
Westfield Terr BA3 ..... 132 D1
Westfield Way BS32 ... 24 D2
Westgate Bldgs BA1 ... 142 B2
Westgate St BA1 ...... 142 B2
Westhall Rd BA1 ...... 101 D7
Westhaven Sch BS23 .. 104 D2
Westland Ave BS30 ... 66 C4
Westleigh Cl Bristol BS10 35 D1
.Yate BS37 .... 27 C1
Westleigh Ct BS37 .... 27 C1
Westleigh Pk BS14 .... 80 B8
Westleigh Rd BS10 ... 35 D1
Westmarch Way BS22 . 89 A4
Westmarsh La BS35 ... 7 B5
Westmead Gdns BA1 . 84 A2
Westmead Rd BS5 ... 65 B7
Westminster Cl 1 BS9 . 49 A7
Westminster Rd BS5 .. 64 D8
Westmoreland Dr BA2 . 142 A1
Westmoreland Rd
.Bath BA2 .... 142 A1
.Bristol BS6 .... 49 B3
Westmoreland St BA2 . 142 A2
Westmoreland Station Rd
BA2 .... 142 A1
Westmorland Ho BS6 .. 49 A3
Westmorland Terr BS11 . 47 D7
Weston All Saints
.CE Prim Sch BA1 ..... 84 A2
Weston Ave BS5 ...... 64 F6
Weston Bsns Pk BS24 . 105 E5
Weston Cl BS9 .... 48 C7
Weston Cres BS7 ...... 49 E6
Weston Dro BS20 .... 58 F8
Weston Euro Pk BS24 . 105 B4
Weston Farm La BA1 .. 84 A2
Weston Ind Est BS24 . 105 B2
Weston La BA1 .... 84 A2
Weston Lock Ret BA1 . 101 C8
Weston Lodge BS23 .. 104 D6
Weston Miniatre Rly
BS23 .... 104 D5
Weston Milton Sta BS22 105 C7
Weston Park Ct BA1 ... 84 D1
Weston Park Prim Sch
BS11 .... 47 F8
Weston Pk BA1 .... 84 C1
Weston Pk E BA1 ..... 84 D1
Weston Pk W BA1 .... 84 C1
Weston Rd Bath BA1 .. 101 D8
.Brean TA8 .... 121 A5
.Congresbury BS49 ..... 91 B5
.Failand BS8 .... 61 C3
.Long Ashton BS41 .... 77 D8
Weston Ret Pk BS23 .. 105 A6
Weston Sixth Form Coll
BS23 .... 104 F2
Weston Way BS24 .... 105 F2
Weston Wood Rd BS20 45 C3
Weston-Super-Mare
.Sea Life Ctr BS23 ..... 104 D6
Weston-Super-Mare Sta
BS23 .... 104 E7
Weston-Super-Mare
.Tech Coll & Sch of Art
BS23 .... 104 D8
Westonia BS22 .... 88 C2
Westonian Ct BS9 .... 48 C4
Westons Brake BS16 .. 38 A1
Westons Hill Dr BS16 . 38 A1
Westons Way BS15 ... 65 F7
Westover Cl BS9 ..... 34 D2
Westover Dr BS9 ..... 35 A1
Westover Gdns BS9 .. 48 F8
Westover Rd BS9 .... 35 A1
Westover Rise BS9 ... 35 A1
Westpoint Trad Est BS15 65 D7
Westview BS31 .... 131 C4
Westview Orch BA3 .. 120 B5
Westward BS41 ...... 62 B2
Westward Cl BS40 ... 92 D2
Westward Dr BS4 .... 64 D2
Westward Gdns BS41 . 62 B2
Westward Rd BS13 .. 78 F7
Westway BS48 .... 59 E2
Westway Sch BS32 .. 14 E8

Westwood BA2 .... 102 F6
Westwood Ave BS39 . 115 C2
Westwood Cl 2 BS22 . 88 F2
Westwood Cres BS4 .. 64 D5
Westwood Rd BS4 ... 80 D8
Westwood with Horch
.Prim Sch BA15 .... 120 F3
Westwoods BA1 ...... 86 B3
Wetherby Cl BS16 ... 37 F1
Wetherell Pl BS8 .... 140 B3
Wetlands La BS20 ... 45 C3
Wexford Rd BS4 ..... 79 D8
Weymouth Ct BA1 ... 102 B8
Weymouth Rd BS3 .. 63 D2
Weymouth St BA1 .. 102 B8
Wharf La BS20 ...... 46 B5
Wharfside BS24 .... 106 B8
Wharnecliffe Cl BS14 . 80 B5
Wharnecliffe Gdns BS14 80 B5
Whartons BS4 ...... 64 D1
Whatley Ct BS8 .... 49 B1
Whatley Rd BS8 .... 49 B1
Wheatfield Dr Bristol BS32 24 D1
.Weston-Super-Mare BS22 89 A5
Wheatfield Prim Sch
BS32 .... 24 D1
Wheathill Cl BS31 .. 81 D5
Wheelers Cl BA3 ... 132 D2
Wheelers Dr BA3 ... 132 C2
Wheelers Rd BA3 .. 132 D2
Whinchat Gdns BS16 50 F6
Whippington Ct 1 BS1 141 B3
Whistley La BS40 .. 128 F6
Whitby Rd BS4 .... 64 C5
Whitchurch District Ctr
BS14 .... 80 A5
Whitchurch La Bristol BS13 79 B5
.Bristol BS13 .... 79 C5
.Dundry BS41 .... 79 A5
Whitchurch Prim Sch
BS14 .... 80 C4
Whitchurch Rd BS13 . 79 A6
White Cross Gate BS39 130 F6
White Hill BA2 ...... 133 F6
White Horse Rd BA15 120 F7
White House La BS26 123 A3
White House Rd BS49 . 91 F8
White Lodge Pk BS20 45 D6
White Lodge Rd BS5 . 51 F4
White Ox Mead La BA2 117 F1
White St BS5 .... 141 C4
White Tree Rd BS9 . 49 B4
Whitebeam Ct BS5 . 64 E8
Whitebrook La BA2 .. 133 A8
Whitecroft Way BS15 66 A7
Whitecross Ave BS14 80 C6
Whitecross La BS29 . 107 A4
Whitecross Rd
.East Harptree BS40 .. 128 F4
.Weston-Super-Mare BS22 104 E6
Whitefield Ave Bristol BS15 65 D5
.Bristol BS5 .... 51 A1
Whitefield Cl BA1 ... 86 B4
Whitefield Rd BS5 .. 51 A2
Whitefields BS37 ... 28 C1
Whitegate Cl BS24 . 122 B6
Whitegates BS36 ... 37 D6
Whitehall Ave BS5 . 50 E1
Whitehall Gdns BS5 . 50 D1
Whitehall Prim Sch BS5 50 E1
Whitehall Rd BS5 .. 64 C8
Whitehall Trad Est 4 BS5 64 C8
Whitehouse La Bristol BS3 63 D4
.Litton BA3 .... 129 D3
.Wraxall BS48 ...... 60 A6
Whitehouse Pl 4 BS3 63 E4
Whitehouse Prim Sch
BS3 .... 79 C5
Whitehouse Rd BS35 . 22 C7
Whiteladies Rd BS8 . 63 A4
Whiteladies Rd BS8 . 140 B4
Whitelands Hill BA3 . 133 B3
Whiteleaze BS10 ... 49 C8
Whitemead Ho 3 BS3 63 A3
Whiteoak Way BS48 . 75 D8
Whites Hill BS5 .... 65 A6
Whitesfield Ct BS48 . 59 D2
Whitesfield Rd BS48 . 59 D1
Whiteshill BS16 .... 37 D3
Whitewall La BS35 . 8 F1
Whiteway Ave BA2 . 101 A3
Whiteway Cl Bristol BS4 . 64 E6
.Bristol BS5 .... 65 A8
Whiteway Ct 1 BS5 . 65 A8
Whiteway Mews BS5 . 65 A8
Whiteway Rd Bath BA2 101 A3
.Bristol BS5 .... 51 A1
Whitewells Rd BA1 . 85 A2
Whitewood Rd BS5 . 50 F1
Whitfield Cl 8 BS16 . 51 D3
Whitfield Fishponds
.Com Sch BS16 ..... 50 F4
Whitfield Rd BS35 .. 8 C2
Whiting Rd BS13 ... 79 A4
Whitland Ave BS13 . 79 B5
Whitland Rd BS13 .. 79 B5
Whitley Cl BS37 ... 27 C3
Whitley Mead BS34 . 36 E3
Whitling St BS40 .. 95 A2
Whitmead Gdns BS13 79 C4
Whitmore Ave BS4 . 65 A3
Whitson Ho 4 BS2 . 141 C3
Whitson St BS1 .... 141 A4
Whiting Rd BS23 .. 104 E4
Whittington Dr BS22 . 88 D2

Whittington Rd BS16 .. 51 C6
Whittock Rd BS14 .... 80 D6
Whittock Sq BS14 ... 80 D7
Whittucks Cl BS15 ... 65 D4
Whittucks Rd BS15 .. 65 C4
Whitwell Rd BS14 ... 80 B8
Whytes Cl BS9 ...... 49 A8
Wick CE Prim Sch BS30 67 B6
Wick Cres BS4 ...... 64 D3
Wick House Cl BS31 . 82 D3
Wick La Camerton BA2,BA3 116 F1
.Lympsham BS24 ..... 121 E1
.Pensford BS39 ...... 97 D3
.Upton Cheyney BS30 . 67 C2
Wick Rd
.Bishop Sutton BS39 .. 113 C3
.Bristol BS4 .... 64 D3
.Lympsham BS24 ..... 121 D2
.Pilning BS35 .... 22 C7
Wickets The Bristol BS15 51 D2
.Bristol BS7 .... 35 F1
Wicketts The 7 BS7 . 35 F2
Wickfield BS21 ...... 57 C2
Wickham Ct BS37 .. 90 D8
Wickham Cl Bristol BS16 50 D5
Wickham Glen BS16 . 50 D5
Wickham Hill BS16 . 50 D5
Wickham View BS16 50 D4
Wicklow Rd BS4 .... 79 E8
Wickwar Rd
.Kingswood GL12 .... 11 E4
.Rangeworthy BS37 .. 17 B1
.Yate BS37 .... 28 B5
Widcombe BS14 .... 80 A6
Widcombe CE Jun Sch
BA2 .... 102 B5
Widcombe Cres BA2 . 102 B5
Widcombe Hill BA2 . 102 C4
Widcombe Inf Sch BA2 102 B5
Widcombe Par BA2 . 142 C1
Widcombe Rise BA2 . 102 B5
Widcombe Terr BA2 . 102 B5
Widmore Rd BS13 .. 79 B5
Wigmore Gdns BS22 . 88 D2
Wigton Cres BS10 .. 35 C2
Wilbye Gr BS4 ...... 79 D7
Wilcox Cl BS15 .... 65 B5
Wildcountry La BS48 77 E6
Wildcroft Ho BS9 .. 49 B4
Wildcroft Rd BS9 .. 49 B4
Wilder Ct BS2 ..... 141 B4
Wilder St BS2 ..... 141 B4
Wildda Cl BS3 .... 63 B2
William Daw Cl BS29 106 F3
William Herschel Mus
BS1 .... 142 B2
William Mason Cl 18 BS5 64 B7
William St Bath BA2 . 142 C3
.Bristol BS16 .... 51 B3
.Bristol BS2 .... 49 F1
.Bristol BS3 .... 63 A4
.8 Bristol BS3 ..... 64 C8
Williams Cl BS30 .. 65 F3
Williamson Rd BS7 . 49 F3
Williamstowe BA2 . 102 C1
Williton Rd BS4 ... 79 E8
Willis Rd BS15 .... 51 F2
Willment Way BS11 . 33 D1
Willmott Cl BS14 .. 79 F3
Willoughby Cl
.Alveston BS35 ..... 15 A4
.Bristol BS13 .... 79 B7
Willoughby Rd BS7 . 49 E5
Willow Bed Cl BS16 . 37 C2
Willow Bed Cl BS16 . 51 B6
Willow Cl Bath BA2 . 118 E8
.Bristol BS34 .... 36 D6
.Bristol BS21 .... 35 E7
.Charfield GL12 ..... 11 A4
.Clevedon BS21 ..... 57 E3
.Long Ashton BS41 . 61 F1
.Portishead BS20 ... 45 C4
.Radstock BA3 ...... 132 E2
Willow Ct BS7 .... 50 A8
Willow Dr Bleadon BS24 122 C6
.Hutton BS24 .... 105 E2
.Weston-Super-Mare BS22 105 E5
Willow Gdns BS22 . 89 D2
Willow Gr 1 BS16 . 51 C2
Willow Ho BS13 ... 79 D4
Willow Rd BS15 ... 65 C3
Willow Sh Ctr The BS15 51 E1
Willow The BA1 ... 137 F2
Willow Way BS36 . 38 C6
Willow Wlk Bristol BS10 35 B3
.Keynsham BS31 ... 81 D4
.Weston-super BS22 . 88 B2
Willowfalls The BA1 . 85 E3
Willows The Bristol BS16 37 B1
.Bristol BS32 .... 36 D8
.Nailsea BS48 .... 59 F3
.Yate BS37 .... 27 D2
Wills Dr BS5 ...... 64 A8
Willsbridge Hill BS30 . 66 A2
Willsbridge Mill BS30 . 66 A2
Willway St Bristol BS2 141 C3

Willway St continued
Wilmot Ct BS30 ....63 D4
Wilmot Cl BS30 ....66 A6
Wilmots Way BS20 ....47 D4
Wilmott Ho BS7 ....47 D4
Wilshire Ave BS15 ....65 D5
Wilson Pl BS2 ....141 C4
Wilson St BS2 ....141 C4
Wilton Cl BS10 ....35 C1
Wilton Gdns BS23 ....104 D7
Wiltons BS40 ....92 D2
Wiltshire Ave BS37 ....28 A3
Wiltshire Pl BS15 ....54 E1
Wiltshire Way BS11 ....85 A2
Wilverley Ind Est BS4 ....64 E1
Wimbledon Rd BS6 ....49 C5
Wimbledon Rd BS25 ....107 F2
Wimborne Rd BS3 ....63 C1
Wimash Cl BS14 ....80 D7
Wincanton Cl
  Bristol BS16 ....37 F1
  Nailsea BS48 ....60 B1
Winchcombe Cl BS48 ....76 A8
Winchcombe Rd BS36 ....38 B8
Winchester Ave BS4 ....64 D3
Winchester Ct BS16 ....50 E6
Winchester Rd Bath BA2 ....101 D5
  Bristol BS4 ....64 D3
Wincombe Trad Est BS2 ......64 A4
Wincroft BS30 ....66 C4
Windcliff Cres BS11 ....47 E7
Windermere Ave BS23 ....104 F4
Windermere Rd BS34 ....36 A8
Windermere Way BS30 ....66 D6
Windmill Cl BS3 ....63 E4
Windmill Farm Bsns Ctr
  BS3 ....63 D4
Windmill Hill
  Bristol BS3 ....63 D3
  Hutton BS24 ....106 A2
Windmill La BS10 ....34 D3
Windrush Cl BA2 ....100 F4
Windrush Ct BS35 ....15 C8
Windrush Gn BS31 ....82 A4
Windrush Rd BS31 ....82 A4
Windsor Ave Bristol BS5 ......65 B6
  Keynsham BS31 ....81 E4
Windsor Bridge Rd
  BA1,BA2 ....101 D7
Windsor Cl Bristol BS34 ......36 E4
  Clevedon BS21 ....57 D2
Windsor Cres BS10 ....34 C4
Windsor Ct Bristol BS16 ......51 E7
  🖼 Bristol BS8 ....62 F6
  Wick BS30 ....67 C7
Windsor Dr Nailsea BS48 ......59 E2
  Yate BS37 ....27 D2
Windsor Gr 🖼 BS5 ....64 B8
Windsor Pl Bath BA1 ....101 C7
  Bristol BS15 ....52 A5
  Bristol BS8 ....62 F6
Windsor Rd Bristol BS30 ......65 F2
  Bristol BS6 ....49 E2
  Weston-Super-Mare BS22 ...88 C2
Windsor Terr Bristol BS3 ......63 F4
  Bristol BS8 ....62 F6
  Paulton BS39 ....131 E5
Windsor Villas BA1 ....101 C7
Windwhistle Circ BS23 ......104 F4
Windwhistle La BS23 ....104 E3
Windwhistle Prim Sch
  BS23 ....104 F3
Windwhistle Rd BS23 ....104 D3
Wine St Bath BA1 ....142 C2
  Bristol BS1 ....143 A2
Wineberry Cl BS5 ....50 D1
Winfield Rd BS30 ....66 C7
Winford CE Prim Sch
  BS40 ....94 F7
Winford Cl BS20 ....45 E5
Winford Gr BS13 ....79 A8
Winford La BS41 ....78 C1
Winford Rd BS40 ....95 F3
Winford Terr BS41 ....78 C5
Wingard Cl BS23 ....104 D2
Wingard Ct 🖼 BS23 ....104 E5
Wingfield Rd BS3 ....63 E2
Winifred's La BA1 ....84 E1
Winkworth Pl 🖼 BS2 ....49 F1
Winnowing End BS25 ....108 A3
Winsbury View BA2 ....99 B2
Winsbury Way BS32 ....24 D1
Winscombe Cl BS31 ....81 D6
Winscombe Dro
  Shipham BS25 ....125 D6
  Winscombe BS25 ....125 A5
Winscombe Hill BS25 ....124 F5
Winscombe Rd BS23 ....105 A7
Winscombe Woodborough
  Cty Prim Sch
  BS25 ....125 A8
Winsford St 🖼 BS5 ....64 A8
Winsham Cl BS14 ....80 B5
Winsley CE Prim Sch
  BA15 ....120 E7
Winsley Hill BA15 ....120 B6
Winsley Rd
  Bristol BS6 ....49 D1
  Winsley BA15 ....120 F7
Winstanley Ho 🖼 BS5 ....64 B6
Winston Dr BS22 ....88 E4
Winterbourne Hill BS36 ......37 D5
Winterbourne Rd BS34 ....36 E6
Winterfield Pk BS39 ....131 E4

Winterfield Rd BS39 ....131 E5
Winters La BS40 ....93 D6
Winterstoke Cl 🖼 BS3 ....63 B2
Winterstoke
  Commercial Ctr BS23 .....105 A6
Winterstoke Ctr 🖼 BS3 ......63 B2
Winterstoke Ho 🖼 BS3 ....63 A3
Winterstoke Rd Bristol BS3 ..63 A3
  Weston-Super-Mare BS23,BS24
  BS23,BS24 ....105 A4
Winterstoke Underpass
  BS3 ....62 F4
Winton St BS2 ....63 F4
Wistaria Ave BS37 ....28 A1
Wisteria Ave BS24 ....105 D2
Witch Hazel Rd BS13 ....79 E3
Witchell Rd BS5 ....64 C7
Witcombe BS37 ....39 C7
Witcombe Cl BS15 ....51 F1
Witham Rd BS31 ....82 A3
Witherlies Rd BS16 ....50 F6
Withey Cl W BS9 ....48 F5
Witheys The BS14 ....80 C4
Withies La BA3 ....138 A8
Withies Pk BA3 ....137 F8
Withington Cl BS30 ....66 C2
Withleigh Rd BS4 ....64 B2
Withy Cl BS48 ....59 F3
Withy Cl E BS9 ....48 F6
Withyditch La BA2 ....117 C4
Withymead Rd SN14 ....70 A8
Withypool Gdns BS14 ....80 B5
Withys The BS20 ....47 D4
Withywood Com Sch
  BS13 ....79 A5
Withywood Gdns BS13 ....78 F4
Withywood Rd BS13 ....78 F4
Witney Cl BS31 ....82 D3
Woburn Cl BS30 ....65 F5
Woburn Rd BS5 ....50 B3
Wolferton Rd BS7 ....49 F2
Wolfridge Gdns BS10 ....35 A4
Wolfridge La BS35 ....14 F4
Wolfridge Ride BS35 ....14 F4
Wolseley Rd BS7 ....49 D3
Wolvers Hill Rd BS29 ....106 E6
Wolvershill Ind Units
  BS29 ....106 C6
Wolvershill Pk BS29 ....107 A3
Wood End Wlk BS9 ....48 C6
Wood Hill BS49 ....91 E6
Wood Hill Pk BS20 ....45 D7
Wood Kilns The BS49 ....74 A1
Wood La Axbridge BS26 .....125 D2
  Clapton In Gordano BS20 ...59 E8
  Horton BS37 ....19 A1
  Weston-Super-Mare BS23 ...87 F1
Wood Rd BS15 ....51 D8
Wood St Bath BA1 ....142 B2
  Bath BA2 ....142 B1
  Bristol BS5 ....50 B2
Woodbine Rd BS5 ....64 D8
Woodborough Cres
  BS25 ....125 A7
Woodborough Ct BS25 .....125 A8
Woodborough Dr BS25 .....125 A8
Woodborough La BA3 ....133 A4
Woodborough Rd
  Radstock BA3 ....133 A3
  Winscombe BS25 ....124 F8
Woodborough St 🖼 BS5 .....50 B1
Woodbridge Rd BS4 ....64 A2
Woodbury La BS8 ....49 A2
Woodchester Bristol BS15 ....51 E3
  Yate BS37 ....39 E7
Woodchester Rd BS10 ....49 C7
Woodcliff Ave BS22 ....88 C1
Woodcliff Rd BS22 ....88 C1
Woodcote BS15 ....65 D6
Woodcote Rd BS16 ....51 B3
Woodcote Wlk BS16 ....51 B2
Woodcroft BS39 ....113 C3
Woodcroft Ave BS5 ....50 D1
Woodcroft Cl BS4 ....64 E4
Woodcroft Rd BS4 ....64 E4
Woodene BS25 ....125 A8
Woodend BS15 ....65 D6
Woodend La BS35 ....38 C7
Woodfield Rd BS6 ....49 B2
Woodford Cl BS48 ....60 A1
Woodford Ct 🖼 BS23 ....104 E5
Woodgrove Rd BS10 ....34 D2
Woodhall Cl BS16 ....51 F6
Woodhill Ave BS20 ....45 D6
Woodhill Ct BS20 ....45 D6
Woodhill Rd BS20 ....45 D6
Woodhill Views BS48 ....59 F3
Woodhouse Ave BS32 ....24 D7
Woodhouse Cl BS32 ....24 D6
Woodhouse Gr BS7 ....49 E6
Woodhouse Rd BA2 ....101 A6
Woodhurst Rd BS23 ....105 A7
Woodington Ct 🖼 BS30 .....65 F4
Woodington Rd BS21 ....57 C1
Woodland Ave BS15 ....51 D2
Woodland Cl Bristol BS15 ....51 E4
  Failand BS8 ....61 B4
Woodland Ct BS9 ....48 C3
Woodland Glade BS21 ....57 E5
Woodland Gr Bath BA1 ....84 C1
  Bath BA2 ....102 E5
  Bristol BS9 ....48 D6
Woodland Pl BA2 ....102 D5
Woodland Rd Bristol BS8 ....140 C4
  Cromhall GL12 ....10 B4
  Nailsea BS48 ....59 E3
  Weston-Super-Mare BS23 ..104 D4

Woodland Terr
  Bristol BS15 ....65 E7
  Bristol BS6 ....49 B2
Woodland Way
  Bristol BS15 ....51 C2
  Failand BS8 ....61 B4
Woodlands Axbridge BS26 ..125 D2
  Bristol BS16 ....51 E6
  Bristol BS32 ....24 D3
  Tytherington GL12 ....16 B6
  Weston-Super-Mare BS23 ...87 D1
Woodlands Ct BS32 ....24 B3
Woodlands La
  Almondsbury BS32 ....24 E5
  Bristol BS32 ....24 C3
Woodlands Pk Bath BA1 ......85 C2
  Bristol BS32 ....24 C3
Woodlands Rd
  Charfield GL12 ....11 A4
  Clevedon BS21 ....57 C4
  Portishead BS20 ....45 D8
  Tytherington GL12 ....16 B6
Woodlands Rise BS16 ....51 D6
Woodlands The BS4 ....116 F3
Woodleaze BS9 ....48 B6
Woodleigh BS35 ....8 C1
Woodleigh Gdns BS14 ....80 C6
Woodmancote BS37 ....40 B8
Woodmancote Rd 🖼 BS6 .....49 E1
Woodmans Cl BS37 ....40 B8
Woodmans Rd BS37 ....40 C8
Woodmans Vale BS37 ....40 C8
Woodmarsh Cl BS14 ....80 A4
Woodmead Gdns BS13 ....79 C4
Woodmead La BS30 ....54 A1
Woodmill BS49 ....74 A1
Woodpecker Ave BA3 ....138 B8
Woodpecker Cres BS16 ......53 C4
Woodpecker Dr BS22 ....105 E8
Woods Hill BA3 ....120 A6
Woodside Bristol BS9 ....48 D3
  Midsomer Norton BA3 .....131 E1
Woodside Ave BS24 ....105 B2
Woodside Cl BS23 ....105 A8
Woodside Gdns BS20 ....44 E5
Woodside Gr BS10 ....34 D3
Woodside Rd Bristol BS15 ....65 C7
  Bristol BS4 ....64 E6
  Clevedon BS21 ....57 E5
  Coalpit Heath BS36 ....38 E6
Woodspring Ave BS22 ....88 B3
Woodspring Cres BS22 ....88 A3
Woodspring Mus 🖼
  BS23 ....104 E8
Woodspring Priory BS22 .....71 C1
Woodstock Ave BS6 ....49 C2
Woodstock Cl BS15 ....65 E8
Woodstock Rd Bristol BS15 ..65 F7
  Bristol BS6 ....49 C2
  Weston-Super-Mare BS23 ..105 B8
Woodstock Sch BS15 ....65 E7
Woodview
  Chilcompton BA3 ....137 E5
  🖼 Clevedon BS21 ....57 F3
  Paulton BS39 ....131 C5
Woodview Cl BS11 ....47 E7
Woodview Terr
  Nailsea BS48 ....59 F2
  Weston-Super-Mare BS23 ..105 A6
Woodward Dr BS37 ....27 B1
Woodward Dr BS30 ....65 F4
Woodwell Rd BS11 ....47 E5
Woodyleaze Dr BS15 ....65 D6
Wookey Cl BS48 ....75 F8
Woolcot St BS6 ....49 B2
Wooler Rd BS23 ....104 E8
Woollard La BS14,BS39 ......98 A7
Woolley La BA1 ....85 A4
Woolley Rd BS14 ....80 E5
Woolvers Way BS24 ....106 B6
Wootton Cres BS4 ....64 E6
Wootton Pk BS14 ....64 E6
Wootton Rd BS4 ....64 F6
Worcester Bldgs BA1 ....85 B2
Worcester Cl BS16 ....51 B2
  Peasedown St John BA2 ...133 D7
Worcester Cres BS8 ....140 A4
Worcester Gdns BS48 ....75 C8
Worcester Pk BA1 ....85 B2
Worcester Pl BA1 ....85 B2
Worcester Rd Bristol BS15 ...51 D1
  Bristol BS8 ....140 A4
Worcester Terr Bath BA1 .....85 B2
  Bristol BS8 ....140 A4
Wordsworth Ho BS34 ....36 A8
Wordsworth Rd Bristol BS7 ..50 B7
  Clevedon BS21 ....57 D2
  Weston-Super-Mare BS23 ..105 A3
Workshop Rd BS11 ....33 C4
World's End La BS31 ....82 C5
Worldsend La GL13 ....2 E7
Worle Cl BS22 ....88 E4
Worle Int Sch BS22 ....88 E2
Worle Parkway BS22 ....89 B1
Worle Parkway Sta BS22 .....89 B2
Worle Sch BS22 ....88 E1
Worlebury CE Fst Sch
  BS22 ....88 D2
Worlebury Cl BS22 ....88 B3
Worlebury Hill Rd
  BS22,BS23 ....88 B2
Worlebury Park Rd BS22 .....88 A2
Wormcliff La SN13 ....86 F3
Worrall Mews 🖼 BS8 ....49 A2
Worrall Pl 🖼 BS8 ....49 A2
Worrall Rd BS8 ....49 A2

Worrel's La BS16 ....37 D3
Worsley St BS5 ....64 D7
Worthing Rd BS34 ....35 F8
Worthings The BS24 ....122 B1
Worthy Cl BS15 ....65 F6
Worthy Cres BS24 ....122 B1
Worthy La 🖼 BS23 ....104 E8
Worthy Pl 🖼 BS23 ....104 E8
Worthy Rd BS11 ....33 D7
Worthys The BS34 ....35 F8
Wotton Rd Charfield GL12 ....11 B5
  Iron Acton BS37 ....26 F5
  Kingswood GL12 ....11 B5
Wrangle Farm Gn BS21 ......57 E2
Wraxall CE Prim Sch BS48 ...60 B4
Wraxall Gr BS13 ....79 A8
Wraxall Hill BS48 ....60 C5
Wraxall Rd BS30 ....66 A6
Wren Cl Bristol BS16 ....50 E7
  Weston-Super-Mare BS22 ..105 D8
Wren Dr BS16 ....51 A6
Wrenbert Rd BS16 ....51 D5
Wright Way BS16 ....50 E8
Wrington Cl BS34 ....36 C7
Wrington Cres BS13 ....79 A7
Wrington Hill BS40 ....92 F5
Wrington La BS49 ....91 E5
Wrington Mead BS49 ....91 E5
Wrington Prim Sch BS40 .....92 E2
Wrington Rd BS49 ....91 F4
Writhlington Ct BA3 ....133 C2
Writhlington Sch BA3 ....133 C1
Wroughton Dr BS13 ....79 D4
Wroughton Gdns BS13 ......79 D4
Wroxham Dr BS34 ....36 C8
Wyatt Ave BS13 ....78 F5
Wyatt Cl BS13 ....78 F5
Wyatt's Cl BS48 ....59 D2
Wyatts View BS4 ....64 E6
Wychwood BS15 ....65 E6
Wyck Beck Rd BS10 ....35 A3
Wycliffe Rd BS9 ....49 B7
Wycliffe Row 🖼 BS3 ....63 F4
Wycombe Gr BS4 ....64 D2
Wye Croft Cl BS10 ....35 D3
Wye Ct BS35 ....15 C8
Wyedale Ave BS9 ....48 C7
Wykis Ct BS15 ....65 F5
Wyllie Ct BS22 ....89 A5
Wymbush Cres BS13 ....79 C5
Wymbush Gdns BS13 ....79 C5
Wyndam Ct BS2 ....141 B4
Wyndham Cres Bristol BS4 ...65 A3
  Easton-In-Gordano BS20 .....47 B4
Wyndham Way BS20 ....45 E5
Wynstones The BS15 ....65 C7
Wynter Cl BS22 ....89 A3
Wyvern Cl BS23 ....104 F7
Wyvern Com Sch BS23 .....104 F7
Wyvern Villas BS9 ....49 A8

Y

Yadley Cl BS25 ....125 A7
Yadley La BS25 ....125 A6
Yadley Way BS25 ....125 A7
Yanel La BS25 ....108 B5
Yanleigh Cl BS13 ....78 C6
Yanley La BS41,BS13 ....78 C7
Yarbury Way BS24 ....89 B1
Yarrow Ct BS22 ....89 A5
Yate Rd BS37 ....26 E3
Yate Rocks BS37 ....27 F7
Yate Sta BS37 ....27 C2
Yatton Jun & Inf Schs
  BS49 ....91 C8
Yatton Sta BS49 ....74 A1
Yeamen's Ho BS1 ....141 B1
Yelverton Rd BS4 ....64 E1
Yeo Bank La BS21 ....72 F1
Yeo Cl BS23 ....105 A5
Yeo Ct Clevedon BS21 ....57 C2
  Congresbury BS49 ....91 D4
Yeo La BS41 ....61 F1
Yeo Moor BS21 ....57 E2
Yeo Moor Jun & Inf Sch
  BS21 ....57 E2
Yeo Valley Way BS48 ....60 B2
Yeo Way BS21 ....57 B2
Yeolands Dr BS21 ....57 B1
Yeomans Cl BS9 ....48 D5
Yeomans Orch BS40 ....92 E3
Yeomanside Cl BS14 ....80 C5
Yeomead BS48 ....61 F1
Yeomeads BS41 ....61 F1
Yeoward Rd BS21 ....57 E1
Yew Tree Cl
  Bishop Sutton BS39 ....113 D4
  Langford BS40 ....109 E6
  Nailsea BS48 ....59 C1
Yew Tree Ct BS14 ....80 B5
Yew Tree Dr BS15 ....51 F3
Yew Tree Gdns
  Easton-In-Gordano BS20 ....47 C4
  Nailsea BS48 ....59 C1
  Sandford BS25 ....108 A4
Yew Tree La
  Compton Martin BS40 ......128 A7
  Kingston Seymour BS21 .....73 B3
Yew Tree Pk BS49 ....91 D3
Yewcroft Cl BS14 ....80 A4
Yewtree Batch BS40 ....94 A1
Yomede Pk BA1 ....101 A7
York Ave BS7 ....49 E4
York Bldgs BS3 ....63 C4
York Cl Bristol BS16 ....37 F1
  Bristol BS34 ....36 D4

York Cl continued
  Weston-Super-Mare BS22 ....
  Yate BS37 ....
York Ct BS2 1
York Gdns Bristol BS8 ....
  Winterbourne BS36 ....
York Pl Bristol BS1 1
  Bristol BS8 ....
York Rd Bristol BS16 ....
  Bristol BS3 ....
  Bristol BS5 ....
  Bristol BS6 ....
York St Bath BA1 1
  Bristol BS2 ....
  🖼 Bristol BS2 ....
  Bristol BS2 ....
  Weston-Super-Mare BS23 ...1
Youngs Ct BS16 ....
Youngwood La BS48 ....

Z

Zetland Rd BS6 ....
Zig Zag BS21 ....
Zinc Rd BS11 ....
Zion Hill BA3 1

NH NJ NK

NN NO NP

NS NT NU

NX NY NZ

SC SD SE TA

SH SJ SK TF TG

SN SO SP TL TM

SS ST SU TQ TR

SX SY SZ TV

Any feature in this atlas can be given a unique reference to help you find the same feature on other Ordnance Survey maps of the area, or to help someone else locate you if they do not have a Street Atlas.

The grid squares in this atlas match the Ordnance Survey National Grid and are at 500 metre intervals. The small figures at the bottom and sides of every other grid line are the National Grid kilometre values (**00** to **99** km) and are repeated across the country every 100 km (see left).

To give a unique National Grid reference you need to locate where in the country you are. The country is divided into 100 km squares with each square given a unique two-letter reference. Use the administrative map to determine in which 100 km square a particular page of this atlas falls.

The bold letters and numbers between each grid line (**A** to **F**, **1** to **8**) are for use within a specific Street Atlas only, and when used with the page number, are a convenient way of referencing these grid squares.

Example *The railway bridge over DARLEY GREEN RD in grid square B1*

Step 1: Identify the two-letter reference, in this example the page is in **SP**

Step 2: Identify the 1 km square in which the railway bridge falls. Use the figures in the southwest corner of this square: Eastings **17**, Northings **74**. This gives a unique reference: **SP 17 74**, accurate to 1 km.

Step 3: To give a more precise reference accurate to 100 m you need to estimate how many tenths along and how many tenths up this 1 km square the feature is (to help with this the 1 km square is divided into four 500 m squares). This makes the bridge about **8** tenths along and about **1** tenth up from the southwest corner.

This gives a unique reference: **SP 178 741**, accurate to 100 m.

Eastings (read from left to right along the bottom) come before Northings (read from bottom to top). If you have trouble remembering say to yourself "Along the hall, THEN up the stairs"!

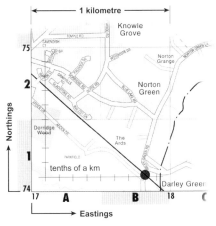

ame and Address	Telephone	Page	Grid Reference

Street Atlases from Philip's

Philip's publish an extensive range of regional and local street atlases which are ideal for motoring, business and leisure use. They are widely used by the emergency services and local authorities throughout Britain.

Key features include:

◆ Superb county-wide mapping at an extra-large scale of 3½ inches to 1 mile, or 2½ inches to 1 mile in pocket edition

◆ Complete urban and rural coverage, detailing every named street in town and country

◆ Each atlas available in three handy formats – hardback, spiral, pocket paperback

'The mapping is very clear... great in scope and value'

★★★★ BEST BUY   AUTO EXPRESS

1 Bedfordshire
2 Berkshire
3 Birmingham and West Midlands
4 Bristol and Bath
5 Buckinghamshire
6 Cambridgeshire
7 Cardiff, Swansea and The Valleys
8 Cheshire
9 Derbyshire
10 Dorset
11 County Durham and Teesside

12 Edinburgh and Central Scotland
13 North Essex
14 South Essex
15 Glasgow and West Central Scotland
16 Gloucestershire
17 North Hampshire
18 South Hampshire
19 Hertfordshire
20 East Kent
21 West Kent
22 Lancashire
23 Leicestershire and Rutland
24 London
25 Greater Manchester
26 Merseyside
27 Northamptonshire
28 Nottinghamshire
29 Oxfordshire
30 Staffordshire
31 Surrey
32 East Sussex
33 West Sussex
34 Tyne and Wear Northumberland
35 Warwickshire
36 Wiltshire and Swindon
37 East Yorkshire and Northern Lincoln
38 North Yorkshire
39 South Yorkshire
40 West Yorkshire

How to order

The Philip's range of street atlases is available from good retailers or directly from the publisher by phoning 01903 828503